'Former Soviet president Mikhail ... tion to events over the past quarte ... the Soviet Union and the emergenc ... the revival of Cold-War-like confrontation with the West and the return of authoritarian governance in Russia itself. Gorbachev deplores the fact that Russia has deviated from the path to democracy that was the aim of his Perestroika, but also points out that US and Western policies have contributed to the current Cold-War atmosphere. Gorbachev's *The New Russia* is essential reading for anyone who wishes to understand why the "Europe whole and free" that Gorbachev and his Western partners tried to create still eludes us. His suggestions for a return to East–West cooperation and for a resumption of democratic reform in Russia itself are timely and much needed.'

Jack F. Matlock, former United States Ambassador to the Soviet Union and Czechoslovakia

'[Gorbachev] has produced a reflection full of an earnest desire that former enemies understand each other and find common ground in a febrile world. This is a reminder of how vast was his achievement in allowing in the light of freedom. Where his contemporary, Nelson Mandela, was great beyond the Whites' deserts in building a post-apartheid nation, Mr Gorbachev was great beyond the deserts of the Soviet Union (and perhaps even of the West, which could barely understand or trust him) in proposing a way for the despotic world to aspire to democratic governance, freely organized civil society and rule of law. That he failed, he keenly knows. Our best hope is that his ideas, in time, succeed.'

The Financial Times

'*The New Russia* is a very insightful book that gives a deep understanding of a country we consider an enemy but know very little about. It is one of the best books on Russia in many years. It is packed with knowledge, analysis and new perspective on Russia. Both students and experts will hugely benefit from reading this. It is a must-read for Western policymakers on Russia.'

The Washington Book Review

The New Russia

Mikhail Gorbachev

The New Russia

Translated by Arch Tait

polity

First published in Russian as *После Кремля/Posle Kremlya*, © Mikhail Sergeyevich Gorbachev, 2015
Hardback English edition © Polity Press 2016

This paperback edition © Polity Press 2017

All images © The Gorbachev Foundation, 2016

Polity Press
65 Bridge Street
Cambridge CB2 1UR, UK

Polity Press
350 Main Street
Malden, MA 02148, USA

Hardback ISBN-13: 978-1-5095-0387-2
Paperback ISBN: 978-1-5095-2361-0

A catalogue record for this book is available from the British Library.

Library of Congress Cataloging-in-Publication Data

Names: Gorbachev, Mikhail Sergeevich, 1931- author.
Title: The new Russia / Mikhail Gorbachev.
Other titles: Posle Kremlya. English
Description: English edition. | Cambridge, UK : Polity, 2016. | First published in Russian as Posle Kremlya, Moskva : Ves Mir, 2014. | Includes index.
Identifiers: LCCN 2015042490 (print) | LCCN 2015049601 (ebook) | ISBN 9781509503872 (hardback) | ISBN 9781509503902 (Mobi) | ISBN 9781509503919 (Epub)
Subjects: LCSH: Gorbachev, Mikhail Sergeevich, 1931- | Gorbachev, Mikhail Sergeevich, 1931---Political and social views. | Presidents--Soviet Union--Biography. | Ex-presidents--Soviet Union--Biography. | Kommunisticheska, a parti, a Sovetskogo So, uza--Biography. | Perestroika--History. | Soviet Union--Politics and government--1985-1991. | Russia (Federation)--Politics and government--1991- | Social change--Russia (Federation)--History. | Political culture--Russia (Federation)--History. | BISAC: POLITICAL SCIENCE / International Relations / General.
Classification: LCC DK290.3.G67 G67213 2016 (print) | LCC DK290.3.G67 (ebook) | DDC 947.085/4092--dc23
LC record available at http://lccn.loc.gov/2015042490

Typeset in 10.75 on 14 Adobe Janson by
Servis Filmsetting Ltd, Stockport, Cheshire
Printed and bound in the United Kingdom by Clays Ltd, St Ives PLC

For further information on Polity, visit our website:
politybooks.com

Contents

Preface:
Perestroika and the Future

This is a book about the relevance of the past. Reflecting on what happened to Russia and Russians at the end of the last and beginning of this century, and what awaits Russia in the future, you inevitably come back to the years of Perestroika. Today, more than two decades separate us from that time, but it is probably still too early to attempt any final assessment. Chou En-Lai is said to have replied to President Richard Nixon's question of how he assessed the French Revolution: 'It is too soon to judge.' He may have been right, yet much can already be seen more clearly.

Today there is again a great sense in Russia of a need for change. Society cannot feel satisfied with the current situation. The attempts at reform undertaken in the past two decades have not been seen through to the end. Of course, we cannot say there have been no changes in people's lives, but many of their hopes have been disappointed and there has been no genuine renewal of life in the interests of the majority of our citizens.

A dead-end political situation, economic stagnation, a build-up of unresolved social problems, violation of the rights and dignity of citizens: all this is only too reminiscent of the state of the country before Perestroika, and people are not happy. Although it has proved possible to temporarily stifle the protest movement that began in December 2011, it is impossible to suppose that those presently in power are unaware of citizens' discontent.

It is no longer possible to say, as we have been doing for very many years, that Russia needs time, that changes of this magnitude cannot be rushed. That is perfectly true, and I have often used that argument in my speeches and in conversations with foreign politicians. Now, however, the process of transition has been going on for two and a half decades, and with every year that passes the argument becomes less convincing.

How should we respond to this state of affairs? What should we do? I am concerned that many are looking for the answer in the wrong direction. They believe it can be found by abandoning the democratic achievements of the Perestroika period. There are attempts to rehabilitate authoritarianism and return to its techniques of administrative pressure and tightening the screws. They extol conservatism and try to turn it into a state ideology, claiming that is more in tune with our traditions and Russia's 'cultural code'.

In President Putin's speeches we hear him quoting conservative Russian philosophers like Ivan Ilyin and Konstantin Leontiev. They cannot be detached from the times in which they lived and contemplated, and we are living in the twenty-first century, a century of new technologies and new challenges. Conservative ideology has no answer to these. Traditional, conservative values do, along with others, have their place in society. But where have conservative policies taken us in the history of Russia? They have led, as a rule, to stagnation followed by upheaval. Sometimes the years of stagnation have been relatively prosperous, living off reforms carried through earlier and favourable external factors. Sooner or later, however, that energy runs out, the external factors change.

The present Russian regime need have no delusions that conservatism is a panacea for our problems, lulling themselves with the belief that for the sake of peace and quiet people will agree to put up with stagnation. They are wrong. I am increasingly convinced that all they are doing is playing for time, clinging to power for its own sake, clutching at the benefits that a minority is able to extract from the current state of affairs.

But people are not blind and their patience is not limitless. They have demonstrated in protest on Bolotnaya Square and Sakharov Prospekt, demanding change. If there is none, the protests will not just be repeated but will become more radical. This would be dangerous and must be avoided. Russia really does not need more turmoil; she needs change, change that opens the way to a genuine renewal of society and improvement in people's lives.

The road will not be straightforward, but in the Perestroika years we did what was most difficult by breaking free of the totalitarian past. At that time and later, we were to live through many moments of high drama, but I am certain that was not in vain.

My message to Russia and the world is a message of hope.

Trying to Bury Me

On 8 August 2013 the newswires of many agencies and media reported: 'Mikhail Gorbachev, the first and last Soviet president, has died, according to a message on the Twitter account of RIA Novosti. He was 82 years old. There is as yet no official confirmation of this information.'

The phone rang. It was Andrey Karplyuk. He reports now for the ITAR-TASS news agency but used to work for Interfax, and we have kept in touch for several years now.

'Mikhail Sergeyevich, I phone you quite often, but this call is not altogether routine.' I sensed he was smiling. 'What I mean is, the reason is a bit unusual.'

'Go on,' I said.

'Well, RIA Novosti is reporting that Gorbachev died during a visit to St Petersburg and I didn't believe it.'

'Neither do I,' I said, and we burst out laughing.

The 'news' was taken off the wire within nine minutes, and the following day I had a letter from the agency staff:

Dear Mikhail Sergeyevich,

We are desperately sorry that hackers have exploited your name in their latest publicity-seeking attempt to discredit the media. Please accept our profound apologies for the shameful sensation caused by the hacking of our agency's accounts on social networks and the posting of hoax information about you.

We do not regard this as a straightforward practical joke or mere act of hooliganism but believe it is a crime that must be investigated. RIA Novosti is sending a statement to the law-enforcement agencies about this hacking of our Twitter channels and we will do everything in our power to ensure that the incident and all the previous hoax reports are thoroughly investigated.

This is not the first time mainstream media have been abused to spread false information, but the latest incident is just too serious, cynical and immoral to be ignored.

Mikhail Sergeyevich, you know how profoundly we respect you and we are deeply distressed that this attack on Novosti has involved you. No doubt attempts to falsify the news and hoax attempts will continue, but we wish to assure you and all our readers that we will do everything we can to quash them promptly.

My relationship with RIA Novosti goes back a long time, and in spring 2013 I gave a talk in their offices to a large number of young people, with the title, 'Does the individual change politics, or does politics change the individual?' I talked about my life, current concerns, and all the obstacles on the road to democracy that Russia has yet to travel. My audience listened attentively and asked plenty of questions. Meeting the young people left me with a good feeling. It always does. A day to remember.

And then this hoax. What was behind it? This was not the first time: Gorbachev has been 'buried' many times, and I know why.

Someone out there has a grudge against Perestroika, and lies are their weapon of choice. Libel, inexcusable fabrications and distortion of the facts. That is how it was all those years ago, and the same weapon is still being used today.

There is no shortage of examples. In December 1990, at the Congress of People's Deputies, Anatoly Lukianov, the speaker of the USSR Supreme Soviet, for some reason almost immediately gave the floor to a certain Sazha Umalatova, who called for a vote of no confidence in President Gorbachev to be put on the agenda. The delegates declined the invitation. In 1991, at the April plenum of the Communist Party's Central Committee, I was subjected to such venomous 'psychological warfare' that I said, 'I give up! How can anyone be the general secretary of two, three or even five Communist Parties at the same time?' The Politburo persuaded me to stay on.

Next, under the pretext of a meeting of representatives of Hero Cities of World War II, a whole gaggle of Party bosses of different levels decided to discuss the 'unresolved problem' of how to topple Gorbachev. In the summer of 1991, as I was meeting with leaders of the Soviet republics to finalize a draft new Union Treaty, three hardline ministers in charge of security and law-enforcement put a proposal to the USSR Supreme Soviet to reassign powers from the president to the prime minister and security ministries. Never a day passed without the warbling of 'anti-Perestroika nightingales' like Alexander Prokhanov.

To this day, insane rumours are spread, hoaxes manufactured for release onto the Internet, and 'documentaries' shown on TV which are a pack of lies and malign invention from start to finish.

From the Gorbachev Foundation website:

In late August 2008 an interview appeared in *Komsomolskaya Pravda* [*Young Communist League Pravda*] in which Pavel Borodin, who holds high office in the Union State of Russia and Belarus, made blatantly libellous allegations against M. S. Gorbachev and Helmut Kohl, former Chancellor of the Federal Republic of Germany.

After contacting Helmut Kohl, M. S. Gorbachev has received confirmation from him that Borodin's allegations were 'a complete fabrication'. The Gorbachev Foundation contacted its lawyers, who took necessary action, and *Komsomolskaya Pravda* has published the following:

Retraction
In Issue No. 127 (24154) of *Komsomolskaya Pravda*, dated 29 August 2008, and on the Internet at URL http://www.kp.ru/daily/24154/369892, an interview with P. P. Borodin, Secretary of State of the Union State of Russia and Belarus, was published under the title 'Pavel Borodin: "If South Ossetia and Abkhazia join the Union of Russia and Belarus, I too will down three litres of wine."' P. P. Borodin alleged that the former Chancellor of the Federal Republic of Germany, Helmut Kohl, had told him that 'for Eastern Europe' Mikhail Gorbachev asked for $100 million 'for his own foundation, 100 million for Shevardnadze's fund, and 100 million for the fund of another comrade'.

This information, as well as the claim that it was communicated to P. P. Borodin by Helmut Kohl, is at variance with the truth. Its intention was to impugn the integrity and reputation of M. S. Gorbachev.

Komsomolskaya Pravda, 28 January 2009

The authorities of the Russian state find me a hindrance. Today's political elite have set their sights on consolidating their right to govern in perpetuity, giving them material wealth and power without accountability. The media subservient to them defame Perestroika, vilifying those who undertook the huge and perilous task of bringing reform and elections to a country weighed down by problems that had not been addressed for decades.

Freedom of speech can be, and is, used not only by people who seek and want to report the truth, but by others who are ill-intentioned and whose consciences are unclean.

To this day I am stunned by the treachery of people I placed in positions of trust, with whom I was bound by years of joint endeavour. The most striking instance of that was the coup by the 'State Emergency Committee' that paved the way for the destruction of the Soviet Union.

By August 1991, after months of severe crises in the USSR, a plan had been devised and agreed by all parties, including the Baltic republics. We had completed work on a new Union Treaty, which was to be signed by the leaders of the republics on 20 August. In the autumn, an extraordinary congress was to move the Communist Party in the direction of reform and social democracy. We anticipated difficulties in the future, but I have no doubt that, but for the coup, the subsequent orgy of destruction could have been avoided.

Democracy is a hard taskmaster, and the free elections to the Congress of People's Deputies in 1989 produced unexpected results. On the one hand, 84 per cent of those elected were members of the Communist Party of the Soviet Union (CPSU), but, on the other, the voters withheld their trust from dozens of Party officials, who found themselves out on their ear. The reactionaries in the Party establishment initiated a campaign of furious resistance to Perestroika. Unable to achieve their goals in an open political fight, my opponents resorted to a coup d'état.

Their putsch failed, but gave the green light to separatists, radicals and extremists, with a string of disastrous consequences. The collapse of the Soviet Union; the rolling back of democracy in almost all the republics; chaos in the economy, exploited by the greediest and most unscrupulous, who succeeded in plunging almost everyone else into poverty; ethnic conflicts and bloodshed in Russia and other republics; and, finally, the shelling of the Supreme Soviet of Russia in October 1993.

People often ask me if I feel all this was my fault. They say that in late 1991, after the Belovezha collusion between Yeltsin and the leaders of Belarus and Ukraine to undermine the USSR and replace it with a 'Commonwealth of Independent States', I should have acted more decisively. My answer is that I fought for a Union State until the last, but it would have been unforgivable to allow a slide into civil conflict, and possibly civil war. We can imagine what that could have meant in a country bristling with weapons, not only conventional but also nuclear. That is why, after long deliberation, I took the decision that I still believe today was the only right one in the circumstances: I announced that I would cease to perform the duties of president of the USSR.

To the Citizens of the Soviet Union
A Broadcast by the President of the USSR, M. S. Gorbachev
25 December 1991
Dear fellow countrymen and fellow citizens,
In view of the situation that has developed with the formation of the Commonwealth of Independent States, I am terminating my work as president of the USSR. I am taking this decision for reasons of principle.

I have strongly supported the autonomy and independence of our peoples and the sovereignty of their republics, but also retention of the Union State and integrity of our country. Events have taken a different course. A policy of dismembering the country and disuniting the state has prevailed, which I cannot accept.

After the Alma-Ata meeting and the decisions taken there, my principles remain unaltered.

I am convinced that a decision of this magnitude should have been based on an expression of the will of the Soviet people.

Nevertheless, I will do everything in my power to ensure that the agreements signed there bring about genuine harmony in society and facilitate the finding of a way out of the crisis and continuation of the reform process.

Addressing you now for the last time as president of the USSR, I consider it incumbent upon me to give an assessment of the path we have taken since 1985. This is all the more necessary in view of the many contradictory, superficial and biased judgements that have been heard.

Fate decreed that by the time I found myself in charge of the state it was already clear that something was wrong with our country. In terms of land, oil, gas and other natural resources, we had so much wealth, and no cause to complain as far as intelligence and talent were concerned, and yet our standard of living was far below that of developed countries and we were in the process of falling further behind.

The cause was already clear: society was suffocating in the clutches of a bureaucratic command system. Doomed to serve ideology while bearing the terrible burden of the arms race, it was close to breaking point.

All attempts at piecemeal reform, of which there were many, failed one after the other. The country was heading nowhere. It was impossible to go on like that. Everything was in need of radical change.

That is why I have never regretted that I did not take advantage of the position of general secretary of the CPSU merely to preside for a few years. I would have considered that irresponsible and immoral.

I understood that beginning reform on such a scale and in a society like ours was a difficult, and even dangerous, undertaking, but to this day remain convinced that to institute the democratic reforms that began in spring 1985 was historically the right thing to do.

The process of renewing the USSR and fundamental changes in the international community proved far more complex than could have been foreseen, but what was done should be judged fairly.

- Society has gained its freedom and been emancipated politically and spiritually. That has been the greatest achievement, and it is one we do not yet fully appreciate because we have yet to learn how to use our freedom. For all that, what has been achieved is of historic significance.

- The totalitarian system that for many years had been preventing our country from prospering and thriving has been eliminated.
- We have made a breakthrough on the road to democratic reform. Free elections, freedom of the press, religious freedoms, representative institutions of government and a multi-party system have become a reality. Human rights have been recognized as wholly fundamental.
- We are moving towards a mixed economy, with acceptance that all forms of ownership are equally valid. As a result of land reform, the peasantry is beginning to revive, farming has appeared, millions of acres of land are being given to country-dwellers and townspeople. The economic freedom of manufacturers has been recognized in law and we are seeing the growth of private enterprise, corporatization and privatization.

In introducing a market economy, it is important to remember that this is being done for the benefit of our people. At this difficult time, everything must be done to provide a social welfare safety net, particularly for children and the elderly.

We are living in a new world.

- The Cold War has been ended. The arms race has been halted and with it the lunatic militarization of the USSR which distorted our economy, national consciousness and morality.
  The threat of world war is over.
  I want to emphasize once again that during the transitional period I have done everything I could to ensure that nuclear weapons remained securely under control.
- We have opened up to the world, repudiated interference in other countries' affairs and the use of troops outside our own territory, and in return we have been rewarded with trust, solidarity and respect.
- We have become one of the main bulwarks for rebuilding contemporary civilization on peaceful, democratic principles.
- Our peoples and nations have gained real freedom to choose

their own form of government through self-determination. The
search for democratic reform of our multinational state brought
us to the threshold of concluding a new Union Treaty.

All these changes have called for great concentration of effort
and have been pushed through in the face of fierce opposition and
increasing resistance by forces clinging to all that is old, obsolete
and reactionary, both in the former institutions of the Party and
state, the economic bureaucracy, and indeed in our own habits,
ideological prejudices and traditions of psychological dependency
and levelling down. They have clashed with our intolerance, our
low level of political culture and fear of change and that is why
so much time has been lost. The old system collapsed before the
new system could start functioning and that made the crisis in our
society even more acute.

I know how much discontent there is over our current difficulties, how critical people are of the authorities at all levels and of my
own record, but let me stress once again that fundamental change
in such a vast country and with such a legacy is inevitably going to
be difficult, disruptive and painful.

The coup attempt in August this year pushed the overall state
of crisis to extremes. The most disastrous aspect of that is the collapse of our state institutions. I am deeply concerned that today
our people are being deprived of their status as citizens of a great
country. The consequences may be very severe for all of us.

I believe it is vitally important to hold on to the democratic
achievements of recent years. We have paid a heavy price for them
through our history and tragic experiences as a nation. Under no
circumstances, under no pretext, must we allow them to be abandoned, since otherwise all hope of anything better will be lost.

I am telling you all this directly and truthfully, as is my moral
duty. Today I want also to express my gratitude to all those citizens who have supported the policy of renewal and participated in
implementing democratic reforms.

I am grateful to those servants of the state, politicians and
public figures, to the millions of people abroad, who have understood our intentions, supported them, and joined with us in sincere
cooperation.

I am standing down from my position with concern but also with hope, with faith in you, your wisdom and steadfastness. We are the heirs of a great civilization and today it depends on each of us individually and all of us together whether it will be reborn to a new, modern and worthy way of life.

My heartfelt thanks go to all those who have stood beside me in these years for what is right and good. No doubt there were errors we could have avoided and much we could have done better, but I have no doubt that sooner or later our joint efforts will bear fruit and our peoples will live in a flourishing and democratic society.

I wish you all the very best.

The Belovezha plot is a history of deceit and, moreover, of self-deception on the part of those who connived at it, especially on the Russian side. They hoped that the 'Commonwealth of Independent States' they had invented would be a Union without Gorbachev, but that was not what happened. The provisions included for appearances' sake in the Belovezha document about coordinating foreign and defence policy were promptly forgotten. I appealed again and again to the sense of responsibility of our parliamentary deputies to serve those who elect them, to be answerable to them and not subservient to political opportunists. At that time it was they, the Supreme Soviets of Russia, Ukraine and Byelorussia, who almost unanimously, including the communists who today lament the disintegration of the USSR, ratified the Belovezha Accord and deceived the people. Why do we overlook that?

The very thing I was doing my utmost to prevent duly happened. The unity of our state was destroyed. In those final days of my presidency, I saw my role as being to try to ensure this did not lead to a further splintering of society, rupturing of economic and human ties, and acceleration of the trend towards disintegration. I used my international contacts to appeal to Western leaders to help Russia, phoning George Bush Senior, François Mitterrand, John Major and Helmut Kohl. I urged them to forget the standard ways of doing things and support the Commonwealth, especially Russia. It was crucial that they assisted our efforts to reform.

I forget when it was that I read an article in *Komsomolskaya Pravda* giving statistics about the ascent of Everest. The numbers were startling: of 1,500 people who have successfully climbed the mountain, some 200 have died. Most of them perish shortly after making it to the top, on the first section after their successful ascent. Those who reach the summit are not always able to find their way back down.

A new phase was beginning in the life of our country, and in mine too. I had no illusions and knew it was going to be grim. A deluge of lies and libels rained down on me. As the economy's problems worsened, it was wholly predictable that the politicians now in power would be looking for a scapegoat. Gorbachev was the obvious candidate.

What kept me afloat during those first months after the Kremlin? Why did I not buckle under the strain? I was firmly committed to my principles, I was tough, and in the course of my life I had learned to fight. In addition, I had the support of those close to me, my wife Raisa and the rest of my family. I had the support too of friends and allies from the Perestroika project, and of others who became friends in later years, who helped in my work and new projects for love, not money.

Above all, what kept me going was the certainty that Perestroika had been and remained historically essential and that, having taken on a far from light burden, we were bearing it with the dignity it deserved. For all the mistakes and failures, we had led our country out of a historical impasse, given it a first taste of freedom, liberated our people and given them back the right to think for themselves. And we had ended the Cold War and nuclear arms race.

It was important to me at that time, and still is today, that many of my compatriots recognized that; and so I would like to publish just a few of the letters I received from people I never knew, but to whom I am immensely grateful.

You have a great many supporters

Responses to the resignation broadcast of the president of the USSR, 1991

Thank you for telling us the truth, and for your courage.

Captain Filimonov
on behalf of the White Sea fishermen, Belomorsk

This New Year will be very sad for us. We have always been on your side, admired you, sent telegrams of support and given what help we could. May all the other presidents find work worthy of you. We wish you and your family good health and happiness.

A. P. Valikova
Artist, Moscow

We have learned with regret but understanding of your resignation. The seed of democracy, freedom and Glasnost sown five years ago has already sprouted, and we are confident that, as the years pass, it will mature and yield good fruit. We hope you have a good holiday, recharge your batteries, and continue the work you have begun.

V. S. Goncharov
The Farm, Kantemirovka, Voronezh Province

We are grateful to you for the freedom with which you think, reflect and speak. Everything else will follow.

Staff of the Far East Branch of the Russian Academy of Sciences
G. Glukhomanyuk and P. Logvenchev, Vladivostok

Forgive us if you can. I wish you health, spiritual strength and happiness. God Bless you!

Koshulko
Adamovka, Orenburg Province

I   AFTER PERESTROIKA

The 1990s: Defending Perestroika

What is it like when, after fate has raised you to leadership of a superpower, you find yourself in the kind of situation I was in during the first months of 1992? Not much fun, I can tell you.

My last month as president was tense and dramatic, but I continued doing all I could to keep open the prospect of renewal of the Soviet Union, and of cooperation and continuing ties between the former Soviet republics, which by then were already independent states. I did not cling to power at all costs, power for its own sake.

It was a bitter blow that Perestroika had been halted halfway, indeed when it was still only beginning. Already I was aware of just how deeply rooted the legacy of totalitarianism was, in our traditions, in people's mindset and morality. It had seeped into almost every pore of the social organism. That deeply troubled me in those days and, more than 20 years later, still does.

My last day in the Kremlin

On 26 December 1991 I arrived at my office in the Kremlin, having agreed with Boris Yeltsin that I would vacate it by 30 December. There were papers and personal possessions to be sorted, but I was primarily interested in the responses coming in from different parts of the country to my announcement that I was standing down as president. I looked through the newspapers and letters and telegrams from Soviet citizens. Most were sympathetic and wishing me well, although there were others. The machinery of slander and lies was already grinding away on the subject of supposed Swiss bank accounts and villas abroad.

It struck me that many people did not yet know they were being deprived of their country.

Here is a summary of those first telegrams and the reactions reported to me.

Most correspondents could understand the reasons for my decision. Many wrote appreciatively that they had been freed from the threat of nuclear war, from fear of a tyrannical government. They were thankful for the breakthrough to democratization and freedom and hoped I would soon return to national politics. There were calls for leaders of the former Soviet republics to 'find a job worthy of Gorbachev', many good wishes for the New Year, for good health, 'inner peace', and invitations to come with my family to visit.

Other telegrams criticized my decision because 'the process of Perestroika is not yet complete'. There were doubts that the Commonwealth of Independent States would prove capable of uniting the peoples incorporated in the Soviet Union, of guaranteeing harmonious relations and genuine equality and making life better for them. There was much criticism that decisions about establishing the CIS had been taken in haste and were of dubious legality. Some hoped I would support the Commonwealth, or at least not try to hinder it. There were also accusations that I had caused the break-up of the country and wrecked the economy.

People wrote about the lack of bread, milk and other food supplies in the provinces for weeks at a time; about having to queue for hours in shops; about inadequate preparation being made for the winter; interruptions in the supply of electricity, fuel and heat; about how cold it was in their apartments. There were desperate pleas for urgently needed medicines and complaints about shortages of them. People wrote of the importance of paying urgent attention to the situation of troops in the former Soviet republics, and the social welfare of servicemen. Several correspondents urged me to appeal for support to the army, whose job it was 'not only to defend the state, but the lives of all the people'.

I signed photos for the closest members of my staff, adding a message: 'We have made a start, life goes on, and anyone who thinks the Gorbachev Era is over had better think again. This is only the beginning.'

While I was going through the mail, Raisa called in some distress to say the managers sent by Yeltsin's administration were demanding we should move out of the presidential apartment in Moscow as well as the official country residence, while refusing to provide transport for the removal. I had to put the overzealous commandants in their place in a stoutly man-to-man and Russian manner.

I recently found the following note in my archive:

Privatization of Apartment
M. S. Gorbachev and R. M. Gorbacheva on 28 December 1991 have concluded this agreement with the Committee on Housing Policy of Moscow City Council whereby in accordance with Article 7 of the Law on Privatization of the Housing Stock of the RSFSR they have each and severally acquired rights of ownership to an apartment occupied by them on Kosygin Street which has a total usable area of 140 (one hundred and forty) m², of which the residential area comprises 65.1 (sixty-five point one) m². Citizens M. S. Gorbachev and R. M. Gorbacheva will service and maintain the privatized apartment at their own expense. The apartment was previously occupied by members of the bodyguard of the president of the USSR.

The woman notarizing a copy of the privatization contract on 29 December 1991 asked my assistant in surprise: 'Is it really true that this extremely modest apartment is all the Gorbachevs now own?'

The presidential apartment we had been living in and were required to vacate with such urgency was, I heard, looked over by Yeltsin, but he did not care for it. With the approval of the new authorities, it was subsequently sold and resold several times.

That same day I gave the first interview since my resignation to Italian journalists from *La Stampa* and *Repubblica*. To their first question, 'How are you feeling?' I replied: 'Once a decision has been taken, one usually feels better. Changes in my living conditions do not trouble me. My family and I are not being spoiled.' Giulietto Chiesa, the correspondent from *La Stampa*, took the opportunity to ask some broader questions.

Q: Do you still call yourself a socialist? Do you think socialism
      is still a credible project?
A: It is not socialism that has been defeated but Stalinism dis-
      guised as socialism. What has been defeated is a model that
      levelled everything down and ruled out innovation. I feel that
      what I participate in is, on the contrary, a collective search for
      justice, freedom and democracy. Mankind will continue that
      search, as do movements professing a wide variety of ideals.
Q: You sound like Sakharov.
A: Yes, the theory that the communist and capitalist worlds are
      converging ... The thought and moral authority of people like
      Sakharov is very important to me.
Q: Are you feeling safe? Are you not afraid you may be used as
      a scapegoat if things go wrong?
A: That has happened often enough in the past. When politi-
      cians in power suffer reverses or find themselves unable to
      control the situation, they try to divert their citizens' attention
      to other problems and energetically seek someone to blame for
      their own mistakes. Nothing can be ruled out.

Russian and foreign journalists were interested to know
whether I was planning to lead the opposition. I could see no jus-
tification for joining it, neither from a political point of view nor
from that of the country's interests. It was out of the question that
Gorbachev might oppose the policy of reform in Russia. I said I
might offer advice, express my opinion, but I supported the basic
direction of the reforms and declared that we should support
Russia's leaders.

'I cannot even imagine going over to the opposition. Opposition
to what? Democratic reforms? Opposition to myself? That is not
the kind of person Gorbachev is, as everyone well knows.' I
repeated that in almost all the interviews I gave in my last weeks
as president, and said the same thing to Yeltsin.

On the evening of 26 December, I attended a farewell reception and briefing for journalists, arranged by my press office at
the October Hotel. (The new authorities renamed it the President
Hotel.) The journalists, Russian and foreign, applauded when
I came in, and for more than two hours I answered questions,

signed autographs, and received many good wishes. These are the main points I made to them:

> We need now to put aside all political affiliations, and perhaps even our disagreements. The top priority must be to help the country keep reform moving forward. That is the most important thing. I have invited my colleagues to do the same, particularly those who bear the burden of state responsibilities.
>
> Our foreign partners are also involved, because what happens here in the coming months will have repercussions for the entire global process. We want the policy of transformation to be carried forward. We want the reforms to continue and democracy to grow stronger, so I would ask our foreign partners to join in supporting this country, perhaps even to turn a blind eye to some things, because the stakes are very high for everyone. As the top priority I would put the need for material support for Russia, not only political, but in every other respect. She will have a great and influential role to play in the future.

The journalists asked me about my personal plans and I told them, as I told everyone during this period, that I had no intention of running away to hide in the woods or abroad. I would not be abandoning politics and public life, and continued to believe my main objective must be to do everything in my power to promote democratic reform in Russia, now in my new capacity, and to promote New Thinking throughout the world. I hoped these ends would also be served by the International Foundation for Socio-Economic and Political Studies that I was establishing.

I had an interview with Japanese reporters scheduled for the morning of 27 December and decided to conduct it one last time in my Kremlin office. The journalists were already waiting, but, as I was approaching the Kremlin, I was warned over the car phone, 'Yeltsin, Poltoranin, Burbulis and Khasbulatov have been sitting all morning in your office. They've drunk a bottle of whisky and are having a party.'

Yeltsin could not wait to occupy the presidential office, which those initiated in Kremlin affairs called 'the Heights'. Unable to contain himself for the three days before 30 December, he and his company had prematurely stormed the heights and were having a booze-up to celebrate their victory. Two years later, these same men would be firing at each other as they destroyed parliament! Just before their importunate arrival, the remaining personal belongings of the president of the USSR had to be whisked away in a cart. I never set foot in the office again.

A new beginning, without presidential immunity

My new workplace was, and to this day remains, the Gorbachev Foundation. On 30 December 1991 it was registered at the Ministry of Justice as The International Foundation for Socio-Economic and Political Studies ('Gorbachev Foundation'), with M. S. Gorbachev as its president.

The registered stakeholders were the Russian Branch of the International Foundation for the Survival and Development of Mankind, headed by Academician Yevgeny Velikhov; the Foreign Policy Association, headed by Eduard Shevardnadze; Academician Stanislav Shatalin's Foundation for Economic and Social Reform; and Russian citizens Mikhail Gorbachev, Grigoriy Revenko and Alexander Yakovlev. I became president of the Foundation and Revenko and Yakovlev, my fellow protagonists of Perestroika, became the vice-presidents.

On the instructions of the president of the Russian Federation, the premises of the former Social Science Institute of the Central Committee of the Communist Party of the Soviet Union were placed at the Foundation's disposal. Maintenance of the buildings and all the Foundation's activities were to be financed without any further material support from the state. Highly respected economists, sociologists and political scientists, specialists in the major areas of the humanities and public figures in Russia and a number of European countries, the United States, Canada and Japan all announced their intention to contribute.

My vision was that the Foundation would analyse the processes and publish reports on the history, successes and failures of the democratic restructuring of the USSR, and dispel all the nonsense, libels and falsification that had been thrown at it. Additionally, there would be a need for research to monitor the main processes at work in the life of post-Soviet Russia, and to consider options and alternatives as to how it might develop. Finally, the third major line of enquiry was to be the international and global processes in which our country would be living and developing.

Yeltsin raised no objection and, evidently in the first flush of victory, signed the needful decree. He did warily ask whether I was planning to turn the Foundation into an organization for opposing him. I said that, for as long as democratic reform continued in Russia, there could be no question of opposition on my part. On the contrary, I would support and defend it. He continued, nevertheless, to be apprehensive about opposition, and I presume that lay behind his announcement, when the presidential documents were being transferred, that there could be 'no question' of immunity from investigation and prosecution for the president of the USSR. 'So,' he added, 'if you have anything on your conscience you would do well to repent while you are still the president.' I never did ask for presidential immunities from Yeltsin or his successors. He did not take kindly to that.

Incidentally, when Yeltsin himself retired, he made sure he obtained presidential immunity for himself by a special decree signed by V. V. Putin. Meanwhile, for more than 20 years now, I have been living, working and standing up for my beliefs without any guarantees of immunity from prosecution. Since 1999 I have had my daughter, Irina, at my side as vice-president of the Gorbachev Foundation.

My closest colleagues and assistants from the Office of the President of the USSR came to work at the Foundation, including Anatoly Chernyaev, Georgiy Shakhnazarov, Vadim Medvedev, Vadim Zagladin, Pavel Palazhchenko, Georgiy Ostroumov, Alexander Veber and Viktor Kuvaldin. They were all top-level professionals with distinguished titles and academic degrees. My technical assistants also came over, as did my irreplaceable shorthand typists, Irina Vagina and Tamara Mokacheva. Their motives were altruistic and based on conviction rather than the pursuit of money or other rewards: their salaries in the Foundation were substantially lower than they could have commanded as government employees. None of those who had worked with me in the Kremlin or at Communist Party headquarters in Old Square ended up with palatial mansions and luxurious villas, or had foreign bank accounts.

At this time, or a little later, the Foundation was further augmented by former staff from the Social Science Institute: Alexander Galkin, Yury Krasin, Vladlen Loginov, Irina Malikova and Yekaterina Zavarzina. From academic institutes we were joined by Valentin Tolstykh, Yelena Martynova and the Foundation's present executive director, Olga Zdravomyslova.

The Foundation receives no support from the state. Its main source of funding consists of fees from my lectures, royalties from my books and individual donations. The remuneration of the staff is very modest, and bears no comparison with the income of officials in the bloated Russian bureaucracy, who again recently received a substantial pay rise, at a time when many of our citizens are finding life very difficult.

Shock Therapy

Russia and the other republics of the former Soviet Union were entering an unknown future. What could they expect? A radical break had occurred in the life of the country and of tens of millions of people. Was there hope we could overcome the negative effects of the rash, unlawful decision to 'disband' the Soviet Union? That we could get on track to develop the economy along free market lines, and find new arrangements for nations that for centuries had been living in the same country to collaborate? I have to admit that at the time I had no answers to these questions. When I speculated about the future, my main feeling was disquiet, not for myself, but for the country and our people. I tried to remain optimistic.

In his New Year speech on television, the president of Russia said the coming year of 1992 would be different: 'Our task is to lay the foundations for a new life. I have said before and will say again: we have a difficult time ahead, but it will not last long. We are talking about six to eight months.' Did Yeltsin believe his own rhetoric? He was, of course, being advised that the difficulties would be overcome in miraculously short order, and was being plied by foreign experts with news of how beneficial the experience of 'shock therapy' had been in a number of countries in Eastern Europe, Latin America and elsewhere. What is certain is that neither Yeltsin nor Yegor Gaidar, to whose team he entrusted implementation of the economic reform programme, can have imagined that the promised six to eight months of economic discomfort would, for most of Russia's population, drag on for many painful years. For almost 15 years Russia's standard of living was to remain lower than in the Soviet year

of 1990. In some years it was catastrophically lower, at half the
level.[1]

The Russian deputy prime minister, Yegor Gaidar, commenting on the 'freeing' of prices in the Russian Federation on 2
January 1992, stated in an interview for Russian journalists: 'In
the most favourable scenario, prices will increase in January and
February by approximately 100 per cent in each month.' In fact,
the price of most basic goods immediately rose by 5–10 times
compared with December 1991, and by 10–20 times compared
with January 1991.

In early 1991, the minimum level of pensions and wages was
stable, at 100 roubles, while the average salary was between 200
and 250 roubles. In early 1992, incomes of the lower paid rose
by 350 per cent and that of those on middle incomes by 150–200
per cent. Against that, the price of bread went up by 1,000–1,500
per cent, milk by 1,500–2,000 per cent, butter and sour cream by
3,000 per cent, potatoes by 1,000–2,000 per cent in the shops and
by 5,000–10,000 per cent in the markets.

The price shock of January 1992 had been preceded by a complete emptying of the shelves the previous December. Matches
and salt had disappeared. Cereals and sugar were bought up by
the sackful. A considerable contribution to this state of affairs
was an announcement to the whole country by the president of
the Russian Federation in October 1991 that he had decided in
favour of 'radical economic reform'. People realized this would
inevitably result in price rises and rushed to stock up. In antici-
pation of higher prices, producers and trade organizations held
back goods in their warehouses and distribution centres. As a
result, expectations of inflation soared and in the final months
of 1991 commercial activity was at a virtual standstill. Blame for
the long hours of queueing and empty shelves was laid squarely
on 'Gorbachev's Perestroika'. That was easy. It was less easy
to blame Gorbachev for the fact that average consumption of

[1] According to official figures from the Russian Federal State Statistics
Service, the population's real income returned to the level of 1990, the
penultimate year of Perestroika, only at the end of 2005.

foodstuffs in Yeltsin's Russian Federation approached the corresponding level in the Soviet period only in the mid-2000s.

The price rises were painful in the extreme. As early as the first week of January 1992, the social and political situation in many Russian cities became tense and protest demonstrations broke out. President Yeltsin decided to travel to the Volga region to see, as he said, 'at first hand the state of affairs in the provinces, how price liberalization is being implemented, and whether anything is being overdone'. Andrey Cherkizov, a journalist travelling with him, wrote: 'The reform is causing distress. It is a harsh reform, with almost no accompanying safety net, a reform that is sailing very close to the wind.' He saw this as explaining the president's desire to 'frantically find additional propaganda resources'. Instead of looking for ways to provide people with support and mitigate the impact of price increases, Yeltsin suddenly started talking about the Black Sea Fleet in Crimea and making remarks about not granting autonomous status to the Volga Germans. 'First they started playing the Black Sea card, now it is the German card', and all this delivered 'in a steely tone of voice'. It seemed, Cherkizov concluded, that 'the Yeltsin-Gaidar economic reforms need someone to confront'.

Indignation at rising prices was growing, but I believed it was best not to jump to conclusions. As I told the journalists who surrounded me at the entrance to the Foundation: 'Eleven days into the start of price liberalization is too early to judge. I think the first priority for Russia's leaders should be to demonopolize production and mitigate the effect of price rises on the population.'

The search for a scapegoat, threats

With every passing day, however, it became clearer that Giulietto Chiesa had been right in anticipating that the new Russian government might start looking for a lightning conductor, or rather a scapegoat. Help came to them from a seemingly unlikely quarter. The leaders of the Communist opposition now thunderously proclaimed – as, until recently, the radical liberals had been doing – that the name of the 'main and basic culprit of all the ills of Russia and the Russian people' was, wait for it: 'Mikhail Gorbachev'!

In Moscow the Russian Communist Workers Party, the Communist League, and Workers' Russia called on people to demonstrate on Manezh Square against the 'ridiculous' free market, 'ridiculous' privatization and the collapse of the country and army, but loudest of all they called for Gorbachev to be put on trial. Here is how *Den'* [*Day*], a newspaper edited by that longstanding opponent of Perestroika, Alexander Prokhanov, put it in a special issue:

> The square demanded prosecution of this appalling man who has betrayed everybody. In accordance with the will of this most magnificent meeting in the world, people were chosen who have begun investigating the case against Gorbachev. Viktor Ilyukhin heads a commission which is already elucidating the role of the former general secretary and president in the unprecedented wilful destruction of the country in the interests of other powers, his foreign policy which has destroyed our allies and partners, and his domestic policy which has pushed crazed citizens to the brink of civil war.

I should mention here that the author of this literary gem is today an all but permanent fixture on the screens of the state television channels, appearing in the second decade of the twenty-first century as an active supporter and would-be ideologist of the current Russian government, developing a new 'National Idea'. Many active in the United Russia Party are zealous disciples of Prokhanov and have taken up not only his anti-Gorbachev rhetoric but also the threats directed at my person.

These were first heard in early 1992. The Moscow Organizational Bureau of the Russian Communist Workers Party appealed to the Supreme Soviet and the forthcoming Congress of People's Deputies to

> prevent attempts by Gorbachev to leave the territory of the Russian Federation prior to open and legal consideration of the charges brought against him by Prosecutor Viktor Ilyukhin and

the public, and also until final completion of investigations into the State Emergency Committee. Actions undertaken by any individual, state or public organization to facilitate the flight abroad of the former general secretary of the CPSU, former president of the USSR, former commander-in-chief of the armed forces of the USSR, Mikhail Gorbachev, will be considered hostile and criminal acts against the peoples of Russia and other republics of the USSR.

The Communists were joined by lawyers acting for those accused in connection with the State Emergency Committee case, who demanded interrogation of Gorbachev and a ban on his travelling abroad. This was followed by the first threats from the new Russian government. Deputy Prosecutor General Yevgeny Lisov, in an interview for the New York *Newsday*, announced that he considered Gorbachev 'a suspect' in a case investigating financing by the CPSU of foreign Communist parties.

Later, at hearings into the financial affairs of the CPSU, Lisov admitted that there was no direct evidence of Gorbachev's involvement in the case, but claimed he bore 'collective responsibility' because at Politburo meetings where such matters were discussed he 'never voted against'. Altogether, attempts were made from all directions to create a negative aura around me.

I reacted to it as any man with a clear conscience and strong nerves should. I had no intention of 'fleeing' anywhere and these people could not intimidate me. What did disturb me was that Raisa and my family and friends were being greatly upset by what was going on.

I was often asked during this period for my assessment of what was happening in Russia and what the response should be. This was a matter of interest to our Western partners also. When I met Rodric Braithwaite, the British Ambassador, in January, I said the reforms in Russia and other CIS countries were being carried through under difficult conditions and with considerable costs, but were in need not so much of commentary as of material support. I reminded him of the agreements reached during my participation in the London summit of the G7 leading industrial nations in July 1991, and again called for maximum support for Russia's radical economic reforms, because if they failed that would affect all democratic forces. As regards the future of the Commonwealth of Independent States, the most important thing was to help it become a commonwealth not only in word but also in deed.

The Gorbachev Foundation: its first reports

The Gorbachev Foundation was hard at work even before its official launch. We attracted authoritative research specialists to analyse the situation in Russia, and my colleagues associated with Perestroika joined in. At the end of January we met up to try to evaluate what was happening, to probe what was driving events and suggest steps to mitigate negative tendencies. Some of those assessments were to prove only too accurate. It is a pity they were ignored.

The experts were particularly exercised over whether integration of the republics of the 'disbanded' Soviet Union was still possible. The historian Grigoriy Vodolazov put forward the idea of organizing the CIS as a 'multi-structural community'. 'Currently,' he said, 'the prevailing intention is to set up the CIS with a standard pattern of association of the republics, but I would recommend providing for less intimate relationships within its framework, alongside closer links where possible.'

I was naturally concerned about these longer-term problems, but also about the course being taken by the economic reforms, which amounted to no more than price liberalization, indiscriminate privatization, opening the market to imports and hoping for foreign aid. My attitude was becoming increasingly critical, and in an interview for the Italian weekly *Panorama* and Russia's *Literaturnaya Gazeta* [*Literary Gazette*], I reminded their readers that in my last conversation with Yeltsin in December 1991 I had said I was not planning to develop an opposition movement, but that did not mean I would abstain from criticism of weaknesses and mistakes. Of these there had already been plenty within the past month. I did not pull my punches:

I believe that before price controls were lifted there should have been measures to stimulate production and adjust tax and credit policies. The growing social unrest is worrying. If it reaches the point where people take to the streets, the stark question will be how to stay in control and carry on governing. That is why action is needed immediately, before it comes to that. I again urge the need for consensus. We cannot allow representatives of different political tendencies to carry on staging pitched battles.

I still consider the worst strategic mistake to have been terminating the Soviet Union as a unified country, with the accompanying destruction of culture, the economy and national defence, and the disruption of human relationships.

In an interview for *Komsomolskaya Pravda*, I explicitly warned that, if no adjustments were made to fiscal policy, no measures taken to stimulate production, and no effective institutions established capable of controlling the economic and political situation in the CIS, we might find ourselves facing a major political crisis.

December 1991: politics and morality

For most of January I worked on my book *December 1991: My Position*.[2] It is a documentary account of my efforts to save the Soviet Union in the aftermath of the August coup. Work on the book was hard-going, primarily in emotional terms. Everything was still raw in my memory, but I had a tremendous urge to tell the truth about that period and to think through everything soberly. In my introduction I wrote:

I want to present my position during the course of the December events, because it remains unknown to many citizens. My arguments did not suit everybody and so, contrary to the principles of Glasnost, my speeches were either not reported at all or were 'edited' out of all recognition.

These events have roots both in our distant history and in the years of Perestroika, but already there is no mistaking the fact that one of their main causes was a loss of social cohesion, which became increasingly damaging after the August coup. Even now

[2] M. S. Gorbachev, *Dekabr'-91. Moia pozitsiia*, M.: Novosti, 1992.

you will hear it claimed that the coup plotters were acting to prevent disintegration of the USSR and maintain the integrity of the state. Some even try to represent the coup as an attempt to ensure the democratic reforms succeeded. That is codswallop. The real aims of the plot were obviously to retain and resuscitate the old ways, even if that meant resorting to the most extreme measures. Through their actions, the coup plotters disrupted the signing of the Union Treaty, implementation of the programme to counter the crisis, and reform of the Communist Party.

In this book I present my position as it was declared during those days and weeks in December 1991, not titivated or revised in the light of the events of this new year.

Just before the book was due to be published, I decided to add a kind of second preface, and felt a lecture I gave during my visit to Germany on 8 March 1992 in Munich fitted the bill. Here are the main points I made:

During the Perestroika period there were, of course, mistakes, tactical miscalculations. There is no denying that, but I would like to highlight one issue of principle, because it explains a lot in the past and present. That is the relationship between politics and morality.

From the earliest stages of Perestroika, when we were only beginning to think about it, when the idea of a profound, revolutionary restructuring of our entire society was taking shape, I vowed to myself, and declared publicly, that I would do all in my power to ensure that the transition, although revolutionary, would, for the first time in the history of a country like ours, be peaceful, without bloodshed, without categorizing people as Reds and Whites, or Blacks and Blues. ...

New Thinking as the philosophy of Perestroika was based on universal values, not a class approach, which leads only to social confrontation, divisions and conflict. To this day I firmly believe that was the only correct position and I have adhered to it throughout my political career. I see it not as a sign of weakness but of strength and determination.

As president I was criticized for not making full use of my powers. What matters most, however, is not the president's powers or how he uses them, but his moral position. Once we had recognized the legitimacy of pluralism in economic and political life, and indeed in every aspect of society, it was essential to stop resorting to 'administrative' approaches and resolving the problems that arise in any society by force. That too was a skill we had not fully mastered and had to acquire as we went along. It was not easy.

It took immense faith that we were moving in the right direction, and immense stamina not to renege on that initial decision.

I am reminded of an example from Russian history. Who was the right-hand man of Tsar Alexander I at the beginning of his reign? Mikhail Speransky, an architect of reform. And who was running the show at the end of his reign? Alexey Arakcheyev, renowned for his brutally repressive regime. That is the kind of volte-face reformers tend to succumb to under the pressure of events, ending up very far away from what they initially sought to achieve.

Remaining true to your moral convictions is extremely trying, but I did not go back on this most fundamental political and moral choice. I believe that ultimately this 'indecisiveness' and this 'tardiness' of President Gorbachev (and I confine the words firmly within quotation marks), in other words, my approach, my strategy, are what has enabled society to build up strengths which, as people are now saying, are the foundation for preserving and building on our democratic changes.

We managed occasionally to get out to the theatre. On 27 January, Raisa and I were invited by Oleg Yefremov to a function at the Moscow Art Theatre. On 29 January, we attended a celebration of *Nezavisimaya Gazeta* at Cinema House. Since stepping down from the presidency, this was my first major public appearance and opportunity to meet a large number of people. Many shook hands, and I was able to talk to some, to reminisce and discuss. Members of the intelligentsia had reacted in a variety of ways during Perestroika, and relations with many of those in Cinema House that day were also to develop in different ways. That evening, however, was a celebration of Glasnost and freedom. Speaking to the gathering, I said that this achievement of Perestroika needed to be protected and defended, whatever zigzags might lie ahead for Russia's historical development.

On 28 February I had a meeting at the Gorbachev Foundation
with young members of democratic parties who were attending
courses at the Foundation's Social Science Centre. Most were
from the Democratic Party and the Free Russia People's Party.
The budding politicians impressed me favourably. They were not
interested in so-called 'political technology', which later came so
much into vogue and was often no more than political chican-
ery, but in the real problems of the country and how it could be
reformed. I supported that:

> A competent democratic politician does not defer to ochlocracy,
> while demagogues go out of their way to provoke mob rule and see
> what fish they can catch in muddied waters. That is the approach
> today of both our extreme left and extreme right. It has to be said
> that our democrats who are presently themselves in or close to
> power are behaving very oddly in this respect.

I felt it important to add:

> I want you to know that I am hoping the Yeltsin government will
> be successful in continuing democratic reform, because if it does
> not succeed, all of us and Russia will face serious trouble. In terms
> of foreign policy it is essential to continue in the spirit of the New
> Political Thinking, along the path embarked on in the second half
> of the 1980s, and not try to reinvent everything as if history began
> in December 1991, as Burbulis claims. We must not repeat the sce-
> nario of 1930s Germany when the democrats bickered and fought
> each other, and allowed Hitler to come to power.

Among the questions asked was one about ownership of land.
It was tempting to latch on to simple solutions in agrarian matters
and there were a lot of illusions around. I replied:

> I am all in favour of coexistence of different forms of land use, col-
> lective and private, where that is justified in practice. Incidentally,
> in traditional Western agricultural countries like Italy, France and
> Spain, individual peasant holdings are enmeshed in a whole net-
> work of cooperative relationships.

I talked about how the situation was developing in the country in the first months of 1992 in an interview for *Komsomolskaya Pravda*. In February the government adjusted its policies, and by the end of the month the situation was less acute. I remarked on this, because I do not gloat when things get worse.

At the same time, I decided to take the opportunity to speak loud and clear to the whole country, through a newspaper with a circulation of many millions, against the smear campaign I was being subjected to by the Communists under Gennadiy Zyuganov and their supporters. The situation was ludicrous: the Communist Party's reactionaries were denouncing Gorbachev the Democrat, while the radicals were denouncing Gorbachev the Communist Party Boss. Every newspaper every day could be relied on to vilify Gorbachev. Responding to the lot of them, I said:

> The reactionaries who were defeated dream of taking society back to the pre-Perestroika era and are busily trying to blacken the reputation of all who introduced reform. They focus on the most serious difficulties in people's lives, exploiting tensions and trying to present me as the cause of all ills.
>
> I wish, through your newspaper, to invite the world's bankers to reveal all the information at their disposal about my supposed foreign bank accounts. Please reveal every detail of the amounts and dates of any deposits. Go ahead, publish it all!
>
> Rumours to the effect that Gorbachev wants to emigrate, to live abroad on all the money he has supposedly squirrelled away, have gone beyond the bounds of all decency. I have to disappoint you! I have no intention of running anywhere. Here is where I have lived and shall live my life. Many might like to see the back of me, but that is not going to happen.
>
> The views of the president of the USSR were not reported in December, and there are attempts to misrepresent my position now. One letter-writer advised me to shoot myself, but hundreds of others support me. For as long as it seems to me that I can be useful to my country, I will not be silent. In 1974, Shchelkov tried to crush me when I began sacking bribe-takers in the militia in Stavropol. Even when I was a member of the Politburo, false testimony was fabricated against me. Shortly before he died, a deputy

interior affairs minister told me all about it. Those people have not gone away! Are they hoping now to get the people of our country to join in their harassment?

I have every intention of continuing to work in politics and public affairs to promote New Political Thinking and, needless to say, to facilitate reforms and democratic change within our country. That is what I told Boris Yeltsin.

Salvation in work

I celebrated my 61st birthday at home with my family. There were many greetings, often from people I had not previously known, and the apartment was overflowing with flowers. There were telegrams from all over the place: from big cities and the distant provinces. Some were short, just three or four words wishing me good health and fortitude. I and my family found that particularly touching. People understood that we were in a difficult situation and wanted to lend us support. Some of the letters were very carefully considered and thoughtful. We were cheered to see that people, citizens, understood that change was essential and that life could be better.

On 3 March 1992 we held the official launch of the International Foundation for Socio-Economic and Political Studies, the Gorbachev Foundation. That day, hundreds of invited guests streamed towards our headquarters on Leningrad Prospekt. There were representatives of Moscow academic and artistic organizations and public figures, among them Eduard Shevardnadze, Yevgeny Primakov, Yevgeny Velikhov, Alexander and Yegor Yakovlev, Nikita Mikhalkov and other famous people. There were many foreign guests, journalists and diplomats, in total some 1,000 guests. The Russian government was represented by Vice-President Alexander Rutskoy. In a brief speech, I said:

> We are witnessing a change of eras. That is why we have decided to continue the intellectual effort that ushered in a new understanding of the present day and major changes in the world, opening new opportunities for relations between countries and

peoples. Hence the motto of our Foundation, 'Towards a New Civilization'.

We are not a governmental, but an academic organization. We have no levers for exerting direct influence on policy, and we make no claim to participate directly in the political process.

Our Foundation is not going to be an ivory tower dispassionately observing the situation in the country. The Foundation's aim is to provide analysis and research to help Russia emerge from crisis.

To investigate objectively what was happening in the country and the world, to provide a platform for intellectual searching with the involvement of representatives from a broad spectrum of political forces, except, needless to say, the extremists – such was the mission I and my associates envisaged for the Foundation. Looking back, I can only say the Foundation has been fully up to the task. It has been a success.

The Foundation began work, and has continued all these years, under far from easy conditions. The first priority was to raise funds for its research and charitable projects. We received, and still receive, no financial support from the state. With time, the main source of funding came to be from my lecture tours abroad. That is nothing to be ashamed of. Giving lectures is not just a way of earning fees, but an opportunity to talk to people about what is happening in the outside world and in Russia. Despite the difficulties of the present situation in our country, despite my critical attitude towards many aspects of what goes on, I always tell my audiences, be they academics, students or businessmen, Russia will get back on her feet; she will be a major player in global processes. There have been times of trial and times of troubles in her history before, but she has always been reborn and given much to mankind. So it will be this time also.

Attempts to 'destabilize' me

Gradually, my post-presidential life developed a routine and I found myself with a busy schedule. There were many invitations to speak abroad, from Germany, the United States, Japan and

Italy. Preparing for these visits took up a lot of time. I consulted academics and experts, and worked on important addresses to the German Parliament and US Congress.

Meanwhile, attempts to neutralize me continued with various 'charges': I had been involved in a conspiracy connected with the State Emergency Committee's coup; I had been embezzling the CPSU's funds; and so on. Someone evidently saw all this as a high priority. While the libels were coming from the likes of long-forgotten Deputy Sergey Belozertsev, they could be ignored. When, however, they came from the president of Russia, I asked Prosecutor General Valentin Stepankov to conduct an enquiry into the substance of the charges.

On 15 March 1992, the prosecutor general, replying at a press conference in Moscow to a question from Andrey Pershin, correspondent of the Interfax News Agency's *Presidential Messenger*, said the prosecutor's office had conducted an investigation at my request. No hard facts had been found in the files on the case of the State Emergency Committee or been presented by Belozertsev. A document to this effect had, the prosecutor general stated, been issued to Gorbachev.

I also talked to the prosecutor general about the 'case of the Communist Party Finances'. I had nothing to hide, and it was clear from the outset that there was a great deal of groundless speculation in the allegations. I could see that certain people were trying to exploit the law-enforcement agencies and courts against me, but considered it important to demonstrate respect for them. Our discussion was conducted in a civilized manner, and there was no talk of 'restrictive measures' like a ban on my travelling abroad. We agreed to meet a second time. This took place in early April and lasted about an hour and a half. Here is the Interfax agency report:

> Mikhail Gorbachev said that he was prepared to cooperate with the Prosecution Service to establish all the facts in connection with the case on the CPSU financial resources. Gorbachev stated that, by visiting the Prosecution Service, he wanted to demonstrate that respect for the law should be the 'norm for everybody' in the country.

Mikhail Gorbachev stated that no specific charges had been laid against him in the course of his interview at the Prosecution Service. He expressed doubt that the investigation would reveal concealment or illegal transfer of CPSU funds to banks in other countries.

I also answered questions about the case of the CPSU's money put to me by Vadim Belykh and Valeriy Rudnev, reporters from *Izvestiya* [*The News*]:

Q: Mikhail Sergeyevich, so much has been talked and written about the Party's finances, but everyone is waiting to hear what you have to say.

A: Frankly speaking, there has been too much noise and too much invention in the newspapers and gossip about this issue. I support the efforts of the team of investigators: we need finally to understand everything and dot all the 'i's. There is no need for all this sensationalism. We should also ensure that the investigators' findings are made public. There should be no secrets about the Party's financial affairs.

In recent years there have not been any. Of course, in the past the budget of the CPSU was not made public. Not even all Party members knew our income and expenditure, but at the Twenty-Eighth Congress we made all the Party's accounts openly available to Party members.

How well we managed the money is another matter. Initially, the Party's funds just lay as dead weight in the bank. Later, when we reduced the membership dues, we naturally lost some income, actually, a very considerable part of it. The question arose of how to make up the losses, and we began to study commerce. We reduced the size of the Central Committee and provincial Party administrations, and started investing money productively. We put it into circulation to bring in income for the Party. I emphasize that we did all this in accordance with the law. How competently we did it is another matter.

Q: But in the lawsuit regarding the CPSU cash there is talk of abuses and personal enrichment.

A: Exactly. There is talk. There is much rumour-mongering

and just plain malicious tittle-tattle around my name. You are
welcome to investigate using whatever judicial, undercover or
journalistic means you choose: my conscience is clear.

There was an attempt to use the opening of the CPSU archives
against me. The new government's propagandists proclaimed
that when they threw open the Central Committee archives they
would find there such dirt on Gorbachev as would make the
whole world shudder.

And then in March there was a presentation at the Centre for
the Preservation of Contemporary Documentation, created on the
basis of the archives of the Central Committee. It was announced
that more than 160 million documents from the Party archives,
'reflecting the mechanisms of governance that existed in the
USSR prior to August 1991', would be made accessible to almost
anyone interested in reading them. The media reported:

> The exhibition organized in connection with the launch dis-
> played minutes stamped 'Top Secret' of meetings of the Central
> Committee's Politburo, including some dated 1990; the personal
> files of Party leaders and of such top officials and military lead-
> ers as Eduard Shevardnadze, Georgiy Zhukov and Konstantin
> Rokossovsky; the original Party membership and record cards of
> Vladimir Lenin, Joseph Stalin, Nikita Khrushchev, Yury Andropov,
> Konstantin Chernenko, Mikhail Gorbachev and other documents.

What can we add to this report today, after more than 20 years
have passed? Many important documents 'disappeared' into foreign archives, but to this day no compromising documents against
Gorbachev have been found. We talk of something being 'as difficult as finding a black cat in a dark room'. That is even more
difficult if the cat is not there in the first place.

The 'Trial of the CPSU'

Meanwhile, the situation in the country was developing unpre-
dictably. The reforms were increasingly being implemented in line
with the 'shock therapy' approach, devised by the International

Monetary Fund for countries whose economies were fundamentally different from that of Russia, but accepted by our reformers as virtually a panacea. In some countries the schemes worked, if at a high price, but in Russia implementing them brought about a sudden fall in production and mass impoverishment of the population. One of the consequences of this was increasing friction between the Supreme Soviet of Russia, which until recently had given Yeltsin unconditional support, and the president's team, who insisted on a 'resolute' continuation of shock therapy. In April, these tensions almost boiled over at the Congress of People's Deputies of Russia.

The hawks among Yeltsin's supporters and advisers told him he should disperse the Congress. He did not take their advice, and gave a fairly conciliatory speech there, stating after it was over that he had succeeded in rescuing the reform programme. At a press conference in Moscow, I said: 'If the president had followed the advice he was receiving and dispersed the Congress, the consequences for society would have been tragic.' On this occasion the worst was avoided, but I found myself increasingly at odds with the policies the government was so aggressively pursuing. At the same press conference, I warned:

> Yes, the times call for tough measures, but they cannot be implemented at breakneck speed. Our people were once herded into collectivization, then into industrialization, and now they are being driven into Burbulization. In the past it was all ostensibly done, and is again supposedly being done, for the greater happiness of the people.

I commented that there was a current vogue for resolute politicians, 'but resolute people alarm me. They could easily wreck everything that has been achieved in the past seven years. It is vital to base policies on what is possible in terms of the actual economic, political and social situation.'

As time passed, however, it became increasingly obvious that the president and his team had decided to race ahead regardless of the consequences. The economy responded to their 'resolute action' by collapsing at an accelerating rate, and the life of ordinary people became increasingly hard. This was evident when someone came up with the idea of distracting attention from the rigours of the transition to a free market by 'putting the Communist Party on trial'.

The occasion was a petition to the Constitutional Court by a group of deputies, former Party officials, asking the court to examine the legality of Yeltsin's decrees dissolving the Communist Parties of the Soviet Union and of the RSFSR [Russian Soviet Federative Socialist Republic]. In response, Oleg Rumyantsev, the secretary of the Constitutional Commission, filed a counter-petition to review the legitimacy of the CPSU itself. The Court decided to consider both matters jointly. Thus began the saga of the Trial of the CPSU, a pernicious enterprise from the outset, which served only to deepen the divisions in Russian society.

In late May, at a meeting between Yeltsin and the represen-tatives he sent to attend sessions of the Constitutional Court (Secretary of State Gennadiy Burbulis, Member of the Supreme Soviet Sergey Shakhrai and Director of the Intellectual Property Agency Mikhail Fedotov) the idea was proposed of turning the trial of the Communist Party into a 'new Nuremberg Trial'. This was confirmed the same day by Shakhrai at a press conference. As the Constitutional Court considered the 'case', it became clear that those who had instigated it, in fact both sides, were eager to turn the Trial of the CPSU into a Trial of Mikhail Gorbachev.

There could be no two ways about it: this was an attempt to exploit the Russian judicial system to exert pressure and settle scores in a political struggle. There is no need to dwell on the absurdity of the intention of delivering a legal assessment of Soviet history and the constitutionality of the Communist Party. My decision was unequivocal and irrevocable: I would take no part in these antics.

Not everybody understood my reasons, and even some of my colleagues urged me to show respect for the court and find some manner of means for taking part in the 'trial'. That would have had me playing for both teams at the same time, and moreover, both were equally determined to blame all the country's ills on Gorbachev in order to exonerate themselves. By this I mean the reactionary wing of the disbanded Communist Party and the extreme radicals in Yeltsin's entourage. If I allowed them to lead me by the nose, I would only be contributing to a further heightening of social tensions, a splitting of society into opposing camps and diversion of attention away from pressing problems which were snowballing.

The signals emanating from Yeltsin at this time left no doubt as to his intentions towards me: he wanted to humiliate and, at the very least, silence me. On 2 June the president's press secretary, Vyacheslav Kostikov, issued the following statement:

> The utterances of the former president of the USSR have of late been adopting an ever more didactic tone towards the government and the president, and a number of recent statements by Mikhail Gorbachev cannot be interpreted otherwise than as an attempt to heighten political tension, in effect, to destabilize the socio-political situation in the country.

The statement continued that Boris Yeltsin, noting that such utterances by M. Gorbachev were both dangerous and intolerable, would be forced to 'take the necessary legal steps to ensure that the reform programme was not harmed'.

So that was what was threatening reform in Russia!

My response to this warning shot took the form of a statement from the Press Service of the Gorbachev Foundation:

> M. S. Gorbachev has in recent weeks repeatedly drawn the attention of those he has spoken to, including those abroad, to the extreme importance of stabilizing Russia and ensuring the success of the reforms. He has emphasized that, in the face of serious difficulties, we must remain firm. He has, in the process, noted that his proposals 'come from someone with a strong interest in seeing that everything that has been initiated should be carried through to completion, and that Boris Yeltsin and the government should succeed'. Yeltsin's team was meanwhile busily preparing for a trial in the Constitutional Court. Representation of the president's interests was delegated to officials close to Yeltsin, under Secretary of State Burbulis. On the day before the trial, he publicly expressed his confidence that the court would arrive at a verdict 'conducive to

continuation of reform by Boris Yeltsin's team' and would uphold
the constitutional ban on the CPSU, and that this would 'prove the
path to normal state governance in the Russian Federation'.

With the beginning of the politically motivated Trial of the
Communist Party, I found myself again under fire from two
directions. More precisely, I was under a synchronous political
and propaganda attack from all directions by radicals of the left
and right. *Den'*, the mouthpiece of sundry anti-reform forces,
demanded that Gorbachev should be put in the dock for having
instigated the State Emergency Committee coup, while simultaneously demanding that all the coup participants should be released.

Yeltsin's side were threatening to 'take measures', to discredit me, and intriguing to force me to leave the country. Both
sides were eager to take it out on Gorbachev in order to divert
public attention from their own very serious failures and the
consequences of their policies.

On 29 July, literally the day after I announced my decision on
moral grounds to have no truck with the trial at the Constitutional
Court, the Finance Ministry of the Russian Federation, through its
Audit Department, set up a special commission to scrutinize the
economic and financial activities of the Gorbachev Foundation.

The Commission, which comprised no fewer than ten
experienced auditors under the direction of the Chief Audit
Inspector of the Finance Ministry, began a total audit of the
Foundation's financial records. And all this within five months of
the Foundation's official opening and almost six months before
the accounts for the fiscal year were due! It was obvious that
such an extraordinary inspection could only have been initiated
by the man at the top. That fact, against a background of major
economic and financial upheaval, the embezzlement of billions of
roubles of public money and property, bureaucratic malfeasance
and rampant corruption in every sector of the economy and government of the country, speaks volumes about the character and
the moral and intellectual level of the Russian government of the
time.

Unfortunately, the same sort of thing goes on in front of our
eyes even today.

First results of shock therapy

Summer was coming to an end, but this year August at least brought no catastrophic events, other than that the economic situation was approaching crisis levels. The decline of industrial output continued, due mainly to the policy of shock therapy and the rupturing of economic ties between the republics of the former Soviet Union. Reminiscing about that period, Boris Yeltsin wrote later: 'In September 1992, I looked at the statistics for the economy over the first nine months. They were horrifying.' In the same place he comments:

> By the end of summer, it was clear the economy was breaking down ... The danger finally became clear that the period of galloping inflation could drag on for years ... Whole strata of the population were sliding towards the poverty threshold ... And at the same time there was acute social stratification. The wealth of some was in stark contrast with the poverty of others. Society was entering a difficult period of social alienation.

I could not put it better myself. The only plus was 'elimination of shortages of goods'. What a price that came at! By the end of the year, prices had risen 2,600 per cent and inflation was running at 5–7 per cent a week. The savings of those who in the Soviet period might have been categorized as middle class had been rendered worthless. Instant liberalization of prices and hyperinflation had effectively expropriated the population's savings to the tune of some 800 trillion roubles, or $160–170 billion. In 1992, Gross Domestic Product fell by almost 20 per cent and industrial production by 18 per cent.

The government was now pinning its hopes on swift privatization of state property. Behind closed doors, a voucher privatization scheme was hastily drafted over the summer. It differed substantially from the 'popular privatization' plans being worked on by academics in the Supreme Soviet, the Moscow Mayor's Office and other institutions. Once again, the policy was to rush it through without consultation. On 23 August, the president signed a decree introducing voucher privatization

on 1 October, with the intention that it should come into force
within a week, before the Supreme Soviet deputies returned from
their summer break. This was a straightforward violation of the
constitution, under which privatization of state property fell
within the competence of the Congress of People's Deputies and
the Supreme Soviet.

A year after the coup

On 17 August 1992, I arranged a press conference for the numerous journalists who had asked for interviews in connection with
the first anniversary of the August coup. Today, when many
years have passed, I reflect on how many of these anniversaries
there have been, and how every time they provide an excuse for
unfounded conjecture, defamation and libel. In 1992 that was just
beginning. The coup plotters, newly repentant, began one after
the other to offer up new accounts of the events with the manifest
purpose of whitewashing themselves and discrediting Gorbachev.
Meanwhile, the consequences of their mischief-making were
becoming only too evident, and that was the main point I made at
the news conference.

The State Emergency Committee coup, I said, was a criminal
escapade rejected by the citizens of Moscow and the country
at large, but which, ultimately, played into the hands of those
opposed to maintaining a single unified state. I included among
those complicit in destruction of the Soviet Union the government
of Russia proper, which, in December 1991, torpedoed the possibility of concluding a new Union Treaty of the sovereign states
that had comprised the USSR.

In reply to a question about the possibility of another coup, I
said, 'Only a crazy idiot would embark on such a course', but I
warned that the growing levels of mass discontent had the potential to generate forces far from democratic. 'I think,' I said, 'that
the present government is at risk of losing out in exactly the same
way Gorbachev lost out: by falling behind on key political issues.'

I also said I was shocked by the levels of corruption in the
current state institutions, to which we had entrusted the reforms
and our own destiny. 'It has come to such a state of affairs that

a guidebook has been published in America listing the names of officials in our new government and other institutions and specifying the number of dollars they require as bribes for resolving issues.'

Under the guise of 'popular privatization', there are plans to rob the population. Everybody will be given a voucher equivalent to a month or a half-month's salary, and those who have been stealing and looting the economy will buy up the securities from the people and seize, first, economic and then political power.

My judgements were harsh but, unfortunately, proved only too accurate.

I had also to mention the discreditable role of the press: 'My statements to the people are often simply ignored and suppressed. If anything does get published, it is only in a much curtailed form. The press has become subservient to the government. It too toes the line, aiming only to survive.' What was needed, I said, was a programme of emergency measures for Russia: 'We need a new economic reform programme around which all patriotic democratic forces can unite. On a basis of consent it will be possible to take wide-ranging, radical decisions to stabilize society and avert a rift and further deterioration of the situation.'

My stance

The pressure on me was ramped up. It was insisted I must take part in the charade of the Trial of the Communist Party, whose dangers were becoming increasingly obvious. I decided I should state my position publicly in the form of an open letter to the Constitutional Court. Here it is in its entirety:

Dear president and members of the Constitutional Court,
In connection with your decision of 30 September to summon me to attend the court as a witness, I wish to make the following statement:
    I stated my position on this trial some time ago, and gave my grounds for not participating in it, which seemed to meet with understanding. Since, however, for unknown reasons the Court

has nevertheless decided to summon me, I feel obliged to lay out my reasons in the form of an open letter.

Despite my deep respect for the Constitutional Court as an important democratic institution of Russia, I do not find it possible to take part in its trial of this case. By agreeing to consider it, the Constitutional Court has become embroiled in actions inappropriate to its status. It has become a hostage in a political conflict, to the detriment of its authority. At the same time it is contributing to aggravation of the social and political situation in the country. Accordingly, no matter how professionally, from a technical point of view, this trial is conducted, it cannot be free of the character of a political trial. It is by now obvious that it is being exploited by the parties in a conflict in their narrow political interests.

One side is seeking to destabilize the situation by trying surreptitiously to rehabilitate those members of the Party leadership, the Secretariat of the Central Committee of the CPSU and other Party institutions who supported the coup of August 1991, or who even directly participated in it; a coup that dealt an irreparable blow to democratic reform, disrupted the signing of a treaty for a Union of Sovereign States, the beginnings of a programme to overcome the crisis, and the holding of an extraordinary congress of the CPSU to complete democratic reform of the Party.

The other side, losing public support for its policies and seeking a scapegoat, wants to put our history in the dock and to argue that the Party was unconstitutional. These efforts could signal a return to suppression of dissent and recreate a climate where reprisals for the holding of political views and beliefs is seen as legitimate. I spoke out strongly against that kind of approach in the Supreme Soviet of the RSFSR after the coup and adhere firmly to that view.

One further point. I cannot participate in this trial, on moral grounds. At this time society is in a state of crisis. As winter approaches, people are greatly concerned about the provision of food and heat. The economic reform as currently implemented has not delivered on the promises made to the people, millions of whom are already experiencing poverty. There is increasing uncertainty in the country about the ability of the current leadership to conduct affairs, about what policies it is currently planning to implement and about whether it will really prove capable of delivering cooperation with other states of our Commonwealth.

Without this, there can be no prospect either of the resolution of urgent problems or of further progress through reform to ending the crisis. Efforts to revive a lawsuit that had essentially stalled and to give it a sensationalist veneer is nothing short of an attempt to distract our citizens' attention from genuinely vital issues. What is needed now is not a deepening of society's divisions, not inciting people to attack each other, but consolidation and unification of the forces of reform and democracy.

As a Russian citizen, I respect the law and the constitution of my country. I participated as a witness in the investigation by the Prosecutor's Office of the activities of the State Emergency Committee and the finances of the CPSU. I met the investigators and gave evidence. I do not believe I gave any grounds to suspect me of a lack of respect for the law.

Nevertheless, I am not prepared to become involved in a political trial whose consequences can only be uniformly negative. I find that unacceptable.

As regards history, no matter how tragic it has been, treating it as something amenable to legal proceedings strikes me as futile. It has been attempted in the past and resulted only in bathos.

Respected Constitutional Court, I hope that the reasons and considerations I have given, and no less my moral position, will be received with due understanding.

Yours sincerely,

Mikhail Gorbachev
28 September 1992

My open letter to the Constitutional Court enraged the instigators and perpetrators of this piece of nonsense, because it undermined the whole sensation on which it was premised: a show trial of the president of the USSR. The court gave a ruling 'officially requiring' me to 'appear when summoned to give witness statements'.

The president of the court, Valeriy Zorkin, accused me of contempt of court. One of the judges, and after him Minister of Justice Nikolai Fedorov, threatened to instigate criminal proceedings against Gorbachev for failing to appear before the Constitutional

Court, although the law regulating the court provides for no penalties other than a fine of 100 roubles. They all seemed to be overlooking the classical principle, going back to Roman law and familiar to every law student, of *nullum crimen, nulla poena sine lege* [no crime, no punishment without a law]. Some Russian judges and courts in the twenty-first century could do with being regularly and loudly reminded of this classic principle.

It finally came to the point where the former president of the USSR was banned from travelling abroad. The announcement was published by the Press Service of the Constitutional Court. They had evidently suddenly forgotten or, on the contrary, had decided to remind everyone, of the effect of being banned from travelling abroad during the Soviet period: that very wall of prohibitions which had been demolished by none other than the president of the USSR.

On 3 October I wrote to the Constitutional Court, the Foreign Ministry and the Ministry of Security asking to be informed by whom and on what legal basis measures had been taken that affected my civil rights, responsibilities and legitimate interests. The Constitutional Court replied, 'All decisions of the Constitutional Court affecting your interests have already been made known to you. You may familiarize yourself directly with the other documents at the Constitutional Court.'

The only conclusion possible from this response was that the decision had not been taken in the Constitutional Court, and they had no documentation to show me. Quite obviously, the measures taken by 'the relevant authorities' had been based solely on the principle of 'law over the telephone' and were hence illegal.

Then, without warning, on the morning of 7 October the Gorbachev Foundation offices were cordoned off by the police and sealed. The Foundation's staff were prevented from going in to work. At the entrance a crowd of Moscow and foreign correspondents gathered; for them, the sealing off of the Gorbachev Foundation was a big story.

More and more people were arriving and I was warned over my car telephone that a regiment of mounted police would arrive shortly. I asked for my request that everyone should remain calm and orderly to be passed on. Arriving at the Foundation, I found myself giving an impromptu press conference. I surmised that the decree, effectively confiscating the Foundation's property, had resulted from my blunt criticism of the president of Russia, and described the government's action as ostentatious despotism. I suggested that the government was on the verge of paralysis and was trying, by this sort of conduct, to assert its authority.

Speaking about the situation in the country, I said that, having flung Russia into an unregulated market, the government now did not know what to do next. Yes, we needed to adopt market relations, but should do so gradually, taking account of the interests of the bulk of the population. It seemed that now the best way forward would be to form a coalition government.

I talked also about the workings of the Constitutional Court, which had undertaken to consider the 'case against the CPSU', even though that was no part of its remit. They had succeeded only in presiding over a political free-for-all, and meanwhile the federation was splitting apart and the economic situation was going from bad to worse.

As later became apparent, the previous day the president of Russia had signed a decree rescinding his own decree of 23 December 1991 and transferring the building and property at the disposal of the Foundation to the beneficial use of the Financial Academy of the Government of the Russian Federation. The Financial Academy was instructed to lease to the Gorbachev Foundation at a price to be agreed premises totalling 800 m². The Foundation had previously occupied 3,500 m² in the building.

Negotiations began between officials of the State Property Agency and the Foundation's managers. The government representatives did eventually agree to allow staff in to collect their work materials and personal belongings.

All this was acted out in front of numerous reporters. Before long, the government representatives were asking the Foundation's staff to calm the press down and bring some order to the reporting of the outrage, which was already echoing round the world. I and my colleagues did what we could, and stated that the Foundation intended to protest against the government's abuse of power solely by lawful means.

My travel ban redounded to the discredit of those who had

come up with such an inane idea. On 9 October, our Foundation was visited by the French Ambassador, Pierre Morel. He conveyed to me the sympathy and support of President François Mitterrand, his best wishes for the Foundation's success and his invitation to visit France at a time of my choosing.

From press reports, we learned that the 'Gorbachev affair' had been raised in London at a meeting between the Russian Foreign Minister Andrey Kozyrev, Prime Minister John Major and the British Foreign Secretary Douglas Hurd. Kozyrev described as an 'unfortunate coincidence' the simultaneous 'temporary moratorium' on travel abroad of the former USSR president and the government measures taken in respect of the Gorbachev Foundation.

Next, following the death of the former German Chancellor Willy Brandt, his friends and the German government invited me to take part in the funeral of this outstanding political and public figure, with whom I had a long history of friendship and constructive cooperation. Chancellor Helmut Kohl addressed a request to the Russian government to allow me to come to Germany for the funeral. Thereupon, 'justice over the telephone' clicked into action, also making it clear who had been behind the ban in the first place.

The president of the Constitutional Court now informed the press that President Boris Yeltsin had requested him to consent to Mikhail Gorbachev's travelling to Germany to take part in the funeral of ex-Chancellor Willy Brandt. The Constitutional Court, Zorkin went on, had decided it was permissible to hear evidence from Mikhail Gorbachev before his trip abroad in connection with 'humane considerations', and after it. This did not mean, Zorkin added, that the Constitutional Court had gone back on its decision to summon Gorbachev to appear in court to testify.

Meanwhile, batches of 'compromising material on Gorbachev' continued to be fed to the press. Nothing was off limits: the tragedy of the South Korean passenger plane shot down in the Far East of the USSR in 1983; the Soviet invasion of Afghanistan in 1979; the August 1991 coup; and, finally, 'the latest sensation – concealment from the Poles and the world of who was really responsible for the Katyn massacre'. This release was saved up for the final sitting of the Constitutional Court in the trial of the Communist Party and came just as I was attending the farewell for Willy Brandt.

Overlooked was the fact that it was I who, during his visit to Moscow, handed over to President Wojciech Jaruzelski of Poland archive documents found by Soviet historians testifying to the fact that Lavrentiy Beria and Vsevolod Merkulov were responsible for the atrocities in the Katyn forest. This was reported in a statement from the TASS news agency of 13 April 1990, where the Soviet side expressed deep regret at the Katyn tragedy, one of the heinous crimes of Stalinism.

When, a few days before leaving the Kremlin, I passed over to Yeltsin the contents of the secret archive of the Central Committee of the CPSU, which contained some 3,000 'special folders', I gave him also the Politburo documents with the signed decisions of Stalin and his immediate entourage on a note from Beria dated March 1940. This had an appendix about the shooting of thousands of Polish prisoners of war. We agreed at that time, in December 1991, that Yeltsin would give these documents to the Poles. I can only guess why he did not do so during the visit to Moscow of President Lech Wałęsa in summer 1992. Perhaps even then he was keeping them back for use in his Nuremberg Trial of the CPSU and Gorbachev.

Despite the pressure to which I was being subjected, I stood firm. I expressed willingness to meet the president of the Constitutional Court, but not as part of any trial. I did so not out of fear for my reputation, or, indeed, my life. Lacking presidential legal immunity, I was prepared for anything. I was guided by considerations of principle, considering that the exploitation of the law and constitutional oversight for political purposes was as unlawful as it was immoral. I considered it tantamount to elevating despotism to a policy, and destroying the fundamentals of modern governance and civilization.

Evidently aware that he had painted himself into a corner, Valeriy Zorkin went on television to deliver a statement, demeaning for a judge and offensive to me:

> I believe that by failing to appear in court Mikhail Gorbachev
> has signed his own verdict ... Perhaps I am infringing the law
> by revealing my own, as it were, personal thoughts, but I find
> myself increasingly inclined to think that Gorbachev in his
> present capacity is effectively becoming an encumbrance for
> Russia.

I protested against these remarks by the president of the
Constitutional Court and, as provided for by the law on information, demanded that I should be given an opportunity to respond
to these accusations and clarify my position in a live broadcast
with the same format and the same team of presenters.

The chairman of the Russian State Television and Radio
Corporation, Oleg Poptsov, on the grounds that Zorkin's broadcast press conference had 'not been organized on the initiative of
RTR', refused to give me airtime. In principle, he went on to say,
he did not exclude the possibility of broadcasting 'within reasonable limits' M. S. Gorbachev's answers in a video recording in
news or other programmes, although this would not be possible in
the immediate future mainly 'for technical reasons'.

Well, that is what happens to people who are not free to act as
they choose, and not prepared to stand up for a matter of principle. Their technology inexplicably breaks down, and they destroy
something of fundamental importance in themselves.

The controversy surrounding the Trial of the CPSU, and the
whole climate in society and politics, were increasingly fraught
with intolerance and authoritarianism. The main features of the
opposed parties, or gangs, were mutual hostility and a desire to
crush all who stood in their way or were political adversaries.
Literally every day of that first post-Soviet year further strengthened my belief that we were heading towards a new setback for
the growth of democracy initiated by Perestroika that might even
bring it to an end.

I decided to speak out publicly about this just as soon as might
be, and the opportunity presented itself at the airport, where I
found journalists awaiting my return from Willy Brandt's funeral.
The vendetta and vengeful behaviour of my political opponents
was not only a campaign to discredit Gorbachev.

It is a premeditated project to mask the absence of any considered and imaginative policy. I can see no constructive responses
to Russia's pressing social problems in President Yeltsin's
addresses to the Supreme Soviet. This situation could lead to
termination of the move towards democracy in Russia, with
far-reaching consequences for our country, the CIS, Europe and
indeed everyone. Both the president and the government like to
call themselves democrats, but have no inclination to listen. ... I
do not want to see Yeltsin fail, but I do want him to find some
means of bringing together all those eager for successful continuation of reforms. If the president neglects to do this, he will go
down to defeat.

That prediction was made less than a year before the Supreme
Soviet of Russia was bombarded by tanks.

The Trial of the CPSU proved a complete damp squib, largely,
I believe, because of the stance I adopted. This was not a matter
of personalities, just that, in the end, the Constitutional Court had
to agree with my points of principle. The Court came to the only
possible logical conclusion: consideration of the constitutionality
of the CPSU should be terminated on the grounds that the CPSU
'had effectively disintegrated' in August–September 1991 and
ceased to be a nationwide organization. Could it not have taken
such an obvious decision at the outset, without all the excited
political shenanigans?

The provocative intentions of those who set up the Trial of the
CPSU had been frustrated, but all the time I was watching what
was going on, I could not help feeling its future consequences
were likely to be very negative.

The slide towards social catastrophe

The efforts of the Russian president and government, and of
orthodox communists stuck in the past, to intimidate and wear
me down with endless accusations and slanders did not, of
course, enhance my life. They were an irritant, but far more
disquieting was what was happening in the country as a result
of the government's rushed and reckless actions. What I read

in the newspapers, and heard when talking to people, painted a thoroughly depressing picture.

At the end of the year, a report, compiled jointly with other research centres, was published by the Institute of Socio-Political Research of the Russian Academy of Sciences. Its main conclusion was: 'The social and socio-political situation developing in the course of 1992 in Russia is nothing short of a slide towards social catastrophe.'

The report's authors had to conclude that the radical reform policies of the past year had been a complete failure. 'We have been unable to discern positive results or progress in any of the directions of the reforms.' This had brought about an abrupt reduction in the number of people supporting the radical course. Society had moved rapidly from faith that the reforms would swiftly yield positive results to alienation and rejection of official policy. This swing in Russian public opinion resulted, the report said, from a catastrophic fall in the standard and quality of people's lives.

The rapid rise in prices, destruction of productive capacity and the government's disregard of the basic social interests of ordinary citizens have led to impoverishment of the majority of Russia's population. Russians have known no comparable fall in the level of social welfare since the Great Patriotic War of 1941–5.

A bacchanalia of disregard for the law and unprecedented destabilization of the economy, bringing about chaos, had led to a sharp rise in corruption and effectively an abdication of power to corrupt individuals and the mafia. From this, the report's authors concluded: 'A government that encourages corrupt elements of the state bureaucracy and black economy operators to seize and share out public property cannot expect to enjoy wide social support.'

Unsurprisingly, the deputies elected just two years previously by a direct vote in free elections reacted against what was taking place. In December 1992, the Seventh Congress of People's Deputies of the Supreme Soviet of Russia sharply criticized both the way the economic shock policy had been conducted and its results. Speakers lambasted the government and First Deputy Prime Minister Yegor Gaidar, who was in charge of economic policy. (The government was formally headed by Yeltsin.)

Gaidar had previously been one of the team working on plans for the Soviet economy's transition to a market economy. He gave the impression of being a serious, knowledgeable, energetic person. I imagine that, if Perestroika had not been cut short, he would have found his place as an academic economist, and perhaps in managing the country's economy. The disintegration of the Soviet Union meant, however, that his potential and that of his young team were exploited by Yeltsin's group in pursuit of primarily political ends. By the time Gaidar joined the government, the country's financial system had been wrecked (not without the connivance of that same Supreme Soviet that was now so highly critical of his record). The mistakes made by the reformers compounded the consequences of the collapse of economic ties between the former Soviet republics. Gaidar was very concerned about what was happening, but not in a position to change the overall policy or make serious adjustments to it.

Yeltsin was, of course, well aware that the deputies' furious criticism was aimed less at Gaidar than at himself. His reaction was fully in character: he sulked and, from the podium, appealed over the heads of those assembled to the citizens of the country, declaring that the congress had turned into 'a mass of total reactionariness'. The president refused to cooperate with the parliament, called for a national referendum of confidence and ostentatiously walked out.

In response, the congress refused by an overwhelming majority to extend the president's emergency powers, but did, ultimately, accept his proposal to elect Viktor Chernomyrdin chairman of the government. Chernomyrdin had served as minister of the gas industry of the USSR and had subsequently headed Gazprom. It was also agreed to hold a referendum in April 1993 on the main provisions of a new constitution, including reallocation of powers between the legislative and executive bodies. Very soon, however, it became clear that this was only a temporary truce in a conflict between two parties, neither of which was inclined to collaborate with the other, to compromise, or to settle for anything less than unconditional victory at any price.

Unlike many, I did not consider the idea of a national referendum constructive or as contributing to stabilizing the situation and consolidating society. In fact, it struck me as positively counterproductive and dangerous. The purpose of the noisy referendum campaign was to divert society's attention from the big question of why the course adopted in January 1992 had brought society to the verge of ruin. I made my opinion clear in an article in the weekly, *Moskovskiye Novosti* [*Moscow News*]. 'Rather than bringing the supporters of reform closer together and extending democracy, the referendum will only deepen divisions and reinforce Russia's centrifugal tendencies.'

The situation was now so acute that I felt compelled to express myself very directly. I described the government's policy towards the people as blatantly cynical. 'The inefficiency of the state bureaucracy and corruption have reached levels unprecedented in Russian history, and indeed in the modern world.'

In the same article, I expressed the opinion that 'further expansion of the Russian president's powers is fraught with the danger of fomenting an openly authoritarian regime'. I drew attention to 'rumours that the president's circle are thinking of declaring a "transitional period", with emergency powers'. A situation might be created, I warned, which 'could be used to justify a "temporary" reduction of free speech and other civil liberties, and suspension of representative bodies while a new constitution was developed and introduced'.

What needed to be done? In order to preserve civil peace, I advised the Congress of People's Deputies to examine the work of the Supreme Soviet and executive arm and seek ways of restoring social harmony. 'If that proves impossible, the only way to resolve the crisis constitutionally is to hold early elections of both branches of government, rather than waiting for a whole year.'

I also felt new elections were needed because the Russian institutions of government had been formed in the days of the USSR, when there was still a centre to the Soviet Union. 'Many active and experienced Russian politicians were not eligible to participate in those elections because they were working in Union, rather than specifically Russian, institutions. Moreover, during the past two years new, fresh forces have come on the political scene in Russia that are capable of assuming responsibility for developing every sphere of life.'

The way events developed showed the risks only too clearly. They were compounded by a continuing deterioration of the situation and increasing hardship in people's lives. This made the conflict between the president and parliament all the more acute and irreconcilable. Serious accusations were hurled by both sides at the other. Yeltsin's kitchen cabinet hinted he was on the verge of dissolving parliament. In response, the deputies denounced the 'Kremlin's court favourites', and called for a campaign of civil disobedience and the establishment of a government of 'national salvation' to 'restore order'. I followed what was happening with growing concern.

On the brink of crisis

Meanwhile, tensions in the country continued to increase. Rumours that the president was planning to declare a state of emergency and strip parliament of its functions proved only too correct. On 20 March, Yeltsin announced in a televised appeal to the citizens that he had signed a decree for an emergency system of government in the Russian Federation until the power struggle was resolved: 'We cannot govern the country and manage its economy, particularly in a time of crisis, by votes, ripostes blurted into microphones, a parliamentary talking shop and endless meetings.' The chairman of the Presidium of the Supreme Soviet, Ruslan Khasbulatov, and the opposition saw the actions of President Boris Yeltsin as an attempted coup d'état. On behalf of the Constitutional Court, Chairman, Valeriy Zorkin declared the president's statement and decree unconstitutional. Outside the Supreme Soviet's headquarters, the 'White House', rallies of those supporting or opposed to the president alternated in the square. Society was split and there was a whiff of burning in the air.

At the request of Interfax, I expressed my opinion of Boris Yeltsin's announcement, describing his decree on introducing presidential rule as a 'serious political miscalculation' that testified to the narrowness of his political power base and the extent of his suggestibility and reliance on the views of people who, as the saying goes, are ready to burn the house down in order to fry themselves an egg. The unconstitutional course of action chosen by the president, despite his promises to eschew force as a political resource, was, I said, 'driving society towards confrontation and could upset the fragile state of peace in society and the state'.

I called on the executive and legislative branches of government to behave responsibly during this critical period of the country's development:

> It is important to allow people to decide for themselves in this situation, and the only way to do that is by holding early elections. ...
>
> It is time for the Congress to speak. It has one last chance to disprove the popular opinion that the deputies are motivated only by an instinct to hold on to power rather than by concern for the fate of Russia. In the present inflamed situation it is vital that the government, and especially the law-enforcement agencies and regions, should not allow themselves to be drawn into a political confrontation between the institutions of government, and should preserve the country from collapse and society from conflict and confrontation.

In what happened subsequently, it seems to me today, what was crucial was less the details of the conflict or even the results of the referendum than the intentions of the parties to the conflict. Did they have the political courage to turn away from a senseless fight and settle down to building the essential institutions of democracy: a strong, responsible presidency; a parliament with extensive powers; an independent judiciary; political parties and the organizations that constitute civil society? Would they jointly find ways to implement difficult but essential economic reforms, while shielding people from their most painful consequences? That was the question.

On the eve of the referendum of 25 April 1993, I commented that, as formulated, it would not lead to a fundamental resolution of the crisis in the institutions of government or the country generally.

The referendum result was formally a victory for the president's team. A majority voted 'yes' to the question of whether they had confidence in the president, and slightly more than half to the question of whether they approved of the government's socio-economic policy. Taking account of the low turnout, this amounted to just over one-third of the electorate. As for the question of calling early elections, 49.5 per cent voted in favour of a new presidential election, and 67.2 per cent in favour of a new parliamentary election.

How should we interpret the result? In my opinion, the referendum result clearly reflected reluctance amongst a majority of people to return to the pre-Perestroika administrative-command past, which, presidential propaganda claimed, was the risk if supporters of the Congress won. 'The referendum results', I said, 'do not allow us to recognize either side as the conclusive victor. Russian citizens are against confrontation: they want stability. They favour continuing the reforms, but with substantial modifications, primarily relief for those whom the reforms have put in special difficulties.'

What next? I had no doubt that a new constitution was needed, 'but it would be unforgivable if it were the opportunistic fruit of the present political conflict'. The constitution should be adopted by a newly elected Supreme Soviet. Any coercion in adopting it would represent disrespect for the opinion of Russia's citizens. 'At all events,' I stated at the end of May, 'everything must be done in a lawful, legal manner. Only that can guarantee stable functioning of the Russian system of governance and safeguard the normal operation of Russian civil society, which is being born with so much travail.'

The Constitutional Convention established to put forward a draft new constitution was unable to do so. There was no substantive discussion at it, and in June I expressed my view that it had become a complete waste of time. I told reporters it was just 'games that are not going to produce anything of value. We need politics, not political games.'

Summer 1993 was very busy for me, with several trips abroad, including to the Netherlands and Switzerland, where I worked on setting up the Green Cross International environmental organization. There was other charitable work too. On 7 June, Raisa and I were present at the opening of Russia's largest and best-equipped department for bone marrow transplants at the

National Children's Hospital, with which she was constantly involved.

In 1990, Raisa became the patron of an international association, Haematologists of the World for Children, created specifically to provide modern treatment for the severest blood diseases in children. In March 1991, she donated a cheque for $100,000 to the Institute of Paediatric Haematology, which enabled doctors and nurses to be trained to use the latest medical technology and for them to work as interns at the most advanced haematology centres of the USA and Germany.

After December 1991, finance for building a specialized department for bone marrow transplant at the Institute of Paediatric Haematology was cut off. Resumption and completion of the building project was made possible when we succeeded in raising $1,000,000 for this specific purpose. Half was donated at my request by Fred Matser, a Dutch businessman and founder or co-founder of many charitable trusts, and the remainder was made up of fees I received for lectures during a trip to the United States in 1992. A further $1,000,000, needed to complete construction of the unit, was found after I made a number of appeals to the Russian government. Other foreign friends gave humanitarian and charitable aid to Russian organizations through the Gorbachev Foundation. On 24 August we delivered medical equipment to hospitals in the Stavropol region, purchased on the initiative of Maria Wilmes and a group of sponsors in Germany.

At that time I also finished work on *Years of Difficult Decisions*.[3] The book contained my talks and speeches, transcripts of interviews and negotiations in the period from 1985 to 1992. Much of the material was being published for the first time (including minutes of sharp exchanges in the Politburo).

We delivered the manuscript of my book almost simultaneously to Russian and French publishers, but the Russian publisher was prevented from bringing it out. It was made very clear that if he did, both the publisher and printer could expect a raid by

[3] M. S. Gorbachev, *Gody trudnykh reshenii. Izbrannoe. 1985–1992*, M.: Al'fa-Print, 1993.

the authorities. The set type of the book was broken up. It was secretly set again from scratch by a printer in Ryazan, but the upshot was that the book appeared in France before it appeared in Russia.

Fateful Decisions, Fateful Days

Meanwhile, the government crisis caused by the irreconcilable stand-off between the president and Supreme Soviet continued and threatened serious trouble. The underlying cause was, of course, the deteriorating situation in the country. At the Foundation we analysed it and our conclusions were dismaying:

> Among the bulk of the population, oppositional moods and mistrust of central government, both the president and the Supreme Soviet, are increasing but a majority, for a variety of reasons, are apprehensive of new, drastic changes. The relative equilibrium of power between the executive and legislative branches in the Centre is highly unstable ('no parliament could work together with the current president in a stable manner').
>
> The ruling elites out in the regions are increasingly recruiting management specialists from among former Party staffers and trying to insure against further possible interference from the Centre. If elections were to be held in the autumn or winter the results would be totally unpredictable.

I, however, remained convinced that only new elections offered any hope of ending the protracted deadlock. The way out of the crisis lay in renewing the federal government. It was essential to bring the country back from its present chaos, and 'only new people will be capable of doing that. In addition, they will be credited a modest, but nevertheless valuable, degree of trust.'

Yeltsin had a different plan, and apparently by the end of the summer had firmly made up his mind to resolve the crisis by getting rid of parliament. The president devoted the whole of September to preparing to remove it by force. Accompanied by the ministers of defence and of the interior, he personally checked the preparedness of elite divisions deployed near Moscow and army units to obey his orders. He started appearing on television wearing military camouflage and a maroon beret, and holding a combat rifle.

On 21 September 1993, the president of Russia signed Decree No. 1400 annulling the powers of the Congress of People's Deputies and of the Supreme Soviet. The president 'recommended' to the Constitutional Court that it should suspend its sittings until the election of a new legislative body, the Federal Assembly, scheduled for 12 December. This fatal decision initiated a chain of events that largely determined the departures from a democratic path of development that we have witnessed over the following years and up to the present day.

That same day, the Constitutional Court ruled that the actions and decisions of the president relating to his decree of 21 September were not in accordance with the constitution of the Russian Federation. They were grounds for removing President B. N. Yeltsin from office or inaugurating special procedures to hold him to account in accordance with the constitution of the Russian Federation.

On 22 September, the Supreme Soviet passed a resolution stating that 'the president of the Russian Federation has instigated a coup d'état'. The same day it resolved to amend the Criminal Code with an article making actions against the constitution punishable by penalties up to and including death with confiscation of property. Yeltsin saw this as a threat aimed at him personally.

The two sides truly deserved each other! I have no doubt that, right up to the last minute before the bloody showdown on 3–4 October, there was some possibility the crisis could have been peacefully resolved. I had no leverage with the parties directly, but tried to moderate their behaviour by speaking out publicly and calling for common sense.

At a press conference in Moscow on 25 September, I stated: 'The best way out of the situation that has developed in Russia is simultaneous early elections for the presidency and parliament, and the sooner the better.' It was essential to return to constitutional politics, since otherwise a very dangerous precedent would be set. 'This kind of treatment of the constitution, wiping your feet on it, is Bolshevism.' Another important point I stressed at the press conference was that, if only one source of government power were to be left and have total control of the media, there would be no possibility of conducting free elections to the parliament.

The root of all this evil was the failure of the policy pursued by the Russian government, both the president and the parliament, since the end of 1991. 'They are each as bad as the other, and are mired in this situation. They must go,' I said. I advised Yeltsin to immediately return the situation to where it was before 21 September. Needless to say, all the latest resolutions of the Supreme Soviet also needed to be revoked.

I thought the stance of the leaders of the West, with their unconditional support for Yeltsin, was dangerous, and supposed they did not understand the situation. The most important thing Boris Yeltsin could do, I said, was 'behave not like the protagonist of a particular political faction but as a national leader'. I believe that was his last chance. He did not take it.

On 29 September, Alexiy II, Patriarch of Moscow and All Russia, appealed to the parties to the conflict not to resort to bloodshed. The church joined the search for a compromise solution. A majority of the members of the Supreme Soviet, meeting in a building surrounded, on the president's orders, by a cordon of troops, were prepared to compromise. Several regional leaders and presidents of republics within the Russian Federation tried to mediate between the Supreme Soviet, the Presidential Administration and the government of Viktor Chernomyrdin. Even those in favour of the presidential decree of 21 September inclined to a compromise solution close to what I had proposed.

On the afternoon of 3 October, however, the situation in Moscow deteriorated. Groups of demonstrators, gunmen and manifest agents provocateurs, led by General Albert Makashov and Viktor Anpilov, broke through the cordon surrounding the White House, seized the Mayor's Office on Novy Arbat and headed for the Ostankino Television Centre.

That evening, Boris Yeltsin declared a state of emergency in Moscow. Shooting broke out at the Television Centre and resulted in deaths and injuries. Dozens of people were killed, including several journalists. Unquestionably, the situation had to be brought under control, and by the morning of 4 October that had been done. I have no doubt that at that point too the crisis could have been ended without further bloodshed, but just then, at 10:00 am, tanks were brought up to the bridge in front of the White House and opened fire on the building! In effect, a brief civil war had been unleashed in the centre of Moscow, which resulted in the death, according to official statistics, of 160 people.

There were about 1,000 people in the parliament building at this time: deputies, members of staff, service personnel, journalists, women and children. The building caught fire. Tongues of flame and black smoke engulfed it window by window and storey by storey. This appalling picture was being shown live on the screens of millions of television sets in Russia and around world. CNN cameras were broadcasting live from several points in blocks adjacent to the Supreme Soviet building.

'What infamy!' I thought, as I watched it on television. At 14:30 people began emerging from the parliament with a white flag. Rutskoy, Khasbulatov and Makashov were arrested. Yeltsin, in a televised address, announced the suppression in Moscow of an 'armed fascist-communist rebellion'.

My reaction to those events, my initial assessment and conclusions are most fully set out in an interview I gave two or three days after the event to *Komsomolskaya Pravda*'s correspondent, Alexander Gamov:

Q: During the assault on the White House, some of our compatriots were on one side of the barricades, some on the other, and the rest were watching what was going on with curiosity and alarm. Where was Gorbachev?

A: Sitting in front of the television, but not in aloof contemplation of the unfolding tragedy. From 21 September I was closely monitoring how the situation was developing and, to the extent that my current position allows, doing my best to react to it. I presented my initial view at a press conference on 25 September, advising President Yeltsin to think things through, return to the situation as it was before 21 September and propose simultaneous presidential and parliamentary elections. I was told by Oleg Rumyantsev, secretary of the Congress's Constitutional Commission, when we met later that the 'besieged Congress' had been prepared to rescind all its recent resolutions and reach a compromise. That was the preferred option of the Constitutional Court, of most of the regions and of several public bodies. Even people who supported the president's actions on 21 September inclined to the same approach. The Orthodox Church also joined the negotiation process, so there was real hope that bloodshed could be avoided.

What happened on the Sunday was, I think, unexpected for many people. Before I knew what was going on at the Television Centre and the Mayor's Office, I sent an appeal to Interfax and ITAR-TASS urging strongly that the army should not become involved. I said that, if troops were deployed in Moscow, there would be bloodshed, a war. I did not know at that moment that a state of emergency had already been declared and troops brought in. Who did? Television and radio were not functioning and nobody had any information. Afterwards, I was accused of supposedly being against measures to halt violent rioting.

Q: Mikhail Sergeyevich, on that murderous Sunday evening your reaction really did seem very peculiar.

A: Not so fast! The way it was presented made it seem that Gorbachev was practically condoning the rioters. My appeal was made during the day but only broadcast late that evening. That is the first point. And then what happened? By the following morning the situation, thank God, was back under control. The White House was sealed off by troops and armoured vehicles, people were going to work and, suddenly, in full view of the whole country, the whole world, they started shelling the parliament! I couldn't believe it!

Literally the previous day representatives of the president were saying Rutskoy and Khasbulatov had taken hundreds of blameless citizens hostage to further their criminal plans. In the White House, with the exception of a handful of opportunists, there were numerous members of the service staff, administrative staff, journalists, deluded 'defenders' and, finally, deputies sincerely standing by their constitutional principles, And these people, cooped up in there, are who the troops began ruthlessly murdering. The actual gunmen and instigators of the rioting, as it turned out, got off most lightly. That is what I was warning against during the day on Sunday 3 October.

By the way, as we now know, Rutskoy and Khasbulatov were trying to continue negotiations through Interfax and Defence Minister Pavel Grachev. They were prepared to surrender. That offer should have been accepted.

In my opinion, what happened at the White House was completely unjustified retribution. Several days have passed and the bodies of the dead have still not been released from the building, supposedly because they are being examined by investigators. That is sacrilege! The impression is that the authorities are trying to conceal the fact that hundreds of people have been killed in the White House. In broad daylight! In front of an enormous crowd! We have descended into the first stages of lunacy. Our army has been forced to shed blood. It is unforgivable. This tragedy has been brought about by the leaders of the Supreme Soviet, the presidency, the executive branch – and it has totally discredited them. Today, none of them have any right to remain in power.

Q: Well, at least the Kremlin is not trumpeting its victory.

A: I am glad they have toned down the triumphalism and war cries like 'Crush the nest of vipers!'

The press is already using the kind of language and tone and expressing the kind of concern that we should be hearing at this terrible time. Many people are aware that, after what has happened, we cannot continue to behave as we have been.

Finally, even the president in his address said this was a tragedy, not a victory. He has declared a period of mourning and spoken the kind of words that are appropriate on a day like this. But for the rest ... One has the impression Yeltsin's aim is to intimidate Russia, to intimidate people even more. And then what? I heard nothing constructive. Nothing more than, in effect, do away with the soviets!

Q: Mikhail Sergeyevich, you keep criticizing the president, but actually some people see a logical chain of development: Gorbachev spawned Yeltsin, Yeltsin spawned Rutskoy and Khasbulatov.

A: That is a very superficial analysis. New movements and personalities have appeared as society is developing. It is historically conditioned.

Q: I am just remembering that in the last years of your presidency there was also talk of declaring a state of emergency.

A: Indeed there was, and when I was president I often heard people demanding I should declare a state of emergency and introduce presidential rule.

Otherwise, they would say, step down! I was under constant siege! But I did not fall for it. For me, the option of shedding blood was unacceptable, dividing society into Reds and Whites, wanting to devastate the opposition. That does not mean things always turned out as I might have wished, but I was guided by deep moral convictions. I tried to hold back those on both sides, move democratic processes forward to the point where they would become irreversible. But now look at the state we are in!

Look! Again we are seeing basic political, economic, social and constitutional rights of citizens violated; again we are seeing Glasnost, transparency, openness throttled. What use are all these manifestos and concepts if, ultimately, we are dragged into a bloodbath?

Q: Do you not think we have to look for the origins of the tragedy not in how Yeltsin behaved, or Khasbulatov or the army ...

A: I do not believe it was possible to implement reform without consulting the people, by just treating them like building bricks for constructing a democratic country. The new government of Russia embarked on a cavalry charge that has brought the state to its knees. Instead of reform we have had 'Mighty Breakthroughs', 'Chairman Mao's Great Leap Forward'. That is neo-Bolshevism.

... Yeltsin and Gaidar started pushing through their shock therapy, their high-speed method of reforming the economy to show Gorbachev and his supporters the proper way to effect social change. But before they could do that, the policy had to be approved by the parliament and congress! Who gave the president the right to issue statutory decrees? The Supreme Soviet and all the deputies in congress assembled!

Do you know when all this free-for-all started? When they saw the results of their joint endeavours! The Commonwealth of Independent States did not work, the country was torn apart, the economy collapsed, centuries-old human ties were ruptured. Seventy per cent of citizens found themselves on the poverty threshold. That was when the president and the Congress started noticing alarm signals. The deputies were more sensitive because most of them live in the provinces and see everything with their own eyes. That is when they started arguing over who was more to blame. They are all to blame: the Supreme Soviet, the Congress of People's Deputies and the president. Instead of recognizing that, they started feuding with each other and have reduced Russia to a state where we are all covered in blood. And to cap it all, the belligerents all see themselves as saviours of the Fatherland.

Q: You are insisting all the current leaders should go, but what if the people do not turn out to vote in new elections? That would be tricky.

A: No, the people are just waiting for new elections and will turn out for them. They will reject these would-be rulers who for the past nine months have been wrestling on the mat of Russian politics and have now started shelling each other. What we need above all else is consensus, to move reform forward in order to promote peace in society and stability. We can achieve that through simultaneous democratic elections of the parliament and the president.

I remain optimistic that Russia will enjoy a rebirth. I have absolutely no doubt of it. I can see how people have changed. More than 60 per cent of managers and business owners now want no return to the old top-down command system. A new breed of entrepreneurs has appeared, not just spivs, but people who really know how to run a business.

We can see that society is eager for normal, healthy, serious reforms within a framework of democracy and firmly

established freedom. That is why I believe we will get out of
this mess, although it may take years, or decades. We can get
out of the crisis sooner than that, especially the current predicament. It will depend on the policies the government pursues.
That is why I want the people, the citizens, to make their voices
heard in free, simultaneous, independent elections of all the
branches of government and local institutions.

A state of emergency is not the way to stability

In the days immediately after the blood-soaked showdown, Russia
was aghast and seemed traumatized by what had happened. It
was important to deny the president any sense of the euphoria
of victory. To consider what had happened a 'victory over a
communist-fascist rebellion' was a dangerous delusion, a mere
propaganda myth. Certainly, some pernicious individuals had
been involved in the events, including extremist groups of provocateurs. There had, however, also been people sincerely protesting
against the violation of the rights and powers of parliament and
demanding a return to the rule of law. And how many entirely
innocent people were victims! After the shelling of parliament, the
government instigated mass beatings of citizens in the approaches
to the White House. Even technical college students who had
rushed to the Krasnaya Presnya area out of youthful curiosity
were attacked, some of them fatally. The mother of one of these
murdered lads, deprived of her sole source of income, came to ask
our Foundation for support. We helped as best we could.

I was astonished and disturbed by a letter signed by well-known
writers supporting the bombardment of parliament. The title
of their letter, published in *Izvestiya*, read: 'Writers call on the
government to take decisive action.' It went on: 'Enough of talking! It is time to learn how to act. These thick misfits respect only
power.' How could Academician Dmitry Likhachev sign such a
letter? Why had this crude, vulgar philippic been signed by Bella
Akhmadulina, Viktor Astafiev and other major writers? These
questions gave me no rest. Many of these people are no longer with
us, but those who still are can hardly be proud of what they did.

Not all our cultural figureheads adopted such a shameful

position, of course. Andrey Sinyavsky, Vladimir Maximov and Petr Yegides published an impassioned article in *Nezavisimaya Gazeta* in which they condemned the slaughter in the centre of Moscow. Perhaps the best response to those demanding the 'vipers' should be crushed was the poem by Andrey Voznesensky:

Snipers aiming downwards at a flood
of human beings cringeing in distress.
Humane values are not written out in blood,
At least, not in the blood of someone else.

Introducing the saga of the 'state of emergency', Yeltsin promised it would lead to stability, pave the way for democracy and facilitate the progress of reform. It very soon became clear that it was having precisely the opposite effect. I wrote an article about this at the request of Italy's *La Stampa*:

The shelling of parliament by tanks, the hundreds killed and wounded, and the way the authorities are behaving under the state of emergency have done irreparable damage to democracy and the cause of reform in Russia.

The lack of a legal opposition will greatly increase the likelihood of errors in the drafting and passing of laws in the implementation of reform. That is extremely dangerous in a critical transitional period and risks further failures, leading to outbursts of mass unrest and a repetition of the kind of events we have already experienced.

One result of those events was the dropping of criminal proceedings against the organizers of the August 1991 coup. The next State Duma, elected in December 1993, voted to scrap the investigation into the massive loss of life in October, simultaneously announcing a political and economic amnesty which extended to the members of the State Emergency Committee. It was a deal of mutual absolution of responsibility of those who shelled the parliament, those who provoked widespread disorder and those guilty of the coup d'état in August 1991. There was a certain logic to this: one lot of coup conspirators (of 1993) amnestied another lot (from 1991). It was all done, as it soon became fashionable to say in semi-criminal jargon, 'with a nod and a wink'.

On 12 December, elections were held for seats in the State Duma, the Russian parliament having had its historical name returned to it. The president and his supporters were confident that the vote would bring the pro-government Russia's Choice Party to power, the first of a succession of pro-government 'parties'. They were in for a rude awakening. The October bloodbath in Moscow sharply reduced the numbers supporting the president and increased the protest vote. The Russian people returned a shock verdict on those who had perpetrated shock therapy on them and the shock of October. They voted in unprecedented numbers for Vladimir Zhirinovsky's 'Liberal Democratic' Party with its extremist slogans. The LDP was well ahead of Russia's Choice and all the other parties.

The overnight telethon organized at the Ostankino Television Centre on 12 December, which was supposed to celebrate the expected victory of the radical democrats, was taken off air shortly after 3:00 am, ostensibly for 'technical reasons'. The real reason was the patently obvious and humiliating defeat suffered by Russia's Choice, which did not bear out the expectations of jubilation of the show's organizers. In my article, 'The election results: what now?', I gave my reading of the situation:

> The inevitable, predictable and widely predicted has happened. Most of those who turned out to vote or refused to do so registered their protest against the policies currently being imposed on them, which have pushed one-third of the population below the poverty line, and another third close to it. Industrial production continues to fall. The country's major factories are at a standstill. We are facing devastating mass unemployment. ... The economy is drifting rudderless.
>
> It was not media failures during the electoral campaign, not even the wrangling among those who claim to be democrats that have caused the rout of Russia's Choice, but the policies for which that party's leading figures are answerable. Disillusionment with those policies and protest against them explain Zhirinovsky's success. It would be absurd to believe that those who voted for him are eager to march off to reincorporate Poland and Finland in Russia, or favour turning Ukraine and the Caucasus into Russian

provinces, or would give their blessing as their sons set off on a campaign of territorial conquest to give Russia access to 'warm seas'. The majority of those who gave Zhirinovsky their vote hardly suppose he can make Russia flourish with a wave of his magic wand. So there is no cause to panic, scaring ourselves and the West with talk of a fascist threat supposedly hanging over Russia. That threat will, however, grow if there is no change of government policy. And that is the crux of the matter: where do we go from here?

The constitution has scraped through. It has been accepted by barely one-third of Russia's citizens, but it has been adopted. If the parties in the new parliament fail to show proper responsibility for the country, if they do not have the intelligence and common sense to turn it into a constructive, active, genuinely independent and competent legislature, the constitution will be exploited to strengthen an already authoritarian regime. It is no longer only journalists who are warning of this.

For his part, the president and the team he chooses, in the light of what has happened, cannot simply ignore the clearly expressed will of the people to which they so often refer. They cannot close their eyes to the fact that the biggest voter is Russia's socio-economic situation, which is continuing to deteriorate with no prospect of improvement in sight. What is needed now is no longer just policy adjustments but a completely new policy, based, of course, on the rule of law and civilized market relations.

On New Year's Eve 1993, I pondered a great deal over what had come about in the year that was ending. My thoughts were mostly apprehensive and gloomy.

Defects of the new constitution

I deliberated a good deal about the newly adopted constitution, discussed it with colleagues, and came to the conclusion that it needed more work.

Even in the fairly well-drafted section on rights and freedoms there were obvious weaknesses. Without an effective mechanism of guarantee, the principle of direct entitlement to rights and freedoms was likely to remain no more than fine words. A careful reading of certain articles suggested that, unless changes were made, we could probably say goodbye to free education and health provision. There was a lack of much-needed clarity.

Other sections, especially those dealing with the relationship between the branches of government, were in need of even greater revision. There was a disproportionate expansion of the powers of the president, together with substantial cutting back of the powers of parliament. In addition, the powers of the president were spelled out in far greater detail than those of the other branches. The legal procedure for holding him to account was so extraordinarily complex as to make it all but impossible.

I thought it very unhelpful to the president to have such an insignificant parliament; it only devalued the gains already made by democracy. A major politician needs strong democratic institutions to safeguard his policies against miscalculation. In their absence, no amount of talk about democracy will prevent its destruction.

Regrettably, my concerns proved only too justified. The new constitution, which started being referred to as the Yeltsin Constitution, was increasingly used to justify and legitimate the president's personal power, with all the inevitable accompanying ills: impunity and unaccountability of his close circle and insiders; arbitrary misconduct towards 'the rest'; underhand intrigues by Yeltsin's 'courtiers'; and so on.

Those drafting the constitution were distinguished specialists in constitutional law. Today it seems extraordinary that they 'overlooked' some of its peculiarities, like the only too well-known provision that the president cannot serve more than two terms in succession but, if he just takes a break, there is no problem! It seems entirely possible that Yeltsin was envisaging just such a possibility, although his age and state of health made it unlikely he would be able to take advantage of it himself. That was done instead, as we know, by Vladimir Putin.

The constitution's major flaw, however, was its 'super-presidential' character. In combination with our monarchist tradition and the deferential attitude to higher authority typical of the Russian national character, this presented a real risk of creating an autocratic regime. Some of the scholars involved in drafting the constitution – for example, Viktor Sheynis – hoped that, over time, the imbalance of power in favour of the executive arm would be adjusted through expansion of the monitoring functions of the parliament, but this, needless to say, did not happen. With every year that passed the tendency became more apparent for the democratic potential of the new constitution to be given only limited implementation, while its authoritarian potential was realized to the full.

1994 Gets Off to a Bad Start

I spent the first months of 1994 completing the writing of *Life and Reforms*, published in English as *Memoirs*.[1] Two years was not long to complete memoirs covering the whole of my life and, most importantly, the years of Perestroika. It was important to ensure as high a degree of accuracy as possible when relating the course of events, to verify assessments and critically rethink what was done. That was important not only for the reader, but also for me. I have often returned to this book since, rereading it, and I believe it will remain an important source for historians and anyone wishing to understand that period.

Like millions of Russians, I could not help wondering what lay ahead for the country after the painful tragedy of October 1993. Would we ever find the road to social harmony? If the president and government set their sights on restoring social consensus and implementing reform on that basis, many past mistakes could yet be put right and much guilt redeemed. I decided to adopt that attitude also to the State Duma's decision to amnesty all those involved in the coup and the shelling of the parliament.

I had a low opinion of this 'mutual forgiveness' of people who had repeatedly broken the law and bore joint responsibility for the predicament in which the country found itself. I had always advocated seeing the trial of the members of the State Emergency Committee through to the end in order to establish all the facts and determine the degree of guilt. Otherwise, I warned, we would learn nothing from the events of August 1991. As I said in an interview for Interfax:

[1] M. S. Gorbachev, *Zhizn' i reformy*, 2 vols, M.: Novosti, 1995; Mikhail Gorbachev, *Memoirs*, NY: Doubleday, 1996.

The country, and I mean the Soviet Union, was irreparably damaged in August 1991. The coup directly affected me personally. It was a drama, but I am prepared to put the interests of Russia and Russians above my own interests, with the proviso only that the amnesty will genuinely help to maintain the unity of the state.

If, however, tomorrow we hear representatives of the Liberal Democratic Party and the Communists declaring that this amnesty represents their victory over democracy, if Russia's Choice again starts calling on people to demonstrate in the squares and demand the dissolution of the Duma, the amnesty will have brought nothing but trouble.

Subsequent events showed that the amnesty was not a step along the road to reconciliation and harmony. The abandoning of the case against the State Emergency Committee was seen by the defendants as a victory and an opportunity to put about their latest version of events, to whitewash themselves and denigrate Gorbachev. Neither did the Russian government get round to doing what would genuinely have facilitated social harmony. There was no change in their behaviour or how they arrived at decisions.

In January 1994, Yegor Gaidar left the government, turning down an offer of the post of first deputy prime minister. In a letter to the president, he wrote: 'I cannot be simultaneously in the government and in opposition to it.' I do not think that was the only reason for his departure. Gaidar had been proposing an acceleration of the pace of reform, but how can you accelerate a process that has already produced only dire results? In an article published in *Izvestiya*, Gaidar himself wrote of the 'failure of democratic government'. 'The country is in a state of profound crisis ... there is no great national ideal, whether realistic or even utopian ... There are no major goals, discipline has weakened, the situation is unstable, and opportunities for self-enrichment are immense.' However, his article was devoted to claiming that the only people not to blame for everything were the perpetrators of shock therapy reform.

In an interview for Interfax, I expressed the opinion that the departure of Yegor Gaidar – and even possibly of other

'figureheads of shock therapy' – would change nothing, because
the government had no clear strategy. If those running the country 'do not take the pulse of life, we can be certain that Russia
must expect more political antics that may have serious social
consequences', I said. I made it clear that I was not advocating a
return to the old system:

> The transition to market relations must continue, but with major
> adjustments. Market relations should be developed through small
> and medium-sized businesses and tough laws should be passed to
> prevent monopolies. The main need, however, is to educate people
> to live in a free market economy, because otherwise it will be
> impossible to introduce market relations without force.

Economists advise, but the government is not listening

In February we convened a conference of major economists at the
Gorbachev Foundation to discuss the economic situation and try
to find a way out of the impasse in which the 'victorious' government found itself.

We wanted to hear the views of economists of different persuasions, from those who on the whole supported the president and
government's economic policy, to those who were critical of it.
Participants included Academicians Leonid Abalkin and Nikolai
Petrakov; corresponding members of the Russian Academy of
Science Vadim Medvedev and Vladlen Martynov; four doctors of
science: Sergey Glaziev (Chairman of the State Duma Committee
on Economic Policy), Alexander Livshits (Analytical Centre of the
President of Russia), Yevgeny Yasin and Andrey Illarionov; and
other prominent academic economists and also journalists.

Participants in the discussion, despite all the differences in
how they assessed the causes and nature of Russia's profound
economic crisis, did their best to present their view of how it
could be resolved. Acutely critical assessments predominated.
Thus, Sergey Glaziev, a former minister in Gaidar's government
who resigned after the shelling of parliament, said: 'From my
viewpoint, the economy has entered a catastrophically destructive
phase, and what is being destroyed is the very industrial sectors

we had hoped would spearhead structural change and have the potential for future growth.' He described the way privatization had been carried out as the most inefficient of all the alternatives, and forecast continuing recession 'until such time as we see the emergence of effective property owners'. Leonid Abalkin put it even more bluntly:

> If we cannot secure a radically new approach to the strategy of reform, Russia will be set back not years but decades.
>
> If we are to believe the law-enforcement agencies, there has been no liberalization of prices and trade in Russia whatsoever. It has been completely commandeered by criminal organizations in a stranglehold more rigorous than we had under the old administrative-command system. That relates both to the flow of trade goods and price formation. As much as 25–30 per cent of bank profits is spent warding off threats from illicit mafia organizations.

Andrey Illarionov criticized the 'reformers' from a different perspective: 'As I see it, we are currently faced with a government entirely lacking any ideological underpinning or realistic plan of action.' He saw inflation as the top priority: 'It is immaterial which government is in power, what its policies are, or what speechifying accompanies them: while monthly inflation is hovering around the 20–25 per cent mark, it stands no chance of remaining in office. No government in world history has been able to.'

In respect of savings, Yevgeny Yasin said: 'I believed from the outset that Gaidar was mistaken in refusing to do anything for savings. Simply to index them would have been unaffordable, but other solutions needed to be looked at, for example, indexing the savings of people of pensionable age. Although even that would have been costly.'

What of the future? Opinions were divided. Alexander Livshits did not anticipate catastrophe: 'Russia is not doomed. It is all just going to cost us a lot and last for a very long time. The knock-on political effects that have been mentioned, the threat of dictatorship and so on, do not seem so self-evident to me.' The majority of the discussants, however, agreed with Academician Abalkin's view: 'The reform and democracy can be saved, but only if there is a radical change of course.'

I spoke twice in the course of the debate. I said:

We will get nowhere by indulging in apologetics or point-scoring. This will lead only to endless disputation and strife, even among those who support reform. That is in the interests only of extremist political forces.

I do not go along with the attitude of some Young Turks who regard the generation of the 1950s and 1960s as hopeless and already consigned to the past. It is largely that supposedly irredeemable segment of the population that is now holding Russia together. We need a consensus that will protect reform and move it forward. That is very important. We have to get away from the old familiar stereotyping and a political culture restricted to the categories of Them and Us, the Whites versus the Reds, Blues, Blacks and Reddish-Browns.

Summarizing the debate, I said:

This conference has brought together very influential people associated with large scholarly teams, important state and public organizations, and with a high profile in the press and on television. ...

Despite the diversity of standpoints and opinions, our discussion has been constructive and full of concern for the country and determination to find solutions. I want to support the predominant view that we are still in with a chance. Our task is not to inflame passions or sweep away the government, but rather to help it make the right choices, to develop policies capable of coping with the current difficult situation, and to supply it with answers, at least for the immediate future. We cannot simply continue to drift as we have since May 1992.

All this is closely connected with the question of what kind of Russia we are hoping for in the future. If we do not have an answer to that, we leave scope both for those who would return Russia to the pre-reform administrative-command system, and those who would blindly follow Western stereotypes and steer the

Federation's future development with no regard for its particular characteristics and traditions. If we do not address that larger question, we shall be unable to find the right solutions for more detailed matters.

I got just one thing wrong, and that was when I said, 'This conference has brought together very influential people.' Unfortunately, neither the president nor the government were interested in paying heed to the advice of independent experts. They brushed their views aside and instead carried on 'firefighting' emergencies as they arose. It was particularly clear they had an allergy to the viewpoint of the Russian Academy of Sciences, which, incidentally, was to be inherited in the years that followed by many in Putin's ruling circle. That approach leads to micro-management and, in reality, to drift rather than thought-through, long-term policies. We seem incapable of freeing ourselves of this. I believe it is one of the great failures of our protracted transition.

Nikita Khrushchev: lessons in courage and lessons from mistakes

I am not a great enthusiast for dates and anniversaries, but one date in 1994 brought to mind someone whose life and experiences had long fascinated me, encouraging me to reflect on continuities and, although they are said always to be misleading, historical parallels. The centenary of the birth of Nikita Khrushchev was approaching.

We decided to organize a conference at the Foundation on the life of this outstanding man. I offered my thoughts about him in an article titled, 'Nikita Khrushchev: lessons in courage and lessons from mistakes'. I wrote that I identified with Khrushchev's fraught experiences.

An undertaking as vast as Perestroika would not have been possible without his example. It is fair to say that in Russia critical thinking about socialism and the relationship between socialism and democracy dates from his period in office. I was conscious of continuing what he had begun when, in January 1987, I took on the Party bureaucracy, which stubbornly resisted political reform.

It is not difficult to find weaknesses, mistakes and faults in Khrushchev's actions, but I would urge, not just to protect him from unfair judgements but primarily in the interests of a historically sound approach to our problems today, that we should not attempt to judge that period with the benefit of hindsight and how we feel today, not impose our perspectives on entirely different historical trends and situations. It is only by going back mentally to that time that we will be able to do justice to Khrushchev's exceptional courage. He struck the first blow against the totalitarian system, and that at a time when the repressive machinery of Stalinism was still functioning, the Party establishment were against change of any sort, there was no place for critical approaches in the way people worked, and officials were ready to fight tooth and nail to retain their privileges, jobs and power. His report to the Twentieth Party Congress in 1956 was not part of some palace revolution: it was an act of great civil courage.

In all the ups and downs of the USSR's domestic and foreign policy of that time, what was at work was not only Khrushchev's level of understanding of the issues, but also the rigid framework in which he found himself and with which he could not but come into conflict.

It would never have occurred to him to renounce the leading role of the Communist Party. That was beyond his wildest imaginings. Nevertheless, he was conscious of the need to reduce its monopoly of power over everyone and everything. He tried to do this in his own way, often taking ad hoc decisions, and this was one of the reasons for his defeat. He tried to make the system work, but by using the system's methods.

That could not lead to the outcome he was looking for. Nikita Khrushchev failed, but there is still much we can learn today from his courage and his mistakes.

Our academic Khrushchev conference was not mere ceremony but a lively, impassioned exchange of views between people, all of whom had their own understanding of this exceptional individual. The participants included, amongst others, Academician Alexander

Nikonov, director of the Agrarian Institute; Khrushchev's son, Sergey; the writer Viktor Rozov; Ambassador Oleg Troyanovsky; historian Roy Medvedev; playwright Mikhail Shatrov; historian Zoya Serebryakova; Khrushchev's American biographer Bill Taubman; Academician Dzhermen Gvishiani; Professor Vadim Zagladin; journalist Nina Khrushcheva, Nikita Khrushchev's great-granddaughter; corresponding member of the Russian Academy of Science and my assistant, Georgiy Shakhnazarov.

Opening the conference, I said we wanted to pay tribute to a courageous politician who had dealt the first blow to the ideology of Stalinism and the totalitarian system. Second, this was an, admittedly belated, opportunity for a serious examination of Nikita Khrushchev's efforts at reform and a frank discussion of the lessons that could be learned from them in the present day.

I shared my reflections and assessments with those attending the conference:

> Khrushchev's attempt was not forgotten. The next generation of reformers had good reason to call themselves the 'children of the Twentieth Party Congress'. During the Brezhnev years of stagnation, timid attempts to change things were firmly confined to the sphere of the economy, but even they got nowhere because the system itself remained sacrosanct.
>
> Our generation has felt duty-bound to resume the process of change and take it further. At the end of 1987, we sensed that the reforms initiated were facing the same fate as befell those following the Twentieth Party Congress. Everything hung in the balance. Officialdom woke up to the fact that ideological and political pluralism undermined its monopoly on power, with all that entailed, and began doggedly resisting. It became clear that, if Perestroika, which was vital for Russia, was to be taken further, thoroughgoing political reform was essential. Through democratization and free elections, the way could be opened for fresh forces, and the Russian people enabled to exert decisive influence on national politics.
>
> That is exactly what happened, but we underestimated the cunning of the forces of the past. We did not manage to continue along the path of gradual, evolutionary change.

The formidable attack Khrushchev launched on totalitarianism was choked off and followed by a period of reaction that was little more than titivated neo-Stalinism. The rest of the world embarked on major structural changes while Russia stagnated and fell decades behind. This is what we need to remember: 'It is not so much for Khrushchev's benefit as for ourselves, for Russia, for the world, that we need to go back to the experience of previous reform initiatives and learn from them.'

The Union could have been saved

Another important project was what the Foundation described as a 'White Paper' titled *The Union Could Have Been Saved*.[2] A white paper consists mainly of documents that speak for themselves. Many were previously unpublished, including records of the negotiations for a new Union Treaty in Novo-Ogarevo and Politburo meetings. Others had been published for limited circulation and now, with hindsight, read differently.

A book launch and press conference were held at the Foundation. Of course, I told the journalists, you cannot turn back the pages of history. Opportunities which had existed in the past were no longer an option. Replying to a question, I said:

> The oligarch groups are all in favour of curtailing democracy. The docility of our representative institutions and lack of public participation suit them nicely, and that is the source of the current state of rampant lawlessness. It is even more pronounced now than when the Communist Party had a monopoly on power. I believe, on the contrary, that democracy is not anarchy and chaos, not dithering and lack of principle, but a very rigorous system under which everybody, from the president to the ordinary citizen, genuinely has to obey the law. That demands an independent judiciary and prosecutors who act in strict accordance with the law, without waiting for orders from above. Everybody who shares that view,

[2] *Soiuz mozhno bylo sokhranit'. Belaia kniga: Dokumenty i fakty o politike M.S. Gorbacheva po reformirovaniiu i sokhraneniiu mnogonatsional'nogo gosudarstva*, M.: 'Aprel'-85', 1995.

and understands it is in the interests of the majority of the population, needs to form a democratic opposition movement. That is the conclusion I have come to after watching the government's intensification of policies that are disastrous for the nation.

The economy: what now?

In the first half of 1994, the government decided to make combating inflation its top priority, and once again tried to solve the problem with a cavalry charge, as if it were an end in itself and, moreover, something that could be over in next to no time. Once again, the result was lamentable, the medicine almost deadlier than the disease.

My colleague, Corresponding Member of the Academy of Sciences Vadim Medvedev, wrote in one of his research reports to me as president of the Foundation:

At the beginning of this year inflation was reduced at too high a price, by inducing a further, uncontrolled contraction of the economy at a dangerous rate. In the first quarter of the year, industrial production declined by 24.9 per cent, in comparison with the corresponding period last year. We have not seen such a shocking fall in industrial output since early 1992. This is, in effect, a new downward spiral. For the first time, the level of industrial production has fallen to less than half the pre-crisis level. The country is closer than ever to a major economic collapse. Major enterprises that are the backbone of our manufacturing capacity, the pride of Russian industry, like the ZIL automotive factory and the Kirov engineering complex, are coming to a standstill, while many others are limping along.

Recent months have seen a rapid increase in mass unemployment. Including part-time workers, the overall level of unemployment according to the State Statistics Committee is currently 8.8 million people, or 11.7 per cent of the workforce.

This results from the fact that, despite the assurances of the leaders of the present administration that they are correcting their former ways of implementing economic policy and that they recognize the unacceptability of shock therapy, they are in effect continuing to implement their belief in the omnipotence of tight monetarist policy while ignoring its effects on manufacturing output.

Meetings in the regions

In 1994, I travelled to St Petersburg, Krasnoyarsk, Vladimir, Ufa and Novgorod. I wanted to talk to people and get a sense of their mood and reactions to what was going on in the country, and also of their attitude towards me.

I went to St Petersburg at the invitation of cultural figures and business circles there, and also of the mayor of St Petersburg, Anatoly Sobchak, and the head of the administration of Kronstadt, Viktor Surikov.

Surprisingly, contrary to the agreed programme, Sobchak was absent from our meetings. We heard later that this had been because of direct pressure from Yeltsin. The Petersburg authorities' arrangements for the visit were coordinated by the city's deputy mayor, Vladimir Putin. He met us at Pulkovo Airport, accompanied us throughout our stay in St Petersburg, was attentive and considerate, and showed he was knowledgeable about the city's problems and much else besides. We enjoyed the company of Lyudmila Putina, who showed Raisa the work of the city's schoolchildren.

We spent an evening at the Actors Club of the Union of Theatre Workers, where we met such outstanding Petersburg actors as Vladislav Strzhelchik, Kirill Lavrov, Andrey Tolubeyev and others prominent in the arts.

I remember Andrey Tolubeyev took me aside at one reception and said very quietly: 'Mikhail Sergeyevich, if you should need a place of refuge, I will hide you in my dacha in the forest. The Devil himself would never find you there. You can rely on me.' I laughed, although I believe the offer was meant seriously. I said I was touched by his concern, but had no intention of hiding anywhere.

Raisa and I went to see Maxim Gorky's *Posledniye* [*The Last Ones*] at the Bolshoi Drama Theatre.

In meetings with some of the city's young entrepreneurs I heard of the extraordinary difficulties they had to overcome for their businesses to survive.

A small group of protesters tried to disrupt my meeting with students at St Petersburg State University. The students had come to listen to Gorbachev and gave them no support. As always when I have meetings with young people, we got on well and I left to warm applause. Incidentally, I noticed one of the girls who had been protesting clapping loudly. She had stayed, listening carefully, right to the end.

I had the rare opportunity of a live television interview on Petersburg-Channel 5, and enjoyed a meaningful conversation with the editors of the St Petersburg press. I was left with a good overall impression. Although initially rather taken aback by Sobchak's 'disappearance', I left St Petersburg in a positive mood.

In the summer, Raisa and I undertook a visit to Siberia, to the banks of the Yenisey. Viktor Astafiev invited us to his 70th birthday party. He was an important writer, a real, modern Russian classic, and although I did not see eye to eye with him (he could sometimes be over the top in his loves and hates), it would have been churlish not to accept the invitation. For the anniversary, our Foundation supported publication of *Russkii Almaz* [*Russian Diamonds*], a collection of his short stories.[3] Our meeting was very cordial.

I visited the city of Vladimir at the invitation of its young governor, Yury Vlasov, and remember completely informal meetings in the streets with local people. Some who came over seemed not entirely sure this really was Gorbachev. A clone perhaps, or just someone with a strong resemblance? But then I was bombarded with all sorts of questions: 'How are you getting on now, after the Kremlin?' 'Where do you live?' Somebody had been busily dunning into people's heads that Gorbachev had emigrated and was now living in Germany, or perhaps America. 'What is going on now, is that what you did Perestroika for?' And again, 'What do you think about the fighting in Chechnya?'

I met people working in local authorities, who had come from every district of the province to Vladimir for our discussion. In

[3] Viktor P. Astaf'ev, *Russkii almaz. Rasskazy. Zatesi*, M.: Iskusstvo, 1994.

the cathedral, quite unexpectedly, a young priest came out to me and the church choir burst into chanting 'O Lord, preserve him, unto many years of life'. They wished me good health and asked after Raisa.

The human warmth of our reception gladdened us, and confuted all the talk about virtually everyone in Russia hating Gorbachev, but I still had a sense of uneasiness.

My travels around the country, meetings, discussions in factories, informal contacts with a great variety of people, young and not-so-young, long-serving workers, owners of small, medium and large businesses led me to the conclusion that people were increasingly losing faith in democratic reform and beginning to pin their hopes on a new 'firm hand'. This prompted me to send an open letter on 26 October 1994 to the media:

Russia is going through extremely difficult times. Millions of Russians are living in hardship, suffering a sense of hopelessness. The security of our citizens and our very state are under threat. People are at the end of their tether. Unfortunately, many believe democracy is to blame for all this. Increasingly we hear it decried, and calls for dictatorship.

It is impossible to restore health to our lives without democratic government based on the trust and support of the majority of Russian citizens. I see the urgent holding of free, democratic elections of the president, parliament and local authorities as an essential step towards establishing democratic government.

We can rely only on ourselves, and I therefore suggest setting up public committees in the Centre and in the provinces to ensure free elections in Russia. Establishing them would be an important step in the struggle for a democratic alternative to both the present regime and attempts by fundamentalists and ultra-nationalists to drag the country back to totalitarianism.

Committees established by the citizens themselves will be able to protest against violations of the Constitution, facilitate the creation of credible guarantees of normal parliamentary and presidential elections, a fair election campaign and open counting of voting results under democratic scrutiny.

Overwhelmingly, the media were deaf to my appeal, my concerns and proposals. *Izvestiya's* political commentator, Otto Latsis, only mentioned it in passing, adding that there was nothing new in Gorbachev's appeal. The government's *Rossiyskaya Gazeta*, quoting just a few fragmentary sentences from the letter, accused me of inciting confrontation with the intention of forming an anti-Yeltsin alliance. There was not a word about the substance of the appeal, the need for free and fair elections. Almost two decades would have to pass before young, concerned people would appear in Russia prepared to actively join the fight for fair elections.

Chechnya: a war that could have been avoided

The last months and days of 1994 have gone down in modern Russian history as the beginning of a protracted, bloody war in Chechnya and Russia.

The pre-history of the war is a whole succession of rash decisions and irresponsible stunts. It all started with the 'Parade of Sovereignties', provoked by Yeltsin in his power struggle with the Soviet Union's central administration. The would-be coup of the 'State Emergency Committee' in 1991 precipitated a serious crisis for the government in Checheno-Ingushetia.

I knew this republic well. They were our neighbouring republic in Stavropol where I lived and worked for many years, and I was fully aware of the many acute sensitivities that had built up there. This whole region requires a supremely cautious and meticulously gauged approach. Shoot-from-the-hip politicking in that part of the world is asking for trouble. Unfortunately, political bungling was precisely what was on offer from the people surrounding the Russian president when they decided to back General Djohar Dudaev, inveigling him into the forcible removal of the Supreme Soviet of the Checheno-Ingush Autonomous Republic under its then leader, Doku Zavgaev. Dudaev found himself with a large quantity of arms at his disposal, left behind by the federal Russian forces who were withdrawn from the republic by the Russian Ministry of Defence. Had it not been for the 1991 coup and disintegration of the Soviet Union, nothing of that sort would have happened.

Dudaev consolidated his position, using the watchwords of sovereignty and independence for the Chechen people, in whom the appalling memory was still very much alive of their deportation under Stalin in 1944. The decline of the economy, growth of criminality, nationalist euphoria and sheer hatred hit the republic exceptionally hard and forced almost one-quarter of the population (nearly all of them Russian) to leave. Opposition to Dudaev's government continued as it became increasingly entangled with mafia networks. For three years the federal government failed to regain political influence and control in Chechnya and the situation became increasingly intractable. The president of Russia decided to resolve the problem by force.

People in the know told me Yeltsin hesitated long and hard over whether or not to negotiate with Dudaev, and seemed inclined to do so until someone managed to inform him 'just in time' about some very unflattering remark Dudaev had supposedly made about the Russian president. Yeltsin rejected a proposal for negotiations and decided the time had come to show his decisiveness and willpower by resorting to the armed forces. 'The president needed a small, victorious war to improve his approval rating': these are the words of a member of Yeltsin's immediate entourage at that time. In other words, he wanted to demonstrate the government's effectiveness and intimidate opposition. Also, of course, to show Europe and the West how tough he was.

On 29 November 1994, Yeltsin issued an ultimatum to the Chechen leaders giving them 48 hours to cease fire and dissolve all illegal armed groups or face the declaration of a state of emergency in the republic. I could only support the call to end bloodshed, but everything else in the document was a gamble on the introduction of a state of emergency and force. This would involve all the accoutrements of a state of emergency: troops, tanks, aircraft, paratroopers, etc. I believed that was the wrong approach.

Reaction of the Russian public to Yeltsin's gamble on a military solution was negative. The press condemned it. The Duma issued a statement calling for a return to seeking a peaceful settlement, and even decided later to set up a commission of enquiry into all the circumstances of the Chechen crisis. The Council of the Federation opposed the use of troops and military operations. Every opinion poll in Moscow and throughout Russia showed 65–75 per cent of citizens to be against deploying the military. The executive, however, demonstrated its authoritarianism by ignoring public opinion.

From the outset I saw great danger in the course the president had adopted, but nevertheless offered to act as a mediator if either of the parties to the conflict so wished. At a press conference in the Foundation on 29 November, I said:

> We could land ourselves with a second Caucasian War. This is the wrong path. Political action and political contact is essential, and we need to meet with Dudaev and initiate dialogue. What we do not need is an attempt to resolve this problem by force of arms. It is a delusion to imagine that will work. Under no circumstances can we permit further casualties on both sides. That is why I am willing to act as an intermediary.

Dudaev phoned me and said he agreed that I should mediate. I have no wish to idealize Dudaev, but he said at that time: 'We do not envisage our future without Russia. We must live together with Russia.' He did not say exactly how, but that would have been the subject of negotiation. Here was the key to conducting a dialogue and seeking ways for us to coexist. That approach, however, proved unacceptable to Yeltsin.

On 30 November, the president signed Decree No. 2137c, 'Disarmament of armed gangs in the Chechen Republic', which initiated large-scale military operations by Russian federal forces. On 11 December a decree was signed on 'restoration of constitutional legality' in the country. Troops of the Ministry of Defence and the Interior Ministry were sent into Chechnya, and the subsequent course of events is well known.

On New Year's Eve 1994, dozens of Russian soldiers died in the course of a failed assault on Grozny. Their bodies lay unburied in the city's streets. On 4 January I called for the convening of an extraordinary joint session of both houses of the Federal Assembly, mandating the appearance of the president. I stated that the war in Chechnya had assumed the status of a national crisis. I called for an end to the bloodshed and the conducting of genuine negotiations, with the real players rather than inventing a puppet government in Moscow and trying to export it there, which I warned would not work. The juggernaut of war was on the move, however, and war has a logic of its own.

For what took place in Chechnya the guilt lies not with the army, the soldiers and military staff, but with the politicians and military strategists. The conduct of our soldiers began, however, to be motivated by revenge. That is understandable: when they saw their comrades being killed, when they themselves had been abandoned, when unburied corpses littered the streets, the motive of revenge developed and grew.

Exactly the same was true on the Chechen side. What are people supposed to feel who have lost their family, their father, mother, children, their home? When everything has been destroyed that had been built up over so many years? It was understandable that they too would take revenge. The longer all this continued, the harder it was to find a way out of the crisis.

The war dragged on, and in February 1996 I made a public statement proposing a plan of action for a political settlement of the conflict.

> Ending the war in Chechnya is now the first priority for all Russians. The solution must be found today, or literally tomorrow. Every day of delay brings new deaths and destruction that threaten to destabilize the whole of Russia.
>
> ... it is essential to recognize realities and face the facts. These are as follows:
>
> - the Russian leaders' attempt to resolve the issue by force has not succeeded;
> - Dudaev's intention of unleashing 'jihad' and separating Chechnya from Russia has not succeeded;
> - the gamble on settling the conflict by electing new leaders of the republic headed by Doku Zavgaev has not succeeded.
>
> The demand for unconditional withdrawal of troops from Chechnya does not promise an outcome acceptable to all. In the

absence of a political settlement, this would almost inevitably result in civil war in Chechnya, with the danger that it would spill over into other regions of Russia.

The way to resolve the problem is direct dialogue between those responsible for the conflict and on whom the possibility of terminating it depends. President Yeltsin, Djohar Dudaev, Doku Zavgaev and, possibly, other Chechen leaders must meet without delay and work out the terms for a political settlement.

In my view this should include an agreement to cease hostilities immediately, a condemnation of terrorism and any forms of the use of force; also detailing of the approaches to the whole range of issues needing to be resolved, and first and foremost the status of Chechnya, taking into account both the interests of the people of the republic and the interests of Russia. Ways must be found of settling other problems, including withdrawal of troops, the holding of free elections throughout Chechnya, formulation of a programme of national restitution, and the resolution of humanitarian issues. ...

Only after one and a half years of futile attempts to resolve the problem by force did the Russian government announce some supposed 'peace plan', promising to 'conclude peacefully in Chechnya'. The presidential election was approaching and the government finally decided to negotiate with the Chechen side. A ceasefire agreement was signed.

Military operations continued, however, only in a different form. After the presidential election, the situation of the federal forces in Chechnya continued to worsen. General Alexander Lebed, appointed secretary of the Russian Security Council by Yeltsin, was delegated to conduct new negotiations. Lebed managed to reach agreement, but at the price of effectively conceding the federal government's defeat.

This was a defeat not for Russia, but for the Yeltsin regime. Its earlier call to 'take as much sovereignty as you can eat', the destruction of the Soviet Union and the shelling of parliament were all steps along a road leading to the war in Chechnya. Everything that followed was a consequence of ill-conceived, reckless policies, resorting to force, and a reluctance to recognize new realities and seek a political solution when it was possible.

Yeltsin authorized the Khasavyurt agreement, but it did not settle the conflict; rather, it was a truce which would inevitably lead to a new military confrontation.

The year 1994 is remembered in history only for a succession of decisions that pushed Russia further towards impasse and saw the Yeltsin government lose whatever authority it still commanded. Life for ordinary citizens worsened relentlessly. Suffice it to say that this was a record year for Russia in terms of 'abnormally high mortality' of men of working age (between sixteen and sixty). In terms of negative demographic indicators, and also in the suicide rate, Russia far surpassed all European countries.

1995: 10 Years of Perestroika

The intelligentsia

In 1995 came the tenth anniversary of Perestroika, but the mood during the first days and weeks of the year was far from celebratory. That made it all the more important to continue analysing the lessons learned during Perestroika and applying them to the new challenges and worries.

A round-table discussion at the Gorbachev Foundation debated one of our most difficult topics: the role of the intelligentsia in Perestroika. It brought together people with different beliefs and of different political persuasions: Academicians Nikita Moiseyev, Vitaliy Goldansky and Boris Raushenbakh; the playwrights Viktor Rozov and Mikhail Shatrov; the film directors Stanislav Govorukhin and Nikita Mikhalkov; actor Anatoly Romashin; journalist Lyudmila Saraskina and philosophers Valentin Tolstykh and Vadim Mezhuyev.

I have had plenty of experience of interaction with the intelligentsia, in public and in private, in wider circles and more exclusively. During Perestroika the intelligentsia was sometimes lavish in its praise, but sometimes turned its back on me and was harshly critical. I was ready for that. Throughout history, reformers have found themselves in the position of being accorded sporadic support, almost worshipped, only then to be vilified. Nevertheless, the intellectuals have the capacity to interpret events and public opinion as they develop. When they have understood what is really happening, they can steadfastly support reformers and help society to understand what is being done and why.

At the round table, I recalled how academics (with few exceptions), writers and media commentators launched a vociferous campaign against our government's intention to raise the price of bread by three kopecks. Nowadays, people would just laugh at that, but back then it was no laughing matter for us. Academicians, doctors of science and journalists anathematized our plans and us personally. Later, those same people were accusing Gorbachev of indecisiveness.

I could have reeled off a long list of instances when the intelligentsia declared Gorbachev was heading in the wrong direction or doing things the wrong way, but serious political action is not based on instant advice. It can take a long time before it becomes clear who has done what, and which route is the most direct. For example, the intelligentsia was largely in favour of the shock therapy begun in January 1992, with dire consequences.

I said I would not like to see us denouncing or blaming the intelligentsia. I considered it unhelpful and even dangerous at the time and still think so today. Society cannot exist without intellectuals, cannot express itself, understand and explain its past and present, or generate guidelines for the future. The intelligentsia are the yeast of a nation, without which the bread is flat. They are the elite seeds needed to grow a good crop. That is why, as we embarked on Perestroika, we were very much counting on the intelligentsia.

There are many conundrums to which no government, including a reforming administration, can find the answer without the support and help of the intelligentsia. By that, I do not mean only the metropolitan intelligentsia, but everybody who works in education, science, medicine, the media and the arts. We are talking about millions of people who are a priceless social asset.

The intelligentsia have a special responsibility for Russia's future, a contribution to make to her renewal and the continuation of democratic reform. Democracy, freedom and culture are what matter most to the intelligentsia, and it is for the intelligentsia to defend them.

Government and society

With the agreement of the chairman of the Duma Committee on Legislation and Judicial and Legal Reform, I forwarded my views to the Duma on a draft law on 'Election of the president of the Russian Federation'. I proposed:

> immediate insertion of essential additions and amendments to the Constitution of the Russian Federation to restore a reasonable balance in the sharing of power and to correct a manifest de facto and de jure bias favouring unaccountability of presidential power, resulting from a hurriedly drafted constitution that was adopted, effectively, as an emergency measure.

Among other proposals, I included an amendment laying out clear conditions and procedure for early elections of the president of the Russian Federation, as well as measures to strengthen guarantees of the democratic nature of the presidential election and scrutiny by voters of how it was conducted and the vote counted. In other words, I demanded guarantees of fair and free elections.

It was impossible to remain silent in those tense months of 1995. I talked a lot to journalists and visited the Russian provinces. Planned trips to Novosibirsk in February and to St Petersburg in May gave commentators grounds to suggest I might be thinking of standing in the presidential election the following year. I decided to take the opportunity to assess the state of society and see how receptive people were towards my ideas.

In Novosibirsk I visited Akademgorodok and met scientists. I met workers at the Stankosib factory, university students and businessmen. I found that everywhere people were very engaged. They bombarded me with questions about topics that were clearly of great concern, and totally dispelled the myth that they had no interest in politics.

I also spent four extremely busy days in St Petersburg. A conference was held at the Mariinsky Palace to mark the tenth anniversary of the beginning of Perestroika. I talked about Perestroika to workers at the Baltika factory, to academics and writers at Kshesinskaya's Palace, and to teachers and students at St Petersburg Pedagogical University. Everywhere the same question came up in one form or another: 'How do you see the future of Russia. How do current policies measure up to your ideas?

Are they a logical continuation of what was begun in 1985?' My
reply was:

> I am very sure that what has happened after December 1991 has
> not been a continuation of Perestroika. Of course, there are pro-
> cesses initiated by Perestroika that are continuing. Take Glasnost,
> for example. It is attacked, attempts are made to distort it by
> applying economic pressures, newspapers are disappearing one
> after the other, independent television stations have their licences
> revoked, and so on. It is very difficult for me to appear on Channel
> One, and here in St Petersburg I have not been given an opportu-
> nity this time to speak on television. Nonetheless, Glasnost, even if
> retrenched, is still there. Much of what people gained, particularly
> in terms of freedom, is still available and advantage should be
> taken of that.
>
> In every other respect, current policies have nothing in common
> with Perestroika.

I had a turbulent exchange of views in Kursk at the Khimvolokno
synthetic fibre factory. The workers and their families there were
in severe difficulties because of a sharp cutback in production.
Their salaries were going unpaid for months. At first, for several
minutes, I was simply prevented from speaking by hundreds of
agitated people who were despairing of getting any justice, including many women with children. I waited for a time, then came
down from the platform and took a few steps across to the front
rows. I asked them, 'Have you come here to make a noise or to
talk? If you just want to make a noise, then perhaps it is already
time to finish. If you want to hear what I have to say, do please
listen!' The hall quietened down and we were able to start a conversation. I made no excuses, and myself asked the audience some
hard questions. Our discussion lasted almost two hours and they
applauded at the end.

In Chuvashia I was scheduled to visit the university and have a
meeting with the lecturers and students. It was moved to the local
concert hall because 'Moscow advised against' politicians speaking in colleges and universities. As a result, the hall was jammed
full of people, standing in the aisles, up by the stage. An attempt

by a small group to disrupt my speech was put down by members of the audience themselves. The stream of questions made it seem our conversation would never end. There were hostile questions too, which I answered frankly.

In the evening I had dinner with Nikolai Fedorov, the president of Chuvashia. Three years previously, as minister of justice, he had threatened to have me brought in handcuffs to Zorkin in the Constitutional Court. He seemed to have mellowed.

My main preoccupation in those months was how to save Russia from sliding into authoritarianism. There were increasingly persistent rumours that the government was looking for a way to avoid elections. In October 1995, I stated that postponing the elections would be tantamount to usurping the people's right to take decisions about their own future. If allowed, it would put an end to democracy in Russia and to her future as a civilized state. The parliamentary elections went ahead in December, evidently in order to test the temperature, assess the balance of power, and then decide what to do about the presidential elections.

The elections brought defeat for the government. The Our Home is Russia Party received just 10 per cent of the vote. The Communist Party gained two and a half times more and came first. Zhirinovsky's 'liberal democrats' came third. For the first time, scaring the electorate with the 'red and brown' threat did not work. The vote for the Communists and Zhirinovsky was very obviously a protest vote. Public sentiment was made clear in opinion polls, which gave Yeltsin an approval rating of just 6 per cent.

The economic situation continued to deteriorate. The budget was coming apart at the seams. To solve the problem of budget revenues while simultaneously bringing in funds for his election campaign, Yeltsin embarked on an unheard-of privatization stunt: 'deposit auctions'.

The mechanism was simple: a small group of bankers were handed Russia's most promising enterprises as collateral (supposedly on a competitive basis). They made 'loans' to the state budget completely incommensurable with the real value of the enterprises. If the state was unable to repay those amounts, the enterprises would become the property of people who soon came

to be known as 'oligarchs'. It all duly happened. In the overwhelming majority of cases, there were legal irregularities in this
corrupt merging of government and business.

In January 1996, Yeltsin announced he would probably agree
to run for a second presidential term. On 1 March, just six months
after the presidential decree pawning the state's assets, he had a
meeting with seven owners of the major private banking institutions. Berezovsky, Gusinsky, Potanin, Smolensky, Fridman, Aven
and Khodorkovsky undertook to do, and indeed did, all that was
necessary to finance Yeltsin's re-election campaign and have him
back as president of Russia.

The banking institutions that entered into this deal controlled,
according to Berezovsky, more than half the Russian economy
and, most importantly, all the television stations and almost all
the media. The government decided to 're-elect' itself with the aid
of big finance, a virtual monopoly of the media and the state's
'administrative resources'. By fair means or foul.

The Need for an Alternative

Throughout 1995, I was constantly being asked whether I would run in the presidential election. I did not underestimate the obstacles and was in no hurry to reply. Most of my colleagues and friends were against my participating, and some, like Alexander Yakovlev and Vadim Medvedev, said so publicly. Raisa was also opposed, but I could not reconcile myself to the election being a choice between Yeltsin and Zyuganov. They were a pretty pair: one had destroyed the Soviet Union, shelled the first Russian parliament, fused government and big business together and given the green light to Russia's criminals. The other had not repudiated Stalinist totalitarianism, approved of the deeds of the 1991 coup conspirators and had persuaded his party to support the Belovezha Accords with their votes in the Supreme Soviet of Russia.

I felt that to stay on the sidelines would be a dereliction of duty. I had to do what I could to unite the truly democratic, healthy forces capable of representing the interests of the majority of citizens and be a civic alternative to the Yeltsinites and Zyuganovites.

For that, however, action was needed. People had to be convinced. There was a need to explain the past and talk about the future. An election campaign provided a unique opportunity for that, and in the end I decided I could not ignore it.

My supporters set up a campaign team in February 1996 and began collecting signatures, of which we needed at least one million. I did not immediately make my decision public, but in an interview, in response to being asked yet again whether I intended to stand in the presidential election, I said the logic of events was inclining me towards doing so.

I invited all the political leaders of centre and centre-left parties to discuss uniting our efforts, and had meetings with their representatives. On 1 March 1996 I sent the media an appeal to all democratic forces titled 'Give the people a choice':

> ... The current government is at bay, and that is very dangerous. No less dangerous are the leaders of the Communist Party, who have yet to break their umbilical link with the totalitarian past. We should not be deceived by the social democratic and liberal slogans currently now in vogue with the Zyuganovites. Knowing these people and the nature of Party officialdom, I fear that if they come to power they will halt reform, take away society's democratic freedoms and, wittingly or unwittingly, open the way to national socialism in Russia. For a country that sacrificed millions of lives on the altar of victory over fascism, that would signal total moral degradation. ...
>
> I see only one way of ensuring the prospect of further progress towards reform and democracy: all reform-minded, pro-democracy leaders, parties and movements must unite and go into the election as a united team, agreeing the distribution of key posts in the future government and making the agreement public. In this way, we shall ensure the legitimacy not only of the next president, but also of the government.
>
> I therefore propose that we should immediately convene a national forum of democrats to agree a common plan of action. It is our sacred duty to give Russia a real choice.

Meanwhile, my supporters were collecting signatures in support of my nomination. The one million signatures were collected quickly and, on 21 March with the number of signatures exceeding 1.5 million, I announced, after long, serious consideration and hesitation, that I was joining the presidential race. In my announcement, I presented Russia's rulers with a lengthy invoice for their failures:

> You have allowed a small section of the population to misappropriate vast riches, while depriving the majority of an anchor in life and even of a meaningful existence.

You say you have filled the shelves with food and goods, but they are completely beyond the reach of tens of millions of people.

With your reckless policies, you have not only failed to provide a means of overcoming the economic crisis, but have doomed Russia's industry to stagnate and die.

You have created an unprecedented situation where, for months, people are not paid what they have earned, while meagre pensions and education grants for the most vulnerable sections of the population condemn them to poverty. Not a word of explanation has been forthcoming from the top of the government about how or why this has happened.

You have abandoned to their fate science, culture and education, forcing teachers, doctors and scientists to go on strike.

You have turned the country into a training ground for, and hotbed of, unheard-of criminality, from which ordinary people have nowhere to seek redress.

You have unleashed a war in Chechnya for no reason the soldiers can discern, causing casualties for no reason mothers and families can understand. One can only speculate why a war the whole country condemns is now in its second year.

You have not even begun to reform the army, undermining the morale of the troops, reducing their combat readiness and eroding society's respect for them.

You have thrown to the winds the legacy of goodwill generated by the foreign policy of the Perestroika period. Your foreign policy is baffling both to our own people and the outside world. It has reduced the country's international prestige and security and does little to promote the economic and political interests of Russia.

You never acknowledge what is obvious to everybody: that the troubles and adversity that have befallen millions of people are the outcome of bungled policies that discredit the concepts of 'reform', 'the market', 'democracy' and 'respect for the government'.

For these reasons, I state my total disagreement with the policies pursued by the present government and insist they must change.

I have the right to put the matter in these terms because I am aware of the degree of my own moral responsibility, not only for what was initiated 10 years ago on my initiative and of my own

volition, but also for what has happened and been done in recent
years without my involvement and contrary to my intentions.

I said I was making no secret of my aims and intentions:

> It is my profound conviction that, both from a political and a moral
> standpoint, the present regime does not deserve to survive. ...
>
> In my manifesto, which will shortly be put forward for discus-
> sion by voters, I start from the premise that reform should be for
> the benefit of everybody and not just one section of society; that
> the prosperity and well-being of each individual and family should
> depend on how hard they work, the extent of their initiative and
> business acumen rather than their adroitness in grabbing anything
> that does not belong to them but is not nailed down.
>
> We need to provide the most favourable conditions possible for
> entrepreneurs, particularly the owners of small and medium-sized
> businesses, to enable them to expand their operations; we need
> to empower the professionals in culture, science and education
> to maintain and develop society's spiritual potential. The urge to
> make Russia a rich, prosperous and democratic country is what
> can and should unite us all.
>
> I publicly declare that I am entering the electoral contest as an
> independent, 'non-party' candidate, free of all group interests and
> obligations. I do not have a party of my own and have no inten-
> tion of creating one. I am prepared to work together with anybody
> who will put the national interests and future of Russia ahead of
> partisanship and personal ambition. My 'party' is all of Russia and
> all Russians, regardless of whether they vote for or against me. My
> priority is to unite a Russia beset by rifts and rebellions and to do
> everything in my power to enable her to stride confidently into the
> twenty-first century.

The Central Electoral Commission registered me as a candidate
for the presidency of Russia on 13 April. Many people, including
friends and those closest to me, tried to dissuade me from joining
the race but, once I had decided to do so, I was very conscious
of their moral support. Raisa, who was not only doubtful but
anxious (as it turned out, with good reason), was with me from

beginning to end of the saga. She did not find the psychological burden easy to bear, particularly because the campaign immediately turned into a contest without rules.

Even before the presidential campaign got under way, violations of electoral law by the Presidential Administration and the other departments of the executive branch become increasingly blatant. The government would stop at nothing, and had the benefit of lavish funding for their own campaign.

Yeltsin's election teams launched a high-cost, large-scale agitation and propaganda campaign with bands, singers and dancers and all the other razzmatazz, complete with catchy slogans previously honed on American voters: 'Choose or Lose', 'Vote with Your Heart!'.

During the campaign, the fees payable to pop stars for concerts went through the roof. My assistant invited a celebrated music group under the direction of a musician I knew well to perform at one of my campaign meetings in Moscow, but the fee he named, considering it honest-to-God 'mates' rates', was well beyond our means.

Then there were the vote-catching promises designed to draw electors to Yeltsin, despite the fact that the backlog of wages, pensions and welfare payments ran into billions of roubles. At the same time, orders were issued by officials in Moscow to local government workers. This was the remit of a team staffed by government officials and representatives of the intelligence services.

Ginger groups proliferated, as did teams, committees and movements, all designed to demonstrate 'universal popular support', all vying to outdo one another. In contravention of electoral law, a council was set up chaired by the incumbent president to coordinate the activities of the teams and associations to re-elect him. It included all the top government officials, from the prime minister to the director of the Federal Security Bureau. They co-opted the head of NTV, the only independent television station, which meant they had total control of television. The election was turned into a football match with one goal, trampling underfoot all moral and legal standards on the principle that the end justifies the means. The only force capable of effectively opposing this aggressive, lawless juggernaut would have been a joint effort by all the opposition's democratic presidential candidates, but they proved to be disunited, unwilling and incapable of cooperating or compromising with each other. That fatal weakness was expertly exploited by the government.

Breaking through the conspiracy of silence

With the start of the election campaign, I again began travelling round the country, meeting people in the streets and squares, in businesses, educational institutions and public associations. I instantly came up against obstruction and attempts to disrupt my scheduled meetings. There were refusals to make premises available, and meetings would be moved at the last minute to less accessible and spacious venues. Meetings were banned at a number of educational institutions, including my own Stavropol Agricultural Institute.

As a rule, I found myself speaking in halls and at other locations that were full to bursting, with people standing in the aisles, sitting on the steps, the stage and the floor. Crowds stood at wide open doors where that was possible, or, sometimes, listened to the broadcast on local radio or from loudspeakers at the entrances.

I was subjected to a conspiracy of silence on the part of the media under government control, and to wild, venomous misconduct by extreme communist and nationalist groups. I came up against cutting discourtesy on the part of provincial leaders afraid to look me in the eye, who failed to appear either to welcome or to bid me goodbye.

In spite of all that, I had no intention of giving up on travelling around the country and meeting the voters. Between March and early June I visited dozens of cities in more than 20 regions and attended many meetings with thousands of people. In a number of cities, television presenters behaved admirably and even, given the circumstances of the time, courageously. For example, in Rostov-on-Don I had a frank discussion with journalist Dmitry Dibrov, broadcast without any 'editing'. In the same city, for over an hour, I answered questions from hundreds of Rostov citizens at an open-air gathering in the city park.

It sometimes seemed that the further we were from Moscow

the more confidently and freely people behaved, including the local civic leaders. In the Altai I had meetings with the governor and the chairman of the regional legislative assembly, held a press conference and spoke on regional television.

Because more than a third of citizens in the Altai voted Communist, I particularly focused on the Party in my speech. Over the months of the election campaign there were plenty of disagreeable experiences. Here is just one. On the morning of 24 April 1996, I arrived in Omsk where a meeting with the city's voters had been announced. The region's leaders ignored the meeting and a hostile crowd had gathered before the meeting at the Political Education Club. Representatives of the local administration suggested I should go in through the back entrance but I flatly refused. I walked calmly through the main entrance and foyer towards the stairs leading to the first floor and a crowded hall, where some 2,000 people were waiting. At this point a sinister-looking young man rushed forward and struck a blow on a part of my head that paratroopers are trained to strike. A security officer managed to push the attacker back and that helped to deflect the blow. At this point a group of individuals who had been standing to one side and watching attempted to free the attacker, who had been detained.

The start of the meeting was delayed and a fairly tense situation had arisen, further aggravated by groups who had infiltrated the hall with the clear intention of disrupting proceedings. This is how the outcome of the incident was described in *Moskovskiye Novosti*:

> When Mikhail Gorbachev came on to the stage in the wake of riot police, he stood silent, listening to the yelling and jeering in the crowd and suddenly roared, 'This is how fascism begins in Russia!'
>
> The hall fell silent, if not immediately. 'Actually, after that I just feel like leaving,' Gorbachev continued. 'Not because I am scared of scum, but because I fear for normal people, and judging from the faces in the audience, I calculate they make up about half of those present. I am concerned for them in this crush, because they need to vote for a new Russia. Leave this fracas, citizens, and remember, the coming four years will determine the fate of our

country for decades to come. Do not allow yourselves to be driven into slavery.'

And Gorbachev departed.

I believe the attack on me and the disruption of my speech to the people of Omsk were deliberately planned. I heard later that Zhirinovsky's 'Liberal Democratic' Party had been behind the incident. A drunken LDP official let that slip at Zhirinovsky's birthday party, saying, 'What a reception we gave Gorbachev in Omsk!' When I heard about that, I forwarded my information to the Prosecutor General's Office, only to receive a meaningless bureaucratic non-response.

In a number of cities, Communist Party representatives tried to disrupt my meetings with heckling and barracking, but I gave them as good as I got, and others attending the meeting shut them up. At these meetings voters were constantly asking about my relations with other presidential candidates: Grigoriy Yavlinsky, Alexander Lebed and Svyatoslav Fedorov. Had we agreed to form a coalition of democratic forces? If you do not come to an agreement, I was told in no uncertain terms, you will just be asking us to waste our votes. I did not regard Yavlinsky, Lebed or Fedorov as rivals but rather as partners, by and large, members of the same team. I believed that as each of us ran his own campaign it would become clear who had the best chance of winning, and we would then agree who should go forward as the unity candidate of the forces of democracy. That seemed to me entirely realistic, and I talked publicly about it. My visits to more than 20 regions persuaded me that a majority of people were entirely capable of seeing through the false choice being imposed on them and that there was a real demand for a third force.

The coming together never happened. My would-be partners lacked the political nous to see they would get nowhere on their own. The government actively fomented disunity among us, targeting primarily Lebed, whose popularity was in the ascendant. They allowed him to conduct his campaign unhampered and, after the first round of voting, seduced him with the offer of the post of secretary of the Russian Security Council. That left me with no option but to soldier on.

For the first time in several years I did get the opportunity of addressing the people on national television. There were no debates between the candidates (and to this day the Russian government evades them), but even a pre-recorded speech allowed me to explain my position to the viewers.

Let me talk about the main thing. The government. The first thing that needs to be done is to bring the government back under control. Its power should come from the people and it should always remain under popular control. Russia needs a president, not an autocrat, and certainly not a dictator. ...

Parliament and the government should function routinely alongside the president, and have all the power needed to do so. At the top we need honest, knowledgeable people.

I intend to take rigorous measures to break the illegal conspiracy between unscrupulous politicians, corrupt officials and the criminal world. Russian citizens should feel they have the protection of the state wherever they are: at their workplace, in the street or at home.

What we must cherish above all else is good relations in this, our shared home. Russia was and remains a world of worlds. Russians, who are in the majority, have always lived in harmony with all our other peoples.

We need to restore the authority of the law, of legality, of the entire law-enforcement system, with support, not interference, from the state, independence of the judiciary, the rule of law above all else. That is what we need.

We can no longer leave our army in its present state. I will restore the prestige of the armed forces.

Social justice. ...

What I understand by social justice is a decent income for those able to work, and support for those in dire need. In Russia, it should finally be more profitable to earn honestly than to steal. Even in our present situation, I believe it is essential to help immediately those who find themselves below subsistence level. By that I am thinking of pensioners, the disabled, students and refugees.

From the Soviet experience, I have included in my manifesto those things that proved valuable: free education, available to every family regardless of their income; publicly available medical care. Of course, we must also improve the private sector, and it too must have the support of the state.

In my Russia, teachers, doctors, scientists and the intelligentsia will not be beggars.

The economy. I see the solution to these enormous social tasks and problems in boosting our own, Russian, industrial output. We cannot leave everything to take care of itself: we need to manage investment and credit, and have a positive policy on taxation and foreign economic links.

I expect private enterprise to play a major role, especially small and medium-sized businesses. All forms of property, whether private or public, will be securely protected by the law. ...

Like everywhere else in the world, we will put all the strength of the state into protecting and supporting agricultural workers.

Today we need to be building not yesterday's but tomorrow's economy, and for that Russia needs to remain a great scientific power.

Foreign policy. To raise Russia's international prestige, I will throw into the ring all the experience and authority I have acquired. In our commonwealth we need to move towards a new union on a basis of mutually beneficial cooperation. At the same time, Russia should not take on greater burdens than she can afford.

Finally, do not believe people who are again promising you the earth, swearing they will 'lie down on the rail tracks' if they do not deliver, that they can find a husband for every woman and all the rest of it. Only we, working together, can rescue Russia and ourselves from this situation. This is the only Russia we have, and we are all responsible for her.

The first round of the presidential election showed that the government had, all the same, succeeded in imposing its choice between the twin evils of Yeltsin and Zyuganov, each of whom obtained around one-third of the vote. A unity candidate of pro-democracy forces would probably have been able to give them a run for their money, but in isolation we picked up a total of only about one-quarter of the vote between us. Although – who

knows the truth of the matter? There was no shortage of outright falsification of results and underhand 'electoral fixing'. The
declared total of votes in my favour in the different regions came
in everywhere at a remarkably similar figure of around 1 per cent.
Opinion polls, and even the initial counts which were presumably
leaked through an oversight, told a different story. It was strain-
ing credibility to claim that a candidate able to muster 1.5 million
signatures for the nomination papers in such a short time could
have received so few votes in the actual election.

There was a revealing and completely outrageous incident
involving my representative, Artur Umansky. He told me over
the telephone from Chechnya that he was coming to Moscow
with documents about serious falsification of the election results.
We learned that shortly afterwards armed men burst into his
house and took him away. He was never seen again. Our numerous enquiries addressed to the Interior Ministry and Prosecutor
General's Office got nowhere.

I have often said that the most honest elections in the entire history of the USSR and Russian Federation were those of 1989 and
1990. No one questioned them: they were simply fair. Everything
after that is a sorry tale of how, instead of genuine, fair elections,
a mere surrogate is set up. Each year has seen increasing application of tricky new techniques and fixes to prevent free expression
of the will of the people. Whose interest is it in? Ultimately, the
economy and business suffer, whose leading figures provided the
funds for Yeltsin's campaign; and the intelligentsia, who failed to
sound the alarm and, for the most part, chose to look away from
all the illegality and abuses employed to keep the Communists
out, which were so successfully trialled during this race.

Letter relating to the 1996 presidential election campaign

Dear Mikhail Sergeyevich,

I know you must be feeling very sad and hope that my heartfelt
letter may help just a little with the burden you bear.

There was a time at the very beginning of Perestroika when it
seemed to me that you were loved by the entire Soviet people. I was

so pleased and excited when you were in France. I rejoiced together with the people of the United States, thousands of whom wanted to shake your hand. I was so proud of you!

There were, though, other times when I was hurt and ashamed. More than that, I was outraged when that massacre took place in Baku, when unarmed people were killed in Tbilisi, Vilnius, and so on.

You bore part of the blame for all those disasters.

I was baffled when you vacillated to the right, then to the left. After 10 years I have come to understand what you were afraid of. From your position up there you could see more than I could.

When you were taken captive in Foros, I was so worried for you. I think today that if it had not been for that accursed 'State Emergency Committee' we would have moved, even if only very slowly, towards democracy, and there might never have been the slaughter in Chechnya or the tragedy in Tajikistan, but history cannot be written in the subjunctive mood.

What happened, happened.

I felt sorry for you, but you were eclipsed by a new hero, Yeltsin. Standing on that tank outside the White House, he was the personification of the victory of democracy over totalitarianism. Again the people (and I with them) exulted.

Reproaches rained down on you, both from the democrats and the communists. Everything was Gorbachev's fault.

I never forgot, though, that it was you who made a speech at the United Nations that ended the Cold War and prevented a third, nuclear, world war. I am certain that a grateful mankind will never forget that.

I follow closely what you are doing now, and know you are doing it not for yourself but for the sake of Russia, for democracy, for all mankind. You are now carrying a heavy cross on the road to your Calvary, and once again I so admire you. ...

With respect, faith and hope,

Svetlana Luchich
Member of the Campaign for Nuclear Disarmament
16 May 1997

I have no regrets about participating in the 1996 election.

Discrediting elections

Yeltsin's supporters were far from sure he would be victorious in the second round. Disagreements worsened within his team, as a result of which financial machinations surfaced, like the notorious 'case of the Xerox box', when it eventually came to light that both the rival factions within his team were carting illicit cash round the regions in boxes, bags and backpacks, and not forgetting to stuff their own pockets in the process. There had never been such discreditable election tactics before, and all for the sake of keeping an increasingly dysfunctional individual in the Kremlin!

None of those in the president's entourage contemplated for an instant the option of giving up power. Among the options they did consider was cancelling the second round. They made no secret of it. Before the election, Yeltsin's security chief, Alexander Korzhakov, publicly touted the idea of cancelling it entirely in order to 'maintain public order'. They decided to go ahead with the second round only after they got the better of Alexander Lebed who, from inexperience, failed to realize they would dump him just as soon as they no longer needed him. I publicly warned him that throwing in his lot with either Yeltsin or the Communists would compromise him politically.

I had no doubt that the second round of the election would see all the irregularities that had marred the first part, only to an enhanced degree. The election, which fell far short of the international standards for fair elections (the West was curiously silent about this very obvious fact) demonstrated that Yeltsin had not gained the support of a majority of Russians.

Personally, I voted in the second round against both candidates (there was such an option at the time, but it has since been removed). It was my protest against the no-choice election. Millions of voters did the same, or refused to turn out for the second round. A poll conducted after the election revealed that 45 per cent of those who voted for Yeltsin did so not because they supported him, but because they did not want Zyuganov to be president.

In the interval between the first and second rounds of voting, Yeltsin was taken to hospital with a heart attack, but this was concealed from the electorate. On the day of the second vote he could not make it even to his local polling station, and voted in the Barvikha sanatorium. It reminded me of the occasion when the terminally ill Konstantin Chernenko voted in a ward at the Kremlin Hospital, which had been hastily disguised to look like an office. Yeltsin appeared in public only on the day of his re-inauguration. The ceremony was curtailed.

Immediately after the election, those who had managed and financed Yeltsin's electoral campaign were appointed to the highest offices in the land. Anatoly Chubais became head of the Presidential Administration, Boris Berezovsky was appointed deputy secretary of the Security Council and Vladimir Potanin got the post of deputy prime minister. Yeltsin had heart surgery, and was unable to return to his presidential duties until six months later, at the beginning of 1997.

Commenting on the election after the results of the second round were announced, I said:

> Boris Yeltsin's re-election for a second term by no means signi-
> fies that a majority of citizens approve of his political approach.
> At least half of those who voted for Yeltsin on 3 July did so only
> because they wanted to avoid letting the Communists back into
> power. They are not at all in raptures over what has happened to
> Russia during the past five years, including the events of autumn
> 1993, the war in Chechnya, rampant criminality and the huge
> social cost of the reforms.

Regrettably, the ruling 'elite' drew their own conclusions from the 1996 election, and decided they could hoodwink tens of millions of people and blithely carry on with a parasitical course destructive for society and Russia. The result of their victory was that, only two years down the line, the regime, and with it the country's economy, faced bankruptcy.

In an interview published in *Novaya Gazeta*, I talked with the paper's editor, Dmitry Muratov, about what people could do who found the current situation unacceptable:

MG: ... The elected president and the government he has
   appointed are hardly going to get away with simply ignoring

the interests of the vast section of society that voted against him and his policies.

DM: Oh, yes they will, and with the greatest of ease! There is no communication between the government and society.

MG: You forget that the regime has the instinct of self-preservation. If they do not change their policies, if people do not feel life is changing for the better then, ultimately, the ruling elite will lose all they have. ....

If you look at who voted for Lebed, who voted for Yavlinsky, if you bear in mind the fact that 3.5 million people (and I imagine it was actually more) turned out and voted in the second round against both candidates, you will see there is a huge social base for a democratic opposition. Despite all the government's efforts, their puppet parties are crumbling and will fall apart. There is a need for a genuine, natural coming together of people.

The Final Years of the Millennium

The Gorbachev Foundation's 'First Five-Year Plan'

In March 1997, our Foundation marked its fifth anniversary with a reception and round-table discussion. The main topic was the work of the Foundation and its search for a way to rescue Russia from systemic crisis. The meeting was attended by guests and partners: prominent academics, public figures, writers, press commentators and people from a broad spectrum of scholarly and artistic Moscow.

Opening the meeting, I thanked everyone who had worked with us all these years, and who had shown solidarity in difficult times when the very existence of the Foundation was under threat. It had been vital for the Foundation's growth, and also very important for me personally.Given the increasing intimacy between the government bureaucracy and the mafia, it was more important than ever, no matter what the difficulties, to protect and cultivate the rudiments of civil society, and that was unthinkable without free speech and democratic thinking. Independent research centres and independent media could do a lot to preserve, develop and affirm democracy and democratic thinking in Russia. Without it, there was no way out of the situation in which we found ourselves.

For the moment, I said, we are very disunited, and that is how the government likes it. It tries to sow dissent between politicians and to split society in accordance with the divide and rule philosophy of ancient Rome. Let us try to find a way, I urged, to overcome this dangerous state of affairs. Our Foundation is open to interaction and collaboration with a great diversity of thinkers in Russia and abroad. Our mission is to work together to find a way out of Russia's current crisis.

Here are a number of contributions by those participating in the round table. They reflect the range of opinions and assessments we heard:

Professor Boris Slavin: I see the Foundation as a unique organization striving, not just in words but in deeds, to develop pluralism of thinking. People of every intellectual orientation, proponents of conservative, liberal or socialist views can speak here and be published. People from a great variety of parties and movements come, and I think that in this way the Foundation is immensely important for democracy.

Professor Yelena Borisovna Vladimirskaya: I represent a sector of medicine dealing with treatment of the most terrible diseases: paediatric oncology and haematology.

So, back to 1991. In Russia, just 7 per cent of children recovered from the most common and terrible paediatric tumours, acute leukaemia. Fast-forward five years. Now the survival rate for recovery from this cancer averages 75 per cent. Nobody any longer begs to be sent abroad for a bone marrow transplant. We can do it ourselves in Russia.

Thanks to the Foundation, we have trained more than 200 paediatricians and nurses abroad. With the help of the Foundation we have held educational courses with top foreign specialists. More than 1,000 doctors from Russia and the former republics of the Soviet Union have attended these courses. In 18 centres, children receive treatment using modern technology, and the results are as good as anywhere else in the civilized world.

Of course, the Foundation on its own cannot provide all the finance for this work, but it does not need to. The Foundation has done what Mikhail Sergeyevich is outstandingly good at: it has drawn attention to us. Because we are associated with Gorbachev, people in the outside world want to help. There has been a steady flow of support.

Viktor Rozov, author and playwright: The Gorbachev Foundation is a miraculously surviving relic of those hopeful, better times when Perestroika was just beginning. All of us were hopeful then, but I feel nowadays that I am living in a foreign country, a country where I am constantly afraid. I am afraid of decrees, of battles in parliaments. I am afraid we may be unable to overcome already very entrenched, dangerous tendencies in the state. Almost every strategic position has been seized and we ourselves are somewhere in the middle of all this. There is total lawlessness and some savage, barbaric, ignorant 'new life' with 'new Russians' is on the rampage.

Oh, yes, we have known brutal, terrible times in the past, but, forgive me, a more iniquitous and dishonourable time than the present day I have not seen in the course of a long life. Today I am afraid of people, and people have started to fear each other.

Alexander Panikin, businessman, CEO of the Paninter clothing company: I want to say publicly that our manufacturing company truly has grown from a seed planted by Mikhail Gorbachev. Ours may be the only cooperative in the manufacturing sector to have developed into a major, serious business group. Today we are able to put up real opposition to the dominance of foreign products on the market in Moscow and to some extent in the rest of Russia, because we have seventy regional representatives across the land.

I want to say that for me, personally, hope for the future of Russia comes not from looking to those in power, not to what they think or come up with, but from everybody doing their own job with all the energy they possess. We have started belonging to ourselves, and for that, thank you so much, Mikhail Sergeyevich.

Georgiy Shakhnazarov, Corresponding Member of the Russian Academy of Sciences: Repudiating the entire Soviet experience, pronouncing it negative from start to finish, we deprive ourselves of a very important part of our history. ... Until we come to terms with the Soviet past, until we recognize that those seventy years are as valuable for the future as all the rest of Russia's millennial history, there will be no new ideas, no breakthrough to the future.

Drawing the discussion to a close, I said:

> I do not for a moment believe, as someone has said here, that
> the intelligentsia has died. I do not want to accept that opinion,
> although I fully share the pain at what is happening to us and
> to the intelligentsia. It seems to me that only demonstrates how
> much Russia needs such centres of independent thought as ours.
> It is splendid that you have come today to remember how the
> Foundation was established, and how it sent out impulses that
> caused other foundations to appear, with which we cooperate and
> discuss specific projects. It is essential to keep the shoots of civil
> society alive.
>
> The Foundation will continue to focus primarily on what is
> happening in our own, native land, and to do all it can to bring the
> ongoing crisis to an end.

The elections fail to bring stability

The end of the presidential election did not bring even temporary
political stabilization. Although the government lost no time in
cynically reneging on their campaign promises, Russia's financial
system was in tatters. There was a rapidly increasing avalanche
of defaults and arrears within the state budget, social inequalities
deepened, the country continued its slide into deindustrialization,
and still there was no sign of a coherent economic and industrial
policy on the part of the state.

It was reported that enormous numbers of working people
in many sectors of the economy and in many regions had not
received their wages and salaries for six months or more. In
October 1996, pension arrears reached 13.3 trillion roubles ($2.5
billion). A conference of Tatarstan judges issued a statement:

'Minimum funding requirements of the court system for
administering justice are not being met.'

January 1997 saw the publication of a statement addressed to
the president of Russia by prominent economists, academicians
and Nobel Prize winners. They saw the state's withdrawal from
its regulatory functions as being the primary cause of the decline,
collapse, plundering and criminalization of the economy. This

had produced 'horrifying social consequences', including a huge increase in the number of completely penurious people.

The inevitable consequences of the policies of the past six years were increasingly obvious. In an article published in *Rossiyskaya Gazeta*, Deputy Prime Minister and Minister of the Interior Anatoly Kulikov wrote:

> Criminal elements have become more organized and quickly moved from disparate groups of gangsters to intellectually and technologically well-supported criminal syndicates with robust security and large-scale ambitions. To demonstrate their power and for purposes of intimidation, extremely dangerous methods and resources have been used, including criminal terror. ... Criminal business methods are increasingly in evidence. ... In this environment the situation of ordinary Russians is worsening. ...

On 6 March 1997, Yeltsin gave an address to the Federal Assembly titled 'Order in the government means order in the country'. It was, of course, impossible for him not to be aware that the people were tired of chaos. It was essential, he said, to restore order, not dictatorial order but democratic order. In response to the president's address, I warned, 'Nothing is said in this speech about what matters most: analysis of the causes of the severe crisis in which our society finds itself.' The impression given was that Yeltsin was again going to back not a change of policy, but increased pressure to force through a course of action that had already led Russia to an impasse. 'If that is the case, if my suspicions and assessment prove correct, we can expect more shocks.'

Opinion polls detected a growing wave of protest, but the president and his 'renewed team' were disinclined to listen to what people thought, and saw the way forward as being a 'more resolute' pushing ahead with the old course. In June, I shared my concerns with the readers of *Novaya Gazeta*:

> After the failure of Shock Therapy, Mk I, a new version of the same thing is to be imposed on Russia. Everything in Boris Yeltsin's recent behaviour indicates that he is intending to remain

as president for life, in disregard of the constitution, society and everything else.

Respected economists have voiced their criticism in unison, but the Kremlin line, personified by Chubais, brooks no deviation. Any who do not fall in with the plans of the Centre will be starved of resources. The upshot is that we can predict rising tension between the Centre and the periphery.

The policy of radical monetarism is being imposed on Russia by all available means. Those in the Kremlin are aware that pushing ahead will encounter universal protests, and that is why the government is so unceremoniously grasping at unconditional support from the media. Television is already almost completely under control, and now it is the turn of print publications. *Komsomolskaya Pravda* has already fallen and the battle is raging to take over *Izvestiya*. The subservient media stop at nothing to ingratiate themselves with their new owners. They even attacked the Russian Orthodox Church after the Patriarch of all Russia, Alexiy II, criticized the results of the reformers' efforts, speaking out in defence of the dispossessed and those deprived of all help and support.

In this climate, the fight against corruption is no more than a pretence aimed at diverting public attention. It is perfectly obvious nothing will come of it, not least because the corruption is rooted in the regime itself.

Russia is entering a difficult period which will see a further increase in conflicts and collisions, both at the top and among the people.

Looking back at the events of 1997 in an interview for NTV, I had to confirm that my worst expectations had come to pass. 'The stunt of trying to revive the economy with Shock Therapy, Mk II, has failed. Gambling on a further round of privatization without economic recovery, without creating and developing the domestic market, without increasing effective consumer demand, is futile.'

It was clear that this phase, without any clear purpose, without a meaningful policy, could not continue for long.

The storm breaks in 1998

The Russian state was in dire financial straits. Foreign debt had risen to 146.4 per cent of GDP. In the first three months of 1998 the state debt in overdue wages and salaries of public employees rose to an astronomical total of 58 billion denominated roubles, about $9 billion. In just two months the population's income fell 7 per cent.

Attempting to find a way of servicing its growing debt, the government tried constructing a financial pyramid scheme, issuing short-term treasury bills at ever higher interest rates. Capital outflow accelerated, increasing pressure on the artificially inflated rouble exchange rate.

In an effort to delay the collapse, the government introduced a rigid restriction of the money supply, which entailed non-payment of wages and pensions, default on government contracts, etc. Economic stagnation worsened, budget revenues were insufficient to cover loan payments, social tensions increased, one strike followed another.

One might have thought it would have been obvious to anybody that a new course and new people were needed, but it was not obvious to the president. The main thing, he declared in a message to the Federal Assembly, was 'to overcome despondency and negative attitudes'. The message abounded with wild assertions testifying to the fact that the president had finally parted company with reality.

At the start of the year I wrote in an article for *Novaya Gazeta*,

> I was astonished the other day to hear the president suddenly say in conversation with Boris Nemtsov, 'Press on regardless!'.
>
> Press on with what? With trying to rob people of all they are worth through new housing maintenance and utility tariffs, through pension reform? 'Press on regardless' piling up domestic and foreign debt, press on with selling off for next to nothing the state assets most vital to the public interest? 'Press on regardless' with raising already punitive taxation to even higher levels?

I was outraged by the Russian government's indifference to people's welfare:

> A few days ago the Constitutional Court ruled that henceforth the priority for all revenue must be payments into the state coffers. Businesses must pay their taxes first and only after that pay people's wages.
>
> This is just a continuation of what they have been doing, seeing their top priority as being to intensify the fiscal take. Here again is that whiff of cynicism that has pervaded all the years of shock therapy reforms. Who cares how high the price? Who cares how people live? Who cares that they are being bankrupted? Who cares about the rise in unemployment? Well, if we do not care about anything that affects human beings, what do we care about? What else matters?

The worsening situation in the country and the lack of carefully considered government policies were aggravating tensions within Yeltsin's entourage. There were efforts to paper over the cracks, but on 23 March 1998 the dam burst: by presidential decree, Boris Yeltsin dismissed the entire Russian government of Viktor Chernomyrdin. A further decree dismissed First Deputy Prime Minister Anatoly Chubais.

This was a turf war between factions. Berezovsky, Yumashev and Diachenko were one gang. Nemtsov was looking for a niche (and supporters), Chubais was looking for his niche, and Chernomyrdin was yet another gang. Everything was falling apart and the president was unable to hold the ring. On top of everything, there were rumours that the president's mental powers were failing. While in Washington, Lebed said as much to the US Congress.

The political motivation for dismissing the government was clear to me: Yeltsin wanted to show how decisive he was and how completely in control. As Chernomyrdin's successor, Yeltsin was proposing Sergey Kirienko, an 'energetic technocrat', young, capable, but completely unknown and lacking sufficient experience to manage a nation.

Yeltsin's decision could open the way to a number of political moves and scenarios very remote from democracy. In an interview for Interfax, I gave a warning about this. The Duma might not approve Kirienko's candidacy, I said, and that might even be the president's intention: to provide himself with a pretext for dissolving the State Duma. Kirienko's candidacy was rejected by the Duma, which twice refused to approve him. Yeltsin proposed the same candidate yet again and had the option, under the constitution, of dissolving the Duma in the event of a third rejection. There has probably never before in Russia been such broad agreement of political forces of every persuasion that the president was the root cause of instability in Russia. It was impossible to predict how the deputies would behave in the third vote.

At the third vote, they did, nevertheless, endorse Kirienko. The new prime minister announced that the government was proposing a new economic policy, whose main thrust would be to revitalize industrial production. It proved to be a mirage. Things could not have gone worse with the economy. The government was incapable of controlling it.

In an interview on 8 August I had to state that the government had failed. With 80 per cent of the population against it, there was nothing it could do. Kirienko had neither a strong team nor the confidence of the public.

A way out of the predicament was possible only by democratic means: 'Let people whom the nation trusts come to power through elections. Without the asset of trust, nobody can get Russia out of her state of crisis. Yeltsin had that asset once, but has it no longer.'

The president and government did not want to admit their inadequacy. On 14 August, Yeltsin was still trying to assure the world: 'There will be no devaluation. I am saying that clearly and firmly. I am not just fantasizing: all the sums have been done.' Just three days later, on 17 August, the government and Central Bank announced restructuring of the national debt through government bonds, which in reality meant a technical default, and a move to a floating rouble. They had to abandon support for the rouble.

This signified a total failure of the macroeconomic policy the Russian government had been pursuing in 1992–8. The economy suffered a further heavy blow: the Russian rouble lost two-thirds of its value, and people again lost their savings in whole or in part. There was a significant fall in industrial output and living standards, and a sharp increase in inflation.

An economy based on speculation, a corrupt government, a rampant crime wave, tens of millions of people deprived of all support: such was the economic legacy of the 'Yeltsin Era'. On 21 August a majority of deputies in the Duma called on Yeltsin to resign voluntarily (only 32 deputies voted in support of him). Plans were afoot in the Duma to have him impeached.

The Impeachment Commission invited me to speak at its meeting on 24 August. I replied that I did not intend to be present in person, because those actively participating in it, and even some of its members, had been supporters of the State Emergency Committee or involved in disrupting the signing of the Union Treaty. I was, however, prepared to submit testimony in writing. In the meantime the Duma passed a resolution advising Yeltsin to cease exercising his authority before completion of his term. The suggestion was timely, and I concurred with it.

How to come out of the crisis?

What was the president to do? Yeltsin decided to bring back Chernomyrdin and appointed him acting prime minister.

I could not see the appointment contributing to lifting Russia out of the crisis because it did not represent any change of policy. The Duma twice rejected the proposal. Given the situation, Yeltsin was now forced to retreat and, on 10 September at Yavlinsky's suggestion, he proposed Yevgeny Primakov for the post of prime minister. That gained parliamentary approval the following day. Yury Maslyukov, a former chairman of Gosplan, the USSR's State Planning Agency, joined the new government along with him. At the same time, Sergey Dubinin was replaced as head of the Central Bank by Viktor Gerashchenko.

I was positively besieged with requests to comment on their appointments. These were people I knew well. 'Yevgeny Primakov', I stated immediately after his nomination, 'is a man well able to form a government enjoying the confidence of the nation, a government expressing the interests of the nation rather than of 10 or 12 or 20 per cent of the population of Russia, or of some group.' I described him as an independent person with broad horizons, with a good understanding of the situation in Russia and the world, and expressed confidence that his government would 'go for a policy of avoiding extreme radical liberalism while also avoiding a return to the past'.

I was sure Primakov was tough enough not to succumb to pressure, to stabilize the situation and create the conditions for early elections. I saw that as the way to bring about an overall improvement of the situation.

Primakov's government introduced fundamental changes in economic policy. It completely abandoned the practice of restricting money supply by failing to pay salaries, pensions and defaults on government contracts. The size of the backlog of debt on public sector wages was significantly reduced over the next few months. The financial situation was brought under control.

Describing the work of Primakov's government, I stated at a Gorbachev Foundation conference in November 1998: 'Even before the August events, we said the country was on the threshold of political change. Now we see that Primakov's government is already something of an antidote to the present system.' It was clear to everybody, I said, that change in Russia was inevitable. 'No matter how long Yeltsin remains at the helm, one year or two, or whether they come up with some kind of presidency for life, that era is now over.'

The only person who did not see that was Yeltsin himself. There was suddenly a discussion of whether he had the right to run for president in 2000, when what needed to be considered was not some fantasy option of prolonging Yeltsin's political career but of planning his departure at an early date and holding parliamentary and presidential elections as soon as possible. Yeltsin was spending a great deal of time in hospital, and if the president is not functioning, I said, the whole system will be limping along. 'In the current situation', I said, 'the right thing is for Boris Yeltsin to resign.'

The growing authority of Primakov and his government gave grounds to speak of the emergence of a strong potential candidate for president. I mentioned this in an interview for *Nezavisimaya*

Gazeta: 'If we can manage to implement Primakov's new approach, I think the country will move forward. And if good fortune accompanies him, he will be the best candidate for the presidency. As far as the office of prime minister is concerned, I believe the most suitable figure is Yury Luzhkov.'

Yeltsin and his entourage, however, did not trust Primakov and his cabinet. They had different ideas about continuity of power, the more so because Primakov was openly talking about his intention of taking decisive action against corruption. The Prosecutor General, Yury Skuratov, had announced that criminal proceedings were being initiated in connection with the financial default and transactions in government securities.

The closer the time came for the next elections, the more Yeltsin and his entourage mulled over what kind of government they would find it easiest to live with. Before long, television commentaries were beginning to resemble bulletins from the front: 'Yeltsin did not shake hands with Primakov', 'the president did not even look in Primakov's direction'.

In May, the question of removing Yeltsin from office was again raised in the Duma. I had ambivalent feelings about the impeachment move, which I explained in an interview for Interfax. Those initiating the procedure would find it difficult to substantiate their allegations, I warned. 'To take one example: the question of wrecking the Union. This was a huge misfortune, but the Belovezha Accords were ratified by the Russian parliament, which was 85 per cent Communist. They all stood up and cheered as they voted to destroy the Union, so it is six of one and half a dozen of the other. The same is true of all the other charges.'

Before the impeachment vote, Yeltsin undertook a pre-emptive strike by dismissing Primakov's government. I described the president's decision as mistaken and said it could lead to the destruction of the new, hard-won stability. The country might be plunged into a serious constitutional crisis. The Duma was evidently reluctant to risk that, although a substantial majority of deputies voted to impeach Yeltsin on account of his actions in Chechnya. The majority was not, however, large enough for the decision to pass. The Duma then approved the president's proposal to appoint Sergey Stepashin as the new prime minister.

He said he would continue Primakov's policies but was silent on the subject of his predecessor's achievements. I immediately detected that the Stepashin government was temporary, a mere tactic. Yeltsin was looking for someone more suitable in terms of his own interests. Once again, the interests of Russia took second place.

Letters of support

Mr President,
I have been an active supporter and sincere admirer of yours, it seems like ever since I was born, because I am 22. I live, study and work in Nizhny Novgorod. Unfortunately we get almost no information about what you are presently doing or about your International Foundation for Socio-Economic and Political Studies, but I would very much like to keep up to date with all this.

I would like to thank you sincerely for the kind of person I have grown up to be. Please do not be surprised, because it is thanks to you and the policy of Perestroika you introduced that it became possible to think freely in our society, and to analyse the past and present objectively. Thanks to you I have had something my parents never had, and I have something that, most regrettably, my current school students do not have.

In my lessons, I urge the children not to act like a bull in a china shop, to think, to deliberate. Unfortunately, today's history books also impose ready-made judgements for the children to memorize, the only difference from the old Soviet history books being that 10 or 15 years ago they said the exact opposite. Nonetheless, there are still kids in our school who are genuinely interested in our country's history, especially of the twentieth century. In this, as a teacher, I find your latest book, *Razmyshleniia o proshlom i budushchem* [*Reflections on the Past and Future*], extremely helpful.[1]

I found a lot in it that coincides with my own thoughts about the history of Soviet Russia. Thank you for this wise, interesting book, which is indispensable today. ...

[1] M. S. Gorbachev, *Razmyshleniia o proshlom i budushchem*, M.: Terra, 1998.

It is no secret that political issues are much debated in our society. And again, to what and to whom do we owe the fact that people still have this desire to reason, to reflect, and express their views on the most pressing issues of the day? Why is there no longer the fear that was so real in the Stalin period, the lazy indifference that characterized the Era of Stagnation? For me the answer is obvious: it is thanks to Perestroika and Gorbachev. ... Ruslan Nikolaevich Kipyatkov Nizhny Novgorod 25 August 1999

Dear, respected Mikhail Sergeyevich,
What I find really surprising is that some people think you are an unsuccessful politician. I do not agree with that and here is why. Our country has ceased to be the totalitarian state it was. That change has taken place everywhere: both in the economy and in the changed psychology of society. Our country has been able to breathe freely. ... Natasha
15 December 2003

Raisa Gorbacheva

In January 1999 I went to St Petersburg with Raisa for, as it proved, the last time. An interview she gave to *Smena* was recently discovered in our archive. I was very moved to read it:

Interviewer: Raisa Maximovna, I have been surprised that you, and sometimes your husband, go shopping. How do people react to you?

RG: When I go into shops, I am always rather taken aback that, after all these years when I have been off the television screen, everybody still recognizes me. Some people just look silently from a distance, but others come over to say hello. I have never been insulted, never. Sometimes people ask how we are getting on, how Mikhail Sergeyevich is doing. They may complain or tell me about something. Sometimes people come up and say, 'Goodness, you look so like Raisa Gorbacheva!' I answer, 'That's because I am Raisa Gorbacheva!' In response they say, 'Oh, but why are you in a shop, on your own, without any security?'

Actually, it is usually our daughter who does the shopping in our family. That is how we share out the chores. She has a car, so she does the shopping.

Interviewer: So, how is your family getting on today?

RG: I suppose we are rather conservative. Our own parents were always there for us, and now my daughter and our granddaughters are with us all the time. Unfortunately, my daughter is divorced. I was very sad about that, but what can you do? They are grown-ups. Things are never simple in this life.

Interviewer: What period in your life was the happiest for you?

RG: The most important period was, of course, when Gorbachev was at the helm of the state. The most cloudless, though, the most carefree, was our youth, the years when we were students at Moscow State University, although we were half-starved, with only our grant to live on and nothing to wear. My entire wardrobe consisted of one all-purpose dress. For a couple of years we could not even afford to buy a raincoat. Still, that was a wonderful time; we were young and in love. It was a time when you are responsible only for yourself. We took our exams, bought ourselves *pirozhok* pies, and went to the cinema or theatre.

Interviewer: Many of Gorbachev's former colleagues parted company with him after 1991. Who are your closest friends today?

RG: For me personally, my husband and children have always been and still are my best friends. We went together through what is probably the worst thing you can experience in this world, betrayal. In order to appreciate and understand that, you probably need to climb to the pinnacle of power, to see those people, and then be on the receiving end of the mass psychosis of betrayal that we endured. In that context, I feel especially close, of course, to those who stood by us. The really good thing was that people rallied to us whom we had never expected to side with us at that most difficult time in our lives.

All these years I have been afraid I might lose faith in people. It was a real ordeal, that experience of betrayal, and on such a massive scale. Thank God, we had and still have people who helped us to get through all that.

Interviewer: One last question. For almost seven years you were the first lady of our state. What advice would you give to other first ladies, now and in the future?

RG: I would like to say that I do not regard the public reaction to me as relating solely to my personal qualities. I see it as coming from the break with tradition my appearance on the scene represented. Before then we simply did not have any concept of 'the wife of the head of state', and suddenly I appeared. Public reaction was mixed. I had thousands of supporters, and from them came letters thanking me for being a worthy representative of Russian women to the world. But there were also the disgruntled and outraged. Today, I would like to say, both to my well-wishers and to the disgruntled, that they need not be ashamed of their first lady, because I have never done anything to disgrace my country, the president or the people of Russia. I send my best wishes to those who are or will be the first lady of this country. May they be worthy of the burden of that role. The crown of Monomakh weighs heavy on the head of the president, but is testing also for those who stand by his side, and there is no instruction manual to consult.

II   WHITHER RUSSIA?

Putin: The Beginning

On 9 August 1999, Yeltsin announced the appointment of Vladimir Putin as acting prime minister and named him as his successor. The 'Putin Era' of post-Soviet history began.

By naming Putin as his successor, Yeltsin was admitting that his time was up. It was a belated admission, and probably forced on him: his physical frailty was only too obvious. Whatever the circumstances, he could have opened the way for a normal competitive election of a new president, and if he had I was prepared to support the candidacy of Yevgeny Primakov.

In the most difficult months after the 1998 default, Primakov, whom Yeltsin had nominated for the post of prime minister, managed to steer a steady course and keep the economy from falling off a cliff. Surveys showed that more and more people had confidence in him, and even after his retirement, or, more precisely, dismissal by Yeltsin, he was still entirely electable.

Yeltsin was not comfortable with Primakov and a media campaign was mounted to vilify and discredit him. Somehow Yevgeny Primakov retreated rather too swiftly, failing to display any great political toughness and will. When Yeltsin resigned on New Year's Eve 1999 and nominated Putin as acting president, it was obvious that the future election result was a foregone conclusion.

Needless to say, there was nothing democratic about Operation Successor, perpetrated by Yeltsin's clique, including Boris Berezovsky. The path was cleared for the designated successor in such a way that the eventual election was a mere formality, the 'ratification' of a pre-empted decision. It was an election without choice. People supported Putin, but it was only too clear that both he and Russia would face major trials.

Putin inherited chaos – in the economy, in the social sphere and in politics. The greatest problem, however, was the chaos in the administrative structures of the Federation, of Russia. In the preceding years, dozens of regions had passed laws and regulations that contradicted the constitution of the Russian Federation. The Caucasus was ablaze, Basaev's gangs invaded Dagestan, in Moscow and Volgodonsk apartment blocks were blown up by unidentified criminals and dozens of people were killed. In August 1999 Putin, as a new prime minister, had to take the very difficult and weighty decision of what to do about Chechnya.

He had the burden of deciding how to stop a fire that had already spread to a neighbouring republic and was threatening to engulf the whole of the Caucasus.

Even today, I have no doubt he took the right decision. It was essential to destroy a hotbed of terrorism in Chechnya. I stated clearly where I stood on this issue, which was at that time probably the most urgent one facing Russia, and declared my support for Putin's decision: 'These people must be severely punished. They must either submit or be struck down.'

Some of my friends were aghast at my stance. Putin was also criticized in the West and, when I was in the United States in December 1999, politicians and journalists put a lot of questions to me about this issue. I told them that doing nothing was not an option: Putin had taken a difficult but correct decision. Quite another matter was the fact that alongside the military aspect there was a political problem, and for that the need was to seek a political solution as soon as possible. I believe Putin was slow to do so.

In late December 1999, Vladimir Putin published a long article in *Nezavisimaya Gazeta* titled 'Russia on the boundary of two millennia'. Few people lay much store by manifestos and declarations, but, as I carefully read the article, I saw a lot in it that was important and gave grounds for optimism. I sensed behind it a feeling of dismay for Russia and the Russian people. Our country, Putin wrote, was today not up there among the states at the cutting edge of economic and social development in the modern world. And, most significantly: 'Throughout the years of reform there has been a steady fall in the real income of the population.' Key to the whole article, it seemed to me, was the idea that Russia's problems could not be solved without rebuilding a strong state. 'We must', he wrote, 'make the Russian state an effective coordinator of the country's economic and social forces, balancing their interests.' He also put forward principles found in the programmes of social democratic parties: 'As much of the state as is essential; as much freedom as there can be.'

One further important point was made in Putin's article: the urgent necessity of fighting poverty. For Russia, he wrote, 'we can effectively exclude any changes or measures that involve a lowering of living standards. In this we are, so to speak, already at rock bottom. Poverty is particularly widespread. ... This is the most pressing social problem.'

This admission, and Putin's tone, differed strikingly from the approach behind Yeltsin's policies. I have to say that in the following years Putin did periodically show he was not indifferent to the reality of people's lives and their problems. Russia's citizens believed that here now was a politician who cared about them and who was wondering what needed to be done to enable them to live a decent life.

The choice of priorities looked right, but the question was, who would flesh out and implement the new policies? Putin was hemmed in by people from the past and these were not their priorities. They wanted again to privatize the state's supreme power in Russia and exploit it to their own ends. Through the media, I called directly for Putin to rid himself as quickly as possible of this dead wood, which posed a danger to him and to the country, to dissociate himself from the ex-president's entourage. The paradox was that he needed to break away from the circle of people who had raised him to his present position of power. That is not an easy thing to do. After the March 2000 elections, President Putin had an opportunity to see through a major reshuffle. He took it, but not all his choices of personnel were felicitous. As a result, the government's actions were all too often at variance with the president's stated objectives.

The first document Putin signed when still only acting president was a decree: 'On guarantees of immunity for the president of the Russian Federation upon relinquishing his powers, and members of his family.' I was asked what I thought about this and replied that I considered the decree in respect of immunity from prosecution of the ex-president was unconstitutional, and that I personally had not needed and had not asked for any special guarantees.

In those first months when, before the March elections, Putin was still only the acting president, I drew attention to his positive features – willpower, intelligence, methodicalness, readiness to assume responsibility and not to flinch – but also pointed out aspects of his personality and style that aroused misgivings. During those months he did make mistakes and blunders, some minor, some serious, but people did not hold him to account and I went along with that. Any politician makes mistakes, and for someone inexperienced in wielding supreme power that was going to be especially true. There were, however, alarming displays of authoritarianism, and at a press conference on 10 March I talked openly about them. I thought, however, that at a time when the country needed strong leadership, a degree of authoritarianism need not cause alarm. At just this time, work on a report titled *Russia's Self-Determination* was reaching completion at the Gorbachev Foundation.[1] The research group was under the direction of my friend and Perestroika colleague, Georgiy Shakhnazarov. Its conclusion was:

> In the immediate future, it is most probable that a moderately authoritarian regime will be established in Russia and will be well received by the public. The political elite is opting in favour of regaining great power status, and Russian society, or at least a majority of it, is again hoping to prosper as a powerful nation.

The report was based on serious analysis and had a robust sociological basis. It painted a complex and in many ways convincing picture, but I could not or, more likely, did not want to, agree completely with the report's assessment of the probability of a transition to authoritarianism. I mentioned this at the launch of the report in the Foundation. The course of history is not

---

[1] *Samoopredelenie Rossii*, M.: Gorbachev Foundation, 2000.

predetermined; a great deal depends on the human factor, the leadership. I saw Vladimir Putin not as someone chosen by a small number of individuals from the former ruling group, but as a popularly elected president.

The new president: hopes, problems, fears

Immediately after the election, which Vladimir Putin won in the first round, I wrote an article for *Obshchaya Gazeta*. I do not have the feeling, I wrote, that the country made a mistake on 26 March. On the contrary, the past presidential election holds out the hope of major changes, not so much because of the personality of the new president as of the mood in society.

The most important revelation of the election campaign was that '70 per cent of citizens have not lost their belief in the possibility of a decent future, in their ability to change the situation, when it had seemed that people had given up hope of changing anything and would never have faith in a national leader again'. Putin's election was a vote for a different kind of government. For the new president, 'a particular test will be how resolutely he fights corruption and the dominance of the oligarchs'.

We should expect no instant miracle from the new leader, I wrote, counselling patience. I knew from my own experience how difficult it is to work when everybody around you is screaming 'Help! Fire! Murder!' Support, especially at first, is more important than even the most justified criticism.

But grounds for criticism and warnings there certainly were. Shortly after the election, an attack was launched against NTV and its Media-Most [Media Bridge] holding company. It was carried out in the style of a special forces operation, which came to be the trademark of other actions by the new government: premises were searched by masked men; people were ordered to put their hands up, lie on the floor, and the like. On 15 May I gave NTV an interview in which I made clear my attitude to the event. Russia, I said, was a country with inadequate experience of democracy. A mechanism was needed to insure against authoritarianism. That role was the role of the media, whose duty was to inform the country objectively, seriously and honestly. I saw the government's operation as kite-flying to detect how society would react. 'This is more than an attempt to put pressure on this corporation,' I said. 'It is an attempt to put pressure on the media in general and on society.' Trying to govern the country by fear, I said, could signal a move down the slippery slope separating moderate authoritarian rule from full-blown authoritarianism. I anticipated that the new president would take a stand and put a stop to the use of violence to intimidate the media.

It was a situation that required me too to take a stand. In response to a request from the management and staff of NTV, I agreed to chair a public council to advise the television station. Its board included the editor of *Obshchaya Gazeta*, Yegor Yakovlev, and of *Novaya Gazeta*, Dmitry Muratov; Academicians Oleg Bogomolov and a former Russian ambassador to France, Yury Ryzhov; the secretary of the Russian Union of Journalists, Mikhail Fedotov, one of the authors of the Russian Federation law 'On the Media'; the director-general of the Russian PEN Centre, Alexander Tkachenko; the artistic director of the Taganka Theatre, Yury Lyubimov; the writer Chingiz Aitmatov; playwright Alexander Gelman; and the dean of Moscow University's faculty of journalism, Yasen Zasursky. The response to these efforts to safeguard an independent television channel was the arrest of the head of Media-Most, Vladimir Gusinsky.

In this incident, there was obviously a power struggle going on between groups exerting influence on the president, one of which was eager to grab a profitable news asset. The main aim, though, was clearly to rein in the media and show who was the boss in control of information in Russia. NTV was subjected to a systematic siege using a whole barrage of approaches, from tax inspections and attempts to bankrupt the channel to the rearrest of the previously released Gusinsky in Spain at the request of Russian law-enforcement agencies.

In my public statements, I did not hold Vladimir Putin personally responsible for actions that NTV's Public Council described as 'deliberate measures to eliminate not only NTV but also other independent mass media as channels for the expressing of dissent and independent views in society'. I tried to leave the president room to prevent escalation of these moves. We had a meeting in late September at which Putin said he was not intervening in the NTV situation, which he described as a dispute between two commercial players: Media-Most and Gazprom-Media. 'I am all in favour of independent and objective media,' Putin declared. Who could take issue with that? In talking to journalists, I passed on the president's assurances that he favoured preserving NTV and its team of journalists. It became clear, however, that events were moving at an increasingly rapid pace in the opposite direction. By the year's end NTV was unmistakably doomed. It fell victim to predatory business interests that pulverized Media-Most and which, shortly afterwards, were themselves elbowed aside by people even more devious and calculating. The Russian media were dealt a heavy blow and everybody was given a clear signal that if they did not submit and do as they were told, it would be the worse for them.

What is Glasnost?

The struggle over NTV in which I took part was, of course, only one battle in a war over the freedom of Russia's media. For me, that was at the time, and still is, a matter of fundamental importance. The issue at stake was a crucial legacy of Perestroika – Glasnost, transparency and free speech.

What is Glasnost? Dmitry Medvedev, during his spell some years later as president, said on one occasion that Glasnost was a 'palliative': 'I am opposed to Glasnost. It is a defective term. What is needed is free speech, but Glasnost is a palliative, cooked up in the Soviet period in order to avoid giving the concept its proper name.' Alexander Solzhenitsyn himself once said, probably in a fit of pique, because he too was pained by what was happening in Russia: 'Everything was wrecked by Gorbachev's Glasnost.' He had forgotten what he himself said in 1967:

Honest and total Glasnost is a prerequisite for any healthy society, including ours. Anybody who does not desire Glasnost for our country is no patriot and is thinking only of his own self-interest. Anybody who does not wish Glasnost for our fatherland does not

want to rid it of its ills but only to drive them inwards and let them
fester there.

In the Brockhaus and Efron Encyclopaedic Dictionary, published between 1890 and 1913, the concept is very precisely
defined: 'In a state governed under the rule of law, Glasnost is one
of the guarantees of the proper functioning of the institutions of
political power and social organizations.' It is not the only guarantee, but it is essential, and before Perestroika we did not have
it in Russia.

To try to set Glasnost against freedom of speech is profoundly
misguided. Glasnost, as I understood it from the very outset,
includes having the opportunity to express your own opinion,
to debate, to criticize the government and demand change, but
encompasses more than that. Glasnost is transparency in all
society's doings, transparency in the government itself, its public
accountability, its willingness to engage in dialogue with the
people. We had none of that before Perestroika. If it had not been
for Glasnost, Alexander Solzhenitsyn would have been chopping
firewood in the state of Vermont for a long time to come and the
majority of Russian citizens would have known nothing of his
books; Dmitry Medvedev would probably still be giving lectures
to university students.

That is why, after standing down from the presidency, I felt
duty-bound to fight for the freedom of the media, for Glasnost,
for transparency of government. I did it in different ways: not
only in speeches, but also by such acts as supporting the NTV
team and becoming involved in the future of *Novaya Gazeta*,
which had been started by journalists from *Komsomolskaya
Pravda* who could not stomach its 'tabloidization'. At the outset,
while they were finding their feet, I gave them support, including financial support; and later, when they were in difficulties, I
gave them moral support, joining in the debate about the future
direction and content of the paper, gave them interviews and
published my articles there. The newspaper has become, it can be
said without exaggeration, the boldest and most uncompromising
of all the Russian press outlets. Its investigative journalism has
been fearless and its sense of civic responsibility has not faltered.

The newspaper faced difficulties on more than one occasion and found itself on the verge of closure. It was not just the difficulties confronting all the press in new circumstances where people increasingly get their news from television, radio and, particularly, the Internet. The newspaper was subjected to pressure in different ways, and the government did not shun even 'special operations'.

When the situation was critical and it was clear that we really needed to put our shoulders to the wheel, I and Alexander Lebedev, a well-known businessman, decided to become shareholders of *Novaya Gazeta*. In the case of Alexander, this involved a serious financial commitment, whereas on my part it was more a matter of moral support. At the same time we agreed not to interfere in the work of the editorial staff. I was very impressed by Alexander's position on that. He is a strong, concerned individual. Having achieved success in business, he entered politics, stood in the election of the mayor of Moscow, became a deputy of the State Duma and was active in social and charitable projects.

His support made it possible to complete the building and equipping of the Raisa Gorbacheva Centre for Paediatric Oncology and Haematology in St Petersburg. The centre opened in the year of the city's tercentenary and is working successfully today, saving the lives of hundreds of children.

The heavy burden of the presidency

Closely observing Vladimir Putin's actions, I continued to give him my support, not unconditional but unwavering. He had, after all, assumed the presidency in very difficult circumstances. Quite apart from major national problems and tasks, the president is immersed in a torrent of day-by-day events that require his constant attention, and these often take a heavy psychological toll. He was not able to bring rampant terrorism instantly under control and organize effective resistance to this inhuman, blatant evil. In August 2000, Russia was shocked by the terrible loss of the submarine *Kursk*. As the result of an explosion, all 118 members of the crew perished. This was a major psychological trauma for the country and a severe test for the president.

The tragedy unfolded in full view of the populace. It seemed at first that some of the crew might be saved, but soon people began getting the impression the sailors had been abandoned to their fate. There was strongly worded criticism of how the military authorities behaved, and criticism also of the president, who was on holiday and did not immediately abandon his vacation. The papers printed photos of Putin waterskiing, which gave the impression that he was either not fully informed or failing to appreciate the seriousness of the situation. It was a blow to the public's trust in the young president. He did subsequently try to put matters right by visiting Vidyaevo, where the submarine was based, meeting the widows and families of those who had died, and enduring a long, difficult, draining session with them.

At that time I was asked a lot of questions about what was happening. Parallels were drawn with the Chernobyl nuclear disaster. I answered these questions in an interview with Natella Boltyanskaya at Echo of Moscow radio. I said:

> The president bears responsibility for everything, in just the same way that nobody can absolve me of at least moral responsibility for everything that happened. The president cannot, however, be held to account for every incident and disaster. His job, his duty and foremost responsibility, is to learn the lessons from every incident and make sure it does not happen again. It is a matter here of the survival and security of the country and the state.

I added: 'I repeat, what is vital is Glasnost, information, a free, independent, responsible press. That is crucial, and we need to give due credit to our media on this occasion.'

I was sure that the president and the public would respond constructively to this tragedy. In Russia, disasters always bring people together, I said, and I see that happening in this case too. 'I hope the government will act now in a way that ensures this sense of common cause leads to greater mutual understanding between society and the government.'

Subsequent events showed that was indeed the crux of the matter.

The main issue during that first year, and indeed of the following years of Putin's presidency, was the matter of democracy. It seemed to me that, overall, Putin was committed to it, and I said as much both to my friends and to Russian and foreign journalists. In a situation where the first priority had to be restoring the standing of the state and stabilizing the economy, tough measures were unavoidable, but what I opposed was moves towards authoritarianism affecting state and public institutions.

Under the constitution, the president of Russia was already endowed with immense power, which made it all the more important not to weaken and undermine those other branches of government, the legislature and judiciary, as well as local authorities in the provinces. Unfortunately, measures adopted by the federal centre were increasingly aiming to do just that.

First, plenipotentiary representatives of the president were appointed for seven federal territories. This move was not properly explained to the public, and the powers and responsibilities of these representatives of the head of state were not clearly defined.

Next, the composition of the Federation Council was modified. It had previously consisted of the popularly elected governors and chairmen of the legislative assemblies of the regions of Russia. Under new arrangements, the Federation Council was to consist of appointed representatives of the governor and legislative body, and it very soon became clear that these people often had no roots in the region and were in effect being appointed by Moscow. As a result, the political standing of the Federation Council, which even before had not been particularly great, was further weakened, and the State Council, set up seemingly by way of compensation and in which the governors sit alternately, never has acquired political weight or any significant role. Its functions are unclear and it meets infrequently.

As regards the lower house of parliament, the State Duma, it was 'tamed' by other methods. Even under Yeltsin it could not play a substantial role in the taking of decisions on the main issues affecting the country. It was hobbled by the lack of strong political parties, without which all the other institutions can be little more than sham democracy.

The political parties in the early 2000s made a dismal

impression. There was the 'party of government', whose name was changed periodically but which invariably represented the interests of the bureaucracy and big business; the Communist Party of the Russian Federation, which chose not to reject the legacy of Stalinism; the 'Liberal Democratic' Party of Russia headed by Vladimir Zhirinovsky, which pretended to fulfil the role of a shrill opposition; the Yabloko Party, which seemed to have lost the will to live; and the Union of Right Forces, irredeemably stigmatized by its association with the 'reforms' of the 1990s which had forced tens of millions of Russians into penury. It was clear to me that, with this kind of political line-up, Russia had little prospect of escaping the clutches of the old, discredited politics.

My social democratic choice

Russia needs the ideas and policies of social democracy. Both in the 1990s and later, I was certain that what was missing from Russia's political spectrum was a strong social democratic party. It would be disingenuous of me to claim that before Perestroika I had the appreciation of social democracy that I ultimately developed.

At first I looked very tentatively at social democracy, trying to gain a better understanding of the philosophy, the political convictions and moral standpoint of people who had devoted their lives to it. I had, first and foremost, a practical question, which was whether it might be possible to begin a dialogue and interact politically with social democrats abroad.

In June 1993 I gave a lecture in Stockholm in memory of the Swedish prime minister Olof Palme, and told my audience about an episode that had occurred during the Twenty-Eighth Congress of the CPSU. During the congress we received news of the assassination of Palme. Opening the next session, the chairman proposed we should honour the memory of this remarkable man with a minute's silence. All the delegates rose to their feet. I believe that minute's silence was an important milestone on the road of our spiritual emancipation, of our recognition of the significance of shared humane values.

In the ideas and experience of international social democracy,

1 *After the Kremlin, 1992. Photo: Herb Ritts.*

2 *Broadcast by the president of the USSR, M.S. Gorbachev, 25 December 1991. Photo: Yury Lizunov.*

3 *Launch of the Gorbachev Foundation, 3 March 1992. A.S. Chernyaev, Irina Gorbacheva-Virganskaya, Alexander Rutskoy, Raisa Gorbacheva, Mikhail Gorbachev, Nikita Mikhalkov. Photo: Yury Lizunov.*

4 *The White House, Moscow, October 1993.*

5 *Launch of* The Union Could Have Been Saved, *Novgorod, 1994.*

6 *Meeting the voters in Volgograd, 9 May 1996. Photo: A. Stepin.*

7 *Discussion with Academicians Alexey Sisakyan and Vladimir Kadyshevsky, Joint Institute for Nuclear Research, Dubna, 30 January 1996. Photo: Yu Tumanov.*

8 *Meeting the voters in Samara, 25 May 1996.*

9 *Laying of wreaths at Mamai Kurgan, Volgograd, 9 May 1996. Photo:*
A. Stepin.

10 *With Leonid Abalkin and Vadim Medvedev at the Gorbachev Foundation, 2 March 1999.*

11 *Meeting with Yevgeny Yevtushenko and Katrina vanden Heuvel, Editor of* The Nation *magazine (USA), Moscow, July 1992.*

12 *Opening of the new building of the Gorbachev Foundation, Moscow, 12 May 2000.*

13 In Mikhail Gorbachev's home village of Privolnoye, August 2005.

14 'Russia and the Modern World'. Answering students' questions after the lecture at Moscow State University, 24 March 2010. Photo: Dmitry Belanovsky.

*15 Mikhail and Raisa Gorbachev at the Gorbachev Foundation, 1998.
Photo: Heidi Hollinger.*

we were seeking something that could be used to reform Soviet society. It was impossible not to see the contribution of social democracy to the policies of social reform that had genuinely improved the lives of workers in many Western countries.

For me, a significant role in that quest was played by my meetings and conversations with prominent social democratic leaders of the West, and in particular with Willy Brandt, a great German politician who for a quarter of a century stood at the helm of the Social Democratic Party of Germany and, for 16 years, of the Socialist International. During the Twenty-Eighth Party Congress I received a message from him which read:

> Despite the differences, of which we are both aware, you should know of the great interest being taken by the parties united in the Socialist International, and by no means only by them, in the proceedings of the Twenty-Eighth Congress of the CPSU. ... It would be improper for us to seek to interfere in your discussions, but needless to say, we are paying close attention to the new and varied interest being shown in the standpoint of social democratic parties and the Socialist International.

After I had already left the Kremlin, I received a letter from Brandt inviting me to take part in and speak at the Nineteenth Congress of the Socialist International. I very willingly accepted the invitation. Brandt was already ill. Unable to attend the congress, he died a few weeks later.

I felt that loss very keenly. For me, Willy Brandt was not only a politician with whom I conducted a continuous dialogue both verbally and through correspondence; he became a personal friend. He fully understood and agreed with the ideals of our Perestroika, and that gave me great moral support.

Speaking at the Nineteenth Congress of the International, I said,

> A number of people were in a great hurry to depict the dramatic events of the late 1980s and early 1990s as the 'victory' of economic liberalism and 'the End of History'. ... This theory has already been much criticized and, in my opinion, rightly so.

Liberal democracy has failed to provide the ultimate solution to the fundamental challenges of existence. Neither the broadening of economic freedoms nor political emancipation can of themselves produce a free, enlightened, moral individual. The institutions of the public sphere are vulnerable to subjection by vested private and group interests.

The downfall of totalitarianism in the former Soviet Union was the collapse of a particular system that was called 'socialism' and seen by many as such, whether from a hostile standpoint or with approval and a sense of solidarity. In reality it was not socialism. The values that usually inform the concept of socialism, however, are as relevant today as ever. They have inspired many generations of champions of liberty, equality and fraternity and have brought vast mass movements into being. ...

I cannot see a fully satisfactory and successful future for Russia that does not involve the values of social democracy. At the same time, I am against dogmatically setting one variety of democracy against another. Pragmatic policy should be based on a synthesis of experience, ideas and values that have been tried and tested in practice in the past.

How I arrived at these views, how I and other supporters of Perestroika gradually overcame the dogmatic thinking and ideological stereotypes of Stalinism, the reader can judge from my dialogue with a friend from my student years at Moscow State University. Zdeněk Mlynář was later to become one of the leaders of the 'Prague Spring' of 1968.

Fate brought Mlynář and me together long before these events. We were both studying in the MSU law faculty, and were not only in the same faculty, but in the same year and the same group, attending the same lectures and seminars and living in the same hostel. In the evenings we passionately debated between ourselves and with other students the problems exercising everybody at the time, and especially the young. Our liking for each other was to grow into a friendship that lasted almost half a century, until Zdeněk's death in 1997.

After I was obliged to forsake the office of president of the USSR, we felt an urge to discuss in greater detail all we had experienced over the course of the past 40 years and agreed to meet up regularly for the purpose. Our priority was to sort out our thoughts and feelings about our political careers, to help each other to better understand what we had done or not done, what we had achieved or failed to achieve and why, and how justified our actions had been at particular moments. Because we had arrived at similar conclusions by different paths, we really wanted to explain to each other our view of the events we had witnessed and participated in and the problems we had tried to resolve. We argued, but this was debate between friends keen to understand each other.

For many years, Zdeněk had agonized over the lessons of the Prague Spring. It had been his finest hour and he remained true to the principles that had inspired the reformers in Prague in 1968. He also, however, had an acute sense of responsibility for the consequences of that movement, not least for the Soviet military intervention. Underlying our discussions was, of course, the issue of our attitude towards communism as an ideology and a system. It was, after all, the starting point of our shared political biography, which subsequently made him a leader of the Prague Spring and brought me to Perestroika.

We talked about the vagaries of socialism in the twentieth century and the future of the socialist ideal. Like Zdeněk, I needed time to gradually overcome, on the basis of my own experiences in life and discovery of other trends of social thought and opinions, a dogmatic understanding of socialism imposed on us in a closed society from our student days.

We did not repudiate socialist values, principally the values of freedom, equality, justice and solidarity, in all their complex interrelatedness. For me, these imply equal opportunities, access to education and satisfactory healthcare, a socially responsible market and a minimum social welfare safety net. This, of course, calls for involvement of the state, which is essential where the market fails to provide.

While still socialists by conviction, we acknowledged that we could not isolate ourselves from other trends of democratic and humanitarian thinking. Fundamentalism in all its manifestations, remaining blinkered when confronted by alternatives and the unfamiliar, is counterproductive and dangerous. It distracts us from addressing serious issues faced by an increasingly globalized world. Reflecting on the experience of Perestroika and Soviet history in its entirety, pondering the realities of modern times and the different ways in which a globalizing world might develop, I came to the conclusion that nowadays we should speak of socialism not as a system but as a policy.

For me, that is a logical conclusion. When I embarked on Perestroika, I saw it as a radical change from a policy of the CPSU that had brought the country to a standstill. Dogmatists of the left and the right to this day reproach me for not having presented a programmatic goal in full detail, for not having put forward an obligatory plan of action. I believed, and still do, that it was fanatical faith in the miraculous power of plans, unchallengeable dogmas and programmes that deprived our great country of the opportunity to develop in a healthy manner.

Socialism, as I understand it now, is an outlook, and I am certain that in today's world it is impossible to formulate policy without socialist values. These values are now particularly necessary. Inequality is seen by the public as an acute global problem, and politicians on all continents cannot but respond to that. Social democratic ideas are back on the agenda.

Russia needs social democracy

In the early twentieth century, social democracy was a major political force in the world, but the fate of Russian social democracy has been particularly dramatic. Stalinism perverted and compromised its ideals and practice.

As a result of the victory over Nazi Germany, and after the historic resolutions of the Twentieth Party Congress in 1956, which condemned the theory and practice of Stalinism, there was a gradual rapprochement between communists and social democrats. During the years of Perestroika a remarkable social democratization of the ideology and policies of the CPSU occurred.

With the abandonment of Perestroika, the policy of shock therapy brought about an abrupt polarization of society. Under the circumstances, what was needed was a party able to offer the public an alternative strategy for developing society, and this was the aim of the Russian United Social Democratic Party (RUSDP), which brought together scattered social democratic associations.

I tried to point the party in the direction of systematic inculcation of such values of international social democracy as freedom, justice and solidarity, and of developing a programme for modernizing Russia. It was to represent the interests not of particular groups or mafias, but of the overwhelming majority of Russia's citizens.

In one of my conversations with President Vladimir Putin, I said that establishing a social democratic party had aroused interest and been welcomed by the public. To this, he responded (and I quote him verbatim): 'What do you mean? Our country is already social democratic!' I do not know what Putin thinks about the issue today: he has said nothing along these lines for a long time, at least not in public.

In Russia, we had to start building a mass social democratic party virtually from scratch. It was important for us that people made their own decision and personally applied to join the party. At the first meetings of our steering committee, it was noted that the two extremes, the Communist Party and the radical 'liberals', were failing to meet the expectations of the public by not providing answers to the challenges facing the country. We were certain that a fundamentally new, genuinely social democratic programme was called for. In our manifesto we wrote:

Russia is in a state of systemic crisis. The economy is crippled by monopolies and protectionism, the state by corruption, and society by organized crime. The small and medium-sized businesses that appeared in the Perestroika years are burdened with unfair levies and taxes, gangster protection rackets and extortion by officials.

The country's fundamental social welfare provision has been undermined. The funds allocated by the state for science, culture, education and health are inadequate not only for these areas to function effectively, but even for them to survive. The income of those in work is insufficient to ensure a decent standard of living, and jobs are constantly being cut. The pauperization of millions of people affects their moral and physical health and life expectancy.

The RUSDP considers that the cause of this systemic, socio-economic crisis is erroneous strategic choices, disengagement of the government from the people, together with a profound moral and intellectual crisis inside it. The government is suppressing people's initiative and thereby generating economic and social passivity and a loss of faith in democracy. If this pernicious tendency is not overcome through the joint efforts of a majority of citizens, Russia will be doomed to a dull existence on the margins of civilization.

Given this situation, the RUSDP proposes not only to its political supporters, but to society as a whole, a social democratic alternative to enable the country to progress. ...

Despite the obstacles placed in our way and our minimal financial resources, we succeeded in creating party organizations and becoming active in most territories of the Russian Federation. That in itself was no small achievement.

I felt that in Russia the Social Democratic Party had to be a mass party, which was largely behind our decision to team up with the Party of Social Democracy, which was initially under the leadership of Alexander Yakovlev and later of Konstantin Titov. Not all members of the RUSDP favoured this merger, many of them alarmed by the radical-liberal bias of its leaders. We did, however, eventually emerge as a united Social Democratic Party of Russia, the SDPR.

Dozens of new regional and local social-democratic organizations sprang up in Russia under the umbrella of the SDPR, but we saw the party's main achievement as the writing and dissemination of its manifesto, which set out the party's strategy and tactics in detail. Our starting point was that reforms in Russia could not be based on neo-liberal ideas about the economy that ignored Russia's history and culture. We were far more in sympathy with the thinking of John Maynard Keynes and Ludwig Erhard, which had made it possible to overcome the pre-war economic crisis in the United States and the post-war crisis in Germany. Their ideas posited active state intervention in the economy, which European social democrats had also supported and which was particularly germane in Russia, where the state has always played a prominent role.

At the same time it was clear there could be no serious alternative to market forces in the Russian economy. Like all other social democrats, we were in favour of a market economy but not of a market society. We proceeded from the view that, in addition to the market, there are always areas in a society outside its reach: science, education, culture. We declared: 'There should be as much of the market as possible, and as much of the state as necessary.'

We saw the main lever for economic development as encouragement of small and medium-sized businesses. We saw these as agents that could rapidly saturate the market with goods and services, reduce unemployment by creating new jobs, and speedily assimilate technological innovation.

We raised the question of where best to apply the revenues from Russia's natural resources. Economists estimated that just the revenues from the sale of oil and gas abroad amounted to five times the total state budget. In our view, these revenues should be spent on state and public needs. The capital presently circulating mainly in the sector of financial speculation, where the highest profits were to be made, should be redirected through tax mechanisms into production.

We offered the public a programme which, if carried through, would give Russia the opportunity to enter the new post-industrial era on an equal footing with developed countries, to master modern technologies and to be a player in global progress. We noted in our manifesto that the highest levels of investment should be in people, their education and training, in advancing science, and that there should be an industrial policy that took advantage of the strengths of the state and big business.

Where the communists and radical democrats go wrong is in talking a lot about people while in fact disregarding them. The communists defer solving their problems to the distant future, the 'bright communist tomorrow'; the radicals, on the other hand, make money the first priority and turn people into 'the workforce', a means of generating profits. We social democrats wanted to move the human being to centre stage.

We were strongly opposed to the expansion of private education at the expense of accessibility, because paying for education violates the principle of equality enshrined in the constitution, and reduces the opportunities for free development of human individuality. The environment and health are high priorities for social democrats. We declared our willingness to cooperate with the 'Greens', and spoke out strongly against the commercialization of healthcare.

In the modern world, ethnic problems remain especially intractable. The success of a nationalities policy hangs on success in implementing two major principles of social democracy – equality and internationalism – and on being capable of listening to the voices and concerns of each nationality.

Our manifesto caught the attention of many active, concerned people and we succeeded in registering the Social Democratic Party of Russia in 83 regions.

I found the atmosphere in the party congenial; it was open and very public. Anyone could say to anyone, including the party's leaders, exactly what they thought about politics, their attitude to the president and government, and debate any and all important public issues.

We managed to establish links with the Socialist International and became an observer member. That was important in terms of ideology and organization. Despite that, because the SDPR had at first no political experience, we were bound to run into difficulties and make mistakes.

I consider our biggest mistake was to decide not to run in the 2003 parliamentary elections with our own party list of candidates. Influenced by Konstantin Titov, a majority at the party congress settled for the 'easy option' of contesting the ballot only in independent-candidate constituencies, in collaboration with the government's United Russia Party. As a result, the SDPR failed to make any political impact in the elections to the Duma. Because the party was so low profile, its independent candidates went down to defeat, while the United Russia candidates were effectively political rivals rather than allies.

The party's fortunes were negatively impacted in other ways by Titov's actions. During the elections he traded his position as party chairman in his own interests, a selfish approach that played into the hands of those who did not want the SDPR participating in the elections at all. Given the situation, I felt unable to continue as party leader and announced my resignation. It was the right thing to do. I did, nevertheless, stay in the party, trying to help, because I felt society really needed a party of the people rather than an appointed, bureaucratic organization that doggedly carried out any decision the government chose to take. People recognized the need even in the Duma, where there was a move at the time to establish an independent social-democratic group.

It seemed to me that the deputies were on the right track, and that all that was needed was to persuade the Presidential Administration of the fact, but I soon discovered I was wrong. The Presidential Administration wanted nothing to do with it. Their aim was to bring all the political parties and groups under direct Kremlin control. Gorbachev and his party were just an irritation. The Kremlin adopted a policy of 'containing' democracy and all political parties in the country that it did not favour. The deputy head of the Presidential Administration actually said to me: 'Why are you wasting your time on this Social Democratic Party? We aren't going to register it anyway.' A new law on political parties allowed the Kremlin to shut down a number of independent political parties, including the SDPR, on purely legalistic grounds.

In combating the Social Democratic Party, the opponents of genuine democracy tested all the means used today to turn democracy into a sham and ensure that the government controls every manifestation of politics in Russia. They claim this delivers stability, but in reality their tactic deprives politics of all meaning and undermines social stability. Artificial parties germinated in Kremlin test tubes, devoid of ideology or mass support, are liable at any moment to wilt, and then what will be left of their whole artificial construct?

I remain convinced that Russian society needs the ideas and values of social democracy. Within the Union of Social Democrats, people with social democratic beliefs continue to analyse and educate, and the need for their work is continually increasing both in Russia and the world.

I will say frankly that I like it when social democrats call each other 'comrade'. We must never forget that this word designates not only membership of a Communist Party, but also a sense of social, human solidarity. I have not the slightest doubt that the voice of social democrats is an essential constituent of a broad civic dialogue. Every social democrat has the ability to contribute to making Russia a modern, democratic country, playing a condign role in creating a new, more stable, just and humane world order.

Issues and more issues

In the early 2000s, I had periodic meetings with President Putin and we talked about many things, including the political system and political parties. One such meeting took place on 17 June 2002, shortly after the Ministry of Justice had registered the Social Democratic Party of Russia. I remember Putin said at that meeting that society needed a centre left party and he was prepared to cooperate with the social democrats. This was exactly what I had been hoping, but subsequent events showed that the Russian government was not interested in interacting with strong, independent parties. It wanted bloodless associations that it could easily ignore, subjugate or eliminate.

The functioning of the judicial system increasingly gave cause for concern. Under the mantle of 'dictatorship of the law', which Vladimir Putin talked about at the beginning of his presidency, 'telephone justice', whereby judges are instructed over the telephone what verdict to reach, became more and more entrenched. The judicial and law-enforcement systems were increasingly used as a means of intimidation, to settle personal scores, subordinate businesses to the powerful and put pressure on political opponents. Without a robust, independent judiciary it was impossible to effectively combat corruption, which the president acknowledged was essential.

With things as they were, it was difficult to envisage a shift from the strategy of stabilization to a strategy of development and breakthrough, but I was becoming increasingly certain that this was desperately needed. A conversation I had with Dmitry Muratov of *Novaya Gazeta* was published on 30 September 2002 and reflects an important strand in my thinking at the time. Here is the gist of our talk:

DM: Mikhail Sergeyevich, Perestroika is over. Instead of 'the framework of the law' we now have 'sorting out a situation'. Instead of Glasnost, we have talk shows. Instead of 'personal freedom', consolidation of the state as a private business enterprise.

MG: For all that, I find much of what is happening now understandable and explicable. I have no reason at present to question the main intention of the president or his actions. It is, after all, a way out of the crisis, away from the chaos he inherited.

We have lived through what was effectively the risk that Russia might disintegrate, or at least relapse into regional feudalism. And, of course, we have experienced the dominance of the bureaucracy, especially the federal bureaucracy, where mafias brazenly made no secret of lending money for elections, for political power, in the expectation that they would be paid back later with public property. They would help themselves to it, and already have. That has had, and is still having, an effect on the moral climate in society. So without an effort to restore public confidence that the government is properly concerned about national issues rather than just servicing these mafias, it will be impossible to get anything done. Governments do sometimes have to be authoritarian, to take action without giving lengthy explanations, and that can make it impossible to understand their measures.

DM: What is there not to understand? They are only too readily comprehensible.

MG: Everything is instantly clear to you young people, but I have seen a few things in my time, and I don't find it quite so easy to know the truth about everything. And with the country in such a state ... the Lord God Himself wouldn't want to get involved. Even He hasn't worked out what is going on yet.

DM: Well, sure. It's the way it always is. We exchange the reforms for freedom, we exchange freedom for property, and the scope for democracy gets narrowed 'in the interests of the people and democracy'.

MG: I'll say it again, there are no grounds to accuse the president of being anti-democratic. I have been in his shoes and I can tell you that what Vladimir Putin has managed to do is in the interests of most of the people.

DM: Okay, let's have some examples.

MG: Take education. The president is in favour of adapting it to the present day, but it needs also to be free and accessible. He intervened in the approach to reforming the public utilities to prevent radical changes being made at the expense of consumers.

DM: Meanwhile, the price of petrol is just soaring, right-hand drive cars are being banned, domestic manufacturers are again being favoured ahead of domestic consumers. Importing old foreign cars is being prohibited. Is that also in the interests of the majority?

MG: There are things in your list I would not have done, but the fact is that the president has to be involved in the battle for the domestic market. That is true also of the richest and most developed countries. See how they fight against letting us into their markets! The European Union has brought more than 60 anti-dumping lawsuits against Russia. Is that what they mean by 'a new chapter in our relationship'? And at the same time, a third of farmers' incomes in the EU comes from state subsidies. In other words, agriculture is being subsidized to make it competitive.

DM: Mikhail Sergeyevich, they have rich consumers who can get by without second-hand, seven-year-old Russian vehicles, but how is our motorist, on a Russian income, supposed to get by without old, but cheap and reliable, cars?

MG: Perfectly true, but we do need to stimulate and encourage our mechanical engineering industry. At present what we still have functioning is mainly the raw materials sectors, metallurgical and chemical industries. Everything else needs to be modernized, and that takes time and needs protectionist measures.

DM: Life is short, Mikhail Sergeyevich. People want to live now, to be able to drive a car. They don't always have enough time to be patriotic.

MG: And the 'life' of a president is even shorter: four years, or at most eight. He needed to make a difference to the country, to let it feel it can get out of this quagmire.

DM: It seems to me there is a contradiction between what you are saying now and what you did as president of the USSR. Gorbachev started a political reform, aware of the fact that without political freedoms and free citizens it is impossible to build a free economy. Now you are to all intents and purposes giving approval to a constricting of politics. Alternatives are out of fashion; nobody has any time for them. Everybody keeps saying there is no alternative, the choices have been made for many years to come. The Federation Council has been all but abolished. The State Duma has become a completely obedient, rubber-stamping body. I repeat, is the price of successful reforms really a reduction of political freedom? Can we honestly say that?

MG: Well, you just have, so freedom of speech is not defunct.

DM: In conversation with you.

MG: Yes ... The situation in Russia is so complex and contradictory that the solutions are necessarily also going to be messy.

What I have seen of the president and the conversations I have had with him convince me that he is committed to democratic governance and has no intention of establishing some kind of authoritarian regime along even the neo-Stalinist lines of the times in which you and I lived and worked. I have absolutely no doubts about that.

I often notice the temperature being artificially raised when these issues are discussed, but I am absolutely sincere in my present position of supporting Putin. I wish the president every success. I think people do instinctively sense that the man is determined to haul Russia out of the morass she is stuck in. ...

To tell the truth, I think our greatest misfortune is that people's morale and faith in the future have been undermined. For us, for the Russian mentality, that is a painful and dangerous state to be in. The way Russia functions is that, if people don't feel valued, if they are again pushed to one side, all these plans for the future will come to nothing.

That means that the whole idea of maintaining the status quo and continuing the inertia of the previous 10 years, with a clique in control of everything, would spell disaster for Russia.

The president is talking more and more about the need for policies of innovation, policies to support grassroots initiatives. In a little more than two years several times more constructive laws have been passed than previously, and they have gone some way towards creating a climate of legality, but you are saying that nothing has changed.

DM: Absolutely. It seems to me that nothing has changed because all the courts are being bought piecemeal and wholesale by large oligarchical organizations to make sure they deliver the right verdicts. Authoritarianism is when you cannot get justice through the courts. It is when justice depends on whether you are admitted to an audience with the president, whether you have his ear or are kept away from him. And is that not the way things stand at present?

MG: What you are talking about is a tendency Putin wants to reverse. The preconditions are in place now to move forward. The preparations for judicial and administrative reforms, the search for a balance in the allocation of powers to get both the regional and local governments functioning are all steps in the right direction. But just see the effort required for every step forward in all these matters.

Without judicial reform and without an effective, independent court system, we stand no chance of combating the bureaucracy and corruption. It seems to me that the president is only beginning to tackle this issue of fighting corruption. And what are we to make of all the bureaucratic delays in trying to get the Duma to pass an anti-corruption law?

DM: What Duma are we talking about? This Duma?

MG: On corruption, yes.

DM: All that is needed is a phone call and the first, second and third readings will be completed in half an hour.

MG: You are wrong. If it was that easy … A draft law, as you know, has been in the Duma's portfolio for a long time, but there is no sign yet of when it might be adopted.

I am not remotely interested in providing an apologia for the president's policies. I have no need of that. I am not one of those who dance attendance on him and compete for access to his presence, but I know from the president himself what his position is on this matter. He is not susceptible to flattery and cannot be swayed by obsequiousness. What we are observing only testifies to a dire shortage of good people. The president did once say that finding suitable people was currently his main problem.

Russia has reached a stage where it is time to replace a survival strategy with a development strategy. Decisions are needed on many matters. It is essential that we should see a thoroughgoing development of small and medium-sized businesses. We need an industrial policy.

What is needed is not a dictatorial approach, but laws. We should support the president so that all of us enjoy success. We should support him. The president and all of us need strength and political willpower. People understand the president, and that is the crucial resource that will enable us to overcome all resistance.

That is how I thought and what I said in September 2002. What was behind my assumptions? Despite failures and mistakes, Putin had succeeded during those first years in gaining and retaining the confidence of the people. He succeeded in stabilizing the situation and beginning the process of emerging from the economic crisis, not at the expense of ordinary people but enabling them to feel the first, admittedly small, benefits of economic recovery. Wages were paid on time, pensions were increased, there was a gradual reduction of inflation; at the time, for most people, these things were crucially important. I had grounds for looking to the future with cautious optimism. However, the doubts, the questions and criticism expressed by Dmitry Muratov and shared by a substantial segment of society were by no means unfounded. Everything depended on what kind of fundamental decisions the president of Russia would take in the years ahead.

The zero years of the 2000s?

We have come to refer to the 2000s as the 'noughties', the 'zero years'. May there not be an intentional or unintentional metaphor in that? Were these not wasted years for Russia, years of missed opportunity? No doubt the final verdict must be left to history. Much depended on the direction taken by the state and society in the first years of the decade, when everything was still fluid and there was heated debate about how the economy and social services – education, science, healthcare and the pension system – should develop. We needed to move from a survival strategy to a development strategy: that was the main point I empha-sized in speeches, interviews, in numerous discussions within the Social Democratic Party and the Gorbachev Foundation, where politicians, experts and journalists assembled. There was concern that in some extremely important areas the policy of the state remained unclear. It seemed to offer no imaginative new pros-pects for developing Russia. Much of what was proposed by the Cabinet of Ministers I found plain alarming.

Economic policy came down to safeguarding macroeconomic stability and budgetary discipline, paying off the national debt and building up financial reserves. All that was doubtless impor-tant, but, without measures to stimulate the real economy or an effective industrial policy, all the achievements, like reducing the budget deficit, foreign debt and inflation, became an end in themselves and helped only to preserve the old structure of the economy with its dependence on natural resources. The recipes that economists close to the government came up with I found profoundly unsatisfactory. They understood market relations as meaning absolutely everything should be privatized, and that the state should abdicate its most important responsibilities towards the population. I found that unacceptable.

In 2001, I was approached by a large group of academics and educationists who were greatly vexed by the government's proposed reform of education. Among them were people I knew well and trusted – people like Academicians Natalia Bekhtereva, Sergey Kapitsa and Boris Raushenbakh; the astro-naut Georgiy Grechko; historian Anton Antonov-Ovseyenko;

and political scientist Fedor Burlatsky. They believed this was the wrong time to introduce a reform; it was academically unjustified and would be disastrous for the Russian education system. I supported their view, and in September our appeal to the president and parliament was published in the newspapers. We raised the alarm, and time was to show that our concerns were justified.

Most seriously, we wrote, the proposed reform was based on false, completely unsubstantiated premises. It was, for example, asserted that Russian education, both in the pre-revolutionary and Soviet periods, was backward, poor and incapable of providing for the advancement of society in the post-Soviet period. In fact, we protested, Russian education was among the best in the world. It had been created and served by outstanding Russian educators, pedagogues and thinkers. The current 'reformers' were suggesting we should adopt a foreign, primarily American, system and privatize education. This would degrade it and open the way for a purely elitist educational system to benefit the rich.

In our open letter we criticized a number of specific aspects of the government's proposed reform, which included the introduction of a so-called education voucher, a single school examination and 'optimization and restructuring' of rural schools – in reality, massive closures. We talked about the wretchedly low level of teachers' and lecturers' salaries.

Something that was totally unacceptable was the fact that the reform was to be imposed without open public discussion. Its proponents demonstrated offhand dismissiveness of the opinion of scholars, major specialists, and teachers and lecturers themselves. I remember we invited the ideologist behind this and other government reforms, the vice-chancellor of the Higher School of Economics, Yaroslav Kuzminov, to a round table at the Foundation. Speaking in a peremptory tone at the beginning of the discussion, he left shortly afterwards, showing a total disregard for the views of the participants. It was an attitude on the part of radical reformers that we encountered only too often.

In an open letter, we concluded that the reform as proposed was not needed. What was really essential was a series of emergency measures to enable us to preserve and develop the existing Russian education system.

Education, as an extremely important aspect of culture, should be one of the country's strategic priorities. It should be accessible and free, from primary through to higher education in state educational institutions; that is, it should be financed from the state budget. Private education should be an optional extra and provide a level of education no lower than that provided by the state. It was unacceptable to force a state educational institution into the private sector. It was essential to revive the principle of education based on the fundamental, classical subjects and, above all, to restore fully effective study in schools of Russian language and literature, mathematics, physics, biology and chemistry. The state should support teachers and lecturers in higher education, paying them at least a living wage. School and further education teachers should enjoy the moral support of the country's leaders and the mass media. It was very important to raise the authority of teachers, lecturers and professors. A top priority must be the allocation of financial resources to equip classrooms with information technology.

I continued in the future to fight for the preservation and development of Russia's education system, to see it properly funded, to prevent its commercialization and the division of education into separate provision for 'the elite' and 'the rest'. Those in favour of universal access based on the best traditions of Russian education did succeed in wringing some concessions from the government and in at least slowing down destructive processes. In some years we succeeded in getting an increase in expenditure on education and improving teachers' salaries. We were hoping for support from Putin, who had repeated on more than one occasion that he was in favour of universally accessible education, but it was not always forthcoming.

Today, the battle over educational issues continues. People have begun more actively to defend their interests and the interests of society. An illustration of this occurred quite recently, in 2013, when the government tried to push through an operation to 'reform', but in reality to eliminate, the Russian Academy of Sciences. The wave of indignation and protest was so great that they were forced to back down, but a law reforming the Academy of Sciences was ultimately passed. I do not believe we have heard the last of the issue.

I was disturbed at that time that no decisive measures were taken to combat corruption. Needless to say, it is not a problem that can be solved with a cavalry charge. Those who demanded arrests as the principal means of countering this scourge under-estimated the complexity of the problem and just how deeply rooted it is in the state, government, economy and social life. The public wanted at least to see some results, and expected to see an end to toleration of corruption at every level of government. That did not happen. I am particularly concerned about the spread of corruption to the law-enforcement agencies.

In May 2001, I had a meeting with Vladimir Putin. I was initially intending to tell him about my trip to the United States, and had interesting information for him. I had met President George W. Bush in Washington, who had recently taken up his duties. It seemed to me he had said a number of things that should be conveyed to the president of Russia. Our conversation ranged much more widely than that, however. We got to talking about the structuring of Russian politics, and the view that political parties should reflect the whole spectrum of views and standpoints in society, left, right and centre. The president said he agreed with that.

I shared with Putin my concerns about government policy on health and education, and expressed the belief that the way to resolve the problems was not to expand 'market relations' into these areas, but to draw on the best experience of the Soviet era and, of course, the new opportunities and mechanisms. I felt this should be done in such a way as to ensure that basic education and healthcare were available to all citizens and that, most importantly, the old, who had worked hard all their lives only now to find life very hard, should not be disadvantaged.

Perhaps my approach seemed out-of-date to the president; I do not know. At all events, subsequent developments showed that the government's plans to redesign the social sphere were not modified. My opinion of the good intentions of the president himself remained unchanged. I believed he was doing his best to develop policies in the interest of Russian citizens and to overcome the inertia of the Yeltsin era, when the government had shown no concern about the social cost of reforms. The group who had decisively influenced policy in the 1990s were increasingly moved away from the centres of decision-making, but at the same time it was obvious there was serious resistance, and no decisive changes in policy were forthcoming.

Would Putin manage to resolve the situation? In April 2002, I looked for the answer to this in the annual Message of the President to the Federal Assembly. I responded to it in *Rossiyskaya Gazeta*:

> I consider it one of the president's strengths that when he is preparing his speeches he does not forget he has a country standing behind him. Two-thirds of the Russian people are living on the poverty line. Where do we go from here? How many billions of roubles are exported out of the country every year? It is time that money was invested in our own economy.
>
> In any case, where do these billions come from? I continue to insist that the country needs a systematic tax on natural resources. ... Perhaps we should set up a Russian sovereign wealth fund for national development, like Norway, to accumulate proceeds from the sale of our mineral wealth. We have the revenue sources: all we need to do is manage them properly, for the good of our people.

The Yukos affair

The subject of natural resources, especially oil, was highly topical at that time. Prices were beginning to rise on world markets. Who would be the beneficiaries: the government, the owners of companies, or perhaps even the Russian people?

The subject came dramatically to the fore when, in 2003, the saga of the Yukos case began, which is still rumbling on today.

There are many issues mixed up in this case: the legacy of the 1990s, large-scale tax evasion, issues of ownership, the relationship between the government and the 'oligarchs'. And, of course, the problem of the legal system, the impartiality of the courts and the extent to which citizens believed they could be trusted.

As the thunderclouds began to gather over Mikhail Khodorkovsky, there was a dearth of information about the exact nature of the charges, and when I was asked about my attitude to the case, I would reply, 'I do not yet have enough hard facts to comment on its merits. The main thing is that action should be taken within the legal framework, that the rights of the individual should be respected, and there should be no damage to the Russian economy.'

Mikhail came over to me one day at an embassy reception: 'Mikhail Sergeyevich, do you remember me?' 'I certainly do,' I replied. 'But do you remember me?'

It seemed to me that Khodorkovsky was embarrassed by that turn of the conversation. How could I not remember one of Russia's first entrepreneurs, who started his business during the years of Perestroika, made a spectacular career, became a wealthy man and made his company, Yukos, one of the leaders in its sector? Khodorkovsky and other so-called oligarchs did everything they could to ensure Yeltsin was re-elected in 1996, and Yeltsin was quick to repay the debt. The 'loans-for-shares auctions' of 1996–7 were an unprecedented act of giving away state property for a pittance to a select coterie of individuals.

The government and this clique co-presided over a share-out of Russia's national assets, knowing full well that they would never be returned to state ownership. In this regard, in the past years, nothing has changed. Most of Russia's citizens consider the privatization of the 1990s to have been iniquitous, and if a referendum were to be held on whether the property given away at that time should be re-nationalized, the result is not in any doubt. As my assistant was told by one of the European ambassadors, if the government decided to annul the results of the loans-for-shares auctions, everyone, including the West, would fully understand. Under Putin, the principle of the government and oligarchs keeping each other at arm's length was declared, but the dependency of big business on the government is unchanged: businessmen can undertake nothing without getting the go-ahead from the government at one level or another.

Keeping my eye on what was happening with the economy at that time, I did not see the operations of Yukos as anything out of the ordinary. I did not pay any great attention to the fact that Khodorkovsky had begun talking about the need for greater transparency in the operations of large corporations, about creating the right climate for investment and fighting corruption. It sounded sensible and timely. At the same time, information began to circulate that in the 1990s his company had underpaid billions of dollars in taxes, and that at a time when millions of people had not been paid their wages and pensions for months. People in the know tell me that was how almost all the major companies behaved, and the government chose, for the time being, to turn a blind eye to tax evasion schemes.

When charges were laid against him, Khodorkovsky tried to shield Yukos by resigning from the company. Viktor Gerashchenko was invited to head it. I knew Viktor well as the head of the USSR State Bank and subsequently of Russia's Central Bank, but the situation was becoming more ominous by the day. Foreign businessmen warned me that a trial of Khodorkovsky might impact negatively on the investment climate. I was astonished and perplexed when Khodorkovsky was arrested in a crude, ostentatious manner by people wearing masks and carrying automatic weapons.

I heard of comparable cases in the United States during visits there. They culminated in different ways, sometimes with large fines, sometimes with prison sentences. The main thing was that there should be no doubts about the court's impartiality and independence from the executive branch, in order to avoid any impression that 'justice' was being applied selectively. Ultimately, I stress again, everything hinges on the political background, on the existence of democratic institutions, strong branches of government independent of each other. Whether we will have them in Russia or not is the big question.

The elections were approaching. Russia and her citizens could feel the results of the stabilization of politics and the economy. Growth rates were gradually improving and wages rising, primarily due to an influx of oil revenues unprecedented in the country's history. Under Putin, life had improved for the two-thirds of the population who had been battered by Yeltsin's radical 'reforms'.

It was clear to me that, in these circumstances, the president had every likelihood of gaining a new endorsement from the electorate by winning in the first round. But how and to what end would he use his power? To move ahead on the path of democracy and modernization, reforming the economy in the interests of all our citizens, or primarily in the interests of the government itself and its cronies?

A party of new bureaucrats

It was plain that new mafias were forming, groups no less predatory than the previous high and mighty individuals they had deprived of power and wealth in their own selfish interests. The mouthpiece for the interests of these people and their associated mushrooming bureaucracy was increasingly the United Russia Party. The only way to combat these negative trends was by developing democracy.

My reflections on these matters were dark and uneasy. Many others were similarly pondering the situation. In November 2003 I again discussed current issues with my invariable conversation partner, Dmitry Muratov. Our discussion was published in *Novaya Gazeta* under the headline, 'Do we need a party of new bureaucrats? I think not.'

DM: Mikhail Sergeyevich, how is it that when you were undertaking the reforms the world came to know as Perestroika, free speech and transparency were helpful to it? Not all that much time has passed since then, but now we find that Glasnost and free speech are a hindrance to today's reforms. How has this happened? To be more specific, why is it, for example, that when you were president the whole country was transfixed, watching live broadcasts of the Congresses of People's Deputies? For the first time people found out many things about themselves, about you and about the Russian people. Now the government party refuses to participate in public debates.

MG: That is a good question. As regards the past, I will say openly that, if we had not first had Glasnost and then free speech, Perestroika as a wholly unique, difficult, risky policy would never have got off the ground. I am sure, even more certain now, that it would never have happened.

Now, about the party in government's refusal to participate in debates. I was shocked. Who is giving them this sort of advice? It would seem that United Russia, which has not yet won the election, no longer wants anything to do with other parties. What are they going to be like after the election? They seem to have a very odd idea of democracy.

In short, not everybody is yet able to withstand the test of Glasnost, freedom and democracy. This also applies to the press. We see often enough that you are all for freedom when writing about other people, but when the media have their attention drawn to something they have published, you all regard it as an assault on free speech and rush to your colleagues' defence.

DM: Well, what do you expect? Of course we do. That is freedom, solidarity, esprit de corps.

MG: Well that lot are just showing esprit de corps in defending their interests! It is a struggle, which is why I really want to emphasize yet again that our greatest achievement, with which everything, the reforms, started, was Glasnost and freedom. I do not think that now, after the painful, difficult years of rule by Boris Yeltsin, which left us only a legacy of chaos, anyone can sensibly still argue that what Russia needs is a 'firm hand'.

In fact, all this talk about a strong state, as if it were something separate from democracy, is ridiculous. The strongest state is a democratic state.

I was talking once to a former prime minister of France. He said, 'I can see that in this situation President Putin cannot avoid using authoritarian methods to resolve certain particular problems.' But, he asked, did I not fear this might lead to an authoritarian regime? I told him that, as I saw and understood Vladimir Putin, that seemed unlikely to happen.

DM: What are these feelings of yours based on?

MG: I said they are feelings. The nous, the intuition of a politician. But let me, nevertheless, try to reply to your remark. Look at what is happening. According to UN statistics, in the last quarter of the twentieth century more than 80 dictatorial or totalitarian regimes disappeared from the arena of history and politics; a wave of democracy swept the world. Think how many such regimes disappeared as the result of free elections in Central and Eastern Europe and the former Soviet Union!

DM: How many?

MG: But right at the end of the twentieth century we see the beginnings of a backlash. That has been worrying me for several years now. In the post-Soviet territories it has become increasingly common to try to resolve complex problems by authoritarian methods, and in some cases we have even seen the establishment of authoritarian regimes. In many countries, even in Europe, the electorate is voting for politicians of an authoritarian bent. Political science scholars gathered in Quebec at their World Conference concluded that the unregulated spread of globalization had generated tensions nationally and internationally. They believed that authoritarian tendencies might not only survive, but actually gain ground.

DM: To put it simply, the twenty-first century is going to be the century of totalitarianism? And that justifies what is happening in Russia?

MG: Let me finish. I don't agree with the political scientists, or with other academics who are making the same case. I think they are jumping the gun. I think they are in a panic. The only way to avoid policy mistakes and miscalculations, both nationally and internationally, is within a framework of democracy. The main argument is that nowhere (and we have only to look back in history), nowhere have totalitarian methods proved efficient.

As far as Russia is concerned, we are in a difficult situation, but we will be able to solve even the most difficult problems if we keep to the path of democracy. No doubt our national peculiarities, our mentality, culture, history, experience, religion, will make their mark on democratic processes, but that is the case everywhere. Everybody accepts that nowadays. I have just come back from a forum on Okinawa attended by representatives of countries that profess Christianity, Islam and Buddhism. They included politicians like Zbigniew Brzezinski, former prime ministers of Japan and Malaysia, and representatives of China and South Korea. They were well-qualified people, and everyone was in agreement that you cannot install a democratic regime in a country by sending in the tanks. Mankind's strategic path to the future can be successful only on a basis of freedom and democracy.

DM: I don't understand, Mikhail Sergeyevich. You seem to be saying democracy cannot be imposed, but that it is indispensable. Please explain.

MG: I'm just saying that where we are dealing with states in transition, we need to remember that it will take not '10 days' or '500 days', but decades, and perhaps the whole of the twenty-first century. That is key to understanding the context in which Vladimir Putin is operating.

I do not think that President Putin's top priority today is suppressing public opinion and subordinating Russia, society and the state, to himself. In the first place, it would be unrealistic and, in the second, I believe it would be contrary to his views. As a warning that we need to prevent a slide into authoritarianism I consider that what the press is saying is justified, but to accuse President Putin of that sin is unfounded.

DM: But the bureaucratic apparatus of government and the way it functions does nevertheless depend on subjective aspects of what the leader does. There is no getting away from that. You tried to dismantle the authoritarian system of appointments to allow society itself to generate new ideas and learn new values. The present government has practically monopolized politics.

MG: But at that time society had been crushed. What did Putin inherit? A state of anarchy, chaos, and a risk that the state might disintegrate.

DM: So what does that mean, that we needed to reinvent a party of bureaucratic officialdom?

MG: No, it means only that I had one problem and he has a different one: to rescue and stabilize the situation and restore the right conditions for moving along the road of democratic changes.

DM: But do you not think that there is a systematic re-establishment of control over civil rights and liberties? If you open the constitution and then look out the window to see which rights are being observed and which not, we see an extraordinary picture: there is only one party, television has been monopolized and the press is under pressure.

MG: You are exaggerating on every count.

DM: How so?

MG: Because there are parties like Yabloko, the Union of Right Forces, Zhirinovsky's party. And, of course, the Communist Party, the Social Democratic Party of Russia and so on.

DM: That is not what I was referring to. I mean that, as far as television access is concerned, with the exception of the debates, there is effectively only one party, United Russia. Everybody has noticed. People find it laughable.

MG: You are largely right about that. The introduction of new requirements of the press just before the election is a mistake. People do not want to be deprived of free access to information. They want to know as much as possible about all the candidates.

DM: I agree with you there.

MG: People do not want to be deprived of the freedom to choose, either, and when they are pressured and have a single party imposed on them, they begin to have doubts about bothering to vote.

People support the president because he presents new policies and tries to act in the national interest. The social situation is in fact improving, if only slowly. That is the main thing. As regards the president's methods, people have a different attitude.

When I read that dialogue today, I detect a lot of anxiety and a lot of criticism, not only on the part of my younger, eternally restive companion, but on my part too. There were good reasons for that, but I considered the only correct strategy was support for the president, albeit not unconditional, albeit critical.

In December 2003, the State Duma elections were held. The candidates on United Russia's party list gained 37.6 per cent of the vote, not all that much for a party presenting itself as the 'party of Putin'. Naturally, the president's popularity and beginnings of an improvement in people's lives favoured the party in power. Half the deputies, however, were elected in contested constituencies, without party lists, and most of them were elected as independents. Immediately after the election they were dragooned en masse into United Russia. As a result, United Russia almost doubled their representation in parliament and obtained a constitutional majority. But, I asked, what about the will of voters? There was a lot of information to the effect that certain 'fixes' were systematically employed in elections to inflate the turnout figures and the number of votes, until eventually people lost patience and in 2011 took to the streets. I increasingly had a feeling that the government had committed itself to creating a subordinate, emasculated parliament.

In an interview on the eve of the presidential election, I said that the crucial question was what President Putin would do after he won the election on 14 March. 'If he only wants to gain power for the sake of it and not in order to bring about a new phase of democratic reforms, that may have serious consequences for Russia.' A lot would depend on what kind of team he chose.

A second presidential term: what for?

The March 2004 election confirmed my prediction: Putin was re-elected in the first round. On the day of his re-inauguration I was thousands of kilometres from Russia, in Latin America. I sent him my congratulations and wished him success:

I hope the next four years will see firm steps on the road of democracy, economic growth, strengthening of the rule of law and the building of civil society. Those were what I saw as the priorities for Putin's second presidential term. Sustained economic growth is impossible without a strong democratic state under the rule of law and an active civil society. Subsequent events were to show, however, that for Russia's leaders developing and strengthening democratic institutions was not a high priority.

It was soon clear that the new Cabinet, headed by Mikhail Fradkov, had no coherent strategy for modernizing the Russian economy, overcoming our dependence on exporting raw materials and making the transition to a 'knowledge-based economy'. This despite the fact that conditions were favourable for introducing worthwhile reforms. The global price of oil and gas continued to rise, generating increased revenues which could have been used not only for building up reserves (which was, of course, important and necessary), but also for infrastructure projects, supporting sectors crucial to the future of the economy, and to finance science, healthcare and the social sphere. It did not happen.

The armed forces too were left in their unreformed state. In the last years of the USSR we had instigated profound changes in the army on the basis of a new defence doctrine and agreements with the West to reduce nuclear and conventional weapons. A start was made on converting the defence industry to peaceful purposes. During the 1990s, the army was forgotten. Far from being reformed, it was simply deprived of funding and left to wither on the vine, abandoning tens of thousands of discharged servicemen to fend for themselves. Little changed in the 2000s. Failing to take painful but necessary measures, the government paved the way for what was to come in later years when, under the pretext of modernizing the armed forces, an exclusive group of individuals dismantled them in circumstances of large-scale corruption.

I was disturbed also by the situation in the Caucasus. In Chechnya the government managed to achieve a military victory over the separatists, but failed to restore any semblance of normality to the politics of the region. Acute problems of interethnic relations remained unresolved. The separatists were able to exploit this, as were extremists and terrorist gangs.

In September, we were all appalled by the tragedy in Beslan. Terrorists acted with monstrous brazenness and brutality. On 1 September they captured more than 1,000 hostages – children, their parents and teachers. For two and a half days they held them in terrible conditions, refusing them everything and tormenting both children and adults. The security forces, having failed to forestall the attack, proved incapable of reacting effectively. The assault on the buildings and crossfire, which began in the afternoon of 3 September, proved to be a disaster, with 334 people killed, 186 of them children.

Vladimir Putin arrived in Beslan on 4 September. He visited the hospital where the wounded were being treated, expressed condolences for those killed and that evening made a televised address to the nation, speaking of the need to defend the country and urging people not to panic. At the same time he announced that action would be taken in the near future to strengthen the country's unity and establish an effective crisis management system. Then, on 13 September, he announced a programme of political reforms, of which the most important were abolishing the direct election of governors and doing away with constituencies electing candidates to the State Duma who were not affiliated to any political party.

I found these measures extraordinary and stated my position in an article for *Moskovskiye Novosti*:

> I still cannot believe what happened in Beslan. It was a terrible tragedy, after which none of us can carry on living our lives the way we did. The first priority must be help for the victims. The Gorbachev Foundation has already transferred money to the account of the Red Cross and now we will try to help particular people and particular families.
>
> I find it wholly unacceptable that the professionals in the special services failed to prevent the terrorist attack in the first place, or the bloody conclusion of the events. I am in no doubt that Patrushev and Nurgaliev must be held personally responsible for what happened. I think the president also understands that and will do what is necessary.
>
> I expected the government to react decisively to what had occurred, and much of what President Putin said in his address strikes me as important and necessary. ...
>
> Unlike the president, however, I believe the terrorist acts of recent weeks are directly related to the military operations in the Caucasus. Back in 1994, during the first Chechen war, I could see only too clearly the catastrophic consequences it would have. Unfortunately, I was right. That means that we need once more to seek political solutions, to negotiate with the moderate militants and separate them from irreconcilable extremists.
>
> I have no doubt that today the government needs public sup-

port for its actions. How is it to overcome all the corruption without a properly functioning parliament or free press, without society at large keeping an eye on everything? Unfortunately there is no sign of movement in that direction, rather the reverse. Under cover of the need to combat terrorism, they are proposing a major retraction of democratic freedoms and to deprive citizens of the ability to give direct expression of their attitude to the state authorities in free elections. We are invited to acquiesce in the effective appointment of governors by the Centre and to give up the election of independent parliamentary deputies, and all this despite the fact that today nearly all the parties are subservient to the Kremlin. I know what I am talking about: when we were trying to set up a social democratic party, we ourselves had the bureaucracy attempting to bind us hand and foot. A system of that sort is going to be a fat lot of use in the fight against terrorism. On the other hand, it will undoubtedly make it easier to impose measures that hurt voters, like abolishing welfare benefits.

I very much hope this is only a possible policy being considered by President Putin, an idea under discussion rather than a final decision. ... Regrettably, it was soon apparent that the president had no intention of listening to doubts and warnings being expressed not only by me. Nurgaliev stayed on as Interior Minister and Patrushev as head of the FSB, while the changes to the political system, with the acquiescence of a docile parliament, were firmly implemented.

My mention of the cutting of welfare benefits was entirely deliberate. On 22 August 2004 Putin signed a law which began with the words: 'This federal law is being adopted for the purpose of protecting the rights and freedoms of citizens.' If only! Whatever the intention of those who drafted the law, its sloppiness was all too obvious. The 'monetization of benefits' variously affected more than 40 million people: people with disabilities, members of the armed forces, veterans of the Second World War, veterans of labour, pensioners and other citizens whose benefits were paid out of federal and regional budgets. Taking decisions affecting such a large number of people, who were already living in difficult circumstances, would only have been reasonable after the fullest possible consideration and public consultation to ascertain the views of those affected by the decision. Instead, the government swooped, adopting wholesale the blueprint of the principal ideologist of monetization, Mikhail Zurabov. The Duma and Federation Council rubber-stamped it and the president, overlooking the fact that this was a political rather than a financial issue, signed it off! Public reaction was extremely hostile!

The protests began even before the president's proposal had been signed into law. At the end of July, victims of Chernobyl rallied in Moscow, and on 2 August a wave of protest demonstrations swept the country. After that, it was obvious that public consultation was essential and that the whole scheme should be reconsidered, and in January 2005, when the impact of monetization hit claimants and pensioners, people took to the streets. The protests were most widespread in large cities, including the twin capitals of Moscow and St Petersburg, where pensioners at one point blocked the major highways of Nevsky and Moskovsky Prospekts. The political parties began declaring their support for the pensioners, as did public figures. Patriarch Alexiy II made an open appeal to the authorities.

The situation was becoming heated and the president needed to act. He had several meetings with the government, proposed reviewing a number of provisions of the pension reform and ordered a pay increase for servicemen. I do not know what turn events might have taken had it not been for these, admittedly belated, actions. It seems to me, I said in an interview for Interfax at the time, that the president should come down harder on the Cabinet's errors in the social sphere. "As time has passed it has begun to seem that the government is implementing a programme quite different from the one declared by the president. I do not know what is keeping him from, if not completely replacing the Cabinet, then at least reacting to its performance." The retreat from democracy I had written about in the article for *Moskovskiye Novosti* was becoming increasingly evident. Dmitry Muratov and I talked about that, but our conversation moved on to broader issues that were important to both of us.

DM: It looks like Russia is becoming an authoritarian country. Do you believe a turn to democratic forms of government is still on the cards?

MG: This is a topic that worries me a great deal, because I have devoted too much of my life to nurturing democracy. Everything will ultimately depend on what choice is made by the present authorities. ...

During the president's first term a degree of stabilization was achieved and a number of steps were taken to improve citizens' welfare. Some control was established over the operating of the state's institutions. I did expect that he would use the mandate of a second term in office to move things on, and in particular to develop the economic, social and political spheres in the interests of the people. This is how democracy begins, but what has begun now makes me very uneasy. You have yourself sensed that, in my recent remarks, even when these were very brief, there has been a great deal of emotion and distress.

DM: But you are not yet ready to swell the ranks of the opposition?

MG: I am ready to point out openly to the president what is going on in the country. And what I am observing is a retreat from what he declared. What is happening is just not what the country expects. How long can people be kept in their current situation? The monetization project shows just how cynically and callously the authorities are dealing with pensioners. All these nonsensical legal draughtsmen with their 'blueprints', driving people to join protest rallies! To hell with these draughtsmen! They should be kicked out now! ... The general public still have no idea what they are supposed to be doing, where they should be going, what documents they need to take. In January there was total confusion, and rage drove sick people out on to the streets to protest in the cold and frost.

DM: What made you particularly indignant during the 'pensioner riots'?

MG: The aftermath. From the very first days they started looking for the 'instigators'. They always look for them among people who just need to go about their business, buy medicine and live their lives! The real instigators are all cosily sitting in their government positions. What sort of administration is this? There was a time when I tried somehow to justify them. I could not believe that the people working on important documents affecting millions of people were so callous and cynical. This was major national policy. I was appalled to realize that policies churning up the fate of millions were being tossed together so brazenly and casually.

Creating Putin's 'vertical of power' has led to chaos. Officials are just sitting there waiting to be kicked out or made redundant and do not know what to do. They are being 'reorganized' out of business. If this approach is pursued further, there is going to be a very big problem. Back in July and August the government took a swing at education and healthcare, by which I mean introducing payment for services. What they are really taking a swing at is the constitution. Right there, enshrined in Article 42, is the right to free education. This is one of the great achievements of democracy: any family, regardless of its income, knows it will be able to educate its children to the end of secondary education. Now the government is thinking of withdrawing that right.

It is just so irresponsible and immoral. We have already had one bout of shock therapy, when privatization was pushed through, robbing the people. All citizens' nest eggs in the savings banks went up in smoke. People were left with tiny salaries. Now we are being told that, according to the latest official statistics, there are hardly any poor people in Russia. They are lying through their teeth! In 1990 we reviewed the poverty threshold in the Soviet Union and raised it. The basket included not just a selection of basic foodstuffs, but such items as the money needed to support children. Under Yeltsin, the government solved that problem very simply by lowering the threshold to half its previous level, and magically halved the number of poor people! Come to that, we could reduce rations to the levels during the Siege of Leningrad and then we wouldn't have any poor people at all. Everything is done purely for effect, cynically, disrespectfully. With that sort of attitude, it is insulting to talk of democracy. ...

DM: The government claims that its reforms of healthcare and education are merely following Western practice.

MG: All these weasel words really make me angry. If you want to shuffle off responsibility for the people, to rid yourself of responsibility for caring for the citizens, who the hell needs you? What are you there for? The comparisons with the West are untenable. If we are going to talk like that, then let the government ensure wage levels are comparable, if not with America then at least with France, Italy, or Germany. Then our people really will be able to say, what the hell, we don't mind paying! If people have plenty of money, they will have no trouble choosing for themselves where to get medical treatment and education. But today they simply cannot afford it. Many people already cannot make ends meet. If policies of this kind continue to be pursued, then, in the near future, we may see serious disturbances.

DM: What kind of disturbances?

MG: I think people will simply not put up with the policy. In any case, it is not even a policy. The people pushing the president in this direction are macroeconomic advisers who always act only from the perspective of the immediate budget, but the budget gets funded by a developing economy, new jobs, the flourishing of small and medium businesses. What do they have to show in that respect? Nothing is happening, or precious little. That is the real issue. The president has a programme he announced to the Federal Assembly, and that is the way we need to go.

DM: Doesn't the present situation in respect of Glasnost remind you of the Era of Stagnation?

MG: Under Brezhnev we had a kind of neo-Stalinism, without the repression but everything was controlled. On one occasion, someone, a worker or an engineer speaking at a trade union congress, said: 'What is the general secretary doing about it? Is he not supposed to be in charge? Does he know what is going on? It is his responsibility!' A meeting of the Politburo was convened: this was an emergency! How could such a comment have been allowed to be heard at the congress? That was how much democracy we had. That was how much Glasnost and free speech there was. There's your answer.

DM: Another instance of déjà vu is the increasingly frequent attacks on the West, talk about double standards. Are we not going back to the times of the Cold War?

MG: There really is a problem of double standards, and it is right to speak directly and openly about it. Pressurizing and megaphone diplomacy are unacceptable in relations between countries. We know from the Cold War period where that leads. What all countries have an interest in is a calm atmosphere, dialogue and cooperation. We need to trade, to exchange technology and knowledge. In isolation, no country can consider itself secure.

DM: We seem to be seeing a weird resuscitation of old attitudes and moss-covered slogans. What is that all about?

MG: I have noticed it too. Is it really normal for the chairman of the State Duma to suddenly start extolling Stalin? I am astounded. By evening, Gryzlov was already backtracking.

In the morning he was shooting his mouth off and in the evening ... No, this is not Stalinism but some kind of hybrid. They have started talking about secret police, 'Chekist methods'. ... They seem to be scared of everything, but what are they scared of? At most, they might lose power. So what? When I began the reforms I said I would work two terms and no more. There was such inertia among the personnel at every level that it was literally holding the country back and the whole situation had to be exploded. But how? Not through Stalinist repression, but by democracy. Nowadays, many people think nobody can any longer be bothered with democracy, and globally, authoritarian politicians seem to be in great demand. In Russia, though, we always go to extremes. Either the far left take power, or the right, who are also practically off the scale. It's madness. I often emphasize that the last thing we need is to end up in a new Era of Stagnation or new era of control freakery and hyper-centralization.

DM: How are things going with your party?

MG: We have, in spite of everything, been creating a new social democratic party. The president publicly supported us, and even said, 'Our country is social democratic'. The officials in the Presidential Administration did not support us, though, and kept throwing spanners in the works. They wanted all the political parties dancing to their tune, malleable, to be able to manage them the way they manage the groups in the Duma, by pager. They were put out that Gorbachev doesn't dance to anyone's tune.

We didn't create the Social Democratic Party the way it is generally done now, when 30 odd organizations are brought together and declare themselves a party, democratic or super-nationalistic or conservative. We admitted only people who wrote their applications personally, which is quite a different approach. People came to us who for many years had shunned the other parties. They were waiting for the appearance of a social democratic party. They came, 32,000 of them. Do you know how interesting our plenums and congresses were? I was positively envious of these young people, so free, so intelligent.

It took me a whole life to grow from writing that essay in tenth grade on 'Stalin is our military glory' to understanding the need to rid ourselves of Stalinism, of his entire legacy, of totalitarianism, of our one-track way of thinking. Today too, we need to free people from fear of the state, because until we do so we cannot have a democratic state. That fear never completely left us and now it has come back again.

DM: Are any of today's political parties capable of leading an opposition?

MG: As of now, no. They need to be created and, of course, from the grassroots up. Attempts to graft something from those already existing are bound to fail. The graft will be the same as its parent. That is how they created the United Russia Party, using the Communist Party as a prototype, and the result has been a shadow of the CPSU! If people with social democratic views genuinely joined together, from the Fatherland party, from the party of the regions, if they took up our idea it would make really good sense.

DM: Are you an optimist, Mikhail Sergeyevich?

MG: Always. They say optimists are an irresponsible lot, but that is nonsense. ... History is not fated: there are always alternatives, alternative solutions. It is not a flood that is unaffected by what we do and the choices we make. We have to find our place in the process of history, which cannot just be abolished. As Bismarck said: 'A statesman must wait until he hears the steps of God sounding through events, then leap up and grasp the hem of His garment.' An optimist is someone who sees everything, analyses and understands, but still goes on to find an answer. Every age has its heroes, people who do, in spite of everything, give an answer.

DM: Do you see any among our politicians?

MG: Not so far, but what of it? I am an optimist about that too. There are opportunities for the president, and not only for him. There is no cause to panic.

A new direction, or more of the same?

The annual Message of the President to the Federal Assembly in April 2005 was considered and substantial. I had the impression that Putin had thoughtfully analysed the events of the past year and drawn some intelligent conclusions about the need to adjust government policy. He had some encouraging things to say about attacking poverty, fighting corruption, supporting small and medium-sized businesses and moving towards a post-industrial society. The priorities announced were education, healthcare, affordable housing and agriculture. The president stated his intention of seeing through nationwide initiatives in these areas. His approach struck me as interesting and very promising: the price rises for raw materials on world markets were providing an inflow of funds that could be applied to rescuing those sectors from their current dire situation. The president's address gave me grounds to reiterate my support for his general approach, but ...

Watching him on television and observing the hall in which the deputies and other representatives of the elite were assembled that day, I had serious doubts. I saw the same bored expressions, the faces with no sign of intelligent interest and involvement in these matters that so affect Russia's future. I could detect no sense of urgency in the hall, no animation that might have indicated a willingness on the part of the deputies and officials to support what he was talking about. I felt I had seen all this before. Thinking back to last year's address, no less considered and responsible, which had outlined similar plans, I believed the president must be in great difficulties.

A year had passed, but instead of settling down to tackle the tasks proposed, the government had plodded along, offering more of the same. It had carried on with the familiar radical monetarist approach, putting macroeconomic stability ahead of social priorities, industrial or agricultural policy, where little had been done. Instead, there had been a monetization of benefits that had outraged and stirred up the entire country. Everything suggested that the government kitchen was still busy baking the same pies: the plans to privatize or semi-privatize education and healthcare, and to raise payment for utilities and maintenance of accommodation above what most families could afford.

'I support the president's overall political approach and policies, but the state of the institutions called upon to implement them raise serious doubts about what will actually happen,' I said in reply to a question from Interfax's reporter. 'I think that Russia and our public are now facing the moment of truth.' Specifically, I stated publicly: 'The situation is such that we need new parliamentary elections and a new government. That is what the president should propose, and I am confident that the public will support him. It is time for action.'

Responses to my call varied considerably. *Izvestiya*, which at that time was still maintaining a respectable level of quality, responsibility and objectivity, wrote: 'Gorbachev's recent advice to President Putin has been something of a sensation.' Needless to say, that was not my aim. I wanted to explain to the public why I considered that to be the right way out of the predicament in which the president and the country found themselves. I gave a long interview to Alexey Pankin, a correspondent of *Izvestiya*:

Pankin: By saying recently that President Putin should dismiss his government and call new elections for the Duma, you blew our planned interview on historical matters out of the water.

MG: I do not know why it was so sensational, because I made the suggestion very calmly.

Pankin: Even so, when the president of the USSR urges the

president of Russia to do something like that, people sit up and
take notice. Why at this precise moment?

MG: My temperament is still a bit volatile, but I never lose
self-control. Every statement I make has been deliberated over
and thought through. That was my considered reaction to the
president's address. It might have been entirely unexceptional
but for what the president said at the very beginning. He said:
'I will not repeat what I said in my last address, and would ask
you to consider these as two instalments and proceed on the
basis of a programme I am proposing for the coming decade.'

I have to say that I paid close attention to the address last
year and, together with the new additions this year about the
state, human rights, the judicial system and political issues, it
really did come over as something of a manifesto. It seemed
a statement of long-term policy and it raised my spirits. I felt
it was a serious project that I could support. However, it was
immediately toned down by commentaries: the president had
supposedly changed his overall policies at the last minute. How
come, if he had begun it last year? I do not believe this is just
some kind of game. The president is, after all, an ambitious
man, a man who knows his own worth, and I believe he meant
what he said.

Moreover, he was clearly finding it all very difficult. When
he read it, you probably noticed, he was thinking very hard
how best to get his point over. He seemed to be choking on
the words, gasping for air. I remember thinking he seemed
to be saying he could not agree with what was happening
and wanted to distance himself. Some people here in Russia,
and also abroad, say he was so stressed because of his incur-
sions against democracy and his attacks on the media and had
decided to put matters right. I don't think that can be taken
seriously. I saw this as a carefully considered choice on the part
of the president.

But how is it all going to be implemented? That is what worries me. Is he counting on parliament? The present parliament
is passing, without proper scrutiny, proposals of huge social
significance, affecting the very part of the population the state
ought to be standing up for. Perhaps some people find that

kind of parliament convenient, but what the hell use is it to the rest of us? It's certainly no use to Russia. Anyway, forget the parliament. Perhaps it can be turned around, although frankly I doubt it.

But what about the Cabinet? This is the government that, early this year, nonchalantly came up with the law on monetization of benefits. At this very moment, what the government is brewing up in its kitchen affects education, healthcare, residential maintenance and the public utilities. Its approach is to pass all the costs on to the general public. I am not convinced this government is capable of implementing the president's programme; I do not believe the government will be up to dealing with everything implied by the address. They are simply not up to it! They are radical neo-liberals no less than the Gaidar government was.

The first step, then, is to send the government packing. ...

Later the conversation turned to history. The year 2005 was the twentieth anniversary of the beginning of Perestroika, so we looked at the parallels between those times and the present.

Pankin: Let's talk about current affairs in the light of past history. Some people see Putin as a kind of new Gorbachev.

MG: We are entirely different people, with completely different careers and biographies. And these are different times. But I said long ago, and still believe, the president has made his mark. Experience has shown he is hardworking and ambitious, but he is in a predicament. He has been pulled this way and that by all these cliques, and still they are wrangling over how to share out state property.

Pankin: But how about this for a parallel? Both you and he appeared after a period of senile, incompetent government. Both you and he were pulled out of the ranks as young men who were somehow to rescue and revive the system. But then you young men got ideas and went off-message.

MG: Putin in his first term worked well. If a competition were held to see who could identify most of his mistakes, I could probably mention more than anyone else. But that is not how these matters are judged. When someone is implementing a particular project, taking decisions about specific, major issues, there will always be instances of too little too late, things that go wrong, and downright blunders.

You need to remember the chaos there was everywhere: in the social sphere, in science and education, healthcare, the army, in relations between the federal government and the regions. There is no counting it all. I think he has already done a great deal. Enough, at least, to have earned his place in history.

But now the question is, what next? How can we avoid continuing downhill out of inertia, which we have largely failed to overcome, in the same rut as Yeltsin? We need to change course now. When he was still only running for a second term, I said that what mattered was what he would do. If he used the power he was given for a second term to consolidate his own power and continue the policy of creating a 'managed democracy', it would ultimately end badly.

Pankin: Here is another parallel with Perestroika. You too consistently took on more and more formal positions, but your real power became less and less. Don't you think Putin is going down the same path: he too is assuming more and more powers ...

MG: The situations are, nevertheless, different. I needed to do that in order to create a different kind of regime through a new constitution, through the political process, through free elections, a regime based on democratic principles and procedures. I needed also to free the state, the executive and other branches from the hold of the CPSU. The problem I faced was creating a state system for managing the country, because we had arrived at the moment when Article 6, enshrining the CPSU's monopoly of power, was going to be dropped from the constitution. For Vladimir Putin that problem had already been solved. He faced a different task, of creating genuine national and federal political parties which could provide the foundation for developing democratic institutions.

I have to say clearly, though, that nothing could be more mistaken than trying to concoct parties in the office of Vladislav

Surkov. A party is formed out of political movements, certain sections of society, large groups of people. Parties form themselves as people discover they have interests in common. ...

Pankin: Another question about parallels. Many people remember the sense of imminent catastrophe in the public consciousness in 1990–1. Everybody was telling themselves that if this or that was not done there was going to be disaster, a civil war. A similar sense of impending doom seems to be growing in Russia now. The mayor of Moscow and the head of the Presidential Administration are allowing themselves to talk about a real danger of the country disintegrating. And what interest there is among readers of *Izvestiya* in the 'coloured' revolutions!

MG: I think the situation has been aggravated by the way the proposed reforms are being introduced. Reform of the government has stalled. Dmitry Kozak's administrative reform has stalled, and we have all these social sector reforms. Resistance to the approaches underlying all these changes did not begin only in January and February 2005. That is when the pensioners came out onto the streets, protesting against the law monetizing benefits, but battle was joined long ago over what kind of educational, healthcare, housing and utilities policies were to be pursued. It is plain that they went about it in the most primitive way possible, burdening ordinary people with all the costs. I think that is what could shake people out of their complacency and acceptance. Russia woke up after the old people protested, and now there are people protesting every day against this measure or that. They are not going to put up with it any more.

Finally, we came to the topic increasingly preoccupying the public as the next elections approached: the possibility of a third presidential term for Vladimir Putin.

Pankin: When Putin says, 'Here is an action programme for the next 10 years', is that an indication that he is intending to stay on for a third term, or hold onto power in some other way?

MG: I thought he had already considered this carefully, and he has said himself that he will not stand for a third term. Observing the constitution is actually a perfectly normal thing to do. At the same time, there are things in it that might need to be clarified. People are raising the question of whether the articles relating to the presidency need to be revised. I think they do. Although Putin says the constitution should be left alone.

Pankin: Revised, in your opinion, in what direction?

MG: My view is that we need a version of the French constitution, adapted for Russia. So the party that comes out on top in the elections forms the government, but at the same time the president is popularly elected. Everybody's powers are clearly set out, and the government is left to get on with its job. The president can come to meetings of the government, as Chirac does, and chair sessions of the cabinet, all as he sees fit. Nevertheless, the government operates under the direction of the prime minister. Of course, he and the president interact.

Some people would like to see a puppet president elected by parliament. Are they going to summon parliament like a plenum of the Communist Party's Central Committee and summarily depose him the way they treated Khrushchev?

Again and again my conviction was reinforced that ultimately everything comes down to politics and the role of democracy. During those years I saw a great deal of my friends Alexander Nikolaevich Yakovlev and Yegor Vladimirovich Yakovlev. They had been my comrades-in-arms – and, not infrequently, my opponents – in the years of Perestroika and subsequently. One and then the other passed away, in 2005 and 2006. They were very different people, with complex personalities, and encountered many difficulties in their careers. They faced many ordeals, overcame illusions and frustrations, but never lost faith that democracy was the path for Russia.

The death of Yegor Yakovlev was a great blow for me. We became particularly close in the post-Perestroika years. Under his editorship, *Moskovskiye Novosti* became a real channel of communication for Glasnost and Perestroika, in many instances helping me personally in very difficult circumstances. Yegor and

I had our arguments and disagreements. Of course we had. I remember shortly before his death, the three of us were reminiscing like old soldiers about past battles and I reminded them that they had demanded my resignation after the Vilnius events in January 1991. The newspaper put me under terrible pressure. They tried to deny it, but I proved it all to them. By the time Yegor arrived at *Moskovskiye Novosti* he had been through a lot of bad experiences and done all sorts of things: he had written about Lenin and edited various publications, been removed from various positions, but always managed to come back. It only toughened him. He was a mature and very deep person, and what he had to say was significant, precise and controversial.

He and I agreed on many issues, except one. He could not understand how I found it possible to justify what was happening, how I could find grounds for supporting Putin. I told him: my dear friend, if you had been in the shoes of a president who had all that chaos, that semi-disintegration dumped on him, you would understand it was no time for textbook democracy. That was a salvage operation. Immediate action was called for.

In 2005, I spent a lot of time working on *Understanding Perestroika: Why It Matters Now*.[2] Together with my associates and colleagues Anatoly Chernyaev, Alexander Veber, Georgiy Ostroumov, Alexander Galkin and Boris Slavin, we reread the documents of those years, recalled events and analysed achievements and mistakes. Revisiting that period, comparing it with what came next, I was strengthened in my belief that, although Perestroika was disrupted before it could realize all its aims, it had nevertheless been victorious. Perestroika brought transformative processes to a point where it was impossible to relapse back into the past. We can, however, never rest. The country must go forward, and only along democratic lines. That has to be fought for. Although my strength was no longer what it had been, with illnesses beginning to take their toll, I felt it incumbent upon me to take part in that battle.

---

[2] M. S. Gorbachev, *Poniat' perestroiku … Pochemu eto vazhno seichas*, M.: Al'pina Business Books, 2006.

Full of Contradictions: The First Decade of the New Millennium

New elections

The political results of 2005 were a mixed bag. I analysed them in an article in *Bolshaya Politika* [*Big Politics*] in February 2006. I wrote about the problems the president had inherited and which had yet to be overcome. At the same time I spoke out about an issue that was exercising me, together with everyone else in Russia, and which the authorities, in my view, were not taking seriously enough:

> Perhaps Russia's greatest bane is corruption. People assert that this is an inevitable consequence of involvement of the state in the economy. They criticize the president for the fact that during his time in office the state has taken back control of the oil and gas sectors. I disagree. I wholly support what the president is doing in this area, but officials should not be given carte blanche. They are there to serve society. They have proliferated out of all proportion and, if that is not stopped, the problem of corruption will become worse. It is a problem that can be dealt with only through democracy.
>
> Now, as the next elections approach, cliques are coming out of the woodwork which are clearly interested in getting control over major revenue streams and exploiting them for their own political ends.
>
> Politicians in office should, as a matter of principle, keep business interests at arm's length. That is all there is to it, and it applies particularly to the president. Politicians should devote themselves to politics because otherwise they will act not in the interests of the country, but for their own personal benefit.

After I resigned I had many invitations to move into business, but I always refused. I long ago chose politics.

I thought long and seriously about the forthcoming elections, and shared some of my conclusions with the readers:

We are about two years away from the next presidential election. This is already being much discussed, and even greater efforts are being made by various groups to safeguard their interests. Increasingly, we hear it suggested that some 'Operation Successor' is needed, or, better still, that a tactic should be devised to enable the current president to stay on for a third term. This is profoundly misguided. ...

I am confident that President Putin will not violate the constitution and will relinquish office at the time it specifies. He will see his biography as president through to a worthy conclusion. ...

Today everyone is still talking about the November reshuffle of the Cabinet and Presidential Administration, and trying to guess which of the new appointees may take the place of Vladimir Vladimirovich Putin. I do not think that merits serious discussion. I do not see the president following his predecessor's example of resigning prematurely and appointing a new prime minister as acting president, with an endorsement of that individual as the future head of state.

As we were to see, one of my predictions proved accurate: Putin did not stand for a third term as president. I was mistaken, however, in the second. The government did once more embark on an Operation Successor, if in a slightly modified form. It was not much of an improvement, though, and I saw and warned of the danger that Russia might step by step turn aside from the path of democracy.

There is a serious risk that the election campaign will be a sham. In my opinion, there have been no fair and free elections in Russia since those of 1989, 1990 and the election of 1991 when Boris Yeltsin became the first president of Russia. All the other campaigns were flawed. The candidates did not face a level playing field, the administrative resources of the state were improperly exploited, and the results were blatantly rigged. I make that claim not from hearsay: during the 1996 campaign I had direct experience of it myself.

Can we compel the authorities to hold elections in accordance with democratic standards? We can and must. Nobody else will do it for us. Civil society must defend its rights. ...

There is, however, another point that troubles me. The elections will be genuine only if there are several strong political contenders. I am sure they will appear, and indeed some already have, but I refrain from naming them. I am only too familiar with the ways of the so-called elite, who will immediately crush them.

Democracy in distress

In terms of economic growth, 2006 and 2007 were reasonably successful, but the nature of the expansion was very questionable. It was achieved, by and large, by an influx into the economy of oil revenues and an increase, as a result, of imports. There were no worthwhile structural changes in the economy, which continued its addiction to oil. No transition to an economy of innovation occurred. There was no sign of administrative action to implement the goals the president set out in his annual messages to the Federal Assembly.

I did not want to believe the presidential addresses were mere ritual, just another piece of PR, to be forgotten as soon as the occasion was over. When I said that I shared the vision of the latest address and supported the objectives set out by the president, I hoped to encourage him to introduce serious measures to implement them. But I could see no current machinery of government capable of making those ideas a reality.

I was disturbed also by signs that the influence of people clearly allergic to democratic governance was increasing in the Russian government. These people had been scared by the 'colour revolutions', especially the Orange Revolution in Ukraine. What alarmed them was not so much the collateral damage and excesses accompanying the turbulent events in neighbouring countries (although they were real enough) as the possibility of a change of government through the ballot box. There began to be talk about 'managed democracy'; sundry artificial groups were funded at public expense, youth groups along the lines of *Nashi* [*Our Team*] and *Molodaya Gvardiya* [*the Young Guards*] and the *Yedinaya Rossiya* [*United Russia*] party. I myself had started out as a member of the *Komsomol* [*Young Communist League*] and was only too familiar with youth policy in the Soviet period. I could not help drawing comparisons. If United Russia struck me as a mediocre imitation of the CPSU, the new youth organizations looked no better, as a tool for manipulation and, on occasion, intimidation. There was ever less sign of democracy in 'managed democracy' and ever more evidence of management, control and constraint. The Russian government clearly did not trust the people and wanted the election results always to be predictable, and in its favour.

At the Foundation and in numerous conversations with friends and colleagues, politicians and journalists, I talked about what was happening. We were not talking about rumours of a tightening of the screws, or pseudo-concepts like 'Cheka-ism' [esprit de corps of the secret police], but entirely real changes that were being made to legislation. Where would they lead, I wondered. In effect the entire first half of 2006 was spent mulling over these disturbing developments, and the result was an article published on 19 July 2006 in *Rossiyskaya Gazeta*. In it, I was outspokenly critical and alarming, and many people were surprised that the official newspaper of the Russian government agreed to publish it. I believe this was evidence that many others shared my concern. In the minds of many people, ordinary citizens and others close to the authorities, doubts and questions were achieving critical mass. I reprint some of the article here:

> In the run-up to the recent G8 summit in St Petersburg, discussions about democracy, which were already taking place in Russia, became particularly pointed. Much of what Western politicians and commentators had to say met with outright rejection in Russia, mainly because people felt that it was our country that was being discussed and our democracy, and that it was for us, rather than the vice-president of the United States, to decide what it should be like and how we should arrive at it. It is high time

the West recognized that attempts to put pressure on Russia are invariably counterproductive.

Rejecting outside pressure, however, obliges us ourselves to analyse and assess all the more carefully and critically the current state of progress in our country towards democracy. My own belief is that Russia can reach the goals we are striving for only by following the path of democracy. At the same time, it needs to be recognized that the transition from totalitarianism to democracy is not taking place in a vacuum, under ideal conditions, but within the context of our history. It is proving difficult and will require considerable time and effort from the whole of our society.

The conditions under which our 'transition to democracy' is occurring were made much more difficult by misguided policies of the Russian leadership in the 1990s. Given impoverishment of the majority of the population, chaos at the heart of government and in the economy and the threat that the nation might simply disintegrate, what chance was there of developing democracy? To all intents and purposes there was none, and it was replaced by a shabby imitation.

Having inherited that situation, Vladimir Putin's first priority had to be preventing the collapse of the country and stabilizing the economy and society. He had to act fast, and inevitably not everything could be done without certain measures that do not feature in standard textbooks on democracy. Overly independent regional leaders had, for example, to be obliged to bring regional legislation into accordance with federal law. Harsh measures were necessary to combat terrorism.

The measures taken dealt with the crisis of the Russian state and led to economic growth, whose results are beginning to impact positively on people's lives. This has changed the situation, but something else is also true: social stability and a noticeable improvement in the economic figures do not of themselves resolve all the issues relating to the state of our democracy. Quite the contrary. If the difficult circumstances, even emergency, that we confronted at the start of the decade have been dealt with, it is all the more time now to examine how far our democratic institutions and current legislative proposals accord with the overriding aim of constructing a new, free, democratic society in Russia.

Here there is cause for concern. Twenty years have passed since the beginning of democratic reforms, yet there are many unjustifiable restrictions, prohibitions and barriers – both old and recently introduced. I do not doubt that Alexander Veshnyakov, the chairman of the Central Electoral Commission, knew what he was talking about when he said recently there was a danger that, instead of a genuine political contest, the election might turn into a farce. The president himself was obliged to remind everyone that the opposition has a right to express its opinions and that it should be listened to. This is a matter of great importance, because competitive elections and a real opposition are essential features of any democracy. ...

Most worrying of all are changes in electoral law.

A law passed last year abolished constituencies fielding independent candidates. This was a retrograde step. In these constituencies the deputy directly represents his or her constituents and their interests. Voting for party lists, on the contrary, the voter sees only the names of celebrities at the top of the list who, as a rule, have not the slightest intention of actually working in the Duma. It is a disgraceful practice, a brazen deception, but there has been no talk at all about abolishing that. The 'merit' of the system is that it enables parties to funnel 'the right people' into the Duma, people whose loyalty is not to Russia's citizens but only to the leaders of their party.

The move to a wholly proportional system of representation could only be justified if Russia had already generated a stable party system, with political parties that, taken together, adequately reflect the interests of all the segments and groups in society. We have a long way to go before that is the case. In the present situation, it is blindingly obvious that the aim of this innovation is to establish a monopoly over Russia's politics.

The law on political parties adopted in 2001 established a rigid state regulation and control of the activities of parties, and was subsequently made even more draconian with additional requirements on the number of parties, the number of regional offices they were required to have, and so on. When I was head of the Social Democratic Party, I reluctantly agreed to these provisions, supposing that any legal framework was better than none. Experience has shown, however, that such regulation is not consistent with democratic principles: the political credibility of parties should be determined by the voters, not by the state.

The process of chiselling away at the rights and opportunities of political parties is still continuing: the entrance barrier for parties to be admitted to the Duma has been raised to 7 per cent of the overall vote, with the manifest intention of obstructing the appearance in parliament of 'undesirable' opposition parties. The new electoral law decrees that, of the 200,000 signatures that must first be collected by any party aspiring to participate in the elections, the permissible proportion of those considered questionable or invalid has been reduced from the previous 20 per cent to 5 per cent. Quite clearly, those conducting the inspection will have no difficulty finding the required number of rejects if they are so minded. There is immense scope for administrative malfeasance.

One of the latest innovations is the removal from voting slips of the box labelled 'Against all the above'. It is claimed that this will raise the sense of civic responsibility among voters, but in reality a substantial section of the electorate is being prevented from voting. In 2003, some 13 million people voted 'Against all the above' and, moreover, most often those who did were educated people protesting against the lack of real choice. The likelihood is that most of them will in future simply boycott the elections.

Even that is not the end of it. The government has resuscitated the provision for early voting, which is a charter for ballot-rigging. Nongovernmental organizations are now excluded from monitoring the elections. Newspapers established by political parties are banned from informing voters about their parties' activities until one month before the election. All these are initiatives proceeding from United Russia, exploiting its majority in the fourth Duma. Their only purpose is to ensure at all costs that 'the bosses' party' is guaranteed a majority in the next elections.

What might look like piecemeal changes to the legislation lead cumulatively to a degrading of the entire electoral system, which is increasingly being turned into a pure formality. This is particularly obvious in respect of the Federation Council, which now consists of appointed officials who often have no connection whatsoever with the regions they 'represent'. Flagrant instances of corruption have been exposed recently. One can only sympathize with the demand of the Federation Council's chairman, Sergey Mironov, for a review of the manner in which this chamber is constituted.

Voters' trust in elections and government institutions has been falling in recent years. Eloquent testimony to this is the low voter turnout in recent elections and referendums.

In fact, however, one has the impression that the ruling 'elite' has a direct interest in reducing citizens' participation. Why else would the quorum for valid elections have been reduced at federal level from 50 per cent to 25 per cent, while for local elections it can be even lower.

Our bureaucrats seem to think that the fewer people who vote in the elections, the surer they can be of obtaining the result they require.

All this is going on against a background of other developments over recent years. I have in mind the restriction on the independence of the electronic mass media to report; the ubiquitous abuse of government administrative resources during election campaigns; the tightening of laws governing the conduct of meetings and demonstrations; the adoption of a law on referendums which has made it almost impossible for them to be conducted other than at the instigation of the state authorities; and intensification of control over the activities of nongovernmental organizations. What does this all add up to in a state of affairs where all the governors belong to the same party?

Is this really justified by national characteristics of our democracy or other external circumstances? I think not.

Of course, democracy must indeed be rooted in the soil of each country, and has its own national peculiarities. There are, however, some universal principles. Restrictions that might be necessary in a situation where people's lives and the very existence of the state are under threat should be regarded as temporary and not perpetuated as basic principles, as is being done by the theorists of 'sovereign' or 'managed' democracy. Such collocations distort the very essence of democracy, no less than it was distorted by designations like 'socialist' or 'people's' democracy.

We are constantly reminded of the need to fight terrorism and extremism. No reasonable person would deny it, but when a law is passed that defines extremism so broadly that it can be used to suppress any opposition or dissent, one has to disagree. The beneficiary of such legislation and restriction of the electoral rights of Russian citizens is the bureaucracy in its campaign to shield itself from public accountability.

There has been a lot of talk lately about the need to rein in the bureaucracy, but the only effective antidote to its high-handedness is a mature civil society with robust legislation and feedback between the state authorities and the population. ...

The first priority is to recognize that with the current legislation in place it is impossible to hold genuinely democratic elections and ensure genuine participation by the people in the political process.

There is still time to put matters right. I believe the president, with his ability to veto, should now make use of his powers and great authority. Decisive action on his part could transform the situation. Much depends at this time on him alone. I am sure the president's actions will be supported by the citizens of Russia.

Ultimately it is for all of us, the people of Russia, to decide whether the country develops in the direction of real involvement of citizens in public affairs or whether the model of paternalistic bureaucratic guardianship prevails. I have no doubt that Russia deserves the former.

The choice of the state authorities was becoming ever more apparent, and the chorus of voices advising Putin to amend the constitution and continue for a third presidential term was increasingly clamorous. The leaders of a number of neighbouring countries joined in, including, to my surprise, Nursultan Nazarbaev of Kazakhstan. Of course, he himself, and Alexander Lukashenko of Belarus, had personal experience of the arrangement, but it seemed to me that Putin was reluctant to copy them. That he could push their suggested amendments through a tame parliament was not in doubt, and although he frequently declared he had no intention of doing so, there was evidently discussion and vacillation over the issue.

The main thing, it seemed to me, was that the elections should provide a genuine choice between candidates with alternative manifestos. Putin was in a position to give the public competing candidates, a proper election campaign and debates, all of which would greatly restore the health of Russian politics and give them a hefty shove in the direction of democracy. It did not happen. Nevertheless, I gave a lot of credit to him for at least deciding not to run for a third term.

'I think he is behaving appropriately and in accordance with the Constitution', I commented in an interview for Interfax. 'I see that as an important sign that we are dealing with a serious-minded person who supports democratic values. If Putin retires as a democrat, without nominating a successor, he will have rendered a further major service to the people. ... We are in the process of forming a new nation and it is important to show the world how we treat the Constitution.' At the same time, other things were taking us in the opposite direction, and I spoke out frankly about them: 'Step by step, United Russia is exploiting its majority in parliament to dismantle many of the positive features of the electoral system and pave their way to success. That is undemocratic, and the president should have intervened.'

The clamp-down on the press continued and even intensified, both in Moscow and the regions. The president stated that the press should be free but also responsible, a formulation I entirely supported. In reality, though, the state authorities wanted media that did as they were told. 'A reaction is taking place', I said, 'when every three months another television channel is re-nationalized.' The upshot was that citizens were deprived of their electoral rights, journalists of their freedom of speech and politicians of any possibility of setting up new parties.

I was not in favour of radical steps or rocking the boat. I did not want to see events developing uncontrollably, and at that time there were no reasons or conditions for mass protests. People were feeling the effects of the current improvement in the economy; many families who had recently been living below the poverty line had a sense of relief and hope. Given the circumstances, if the parliamentary election had been conducted along more democratic lines, with soundly based parties in genuine contention, discussion of manifestos and plans, the ruling party could still have achieved a respectable result, although not an overwhelming majority. Unfortunately, the authorities were intent on ensuring that parliament continued to be 'no place for discussion', as Boris Gryzlov, chairman of the Duma, had once so eloquently put it.

The year 2008 started out looking not to be just another year in Russian politics. The presidential election was going to be an important event, although it was already clear it would not be a milestone in the development of the Russian state and Russian politics. No election whose result is fixed can perform the supremely important function of renewal, providing an influx of new blood, a righting of wrongs and correcting of mistakes made by those previously in power.

I was not alone in the hopes and doubts I felt in those days, which are reflected in my correspondence with Yelena Bonner, to whom I sent good wishes on her birthday. The widow of Andrey Sakharov was a complex and self-contradictory person. We had clashed swords on more than one occasion, but I respect courageous people with strong convictions which they passionately defend. Here is our exchange of letters:

Dear Yelena Bonner,

I very much wanted to wish you a happy birthday by telephone but was unsuccessful, so here are my greetings by letter.

I would like to join with all those who know and appreciate you and who on this day are wishing you all the best. Your heart and mind are always receptive to other people and respond to their pain. You are one of those people for whom politics has never been reducible to ideology or 'spin' but is measured by human, ethical criteria. That is why you are admired even by those who do not always agree with you but share your passionate desire to see our homeland become democratic, a state governed by the rule of law, and to see the world become a more just place.

I believe that these ideals, upheld by Andrey Sakharov, will some day become a reality, thanks to the spirit and energetic efforts of many people, and especially people like you.

I wish you long life, vigour, indomitableness of spirit and the love and care of your family and friends.

Yours,

Mikhail Gorbachev
15 February 2008

Her reply was:

Dear Mikhail Sergeyevich,
Thank you for your good wishes and kind words about my heart and other virtues. When I received your letter, I first thought it was a pity you had not phoned, but a moment later thought better of it, because if you had we would probably have quarrelled again, and on my birthday that would not have been seemly.

I can share your hope that Andrey Dmitrievich's ideals may some day come to pass in our country, but I think the road will be longer and thornier than you do. That does not, however, mean that Russia will never make it: *per aspera ad astra*.

With unfading memory of our departed loved ones, thank you once again, and I wish you, Irina and your family health and all the best.
Yelena Bonner
4 March 2008

Operation Successor

Although the result of the presidential election was never in doubt, was predictable and even 'fated', I felt obliged to go to the polls and vote, to take part in the procedures of democracy. I urged not only my friends and relatives to do the same, but all the citizens of Russia.

Many people were critical of that. I could see for myself that these elections would not bring Russia any closer to genuine, living democracy and said so openly, for example, during an interesting online conference with residents of Chelyabinsk. They asked more than 400 questions and I managed to reply to many of them, not backing away from those that were barbed. One of these asked, 'What do you think about Operation Successor?' My answer was: 'Everything has been done within the letter of the constitution, but not in the spirit of democracy.'

For all that, I saw the objections outweighed by a different argument: even if the machinery of Russian democracy was not perfect, and indeed sometimes warped, we must not turn our backs on politics. That is what I said in an interview for Interfax immediately after the election, which Dmitry Medvedev won in the first round: 'First of all, I want to note the high turnout, with significant participation of young people. One can only welcome the fact that they are not turning their backs on politics but contributing to their future themselves.' Commenting on the preliminary voting results, I said: 'Those who predicted, and I was one of them, that Vladimir Putin's participation in the Duma campaign would largely determine how the presidential election went, have been proved right.'

Putin's popularity was still high. Many credited him with the improvement in the economy, which was increasingly noticeable. I made no secret of being impressed by Dmitry Medvedev: 'He is an intelligent, hard-working man but has, of course, had little experience of working on behalf of the state. I believe his sympathies are on the side of democracy. I said much the same about Putin eight years ago. We will have to wait and see.'

I was thinking hard about the direction events might take, and shared some of my conclusions with the readers of *Rossiyskaya Gazeta* in an article published in early March 2008:

> What is vital is that machinery should be devised for realizing a whole raft of extremely complex changes.
>
> Clearly, to successfully bring together efforts on the federal, regional and even district levels, we need to see a serious improvement in personnel policy. This should not be a witch-hunt. Training personnel, preparing them to resolve completely new tasks must be part of a carefully thought-through system. It is particularly important to recruit young people. If the president and government do not undertake this, many of their declarations and promises will prove empty, and no amount of PR will save the situation.
>
> In the article, I yet again drew the attention of the public and the state authorities to the need for change in the electoral system:
>
> Our electoral system needs not mere adjustment but a complete overhaul. It is essential that there should be changes in the organization of both the presidential elections and the Duma elections, and of the way governors are elected.

As the top priority, I would list the need to return to a mixed voting system, with both proportional voting for party lists and direct election of independent candidates. People should be able to know the particular candidates and choose between them. After the Duma elections in December 2007, 113 top candidates on the lists of successful parties did not take up their mandate as deputies but simply handed them on to little-known people. But 113 seats is just one-quarter of the total! What sort of disregard for the voters is that? We need also to lower the minimum percentage of the overall vote required for a party to be admitted to the Duma to 5 per cent.

I think direct election of governors should be restored, instead of as now having them nominated by the president and confirmed by the regional legislative bodies.

At times I said this more bluntly than in the official government newspaper, remarking that United Russia was turning into a mediocre copy of the CPSU. I was constantly hearing that this was irritating many in power, and worse. The new generation of functionaries wanted an easy life and had no inclination to take criticism on board. Instead of considering how to restore their purpose and democratic nature to elections, what was hatched in offices and meetings in the Kremlin was 'political technology' to develop new ways of emasculating elections and perpetrating outright fraud, as was to be demonstrated in all its glory in 2011.

In spring 2008, I saw two things as supremely important. The first was for the new president to make a good start, quickly gaining experience and confidence. The second was for Russia to have a strong, rejuvenated government. On 7 May I attended the inauguration of President Medvedev. I shared my impressions with ITAR-TASS's correspondent. About Medvedev I said: 'I am increasingly confident he will cope.' I saw him as 'a man who wants to keep in touch, to listen and hear what Russians are saying. I would very much like that to be at the heart of his work in the four years allotted to him as president.' I saw his main task as being to mobilize the executive branch: 'That is very difficult but very important, and the most awkward problem is the staffing and the way all the institutions perform from local to federal level. It is equally important when the government and the president's secretariat are being appointed.' If Medvedev and Putin could cope with that, I said, new perspectives would open up for Russia.

Of course, everybody was curious to see how the cooperation would work out between the new president and now only Prime Minister Putin. Their relationship started being described as a 'tandem'. I knew there were people in the teams of both leaders whose efforts were directed not at facilitating cooperation but at weakening or torpedoing it. All sorts of talk was flying around immediately after it was announced that Putin would become prime minister. I had no doubt this politicking could be disastrous. I wished Medvedev and Putin every success in their joint endeavours.

I am satisfied there was no contradiction between my criticism of the election and my support for the new president and prime minister after it. I was guided by my principles, while taking account of the interests of Russia and the requirements of political culture.

Ideas and people

Much, although by no means everything, depended on the composition of the government. Judging by what we learned from the media, the process of forming it proved far from easy. At the same time, the outlines of the new government's economic policy had to be agreed. What would it be like? In June, the Gorbachev Foundation hosted a discussion on just this topic, with the participation of such authoritative economists as Ruslan Grinberg, Alexander Nekipelov, Vladislav Inozemtsev, Alexander Auzan and Yevgeny Gontmakher. Everybody agreed it was essential to overcome the legacy of failure from the 1990s, and that time was of the essence.

There was a question of priorities: should Russia use advanced technology already available in the West and redirect some of the 'oil money' to purchasing it, or should we rely on our own programmes of innovation? The majority believed we should do both, because if we failed to end the economy's dependence on natural resource exports and make it innovative in the near future, there would never be another chance. We would succeed only in propping up a backward economy.

Another point made was that a major obstacle to an economy of innovation was the backwardness of our social sectors, particularly education and healthcare, and our worsening social stratification. The economists identified the backwardness of state institutions as the main drag on modernization: the legislature, law-enforcement agencies and judiciary, and the lack of effective separation of powers of the branches of government, with an uncontrolled bureaucracy absolutely dominant. This was offered as a serious warning. Would the state authorities be prepared to tackle these problems seriously?

This discussion was taking place only a few months before, first in the United States and then globally, a financial and economic crisis broke that shook the world economy and did not leave Russia unscathed. We shall discuss it below, but for the time being I will say only that at the time neither our people nor the vast majority of economists in other countries predicted anything of the sort. Economics does not yet have trustworthy tools for analysing and assessing many economic processes, including some that are dangerous.

Meanwhile, the process of forming a government was accomplished, and certain indications raised my hopes of changes for the better. I liked a speech made at the St Petersburg Economic Forum by First Deputy Prime Minister Igor Shuvalov. His name was new to me, and some of his ideas were unexpected and held out the promise of a new approach. Of course, I added, behind any reforms, 'we must not overlook the social impact, the very people on whose behalf everything is done ... We do not want the innovation bandwagon to turn into another "great leap forward" followed, as tends to be the case in Russia, by a great crash.'

The research and discussions at the Gorbachev Foundation continued to provide much food for thought. They were highly respected by experts. I was delighted with Academician Tatiana Zaslavskaya's review of *Social Inequality and Public Policy*, the result of many years of research conducted at the Foundation under the direction of my ally from the Perestroika years, Vadim

Medvedev.[1] Zaslavskaya wrote that the book was 'devoted to the principal social problem facing Russia'. Here is her characterization of the situation resulting from the 'reforms' of the 1990s:

> In effect, two social classes coexist today on the territory of Russia. One, relatively small, consists of healthy, free, properly educated and extremely wealthy citizens who enjoy full civic rights. This new court nobility live in a special world they have built just for themselves. They have an exclusive habitat, way, quality and style of life. The second class, however, vastly more numerous, is the bulk of the population, struggling to earn a living. The majority of these are low-income, less educated people with limited rights. They do not enjoy particularly good health, do not receive essential medical care, and are fated to have what, by modern standards, is a short lifespan.[2]

The main value of the book Zaslavskaya saw not so much in its description and criticism of the current situation as in the revelation of its deep roots. She appreciated the report's specific proposals and concludes: 'Russia currently lacks a powerful social democratic movement to make one of its main priorities the battle against unjustifiable social and economic inequality. This book provides substantial material for developing the thinking and political programme of just such a movement.'

The researchers' ideas and conclusions struck me as highly germane and practical. I am sure they remain of importance today.

Life went on, as inevitably as the changing of the seasons, alternately joyful and sad. When I think back to 2008, two events, quite different but each in its own way of great personal significance for me, come to mind. Alexander Solzhenitsyn died, and my great-granddaughter Sasha was born.

Solzhenitsyn and I were bound in a relationship of mutual

---

[1] Vadim A. Medvedev et al., eds, *Sotsial'noe neravenstvo i publichnaia politika*, M.: Kul'turnaia revoliutsiia, 2007.

[2] Tatiana A. Zaslavskaia, *Sotsial'noe neravenstvo i publichnaia politika* [Review], 14 July 2008, website of the Gorbachev Foundation; http://www.gorby.ru/presscenter/news/show_25998/. Accessed 21 August 2015.

respect and critical curiosity and we had public disagreements. We met one time at a reception in the Swedish Embassy in honour of Russia's Nobel Prize winners. Solzhenitsyn was in good spirits and enjoying the attention. He came over and we greeted each other warmly. 'Mikhail Sergeyevich,' he said, 'I may have offended you. In recent years I have made many critical remarks, including some about you. You must understand, it is not from ill-will but because my heart bleeds for Russia.' His tone was friendly and sincere. I replied: 'Alexander Isayevich, this is a good day, honouring you and other winners of the Prize. I believe you and I have many things to talk about and hope we can find the time. Let's meet and talk.'

It was not to be. Either he was ill, or I was, and then the day came to take our farewell of him. I was at the funeral service at the Academy of Sciences and expressed my condolences to Solzhenitsyn's wife, Natalia Dmitrievna, his family and friends. I described my attitude to what he had done:

> We are bidding farewell to a great man and a major writer, a Nobel Prize winner, a man with a unique destiny whose name will remain in the annals of Russian history. He, like millions of other citizens of our country, was subjected to severe ordeals. Solzhenitsyn was one of the first to speak out loud about the inhumanity of the Stalinist regime and about people who were not broken by their ordeals. *One Day in the Life of Ivan Denisovich* and *The Gulag Archipelago* are books that altered the thinking of millions of people, compelling them to re-evaluate the past and present. It is impossible to overstate the contribution they made to overcoming totalitarianism. And in October we had a new arrival in our family: my granddaughter, Ksenia, gave birth to a daughter, my first great-granddaughter, Sasha. She was a sturdy baby, weighing in at 3.9 kilograms or 8.6 pounds, and 52 centimetres or 20 inches tall. Ksenia sent a photo of her new baby to my mobile phone. The little girl looks just like her mother, only with black eyebrows. Olga Vandysheva, a correspondent of *Komsomolskaya Pravda*, asked me: 'Did you know the Buddhists believe that someone who lives to see their great-grandchildren will go straight to heaven?' 'What is there to do there?' I replied; 'I am used to working.'

The second half of 2008 brought world events with the impact of a political earthquake. It was immediately clear that their destructive consequences would last for a long time. I am referring to the military conflict in Transcaucasia and the global financial and economic crisis.

Saakashvili's adventure and the West: my reaction

On the night of 7 August 2008, Georgian armed forces, after firing on Russian peacekeepers, subjected the South Ossetian capital of Tskhinvali to a missile bombardment and occupied it. The Georgian authorities publicly declared that they were beginning to 'restore constitutional order' in South Ossetia. (Their wording exactly mimicked the formulation used by Boris Yeltsin in 1994 when he decided to attempt to resolve the problem of Chechnya by military means.) Russia had no option but to react. In difficult circumstances, with the Russian armed forces not yet fully recovered from the chaos of the 1990s, President Medvedev and the army acted decisively. The Georgian troops were expelled from South Ossetia.

I was on holiday, but of course closely followed the information coming in. I suppose what incensed me no less than the adventurism of the Georgian President Mikheil Saakashvili in ordering the bombardment and attack on a peaceful city was the reaction of many politicians and most of the media in the West, which declared Russia the aggressor for 'attacking little Georgia'. One of the first to expostulate that 'Russian aggression must not go unpunished' was US Vice-President Dick Cheney, thought to be the main instigator of the US invasion of Iraq in 2003.

I responded immediately, first in a brief interview with ITAR-TASS, then in greater detail on 13 August with a major article in *Rossiyskaya Gazeta*. Meanwhile, Western politicians and journalists for the most part continued their mud-slinging. Only after many months was it finally acknowledged in the Tagliavini Commission's report, prepared under the auspices of the Organization for Security and Cooperation in Europe, that the hostilities had been started by Georgia.

I was fighting the Western spin on the incursion literally every day. Very soon, two of my articles were published in Russia and the international press and I was interviewed by Larry King of CNN and by French and Italian reporters. My article in *Rossiyskaya Gazeta* was published the following day in the *Washington Post*, and I was immediately approached by the *New York Times* and *International Herald Tribune*. I wrote for both of them, with my initial reaction and 'preliminary conclusions', and the Russian text was published in *Novaya Gazeta*. In the first article, I wrote:

> The events of the past week in South Ossetia can only cause everyone pain and concern. The deaths of thousands of people, with tens of thousands turned into refugees, the destruction of towns and villages is completely unjustifiable. It is a great tragedy and a warning to everybody.
>
> The roots of the present tragic situation can be traced back to a decision by Georgia's separatist leaders in 1991 to abolish the autonomy of South Ossetia. That placed a time-bomb under the territorial integrity of Georgia. Every time a succession of Georgian leaders attempted to impose their will by force, they only worsened the situation there and in Abkhazia, where the problems are analogous. Fresh wounds were added to old historical grudges.
>
> It would, nevertheless, still have been possible to normalize the situation and arrive at a political solution. For quite an extended period, relative calm was maintained in South Ossetia. A mixed peacekeeping contingent carried out its mission and Ossetians and the Georgians living beside them managed to find a common language.
>
> It is important to point out that all these years Russia's position has been recognition of the territorial integrity of Georgia, but the problem could only be resolved on that basis by peaceful means. There should be no other means of resolving issues in the civilized world. The Georgian leadership flouted that sacrosanct principle. What happened on the night of 8 August, the bombardment of the South Ossetian capital of Tskhinvali from rocket launchers designed for blanket strikes, simply beggars belief. It was impossible for Russia not to react. To accuse her of aggression against 'defenceless little Georgia' is not just hypocritical but inhumane.

It is now obvious that the Georgian leaders' decision to send in troops against a civilian population was an irresponsible escapade that has had tragic consequences for thousands of people of different nationalities. They could never have decided on such folly without believing they had the support and encouragement of a much greater power. The Georgian armed forces have been trained by hundreds of American instructors, and they have been buying cutting-edge military technology in several countries. This, together with promises of NATO membership, made the regime overconfident and gave them a sense of invulnerability that contributed to their hitting on the idea of a 'blitzkrieg' against South Ossetia.

In short, Mikheil Saakashvili was relying on unconditional support from the West, which the West had given him grounds to expect. The resolute repulsing of their military adventure should give food for thought not only to the Georgian government.

What is needed now is to put a stop as soon as possible to the fighting and get on with such vital matters as aid for the victims of a humanitarian disaster very little reported in the Western media, and rebuilding the towns and villages. No less important is to give serious consideration to the best ways of resolving this situation, one of the most volatile in the Caucasian region, which is an area that requires extremely sensitive handling.

I said at one time that the solution to the problems of South Ossetia and Abkhazia was to establish a federation with broad autonomy for the two republics. This idea met furious opposition, especially in Georgia. Later, attitudes changed, but after the present tragic events even that solution would be difficult to achieve.

Memories and pain are hard to bear, and even more difficult to cure. That is only possible after lengthy treatment, involving thoughtful dialogue and completely excluding the use of force. Similar conflicts in Europe and beyond have taken decades to be resolved, and some have yet to be settled. They need not only patience, but also wisdom. The history and experience of peoples living together in the small states of the Caucasus are testimony that tolerance and cooperation can ensure lasting peace and the conditions necessary for life and progress. That is the main thing to remember.

We need political leaders who are fully aware of this and who will apply their energies not to developing military muscle, but to laying the foundations for lasting peace.

Of late, the standpoint of some Western countries has been unbalanced, particularly in the UN Security Council. From the outset that has undermined its ability to function effectively. By declaring the Caucasus, situated thousands of miles away from the American continent, an area of its 'national interests', the United States has made yet another mistake. Peace in the region is in everybody's interests, and elementary common sense requires recognition of the fact that Russia is bound to the Caucasus by shared geography and centuries of history. She is not seeking territorial expansion, but has unchallengeable grounds for declaring a legitimate interest in the area.

The international community might set a long-term goal of creating a system of regional security and cooperation that would prevent any such provocation in the future and the very possibility of crises like this. Establishing that kind of system would be extremely difficult, and could be achieved only by agreement among the neighbouring countries. Powers outside the region might facilitate it, but only if they adopted a balanced and objective approach. Geopolitical games are dangerous, and not only in the Caucasus. That is one further lesson that needs to be learned from recent events there.

My second article, continuing my analysis and conclusions, generated a lot of comment, both on the *New York Times* website and in letters.

Russia was dragged into this crisis. She could not stand idly by.

The acute phase of the conflict, caused by Georgian troops attacking the South Ossetian capital Tskhinvali is behind us, but it is simply impossible to erase from memory the dreadful images: the salvos of rockets raining down in the night on a peaceful city, the barbaric destruction of entire neighbourhoods, the people killed in the cellars of their homes where they had taken shelter, the wrecking of ancient monuments and the graves of ancestors.

Russia did not seek this escalation. The domestic situation of the Russian leadership is perfectly stable and it has no need of any 'small, victorious war'. Russia was drawn into the crisis by Saakashvili's opportunism, in which he would never have indulged if he had not been receiving foreign support.

Russia could not stand idly by. She responded and an end was put to the aggression. President Dmitry Medvedev's cessation of hostilities was a wise and responsible step. During this time, the Russian president acted calmly, confidently and firmly. If anyone was hoping to see Moscow in a state of disarray, they were disappointed.

Now a change of tack is increasingly obvious; whatever the outcome, Russia is to carry the blame for worsening the situation in the region and the world. A full-scale propaganda attack has been mounted against her in the Western, and particularly American, media, without even a pretence of objectivity in the way the crisis was treated, especially at the beginning. The public in the West has been deprived of a full and objective picture.

Tskhinvali was in smoking ruins, thousands of people were fleeing for their lives from a city in which there were as yet no Russian troops, and already Russia was being accused of aggression, repeating the lies of an out-of-control Georgian leader.

Whether the West was aware of Saakashvili's plans is a serious question that has yet to receive a definite answer. At all events, training programmes provided to Georgian troops and massive arms deliveries did nothing to further the cause of peace, and much to foment war.

If this military adventure came as a surprise to the Georgian leader's sponsors, the situation is little better, since it suggests the tail is wagging the dog. How many compliments were lavished on Saakashvili: 'our ally, a democrat', who was helping in Iraq, etc., and now everyone, we Russians, the Europeans, and most importantly innocent civilians are suffering the consequences of the misdeeds of America's 'best buddy'.

Before rushing to judgements about the situation in the Caucasus, and even more before claiming influence there, you need to have at least some degree of understanding of the complexities of the region. There are Ossetians living both in Georgia and in

Russia. It is the same throughout the region: literally every country is a patchwork of different ethnicities, of peoples living side by side. It is unacceptable for anyone to be asserting that 'this is our land', or 'we are liberating our territory'. There are people living on that land, and we have to think about them.

It is pointless trying to resolve the problems of the Caucasus region by force. It has been tried often enough, and each time with disastrous results for the aggressor. A legally binding non-aggression treaty is essential, but Saakashvili has repeatedly refused to sign one. It is now clear why. If the West were to facilitate the adoption of such an agreement it would be a good deed well done. If it chooses a different course, condemns Russia and re-arms Georgia (which some American officials are already suggesting), a new crisis is inevitable that will have even worse consequences.

In recent days, US Secretary of State Condoleezza Rice, and indeed President Bush, have been threatening to isolate Russia. American politicians talk about excluding our country from the G8, closing down the NATO-Russia Council, and blocking our membership of the World Trade Organization. These are empty threats. In Russia, the question is in any case being asked what use all these institutions are to us if our opinion is simply ignored. Just to sit round a well-laid table and be lectured at?

The reality is that, in recent years, Russia has been confronted with one fait accompli after another: this is what we are doing about Kosovo; now we are withdrawing from the Anti-Ballistic Missile Treaty and deploying anti-missile systems in your neighbouring countries; now we are continuing to endlessly expand NATO. Live with it! And all that to the accompaniment of a lot of sweet talk about 'partnership' that is no more than a smokescreen. Who is going to put up with that sort of thing?

There are calls now in the United States for a 'review' of relations with Russia. I think the first thing in need of review is this way of talking down to Russia, ignoring her views and interests. Our countries are well able to develop a serious agenda for cooperation, in deeds rather than just in words. I believe many Americans and many Russians know that. It is time for the politicians to catch up.

A Bipartisan Commission on US Policy towards Russia has recently been established under the co-chairmanship of former

Senator Gary Hart and Senator Chuck Hagel. Its members include some influential people and, judging by its published mandate, they understand what Russia is and how important it is to build a constructive relationship with her.

The Commission has stated that it will produce recommendations 'to advance American national interests effectively in relations with Russia'. If they think only about that, no good will come of the initiative. If, however, they take account of the interests of their partner, common security interests, and add the necessary dose of sober realism, the way may be opened to rebuilding trust and worthwhile cooperation.

Needless to say, I could hardly turn down an invitation from my old friend Larry King, the most authoritative American talk show host. I greatly appreciated his willingness to give me an opportunity of replying to the flood of lies and accusations being made against Russia. I naturally expressed my arguments more emotionally in the interview than in articles for the press and, to judge by the many responses it produced, that made an impression on his viewers.

I particularly valued a letter from former US Ambassador to the USSR, Jack F. Matlock:

> ... We are appalled at the way the press is handling the current confrontation between Georgia and Russia. President Gorbachev's interviews and op-ed articles have been important in drawing attention to the events of 1990–91, which lie at the root of much that has happened.
>
> I hope we can all work together to bring some sanity to the current international situation. Just when I had the feeling that we could soon move in the right direction on the nuclear issues, the situation in Georgia has intruded to make that difficult.[3]

---

[3] Jack F. Matlock Jr., Letter, 12 September 2008. Website of the Gorbachev Foundation; http://www.gorby.ru/en/presscenter/news/show_26114/. Accessed 21 August 2015.

Two weeks after the conflict, Russia recognized the independence of Abkhazia and South Ossetia. Was that the best solution in the circumstances? I had serious doubts at the time and still have today. It will now be even more difficult to find a solution to the political problem in Transcaucasia, but I can only repeat what I said then: responsibility for the tragic events of August 2008 and all their consequences lies with the then president of Georgia, Mikheil Saakashvili, and those who knowingly or unwittingly encouraged him to seek a military solution.

Ordeal by global crisis

Russia, and not only she, was soon to face another test of her resolve, a global financial crisis. When it broke, I was in the United States at the invitation of former President George Bush Sr. Literally on the day before I was to be awarded the 2008 Liberty Medal of the National Constitution Center, which he headed, news broke of the collapse of the Lehman Brothers financial services firm. It was not immediately clear that this was the beginning of a catastrophic collapse, but within two or three days the authorities and ordinary Americans realized that things were bad. It was perhaps the first time the Americans so openly shared their anxieties with us. Moreover, almost everyone pinned responsibility and their hopes on the state, or, as they say in America, the government. President George W. Bush had to cast aside neo-liberal dogma that 'the market will regulate everything' and agree with those insisting on emergency government intervention to prevent a collapse of the banking system.

We returned home in anxious mood. Ten years after the 1998 default, the Russian economy was facing a financial tsunami, which this time came not from Asia but from the very heart of the global financial system. It was certain to affect Russia.

When we got back, however, we found that the Russian authorities and many economists saw nothing all that alarming in what was happening. For several weeks after the start of the crisis, the predominant narrative was that Russia had little to fear and would even be something of an island of stability, a 'safe haven' during the storm. That was the view expressed by Prime Minister Putin at a meeting of the Valdai Club of foreign experts.

I wanted to gain a clearer understanding of the situation and how great a threat it posed. On 29 October, jointly with the National Investment Council, we convened a round table at the Moscow School of Economics. The discussants included influential economists, financial analysts, parliamentarians and journalists, all of whom were agreed that there was going to be no safe haven. Academician Alexander Nekipelov said the crisis had resulted from a huge market failure in assessing and managing risk. The authorities did recognize, if not immediately, that doing nothing was not an option and set to work to deal with the crisis. But how appropriate were their actions? Those at the round table proposed a variety of measures, from supporting the liquidity of the banking system and refinancing mortgages to assisting small and medium businesses and taking social security measures. The general mood can be summarized as a recognition that testing times were ahead.

Economic indicators for the last months of 2008 wholly confirmed that view. In mid-December, the Ministry of the Economy acknowledged that production in Russia was in a decline that would last for, at best, six months. That was, by definition, a recession. 'I fear that two quarters will not see the end of it', the deputy minister said in an interview. Talk of a safe haven increasingly gave way to talk of falling off a cliff.

A group of economists and public figures invited me to participate in an anti-crisis initiative. We expressed our concern in a memorandum released at a press conference at the Interfax agency.

> There is a grave danger that in the very near future the financial crisis will lead to even greater social stratification, a substantial increase in the risk of poverty for the majority of the population, and a significant weakening of the middle class. ...
>
> Increasingly, the impression is that the authorities have no strategy for overcoming the crisis. 'Firefighting' measures are having no effect and financial resources allocated not infrequently disappear into the sand or into someone's very specific pocket. It is plain that

Russia has no modern crisis management capacity or open and effective decision-making methods.

Fifty billion dollars are being used to repay the foreign debts of corporations belonging to Russia's richest citizens, many of whom are continuing to make active use of tax avoidance schemes on their profits earned in Russia. This is money that could be invested in Russia to have an economic and social impact.

More than a trillion roubles has been transferred on deposit to the three largest state-owned banks, and a short time later a further 950 billion roubles was issued as a loan.

Access to these funds is, however, restricted to a small number of beneficiaries. There is no answer to the question of what has happened to the first tranche, for the simple reason that the government has not publicly asked it. There is every reason to suppose that the financial resources issued to the banks have not been passed on to businesses, but are being exploited for speculative refinancing, buying up dollars and the export of currency abroad.

There has also been no system to decisions about protecting the public from the crisis and its repercussions.

It was not enough to confine ourselves to criticism, and the memorandum contained specific proposals.

The first serious anti-crisis measure should be a comprehensive analysis of the domestic causes of the crisis, and public discussion of a draft national anti-crisis programme on an alternative, democratic basis.

This programme could stipulate a set of urgent economic and social measures, of which the following are top priority:

- devising a set of urgent measures to support socially vulnerable segments of the population;
- a change of policy on foreign borrowings;
- support for the rouble and a fight against inflation using all available measures;
- increased support of exports and damping down of imports;
- a freeze on the prices charged by natural monopolies;

- introduction of anti-monopoly policies;
- reduction of state administrative expenditure;
- establishment of a reliable system of national insurance against redundancy;
- urgent measures to reduce levels of corruption.

We proposed uniting the efforts of professional economists and representatives of various civil society initiatives to analyse the situation and formulate the policies needed by the economy and society as a whole. We hoped our initiative would lead to the emergence at all levels of other independent public initiative groups to combat the crisis, because, 'a government cut off from society is incapable of finding optimal policies on its own; it is impossible to come through the crisis without active public involvement and increased confidence'.

Decisions were needed that provided answers to the most acute problems of the present day, and at the same time laid a foundation for the development of Russia for years into the future. Such decisions, the supporters of the Public Anti-Crisis Initiative argued, could not be arrived at in private by a narrow circle of 'officially approved experts'.

That approach still seems correct to me. It may be asked what use such public initiatives are, since the government did ultimately deal with the crisis, Russia avoided major social disturbances, and now economic growth has, after a fashion, resumed. Perhaps that is how it should be and outsiders should not importune busy people with their unwanted advice.

I cannot agree. Take a look at the price Russia paid for getting out of the crisis. In terms of the decline in production and expenditure of accumulated reserves, Russia was one of the most severely affected countries. Brazil, India and China, our partners in BRIC, and most developed countries of the West avoided any similarly severe contraction of GDP. The worst of it was that the opportunity was missed of combining the firefighting and other measures needed to overcome the crisis with resolving the larger issue of developing and modernizing the economy, enabling it to move from dependence on natural resource exports to something more innovation-based.

Some of our recommendations the government did take on board. Vladimir Putin later several times repeated that a very important aspect had been adopting measures to support the population through the crisis. That, of course, was totally absent from the original announcement of the government's plans and was something we urged on them. Unfortunately, many of our other proposals were ignored, and in particular the recommendation of a price freeze for the 'natural monopolies' (privatized utilities and the like), and intensifying the fight against corruption. That was a pity. Yet again, the addressing of issues vital for developing the Russian economy was put on hold.

It was no simple matter for Dmitry Medvedev, occupying the post of president, to make his mark as an independent politician and unconditional national leader. He was immediately battered by the fall-out from the global financial crisis and the conflict with Georgia. Simultaneously, people were waiting to see how Medvedev's presidency would turn out. Would it just be more of the same policies, or would Russia take new steps in the direction of becoming a modern society? Observing the president's actions, I concluded that the desire for continuity was predominating. One could sympathize with the predicament of a young politician who did not want to 'break the furniture' or charge like a bull in a china shop into such a challenging environment. Before taking particular decisions on matters of detail, you need first to be comfortable that you understand their overall context. That is a principle I have always considered crucial.

Together with Dmitry Muratov, the editor of *Novaya Gazeta*, I met President Medvedev at his invitation early in 2009. As soon as we arrived, he said he wished to take the opportunity of offering his condolences to the editorial staff of *Novaya Gazeta* in connection with the murder of our journalist, Nastya Baburova. This brazen outrage was duly investigated and the ultra-nationalistic killers were sentenced to long terms of imprisonment. Medvedev supported the idea of a memorial to the victims of Stalinist repression. We talked about the current state and future development of society in modern Russia and the situation of journalism.

During our conversation, and in his speeches, Dmitry Medvedev expressed important ideas about the need to move to an innovation-based economy, freeing business from bureaucratic shackles and promoting younger officials. These words were not, however, followed up by the establishment of the necessary machinery and strengthening of democratic institutions. The big problems of a poorly developed political party system, the subservient role of parliament and the judicial system, and corruption all remained unresolved.

In the president's entourage and among his main advisers, the tone soon began to be set by the likes of Vladislav Surkov and Gleb Pavlovsky, who promoted the concept of 'sovereign democracy'. At least we did not hear that particular collocation from the president or prime minister, but the inculcation of the expression in the public mind was undertaken with great zeal. I was often asked about it at the time. A correspondent of *Newsweek* once said: 'Please give us your attitude towards this concept. You are, after all, the father of Russian democracy.' I laughed it off by remarking that I was already a great-grandfather. Joking apart, I was very concerned about how the concept of democracy was being emasculated. In the interview I said:

> There either is democracy or there isn't. When a democratic system is being created, a great deal of effort is required to ensure that it grows, matures, takes root, to ensure that all institutions are free and act effectively, and that there is no bias in favour of the executive branch.

I saw no sign of any such efforts being made.

Russian society has no longstanding tradition of people organizing themselves, of forming associations to resolve problems at all levels, from the grassroots to the national. The first shoots of that do appear, but attempts are immediately made to try to crush them. Even in the most favourable conditions, it is a slow process.

In the interview I also said:

> People are afraid that things may get even worse. They do not want to rock the boat, but the new authorities should not delude themselves. People want democracy, and the polls show it. In order to continue moving towards democracy, we need not only mobiliza-

tion of civil society, but also a willingness on the part of the regime to encourage the formation of genuine political forces.

It is all there in the electoral system. What is supremely important is that there should be no electoral fraud, that genuine candidates should be put forward, that there should be competing manifestos, people and parties.

That, however, was the last thing the Kremlin's political fixers wanted, and their influence was visibly increasing.

Defending the credo of Perestroika

For me and the Gorbachev Foundation, the beginning of 2010 was a time for marking the 25th anniversary of the beginning of Perestroika. It was not a matter of just organizing the usual sort of junket. We could see that a political battle royal was being waged around Perestroika, and that it was turning nasty.

For the anniversary, the staff of the Gorbachev Foundation published a volume of almost 1,000 pages of documentary evidence about the foreign policy of Perestroika. In *Otvechaia na vyzov vremeni* [*Responding to the Challenge of the Times*], there were published for the first time records from the Foundation's archive of my conversations and negotiations with foreign politicians, supplemented by records of discussions in the Politburo of the CPSU's Central Committee and other materials.[4] This unique publication makes it possible to judge what principles guided us as we established a new course in international relations. It answers many questions that are still the subject of dishonest speculation on the part of unconscientious commentators. These go out of their way to ignore the Foundation's publications because they find it more convenient, when trying to discredit Perestroika, to confine themselves to fabrications and innuendo.

In March 2010, the book was launched at an international conference in the Foundation. It was highly praised by the Russian and foreign experts, researchers and public figures present.

---

[4] *Otvechaia na vyzov vremeni. Vneshniaia politika perestroiki: dokumental'nye svidetel'stva*, M.: Ves' mir, 2010.

We were preparing another international conference on the foreign policy of Perestroika, planning press conferences and speeches, meetings with students, and editing a collective monograph, *Russia-2010: Russian Transformations in the Context of Global Development*.[5] This was a joint project between the Gorbachev Foundation, the New Eurasia Foundation and the Moscow School of Economics.

The book, to which I contributed a preface, was written by leading scholars from the Russian Academy of Sciences who had been working fruitfully with the Foundation for many years: Vladimir Baranovsky, Dmitry Furman, Viktor Kuvaldin, Yevgeny Gontmakher, Alexander Nekipelov and Vladimir Petukhov. Their views do not coincide in every respect, but we were not striving for unanimity.

I wrote in the preface:

> I was often asked, and still am, whether I would have embarked on reform if I had known then everything we know today. My answer is invariably that things could not go on as they were: the reforms were essential. ... At the same time it is perfectly fair to ask whether it would have been possible to extract ourselves from the Soviet system with much less upheaval. I believe it would.

These were considered judgements, and in the course of answering people's questions at meetings, and in dozens of interviews, I defended them and the credo of Perestroika. I spoke very frankly. Here is an excerpt from an interview I gave *Metro*, a Russian newspaper with millions of readers:

Metro: Was it difficult to foresee all the consequences?
MG: Yes, although in general it was clear enough what was coming. We were probably insufficiently experienced. Nobody had ever made the transition from communism to capitalism before.

---

[5] *Rossiia-2010. Rossiiskie transformatsii v kontekste mirovogo razvitiia*, M.: Logos, 2010.

Metro: A lot of people blamed you for the difficulties our country had to experience. What helped you not to break under the weight of accusations from all sides?

MG: It was hard, but if a person lacks physical, intellectual and moral stamina, he is not cut out to govern a country like ours. I had the stamina both to lead the country and, subsequently, not to be broken.

Metro: How do you feel about people who criticize you?

MG: They may have a point. They are welcome to do so.

In early March, we launched a Foundation report, *Breakthrough to Freedom and Democracy*, which a team of the Foundation's staff had prepared on my initiative.[6] Looking now at the photo of the launch, I recognize many journalists, but also many who paved the way for Perestroika and were active in implementing it.

In April, I had a meeting with the students at Moscow State University, my alma mater. The rector, Viktor Sadovnichy, attended, and students came from the philology, philosophy, law, political science, journalism and global processes faculties. They asked a lot of questions, which I answered for over an hour and a half.

One of the students asked whether democratization is an inevitable tendency in the development of mankind. Is the desire for political and personal freedom an aspiration common to all human beings? What is the foundation of civil society? 'Those are good questions,' I responded.

On your first question, yes, democratization is inevitable, and essential. In the last quarter of the twentieth century, as a result of democratic processes, partly as a result of Perestroika, authoritarian regimes in dozens of states left the stage.

One must, though, particularly if you are a researcher, be honest, observant and take all the facts into account. One fact is that in many countries democracy is being severely tested, and in

[6] *Proryv k svobode i demokratii. Doklad k 25-letiiu Perestroiki*, M.: Gorbachev Foundation, 2010.

some of them there is already a move away from democracy again. That has been and is happening in Russia. In our country we are living through a period of transition.

I think that in terms of our present transition to democracy, we are no more than halfway there. Democratization is one thing, and democracy another. It is one thing when you have a firmly rooted democracy with functioning institutions, but a process of democratization could take 100 years. We are still far away from being able to say we have democracy.

As regards the quest for political and personal freedom, that is a wholly understandable question. A lot has happened, and recent events in our country have shown that you will have to fight for political rights and personal freedoms. These matters have not yet been fully resolved.

Another question: 'When you began Perestroika, what result were you expecting to see? Has much of it been achieved?' 'A lot has been achieved,' I responded.

I am often asked whether Perestroika was defeated. I do not know whether you will agree with me, but my answer is that the process of Perestroika has not failed. I think the politicians, and primarily the main perpetrator of Perestroika (I hope that does not make me sound too arrogant), did fail personally, as politicians. Nevertheless, what Perestroika caused to happen in Russia, and is still causing to happen, is seen around the world as the most important event of recent decades.

The 25th anniversary of the beginning of Perestroika also provoked attacks on it and, of course, me, especially after I confirmed my unflattering opinion of processes currently taking place within our politics. Dmitry Muratov and I talked about this in an interview for *Novaya Gazeta*:

DM: Mikhail Sergeyevich, after your statements in *Novaya Gazeta* and on Radio Free Europe that United Russia has begun to look like an inferior copy of the CPSU, Internet trolls declared war on you: 'Perestroika was a betrayal of the

16 Irina Gorbacheva-Virganskaya, vice-president of the Gorbachev Foundation, Moscow, 7 April 2005. Photo: Viktor Goryachev.

17 Mikhail Gorbachev, Vladimir Putin and Viktor Surikov, head of
the administration of Kronshtadt, St Petersburg, April 1994.
Photo: Yu Chernin.

18 Meeting with President Vladimir Putin, the Kremlin, Moscow, 10
August 2001. Photo: Press Service of the President of the Russian
Federation.

19 Conference of the Social
Democrats Russian political
movement, St Petersburg, 10
August 1999.

20 Joint theory and practice
conference of the United Social
Democratic Party of Russia,
Moscow, 2001.

21 Inaugural congress of the United Social Democratic Party of Russia,
Moscow, 24 November 2001.

22 Interview for Echo of Moscow radio with Editor-in-Chief A.A. Venediktov, 1996.

23 Mikhail Gorbachev, Irina Gorbacheva-Virganskaya and Editor-in-Chief Dmitry Muratov at the offices of Novaya Gazeta, 2000.

24 Inaugural meeting of the Civic Dialogue Forum, Gorbachev Foundation, 15 September 2010. Photo: Dmitry Belanovsky.

25 Press conference at the Gorbachev Foundation, 2010.

26 *Book signing at the Non-Fiction Book Exhibition, Moscow, 28 November 2008. Photo: A. Sharoukhov.*

27 *The launch of the first five volumes of the* Collected Works, *28 November 2008. Photo: A. Sharoukhov.*

28 *The 'Mikhail Gorbachev: Perestroika' exhibition, Manezh, Moscow, 24 January 2011. Photo: Dmitry Belanovsky.*

29 Mikhail Gorbachev and President Dmitry Medvedev of the Russian Federation, after presentation to Mikhail Gorbachev of the Order of St Andrew the First-Called, The Kremlin, 3 May 2012. Photo: Press Service of the President of the Russian Federation.

30 *Speaking at 'The Man Who Changed the World' charity gala concert, the Royal Albert Hall, London, 30 March 2011.*

31 *Irina Gorbacheva-Virganskaya, Ksenia Gorbacheva and Anastasiya Virganskaya at the celebration of the eightieth birthday of Mikhail Gorbachev, 2 March 2011, Moscow. Photo:* Novaya Gazeta.

Motherland', 'Gorbachev danced to the tune of the CIA'. How do you react to this latest storm around your person?

MG: With full awareness that hirelings are being paid money to perform in this way. They should be grateful to me for enabling them to earn their crust of bread. This is a sign of fear. Ordinary people are increasingly becoming involved in the country's affairs. There is a new social climate, people are coming back to normal values. That sticks in the throat of powerful monopolists.

They are scared to death of people having freedom, of a democratic press, of a society emancipated from fear and censorship. Their behaviour might come under scrutiny! The individuals who muscled in on political (which for them is the same as economic) power are defending their ill-gotten gains, in part with all this squawking on the Internet. It is worth adding that our so-called ruling elite takes all the benefits of democracy for itself (the market economy, open borders, etc.), while trying to explain what a terrible thing democracy is for ordinary people. But now people have wised up to them.

DM: In other words, you are not perturbed by these social network attacks?

MG: Well, of course they need to vilify me because they are corrupt from top to toe, and democracy is a very rigorous form of government, which requires a regular turnover of rulers and observance of the law, and does not allow anyone a monopoly on power. ...

Corruption can only be overcome through democracy and an independent judiciary, through society being in a position to know everything about those governing it. That is why they are running scared and attacking anyone who stands for freedom.

DM: Our longstanding dispute: what makes you so sure 'society' wants freedom, that it loves democracy more than a strong hairy fist?

MG: Oh-oh! In a minute we're going to talk ourselves round to the theory that Russia is not ready for democracy. The fact is that we never tried it properly before we started to back off. We need to defeat corruption. We need a rejuvenated electoral system, a change in how the votes are counted, to eliminate ballot-stuffing!

The state authorities at all levels are trying to fraudulently hold on to their top jobs, discrediting the very idea of elections in their own interests. Restricting democracy is restricting the right of people to exercise influence over the government and change life for the better. What other means do people have? Attending protest rallies? The authorities have made it far from easy to hold demonstrations.

DM: The chief of police in Moscow has already recently proposed imprisoning people for 15 days for participating in unsanctioned street protests.

MG: Well, yes – in the USSR when they ran out of arguments they tried to keep life cosy by allowing the security services to imprison dissidents in psychiatric hospitals. They had to stop that in the end.

You cannot allow yourself to be afraid of the people. This lot are scared of their own people and try to hem them in. Why are they scared? Because they know that if democracy starts working in this country, there is a lot they will have to answer for.

DM: And lose office.

MG: At the very least. ...

We have to learn to live in a globalized world, and you cannot be part of it with authoritarian methods. I cannot, and never will, agree with those who distrust the people. That is just a cover for their horror at the realization that public accountability will destroy their corrupt dealings. The state authorities cannot be in charge of their own political future. That is a dead end.

Disturbing trends

The year 2010 was event-filled, including a number of trips abroad, but the main focus of my attention is always what is happening in Russia. In March, the country was shocked by another terrorist outrage, the explosion in the Moscow Metro. I issued a statement:

It is completely obvious that those behind this inhuman act intended to spread panic and intimidate people and the authorities. I am certain they will fail. It would be a mistake to react blindly to this provocation or to appear distraught for even a moment. On the contrary, all of us, both the authorities and society as a whole, must be resolute and take whatever measures may be necessary to block the possibility of villainous terrorist attacks.

There was concern at attempts to use the forthcoming 65th anniversary of victory in the Second World War as part of the creeping rehabilitation of Stalin. The advertising committee of the mayor of Moscow's office decided to display posters with his portrait in Moscow. A reporter from Interfax asked me for my reaction. I replied:

Of course, you can't just overlook facts, and it is a fact that Stalin played a role in the war. I think, though, that we are now fully informed about him, and what was done and how is something that should be written about objectively in textbooks and more generally. If Moscow is suddenly covered in advertising hoardings depicting Stalin, a lot of people will be, to say the least, surprised and baffled. Stalin was, after all, responsible for a lot of mistakes, especially immediately before the outbreak of war and in its initial stages.

Yes, we won the war, but the sacrifices our people made to achieve that victory are a national tragedy from which it will take us a long time yet to recover.

There were disturbing events in the summer also. Again, an interview for *Novaya Gazeta*:

DM: Mikhail Sergeyevich, a hot summer but no shortage of political developments: a mysterious spy scandal, attempts to give the FSB additional powers, aspirations to gain control over the Internet, constant hassle for the protest rallies on the 31st of each month [in defence of Article 31 of the Constitution guaranteeing the right of peaceful assembly], the statement by members of the government about raising the retirement age, and more. You must agree, life seems full of contradictions: on the one hand, entirely proper remarks about the need for modernization; on the other, tightening of the screws, the attempt to control everything, as if the security top brass are getting ready to impose emergency measures.

MG: There is indeed serious evidence of conflict between the state authorities and Russian society beginning to manifest itself. Human rights are ... no longer regarded by most people as something abstract and foreign: people are remembering their rights to medical care, education and housing and are beginning to look for ways to assert them. Pointed questions are being asked about social justice. 'Are the authorities with us or do they live in a different country?' That is what is really getting people agitated.

DM: And do you believe it is possible to continue dialogue? Or are we going back to: first send in the riot police, after which you can put your teeth back in and we'll talk?

MG: Dialogue is indispensable, both for the people and for the state authorities. There is no getting away from that.

It is wrong to separate people out according to their political ideas: 'These young people in the youth movement are a mainstay of the regime, but those others in the awkward squad are nothing to do with "us" and we will just steamroller them!' Some things are more important than ideology: the law and justice are above everything else. Separating society into those who are with us and those who are against us is the royal road to purges and prison camps. The state authorities are in a quandary, and that is pushing them towards mindless use of force.

DM: Are they in a quandary or do they, forgive the expression, not give a toss?

MG: No, they are in a quandary. They are unable to get dialogue going. They are tempted to declare that all those who oppose them are 'enemies'. When you drive somebody out of social and political life, you unbalance the system, and that inevitably leads to a succession of unmanageable social conflicts.

DM: But how can anyone make themselves heard in public or political life when it has all been flattened?

MG: That is precisely why, if society is not to explode, we need a new policy. We hear the authorities making the right noises about modernization, and the courts and freedom. They need to discuss this with the public and get their support, not just silence them. Otherwise there will be nobody to defend these ideas. Only society can defend them, civil society, not the bureaucracy.

On the whole, the current elite of appointees in power are yes-men. They are not material for modernizing Russia. They will filibuster it out of existence, or more likely steal all the funding first. These are the wretched results of forming the present elite on the basis of geographical, professional and commercial affinity.

DM: What do you propose, Mikhail Sergeyevich? Import a new elite duty-free? Create a new party?

MG: We couldn't create a new party. They wouldn't allow it. ... We need to create a new democratic forum. Without delay.

DM: How is that different from a party?

MG: No. It needs to be a non-party movement which, on behalf of the public, can represent their opinion and influence the government. A new, independent partner of government and society, representing the public's interests. Something the state authorities will not be able to ignore.

DM: Why not?

MG: It is in the Federation Council and the State Duma that seats are dished out or simply sold. This forum will be a gathering of authoritative, incorruptible leaders: it will be impossible to ignore them or not to listen to them.

I would like newspaper readers, Internet users and all serious-minded citizens to respond and discuss this proposal. I would like them to nominate leaders, people who might become members of this forum, people who could form a founding group and who, most importantly of all, could formulate the programme the forum might propose to the public and government. The forum should be assembled without party encumbrances, without permissions 'from above', without any knocking knees, within the framework of the Constitution rather than of sham democracy, in order to get away from coups d'état and police-state repression. In short, for genuine dialogue for the benefit of the country.

An Internet portal for the Civil Dialogue Forum was established shortly afterwards, and in September it held its inaugural meeting. It was attended by the businessman Alexander Lebedev; the chairwoman of the Moscow Helsinki Group, Lyudmila Alexeyeva; human rights activist Sergey Kovalev; the head of the Foundation for the Defence of Glasnost, Alexey Simonov; the co-chairman of Solidarity, Boris Nemtsov; the editor of *Novaya Gazeta*, Dmitry Muratov; social and political activist Vladimir Ryzhkov; vice-president of the Russian Union of Industrialists and Entrepreneurs, Igor Yurgens; the Moscow City Council ombudsman for children, Yevgeny Bunimovich; and other public figures. There was widespread interest, and at first the initiative went fairly well.

In October, we issued a statement about the problems of Russian education:

> In 2010, in connection with the passing of a law, 'On the legal status of publicly funded institutions', the problem of education became one of the main focuses of controversy in Russian society. There was strong criticism from representatives of political parties, the Orthodox Church, specialists and the public at large. The law, which, judging by official statements, was seen as central to reforms for modernizing and raising the standards of education, was, in effect, rejected by Russia's citizens.
>
> They rightly saw in the new law an attempt, under the pretext of transferring education to a free market basis, to do away with the all-important principle of 'free and universally accessible preschool, basic general and secondary vocational education'. In recent months, the situation has been aggravated by attempts to modernize the unitary act 'On Education', which encompasses all educational institutions in the Russian Federation, from nursery education right up to the universities. The new project has again raised a storm of protest.

We supported President Dmitry Medvedev's initiative instructing the Ministry of Education to conduct public hearings on the draft law and offered to organize a discussion of the current state of education in Russia and make proposals for amending it, also within the framework of the Forum. Most importantly: 'The Coordinating Council states that unconstitutional abuses are not acceptable and that the newly adopted laws on education must be revised to accord with the Constitution.'

I have to admit that the Civil Dialogue Forum stalled at this point. There were several reasons. First, the following year was difficult for me. My health began to fail and I had to spend too much time doing the rounds of doctors and hospitals. Second, those who had initiated the forum with me proved unable to get themselves organized and settle down to tenacious, purposeful work. It is an old Russian weakness, a national disease, if you like, that undermines many worthy projects. Finally, in 2011 the Russian political class was obsessed almost to the exclusion of all else by the question of how the 'presidency problem' would be resolved. The elections were due to be held in March 2012, but everybody was aware that out of sight of the rest of the world a power struggle had already begun.

My 80th birthday

In 2011 there was, of course, no escaping the fact of my 80th birthday. To tell the truth, I could hardly believe I had lived to be so old. I recalled that Raisa and I found it impossible to imagine being old: 70 seemed an incredible age, and she did not make it even to 70.

For myself, I felt I had somehow just to cope with being this age, to recognize the reality, celebrate it, of course, and then move on. I did wonder whether a fuss really needed to be made, and admitted to a reporter from ITAR-TASS that I would have liked to go somewhere quiet, celebrate my birthday there in a close-knit circle of family and friends, and leave it at that. My friends, however, operating through my family, my daughter and granddaughters, persuaded me a more public celebration was called for.

The celebrations began already at the end of January 2011, when an exhibition, titled 'Mikhail Gorbachev: Perestroika', opened at the Manezh Central Exhibition Hall in Moscow. In Berlin, the German Chancellor Angela Merkel attended the opening of 'From the Family Album', an exhibition of photographs, and we had a friendly and meaningful talk.

On 2 March a gala dinner was held in Moscow to which we invited some 300 guests, including the 'absolutely most important citizens', the president and prime minister, although they were not able to fit it into their busy schedules. Those who did come, however, made the evening unforgettable. Friends who had worked with me all these years gave me a splendid present: a disk made in just ten copies of 'The Favourite Songs of Mikhail and Raisa Gorbachev'. It included two songs I recorded with Andrey Makarevich, 'Old Letters' and 'How Dark the Night'. Our other favourites were there too, performed by professionals: the Ukrainian 'I Marvel at the Sky', the romance, 'Misty Morning', 'Karelia', 'Two Riverbanks', 'How Young We Were', and others.

What touched me most, however, were the good wishes from my daughter Irina. She came up on to the stage with my granddaughters, Ksenia and Anastasia. Everyone there listened to her in complete silence.

You know I don't much care to follow what is written or said about you: it disturbs the memory and, at times, the lies are terribly hurtful. In the last months, though, with your 80th birthday approaching, I have read and listened to practically everything that has been written about you. With every fibre of my being I have relived your and our drama and the triumph of your, and hence of our, life.

It is 20 years now since you were president; those others, just as then, still know everything and the country is exactly where it is. Today, on your 80th birthday, by right of being the only person who has known you closely for over half a century, there are some things I want to say about you as a human being, and that means also about politics.

Our world, now global, is characterized by extreme political cynicism. Big politics is entirely subordinate to making profits, either by big business or directly by the state authorities. Where there are not already mature civil institutions, the prime objective of politics is power itself and personal enrichment. And, of course, spheres of influence. If we look around with open eyes, we observe how calmly, how cynically the unbelievably painful problems of entire countries and peoples are ignored: they are denied basic benefits and freedoms.

Why? Because any transnational corporation finds it a thousand times more agreeable and straightforward to reach agreement with any authoritarian and dictatorial regime, in effect, with just one or two people, than to have to deal with civil society, especially if a country has natural resources. In the early 1980s this general picture of the world was complicated by such factors as the political confrontation of two systems, the real threat of nuclear conflict, an unbridled arms race: the Cold War. The world was divided. In the Soviet Union itself, and to varying degrees in the countries of the 'socialist camp', a totalitarian regime denied its citizens many essentials but could have gone on existing for a long time to come.

And then you came and said that a politics that ignored fundamental human values, and first and foremost the right to live in dignity and freedom, was immoral. That was your personal belief, born of your nature as a human being, but you succeeded in using that conviction as the foundation of a foreign policy that truly changed the course of world history in the late twentieth century, and of transformations in your own country. In your own land you had to reckon with the reality of a country that had never known democracy or free choice, a country where all property was owned by the state, the dictatorship of the Communist Party, terrible shortages, with a real people that had long forgotten, if it had ever known, what freedom and the right to choose even were; and then, when everything kicked off, also with a real balance of political forces, which shifted and where the forms of confrontation became ever more extreme.

All those opposing you were agreed that you lacked determination, that you were insufficiently radical. Those on the right complained you were moving too slowly, those on the left that you were going too fast. They claimed you did not know, or were afraid, to adopt the correct position. Never in my life have I seen you frightened. In the heat of the struggle, none of them paused to reflect that to adopt one of the extreme options might violate your own human nature. You always looked for the true path to reform of our country between the extremes, but truth, like moderation, is elusive, and finding and keeping to that path is as difficult as walking on a razor's edge.

You sought consensus, the position that could unite citizens and nations and nationalities. Many jeered. What was this consensus? What were they supposed to do with it? Most damagingly, who needed it? I never waste my time on the plethora of obscure, muddled conspiracy theories that you were working to some secret plan. That just is not you. If you had wanted to be manipulating everything in secret, you could just have remained general secretary of the Soviet Communist Party. I still remember every outburst of radicalism in those years, every clash, because every time it grieved you profoundly, and us with you.

You never were naive, and I know that for a fact. They say you did not know the Russian people. What nonsense! You were born and bred in the midst of the people: you were hardly going to grow up in a state of rosy naivety. It is just that your knowledge did not alter your beliefs, and your faith in the ability of the people to change for the better if their circumstances changed. Everything went the way it did, the results were what they are; that was what people wanted. Every people made their choice in the light of perspectives that had opened up for them, made the best of new opportunities. Russia's path has proved long and arduous.

You have had the courage not just to stay in a country where you had effectively been deposed, where for years they have been trying to defame not only you, but your wife, where they even tried to represent you as the main culprit for the actions of the Communist dictatorship in the entire 70 years of its existence. Despite all that, you had the courage to carry on doing much work to the benefit of your country and all the people of the world. As a human being, you are far stronger and wiser than those who slander and presume to judge you.

We are proud of you. You are the root of our life in every sense, Your Excellency!

President Dmitry Medvedev invited me to the Kremlin, congratulated me warmly and announced I was to receive the highest award in Russia, the Order of St Andrew. I have to admit this was unexpected. I tried to express my emotions one year later when, on the eve of his departure from the Kremlin, the president presented me with the order.

Dear Dmitry Anatolievich,
I accept this highest award of the Russian state with emotion and gratitude.

My whole life passes before my eyes. I am not ashamed of what I have done. Of myself and those with whom a quarter of a century ago I decided to implement cardinal reforms, I can say in the words of Willy Brandt: 'We did our best.' We embarked on reform not for honour and glory, but because we understood how vitally Russia needed change. People deserved freedom. ...

I received many good wishes, both from Russia and abroad. George Bush Sr sent a good letter, and told the ITAR-TASS reporter there was nothing scary about being 80, and, as for Gorbachev, there was no question of him being old.

At the end of March a gala concert and charity evening was held at London's legendary Royal Albert Hall. To tell the truth, I am not enthusiastic about grand celebrations and had certainly never envisaged anything of the sort. What finally persuaded me was that the gala was to be a fundraising event for charity, at which 'A Man Who Changed the World' awards would be made.

Old friends and colleagues came, people I had known for a long time and others I had come to know more recently. There were speeches by Nobel Prize winners Shimon Peres and Lech Wałęsa; Ted Turner; the former French Prime Minister, Michel Rocard; the Governor of California, Arnold Schwarzenegger; and George Shultz and Bill Clinton sent video greetings. The concert could have extended over several nights.

We listened to my beloved Rachmaninov, performed by Andrey Gavrilov and the London Symphony Orchestra under Valeriy Gergiev; Dmitry Hvorostovsky sang, as did Shirley Bassey, Paul Anka, Andrey Makarevich and Time Machine, Igor Krutoy, Lara

Fabian, The Scorpions, and Turetsky Choir. The gala's presenters were Sharon Stone and Kevin Spacey, magnificent actors I know well and with whom to this day I enjoy friendly relations.

The new prize for a 'Man Who Changed the World', recognizing people who had not been awarded the Nobel Prize but had made a unique contribution to progress for the good of mankind, was awarded in the three categories of Perestroika, Glasnost and Acceleration. The winners were Sir Timothy Berners-Lee, the scientist who invented the World Wide Web; Ted Turner, who founded CNN and changed the face of television; and Kenyan engineer Evans Wadongo, who created the MwangaBora solar lamp which has brought light to millions of Africans.

At the end of the evening, it was time for me to speak. It was hard. I felt very emotional and a long, noisy day had taken its toll. I had to pull myself together.

I came out on to the stage and looked round the vast, crowded auditorium. It had been built by Queen Victoria in memory of her husband, Prince Albert, who died young. I remembered Raisa, and I said that this great hall was a monument to love. Thousands of people fell silent. I thanked the performers, guests and audience for a wonderful evening that had touched me deeply, and then invited them all to come back for my 90th birthday party. The hall exploded with applause. I felt they wanted to show their support for me, and that they believed the will to live, the desire to do good and continue to fight for what you believe in is stronger than ailments and illness.

Russian politics in a quandary

Meanwhile, Russian politics had not gone away. Politicians, journalists, colleagues, friends and acquaintances all wanted to know what I thought about the events unfolding one after another. The moment was approaching when the public needed to know who would be contesting the presidency, if, indeed, there was to be a contest.

I felt this touched on some much broader issues of Russian politics, and spoke out at every opportunity, in many interviews, including those in connection with my anniversary celebrations.

Lyudmila Telen, a journalist, commented:

On the threshold of his 80th birthday, Gorbachev does not mince
words or avoid questions, even if they are clearly not to his liking.
He is not just critical, he is almost irritated and untypically blunt
in his assessments. These are the assessments of someone who can
afford not to be intimidated and not to worry how others may
react.

'Just take a look at how the country's leaders are being chosen
nowadays', I said in her interview. 'You promote your pals,
people you studied with, people who lived on the same street,
who played football with you or whatever, and perhaps still
do. In other words, the main criterion is personal loyalty, old
acquaintance, friendly relations. I find that approach unacceptable. Totally!'

Lyudmila Telen counters, 'But friends do not betray you,
and in August 1991 you were betrayed by your immediate
entourage.'

MG: Well, does it not matter that these 'friends' are betraying
the Russian people? Helping themselves to everyone's property
and quietly moving money abroad? Instead of a fight against
corruption, we have a pretence, and what is the result? The
same pants, only back to front, as the saying goes.

LT: What is your main gripe against the current Russian state
authorities?

MG: They are taking too long to introduce democracy.

LT: Too long? You put that very mildly. Why do you think the
situation is as it is?

MG: Our rulers like to keep everything on manual control, and
to stay in peak physical condition they need to work out by
breaking democratic equipment.

LT: Why are the people who have come to power in Russia
far removed from what is commonly called the ideals of
Perestroika?

MG: Because they were not elected. Those who have come to
power were not elected in democratic elections and have no

mandate from democratic institutions. Since 1989 and 1990, when democratic elections were held for the first time in the Soviet republics, we have had no more free elections.

LT: But Vladimir Putin won in the elections. Even if we allow for a certain amount of fraud, there is no disputing the fact that a majority did vote for him, both in 2000 and in 2004.

MG: If the election campaigns had been more free, he would have been facing competition from a considerably greater number of representatives of the opposition. The elections would have been more full-blooded, and then it would be a completely different story, with a different political climate. Take those countries that do have a mature democracy. There will be several parties represented in parliament, none of them with more than 40 per cent of the seats, and those with most seats are obliged to negotiate with the opposition.

LT: Why do you think governments in Russian traditionally tend towards authoritarianism?

MG: It depends on who comes to power.

LT: On the individual?

MG: Yes, on the person, his personal qualities, his experience. What experience do ours have? Only of manual control. They are accustomed to keeping people in their place by fear. That is why I am now saying that our main problem, our number one problem, is that we need a revamped electoral system that would give people a real choice.

LT: The political situation in Russia seems unlikely to change any time soon. Would you care to predict how political events will unfold in Russia?

MG: No.

LT: Perhaps just for the next decade?

MG: No. The main thing right now is to get robust democratic procedures operating, and for them to disempower those who want to gnaw away at political freedom and property rights.

LT: Would you wish for Russia to have, for example, Vladimir Vladimirovich Putin elected president again in 2018?

MG: No. I think it is essential that we should all firmly agree that nobody should occupy that post for more than two terms.

LT: Do you see any prospect of genuine political competition in the 2012 presidential election?

MG: Not so far. So far the Russian elite is so obsessed with power ... The government is above God! First they get up to all sorts of things, then go to church, take some candles and pray to the Almighty to forgive them their sins. I do, though, have a sense that we already have a whole stratum in the population who will identify and put forward someone with a credible claim to become president.

LT: You must yourself have been tempted to try to hold on to power at all costs.

MG: Is it really so difficult to see that even during the Soviet period Gorbachev began delegating power, giving more and more of it to others? I think I did the right thing there. I am certain of it. That was my choice.

Here is another candid interview, where we started discussing the already impending presidential election. I gave it to *Kommersant*, another offspring of Perestroika. Stanislav Kucher asked me a lot of questions, both about Perestroika and about the current state of affairs. I made no attempt to duck them, and was even deliberately provocative.

SK: People think Medvedev should be the engine for reform. Mikhail Khodorkovsky said last year that Medvedev had become a symbol of reform, but not its engine. Now people are urging him to show some political will and get rid of Putin, one way or another. Legally, of course. Those against that idea say that then Medvedev should accept he would find himself in the role of Gorbachev, that the process he initiated would end up sweeping him off the political stage. If Medvedev starts the process, there is no guarantee the wave will not sweep away not only Putin, but him too, and in such a way that he would be forced to emigrate from Russia because he is a part of the system. What do you think about these parallels?

MG: In the first place, I think their regular and increasingly frequent remarks about coming together to talk and agree everything at the appropriate time testifies, at the very least, to a lack of humility on their part. They have no right to behave in that manner. They were elected by the Russian people and it is not for them but for the people, the electorate, to decide.

SK: That is what is supposed to happen, but not the way things are in reality.

MG: If it is what is supposed to happen, that is how they should behave.

SK: True, but they think they are going to decide.

MG: Who cares what they think. How do they think they will decide? They do, after all, face an election.

SK: Well, you know yourself how elections are conducted in Russia. Hardly anybody believes in fair elections any more.

MG: Well that is just not how it should be. It is something that concerns all of us.

SK: So what should be done, Mikhail Sergeyevich?

MG: We need a completely new electoral system, in which it should be firmly established that two terms is the maximum and that is that.

The arguments about the presidency continued. Some said Putin would stand, others continued to pin their hopes on Medvedev. I was asked to sign a letter to Medvedev urging him to declare his intention of running for a second term.

That was logical enough. After the amendment to the constitution (how easy it is for us to do that!), he could claim six years in office, which would be sufficient to pave the way for a serious move towards real democracy. It would see the formation of genuine, competitive parties, an even playing field for all candidates in the election campaign, introduce essential changes to the electoral system and, most importantly, create a sense of pluralism and genuine alternatives. I believe Dmitry Medvedev would have been all in favour of that, but I was not at all certain he had the will, tenacity and independence to go for it. In any case, I would have preferred to see, not this manoeuvring around which of the two, Medvedev or Putin, would 'get to be president', but a genuine contest, with the emergence of new candidates.

Of course, the loophole in the constitution, allowing a former president who had been in office for two terms to be back in office after a break, was a major flaw, and I suspect the oversight had been entirely deliberate. During my years in power and subsequently I had a very different approach to the issue. I thought, and still think, that the opportunity to constantly replace and renew the group in power is imperative in modern politics. When talking to journalists, I made no bones about it: failure to replace the state authorities took us back to the old ways. Putin's Petersburg team had run its course.

As regards the relationship between the president and prime minister, I was not in favour of trying to 'split the tandem'. I considered that, if they were genuinely working together in a coordinated manner, any such split would be downright harmful for the country. The difference in their approach to Russia's problems was nevertheless substantial and, with the passage of time, becoming ever more apparent. Getting back to normal in the summer after surgery on my back, I began drawing attention to this. In an interview with my old British friend, Jonathan Steele, the correspondent of the *Guardian*, I decided to call a spade a spade:

The president's plan for modernizing the economy, politics and other areas is all well and good, but his options are limited. A coalition with the democratic forces of civil society is essential.

I can see, though, that Putin is outplaying him. He is setting up all sorts of fronts, a so-called 'Popular Front'. I don't know how many of these fronts he will come up with, but it does indicate that he has little faith in what United Russia can achieve, and at least he is right about that. He can see that United Russia is incapable of winning on its own.

Again, what is going to be the mainstay of modernization? Vladimir Vladimirovich is calling for stability. He thinks we should maintain the status quo. We say, 'No! If you want to keep the status quo, where does modernization fit in?'

I went on to be even more explicit:

We need now to realize that we are facing a wave of social problems that will determine Russia's future, the situation in education, healthcare and other areas. If we cannot find solutions to these problems, Russia will not modernize. We need a different pro- gramme from that advocated by Putin.

I have criticized Putin for bumptiousness. I respect him as a political leader and a person, but I believe his current policies are an obstacle to progress.

The summer holidays were not yet over, but already debate was raging in Moscow over who it was going to be: Putin or Medvedev? Gradually, opinion was inclining towards Putin. I do not know how, ultimately, the decision was taken. Was there really an understanding from the outset, as Putin once hinted, that Medvedev was a 'caretaker president', or did that decision come later? That is not now particularly important. What is important is that the decision was taken without consulting the country's citizens. They, just like the 'political elite', were presented with a fait accompli. Evidently, Putin had more of a specifically Russian kind of political expertise and willpower.

There was one occasion in late 2010 when Dmitry Medvedev did demonstrate a strong will, and that was when he dismissed the mayor of Moscow, Yury Luzhkov. I knew Luzhkov quite well. At a difficult time for the country, after the August 1991 coup, he was one of the leaders of a Management Committee of the USSR Economy, and did a great deal to maintain essential supplies and keep the situation under control. He also achieved a lot as mayor of Moscow. For all that, Luzhkov was a living example of why no one should hold high office for decades. After becoming encum- bered by clannish ties, personal and family interests, and too many automatic, well-practised moves, a politician becomes incapable of resolving problems purely on the basis of the public interest. As time passes, the more those other interests encroach, and so it was with Luzhkov. My understanding is, however, that this is not why he was dismissed, but because he got involved rather too soon in the intrigues surrounding the presidency, openly and energetically making clear his support for Putin. Perhaps he knew or had heard something. Perhaps in his own way he wanted to thank Putin for not sacking him in the summer of 2010 when, during the forest fires that engulfed Moscow in smoke, Luzhkov failed to return immediately from his holiday. Whatever it was, he got on the wrong side of Medvedev. His dismissal was for personal, rather than sound political, reasons.

A new Era of Stagnation?

I have a different idea of the proper way of 'doing politics', and I expressed it in an article published on 21 September 2011 in two large-circulation newspapers, *Moskovsky Komsomolets* and *Novaya Gazeta*:

> The more I meet people, read, observe the way events are developing and the public mood, the more I sense a growing unease. Recognition that the state is being degraded and society demoralized is becoming widespread. ...
>
> Even many of those who recognize the need for change hope reform will come from above and are waiting for it to be delivered by the Kremlin. Are we still in this day and age relying on a reforming tsar rather than on our own strengths? Do we still look down on the people as cattle?
>
> Others call for 'gradual, evolutionary' change. I myself am an enemy of 'clean sweeps', but there are some changes that simply cannot be gradual. How, for instance, could you introduce the rule of law a step at a time? Would the protection of the law be extended first only to certain categories of the population? If so, to whom precisely? And in the meantime, what about the others: would they be in a grey zone? Or treated as second-class citizens?
>
> And how would you manage an 'evolutionary' introduction of the principle of political competition? Who would decide who was eligible and who was not?
>
> Reluctance to initiate reform or a desire to restrict it to half-baked changes are often claimed to stem not from a fear of losing power, but from a desire to avoid a new collapse of Russia. Instead, however, it is the lack of change that is threatening to create instability and jeopardize the country's future.
>
> The election campaign is under way and, already noisy and scandalous, is shaping up to be one more Potemkin Village with

false façades. The regime is not even trying to conceal its determination to shield itself from fair competition and ensure its self-preservation. For the rest of its life?

All this reminds me of the 1980s, but back then we mustered the strength to break through the iron hoop of unfreedom constricting society, and released an unprecedented surge of political enthusiasm. People marched with growing resolution, and their demands effectively came down to one slogan: 'This is no way to live!'

The leaders of the USSR recognized that the Soviet system was inefficient and blocking progress. We embarked on cardinal reforms, despite all the risks and dangers. We began dismantling the Communist Party's monopoly on power and organized the first genuine elections in Soviet history.

In short, Perestroika was the answer to the impasse of that time. For the first time in Russian history, people had an opportunity to express their wishes. Contrasting that with the current torpor of the political scene and our sullen public, those days look like an amazing triumph of democracy.

Alas, we, the then government and society as a whole, were unable to see Perestroika through and create a system based on political competition and the guaranteeing of freedom and transparency. Perestroika was halted, and in the 1990s the power of the state fell into the hands of people who, hiding behind a screen of democratic slogans, turned back the clock. Additionally, a new autocracy was bolstered by oligarchic capitalism with a tinge of criminality.

The 2000s, creating an illusion of stability and prosperity, were a period when Russia's natural resources were squandered.

The regime locked itself in a bunker and erected an impenetrable shield consisting of all manner of trickery, abuse of state administrative resources and hypocritical legislation that makes a change of regime impossible. Russia is being pushed back to the Brezhnev era, forgetful of how that period ended. People trust the regime less and less, are losing hope in the future, and are humiliated by poverty and deepening social divisions, unlike a celebrity set who are rolling in money.

Another five or six years of this and Russia is unlikely ever to be able to escape from this dead-end situation.

How is Russia to get out of it? It would be naive to imagine that economic reform alone will suffice. ...

We need to lay the foundations for a state and a system that will serve society and not vice versa. It will be the first time this problem has been solved in the history of Russia, and today nobody has a ready blueprint of how to do it. That is why a wide public debate is needed on how to build a new Russia.

Any such discussion was, however, the last thing the authorities of the Russian state wanted.

The Presidential 'Reshuffle' and the Duma Elections

Everything was settled. On 24 September 2011 a 'reshuffle' was announced at the Congress of United Russia, an event strongly resembling, and even surpassing, the choreographed congresses of the Brezhnev and perhaps, indeed, Stalin eras. Putin would be elected president and Medvedev would become prime minister. The Russian bureaucracy heaved a sigh of relief and responded ecstatically. After all, many of its members were fearful that a second term with Dmitry Medvedev as president might see changes in the direction of real democracy, and then their cosy careers would come to an end. Putin was a much better bet. Democratically minded citizens, on the other hand, felt they had been cheated and no amount of trying to finesse what had happened, like Medvedev claiming the reshuffle was 'legitimate both from a legal and moral point of view', caused them to change their minds. It did not change my mind either.

The first act in the scenario devised in the Kremlin were elections to the Duma on 4 December. The regime needed a predictable result and made its preparations accordingly. It brought into play every available power and method: the infamous 'administrative resources' of the state, sordid election-fixing techniques, control of the media. They put in place crude, brazen methods of outright falsification of the election results: ballot-rigging, fraud, bussing people around to 'vote early, vote often', and direct pressuring of voters. Assuming that everything would go according to plan, that a docile parliament would result and that the citizenry would shrug it all off as only what was to be expected, the regime was in confident mood. They thought everything was under control and failed to detect the tremors of social dissatisfaction.

I well remember how on 5 December, the day after the election, from early morning before the official results were declared, the regime's tame propagandists were trumpeting victory on the radio and television. If United Russia's share of the vote was admittedly somewhat lower than in the previous Duma election, the party still had a majority and that would allow the regime to feel secure in parliament. 'No need to change anything. We are doing everything just right.'

I have to confess that in the first hours after the election I felt the results would have to be considered water under the bridge and it would now be time to analyse the results and see how the balance of political power was distributed. Despite the bad electoral legislation, the unequal treatment of the candidates and the violations of democratic standards, I had voted in the election myself and urged others to do the same. Accordingly, we must accept the results. I was soon to have to abandon that stance.

When I arrived at the Foundation, I started checking to see how the declared results had been arrived at. Suddenly I was deluged with phone calls. Their common theme was outrage and alarm. Within a day, the picture was crystal clear. I was advised to look at videos on the Internet, which showed evidence of incredibly arrogant falsification and ballot-rigging. I looked at some and was shocked to the core! Then information began coming in that this had been massive and ubiquitous. So, my first impression was wrong and I needed to decide how I felt about what had been going on and what position I should now adopt. It did not take me long to conclude that it was impossible to accept the result of the elections. It was insufficient to demand a recount of the results in particular districts and polling stations: what was needed was an entirely new vote. Any other approach would show a complete lack of respect for the millions whose votes had been stolen and misrepresented.

As it happened, the first person to hear of my decision was Fiammetta Cucurnia, an Italian journalist. We have been acquainted for many years and she has my telephone number. She called me on 6 December. The previous evening demonstrations had begun in Moscow demanding annulment of the election results. I told her:

The government must admit that there have been numerous instances of falsification and ballot-rigging. In other words, the results do not reflect the will of the voters. After the criticism and protests at Chistye Prudy, it is clear there is a growing refusal to accept the way the votes have been counted in favour of United Russia. There is a firm conviction that, as the demonstrators are saying, Putin's party collected no more than 25 per cent of the vote, and certainly not 50. This is very serious. The Kremlin has come up against a red line. The situation is grave. There must be no aggravating of the confrontation, no further heightening of the tension. I am convinced that the prime minister and president must come up with an initiative to keep everything within democratic procedures. We have difficult decisions to take, major unavoidable changes to introduce, and that cannot be done without our citizens or against our citizens. Deceit destroys trust in the state authorities. That is why I consider it essential to annul the results of this vote and declare new elections.

I was one of the first to make that demand, and did not back down. This evoked a veritable squall of abuse. United Russia went on the attack, not shunning direct or indirect threats, declaring that Gorbachev had been responsible for wrecking the Soviet Union, was now trying to wreck Russia, and would do well to remember that the Russian people had so far let him off lightly! That gem came from the speaker of the State Duma, Sergey Naryshkin. This was the level of political culture in the higher echelons of the Russian state. If he was hoping to intimidate me, he was out of luck.

On 10 December, tens of thousands of Muscovites took to the streets in the most massive protest demonstration for many years, demanding annulment of the election results and the holding of new elections.

For fair elections!

In the days that followed, I defended my position in interviews on radio, for the news agencies and newspapers. The provisional score was reviewed in an interview for *Novaya Gazeta* on 23 December.

Dmitry Muratov: There is a protest rally on 24 December. What do you think, why will people be going there?

Gorbachev: I was hoping to ask you that question.

DM: I can tell you that all of us in the editorial office who were not involved in producing the current issue of the newspaper, and some who were, went to the meeting on Bolotnaya Square. They all had just one wish, I think, and that was to show that we are human beings, that we cannot be manipulated, and we are modern citizens of a modern country. ...

MG: I want to say once again, I am delighted with this stand by our citizens. And if they again try to intimidate us, they will fail. I am sure of that. Look at how many thousands of people came to Bolotnaya Square!

DM: The mood of the public has changed, don't you think? The sense of glumness has gone.

MG: Yes, the mood has changed. People are coming out of their despondency. Our time has not been wasted! We have been kicked about for Perestroika, they have tried to break us, called us every name under the sun, but now the link is being re-established with everything we began so altruistically, for which we took such risks. Freedom, personal honesty – the things we wanted.

We did not by any means succeed at everything; we did not see Perestroika through to the end, but today I'm amazed by the main ...

DM: The fact that the 'freedom gene' can be found in Russian people? It was inserted, and here it has reappeared a generation later?

MG: Absolutely! And that's that. Now they can't blame everything on the backwardness of a people who 'cannot be left to decide anything for themselves, do not know what is good for them, are happy as they are as long as they have vodka ...'. That is denigration of our people. I was very struck at Bolotnaya on 10 December by the fact that when these 100,000 people left, they took their rubbish with them. They left the square clean! There were provocateurs attempting to stir up trouble, but they failed. People quickly put them in their place. By the way, that is something to bear in mind for the future! That mischief, possibly on a larger scale, may be repeated.

DM: Do you think there may be plain-clothes troublemakers on Saturday, on 24 December?

MG: I think there may well be provocateurs, because civic activism is something a lot of people do not like.

DM: Will the trouble-making be instigated by the authorities or by the radicals?

MG: Tut-tut! How can you even think such a thing? The authorities provoke trouble? How can you be so ignorant, you, the editor of such a well-known newspaper, a well-informed citizen. You of all people should know that!

DM: Mikhail Sergeyevich, you were the first to say the results of these elections should be annulled. Do you stand by that?

MG: I am still staggered by what I saw and heard. That day and the following night I closely monitored everything that was going on. I heard everything that was being broadcast 'from both corners', and saw all that alchemy with the voting and vote-counting.

DM: We passed you a lot of documents too …

MG: That picture our press gave me really shocked me. Russian citizens had their right to vote stolen from them, and at just that moment, a wizard materializes. I refer to Churov, the chairman of the Electoral Commission.

DM: On the Internet he is being called the Churodey.[1]

MG: I can think of a few other names he could be called. He kept repeating, 'We will be holding the very fairest of elections.' He seems to have convinced himself of that and tried to get the public at large to believe it. I believe he managed to fool the president.

DM: You mean Churov was the hatchet that laid himself under Dmitry Medvedev's compass and threw him off course?

MG: You ask such difficult questions!

DM: What is so difficult about it? Medvedev, whom I greatly respect, suddenly turned up in charge of United Russia, and it

---

[1] '*Charodey*' is a wizard [translator's note].

was United Russia that was having all those votes attributed to it.

MG: I do not believe he knew everything that was going on. He does not yet have enough experience for that. You need to go through a lot, get bumps and bruises, and even wounds, before you understand quite how all that gets done. What was it he said exactly?

DM: He congratulated United Russia on getting over the threshold to be admitted to the Duma.

MG: But in the press he said, 'I have no comments or doubts about the elections.' At that point, I think Dmitry Anatolievich did himself no good at all.

DM: I feel sad about that.

MG: So do I. He just needed more time. Now he is in a difficult situation. People are laughing at him. Well, he will just have to learn to put up with that too.

DM: But to come back to your call to annul the election results. Does that still stand? Or is it already unrealistic?

MG: It stands! ...

DM: On Echo of Moscow radio and in *Novaya Gazeta* you said annulment of the election results should be initiated by the authorities, but they have refused. So where do we go from here?

MG: Frankly, I was looking for a way to hand the initiative to them, to let them do it themselves.

DM: But they have refused. The two weeks they were given by Bolotnaya Square have passed. Are you proposing to appeal to them again?

MG: I am not yet making any proposals. We have not reached that point. In the first place, those two weeks between 10 and 24 December have taught us many lessons.

DM: Like what?

MG: About Russia, about the regime, about society. Society is being renewed, it is changing!

DM: Can we take pride in it again?

MG: It has spoken!

DM: I was certainly proud of what I saw at Bolotnaya. What faces! I recognize them: those are our readers! I was so pleased.

MG: That is the first thing. We saw our own country, our own people. And again they were saying, 'This is no way to live!', with the people debarred from deciding the country's future because they are supposedly completely hopeless.

DM: Well, evidently Stanislav Govorukhin thinks this is just the right way to live. He agreed to head the election campaign of Vladimir Vladimirovich Putin.

MG: I can only express regret. I do not just respect him, I consider him a friend. He will have to sort all that out for himself.

DM: Still, what do you think people should do on 24 December?

MG: I think the most important thing is to link this with the campaign for the presidency.

DM: You mean, link the demand for the annulment of the Duma election results to the forthcoming presidential election?

MG: Let me explain: we can trust with our votes only those candidates who raise the question of annulling the Duma election results.

DM: 'Raise the question' or annul them?

MG: Annul them! Give a commitment to annul the results of the Duma elections. We cannot tolerate for five years a Duma elected in this manner.

DM: I have another question: who are these people who will come out again to the square to protest? In addition to the fact that these are free people who love their country and are protesting for Russia, who are they for you?

MG: A new generation. They are voters. They are already a powerful civic association of voters!

DM: With a lot of different views, not members of United Russia, but people with a constitutional human right to a fair election?

MG: I will say without any ifs and buts, those voters are patriots!

DM: The social networks – Facebook, for example – are voting for who should speak at the 24 December rally, and they are not choosing spokesmen for the current regime or the present opposition. The networks are preferring Leonid

Parfenov, Boris Akunin and Yury Shevchuk. Citizens, not politicians. Nobody trusts politicians, and not just those in power. Why?

MG: Because many politicians are not prepared to listen to citizens. To take an example, Gennadiy Zyuganov is calling the protesters, people who are standing up for their constitutional rights, 'that orange plague'. ...

As for the regime, look at Putin's talk on television after Bolotnaya Square. The whole purpose of the show was to mislead people. It was embarrassing, and disgraceful. I feel ashamed now. I feel associated with Putin, in the sense that initially, when he first came to power, I actively supported him here, and abroad – everywhere ... And now?

DM: The regime is giving the organizers of the rally, social activists, newspaper editors, to understand that 'if blood is spilled, the opposition will be held responsible'. As if it is not because of the regime's own machinations that people have rallied in the square!

MG: It is the duty of the state to ensure that people are safe. The people have begun to be personally involved in important matters of state. That is their right. So, protect them!

DM: The meeting will be held on Saturday, then the New Year holiday will begin, people will go away. Christmas trees, presents, hangovers ... And then what? Do you think the rally, which is going to be on Sakharov Prospekt, should set up some kind of permanent organizing body?

MG: I would say that is absolutely essential. The people who were on the organizing committee that took the initiative in the first place could head it.

DM: Don't you think they will squabble among themselves, Mikhail Sergeyevich?

MG: Well, they haven't as of now. Perhaps this will be the beginning of democrats managing to cooperate.

DM: Up till now they have only been capable of splitting into factions.

MG: Yes. But now there is a situation which will enable other things to grow through. All these outmoded, purely ideological attachments will wither and the issue of elections will be central. Whichever way you look at it, this is a serious issue, in fact the top priority for Russia right now.

DM: The current government is claiming that free elections would see the Communists or Nazis come to power, and then we would realize how much better the present regime was. That's their argument.

MG: In every country, in every society there are nationalists. I think the concerns of normal nationalists are feelings for which there should be a place in a different social climate.

DM: Do you actually know any normal nationalists? I don't.

MG: A normal nationalist in Russia is a person whose heart bleeds for his people, but who understands that Russia is a country of many worlds, of different cultures, a complicated state, a society formed over centuries and which, incidentally, existed and developed as such.

DM: Well, for me the modern nationalists are the people who killed our journalist, Nastya Baburova, and the lawyer Stanislav Markelov, people who knife Tajiks and migrant workers. That's who they are.

MG: I cannot agree that those are nationalists: they are criminals.

DM: Nevertheless, that is the regime's scare story: if it does not stay in power and maintain what it calls stability, the Communists or nationalists will come to power.

MG: They are trying to impose the same false alternatives as in 1996, when people were told to vote for Yeltsin or the Communists would get in.

DM: And do you think it would be better if the Communists did get in?

MG: They got away with that scare then and want to use it again now. It is a false choice! If elections are fair, you do not need to be afraid of the results. If there are fair elections you get a change of governments.

DM: Well, back to the rally on 24 December. What needs to happen?

MG: The first thing on that day is to approve the slogan, 'For new, free and fair elections!' The condition for supporting any presidential candidate will be for him to agree to that slogan.

The second thing is for a Voters of Russia organizing committee to be set up and a day agreed for a Congress of Voters of Russia. These will be people with differing political views but who have in common a conviction that elections must be fair, the press must be free, and the government must be accountable to society.

DM: Mikhail Sergeyevich, still, do we or do we not have to be afraid of the unpredictability of the results of fair elections?

MG: We do not. And we should take part in new elections after annulment of the sham ones.

Society awakens

The rally on 24 December took place. There was truly a mass turn-out: on a cold, dank December day, tens of thousands of people gathered at Sakharov Prospekt. It was a sight such as Moscow had not seen for many years. It was determined, but peaceful, a protest demonstration to demand fair elections. It was clear that politics in Russia could not stay the same; the authorities would have to respond to the demands of the people. How would they react? That was the big question.

Their reaction was ambivalent. In his final address to the Federal Assembly, President Dmitry Medvedev proposed a number of changes to the political system, including a move to direct election of regional governors by local residents; a simplified procedure for registering political parties on application by 500 people representing at least 50 per cent of the regions of the Russian Federation; reduction of the number of voters' signatures required to stand as a candidate in the presidential election to 300,000, or for candidates from parties not represented in parliament to 100,000. Although the detail of how these changes would be implemented was left unclear, they could be a step forward. Even more important was the fact that the outgoing president had shown a willingness to listen to people and, judging by the style and tone of his speech, he did not see those who were dissatisfied as enemies.

President Medvedev's message clearly fell short of a reform of the Russian political system, and that was precisely what it was proclaimed to be by experts close to the government. Many of these were almost beside themselves with joy.

I could not join in this chorus of praise, not least because it was obvious that Vladimir Putin had his own views on the situation and his opinion would now be decisive.

After the long New Year holidays, the situation began to become clearer. My apprehensions proved justified. The detailed implementation of Medvedev's proposals showed up their inadequacy, even weakness, and the positive elements in them were increasingly sidelined. Something very different came to the foreground, and that was the tone adopted in his speeches by Vladimir Putin and his attitude towards the impending presidential campaign. There was a whiff of the stale breath of the past. Russia's prime minister refused to take part in debates with his rivals. Television programmes showed how busy he was, directing the situation in one area, then in another, 'restoring order'. Except that nobody interviewed him rigorously, nobody asked awkward questions. On the TV screens, the other candidates appeared inconsequential and fussy. Viewers were surreptitiously being indoctrinated to wonder who these people thought they were, what had they to offer against this person who was resolving problems every day? Putin's frontmen went to great lengths to emphasize the absence of alternatives and, what was even worse, to insinuate that any opposition to Putin was wicked, the act of enemies. At the final election campaign rally, when Putin did finally appear as a candidate, he spoke along those lines himself.

The slogan for the rally was 'Defend Russia!'. In his speech, Putin compared the situation in Russia to that during the 1812 war against Napoleon. 'The battle for Russia continues', the prime minister announced. 'Victory will be ours! How in this connection can we not recall Lermontov and his wondrous heroes who before the Battle for Moscow swore to be faithful to the fatherland and desired only to die for it.' At this point he quoted from Lermontov's 'Borodino': 'We shall die before Moscow, as died our brothers! To die we swore, and our oath of fealty kept on the field of Borodino.'

I found the whole tone of the thing distasteful, and did not hide the fact:

Lately one of the candidates has been urging us to die for the fatherland. We need to live for the motherland, to fight for her democratic future. We need to safeguard our citizens' right to further develop peaceful ways of expressing protest.

And we will have fair elections!

Unfortunately, the rally in support of Putin was the harbinger of a strategy of confrontation with the substantial section of society that was demanding change. The entire first year of Vladimir Putin's third presidential term was overshadowed by that confrontation.

Putin's positive proposals were outlined in a series of his articles published in various press outlets. Much in them was good, although there were also questionable provisions. What remained obscure was what resources would be available to realize the programme's objectives, what public support the president expected to draw on. Judging by his actions, he had decided to rely primarily on the support of the passive, conservatively inclined 'silent majority', while increasingly alienating the critically thinking section of society.

Speaking on Echo of Moscow radio, I said I considered Vladimir Putin's decision to run for a third presidential term to be a mistake. A regular changeover, a periodical renewal of the political establishment, was essential and Putin could set an example of the principle in action. 'New people would appear who could move the process on. He would be leaving a legacy with much that was positive.'

Oh, dear, that put the cat among the pigeons! United Russia stalwarts, rancorous Internet trolls, professional political fixers, the whole motley crew took as one to berating Gorbachev, as if I had said something subversive, something 'un-Russian', something damaging to the state. The first months of 2012 persuaded me that the state authorities were incapable, scared of conducting an honest election campaign. I presented my conclusions in a talk I gave to students and lecturers at Moscow International University.

What is needed is not cosmetic, but radical changes. We need to change the constitutional provisions governing the structure of state power relations so as to prevent any individual or group from gaining a monopoly of power.

We need to ensure independence of the judiciary from the executive branch and freedom of the media.

And finally, and very importantly, we need political parties that reflect the real interests of people and the intellectual and political trends in society, social democratic, liberal, conservative and others.

The outcome of the presidential election and what happened in society in the weeks preceding it called for detailed analysis. I gave my first impressions in an interview for the Euronews television channel:

"I think this election has differed from the last elections in that it became evident during the campaign that society is emerging from a state of, I would say, torpor. The voters are beginning to participate in shaping the agenda."In the course of a few weeks, a protest movement sprang up. I was asked what would happen to it. How would this new force operate and how would the state authorities behave? These really were crucial questions. I gave my reply in an interview for Radio Liberty.

RL: Will the movement that began on Bolotnaya Square and Sakharov Prospekt develop, or run out of steam after the election?

MG: It will expand.

RL: Does Putin understand that?

MG: I believe he does. He senses it. After all, up till now nobody has taken to the streets, other than the old people when they were deprived of their welfare benefits. They, incidentally, were the first to come out in the freezing cold to block roads. They set an example for the young to follow. I am quite sure there will be no progress without increasing pressure. And it will increase, and become more organized and more politicized. Putin will not be able to ignore that.

Was this a prediction or more a wish I was expressing to the newly elected president? Probably a bit of both.

A decision to tighten the screws

The political situation was different after the presidential election: there was no longer the Medvedev–Putin tandem: Putin's 'vertical of power' was recreated in unregenerate form, without any of the 'uncertainties', real or imagined, of the Medvedev period. In the circumstances, it behove, in my opinion, both the government and opposition forces to avoid creating or worsening a split in society. Unfortunately, the situation moved in the opposite direction. There was increasing mistrust and hostility. Who was more to blame? I am far from pronouncing the opposition blameless, but think the government bore more responsibility. After winning the election, it should have done everything possible to start healing the wounds and seek a basis for social harmony.

As for the protest movement, I advised that it should remain a movement for free and fair elections. On that basis, it was possible to present the necessary united front. Beyond that, however, the question inevitably arose of how both the protest movement and society as a whole should be structured. Accordingly, I reiterated the need for strong, ideologically meaningful political parties. The current ones were useless. Above all, there was a need for a party professing the ideals of social democracy, which already had a historically validated record, particularly in Europe. I was entirely willing to facilitate this to the best of my ability, but, of course, could not and did not want to take on the role of leader: my age and health simply did not allow that. I have to admit that one of the greatest disappointments of recent years has been the absence of people prepared to take on the task of realizing this political alternative. We are still deficient in the skill of organizing ourselves to implement major, long-term political projects. The regime, meanwhile, having bolstered itself with a new elite of officials, most certainly does have a project: keeping things the way they are.

On 6 May, on the eve of the presidential inauguration, tens of thousands of people took to the streets of Moscow to demand change. What happened at that rally? According to the police report, which became public knowledge a year later, there were no major incidents, let alone mass riots on Bolotnaya Square:

'As a result of the measures taken by the Interior Ministry agencies in Moscow, the tasks of ensuring public order and safety were implemented in full and no serious incidents were able to develop.' From the same report, we learned that to maintain order almost 13,000 law-enforcement personnel were drafted in!

The vast majority of the protesters were calm and behaved peacefully, but a criminal case was manufactured out of a few incidents, and the proceedings dragged on for over a year. Dozens of people were arrested.

A month later, the Duma adopted as an emergency measure, and the president signed, a law on meetings that introduced a whole raft of sanctions, with fines from 300–10,000 roubles, and even restrictions on 'simultaneous mass presence of citizens in public places'. Moreover, the wording of the law was such that it left scope for the authorities to interpret it to prohibit anything they pleased. The fact that the law flagrantly contradicted the constitutionally guaranteed principle of freedom of assembly was so obvious that I, like many others, had hopes until the last moment that the president would not sign it. When he nevertheless did, I said, 'This is an error and it will have to be corrected.'

At the same high speed, an emergency law was passed on 'nonprofit organizations performing the function of a foreign agent'. Its avowed aim was to prevent foreign states from interfering in Russian politics, and ensuring transparency in the activities and financial affairs of public organizations. These would seem to be commendable aims, and there was nothing to prevent their being achieved within the framework of existing laws. However, the wording the Duma so hastily rubber-stamped without discussion, and which the president signed into law, the use of the words 'foreign agent' and the fact that there immediately followed mass 'inspections' of nongovernmental organizations with involvement of the State Prosecutor's Office, and the treating of all public activity as political, left no doubt that the intention was to straitjacket every social initiative not approved by the regime.

By late 2012, the intention of the Russian state authorities to restrict civic activity and wholly subordinate society to its own purposes was unambiguously clear. Among the zealous defenders of this policy was the president of the Constitutional Court,

Valeriy Zorkin. I could not leave his stance unchallenged. My response was published in *Nezavisimaya Gazeta*.

To the president of the Constitutional Court of the Russian Federation, V. D. Zorkin:

Esteemed Valeriy Dmitrievich,

Your article 'There is no morality in chaos', published in *Rossiyskaya Gazeta* on 11 December 2012, came to my attention after some delay. I will not disguise the fact that much in the text surprised me precisely because it was written by the president of the Constitutional Court of Russia and published in our government newspaper.

Polemicizing with the highly subjective judgements of the American political scientist, Leon Aron, 'On moral and personal choice in constructing the Russian state' (*Nezavisimaya Gazeta*, 28 November 2012), you ascribe, absolutely without foundation and contrary to the well-known historical facts, an absence of any positive moral values to Gorbachev's Perestroika. You find it 'guilty' of sedition, as a form of chaos devoid of morality.

As if there had not been the first free elections with alternative candidates for decades of Russian history in 1989 and 1990! As if there had not been Glasnost, which allowed people to say freely what they were thinking!

As if there had been no opening up to citizens of access to information and the wealth of Russian and world literature! As if there had been no introduction of the freedom for citizens to leave and return to their homeland!

And what of the law on freedom of conscience and religious organization, the return of places of worship to believers and the extensive celebration of a millennium since the Christianization of Russia? Why do you overlook the resumption of the suspended rehabilitation of victims of Stalinist repression and the release of political prisoners? To say nothing of the ending of the Cold War and real steps towards removing the danger of nuclear war and towards arms reduction. Can you not see 'positive moral content' in this?

I can well imagine whose interests the clarion calls and orders to vilify Perestroika served, and why they are now being reissued.

I did not expect, however, that a writer of your level of authority, ranting against those who 'extol' Gorbachev's Perestroika,
would literally in the next phrase start trying to identify it with the
upheavals and crimes of the 1990s and use that to denigrate the
new 'Perestroika sedition' which is supposedly aiming to 'further
this degradation of society'. ...

The climate of opinion that leads to movements like Perestroika
arises less at the volition of seditious troublemakers than as a consequence of the failure of a political system and ruling elite to keep
abreast of the demands of a developing society and the maturing
civic consciousness of a population. To be unable to recognize the
steady rise of civic protest in conditions of political stagnation, to
attempt to write it off as due to moral and legal 'inadequacies' on
the part of your 'overly demanding fellow citizens' is dangerously
short-sighted and profoundly mistaken. That way we really can
expect dramatic upheavals and revolutions.

As regards the assessment of Gorbachev's Perestroika given
in your article about chaos-devoid-of-morality, in the interests of
objectivity I will permit myself to quote some rather different writing and acknowledgements from an official government telegram I
received. It reads:

'Dear Mikhail Sergeyevich,

Please accept my cordial best wishes on your 75th birthday.
Everyone knows how much effort you put into enabling our country to take a historic decision to turn in the direction of democratic
reform, for the emergence of civil society and the construction of a
state living under the rule of law.

I wholeheartedly wish you good health and inexhaustible
reserves of optimism and faith in the future. I wish you success in
all you undertake, and happiness and prosperity for you and your
family.

V. D. Zorkin
President of the Constitutional Court of the Russian Federation
2 March 2006'

What has prompted you so abruptly and diametrically to
change your judgements and assessment? May it perhaps be the
fact that in recent years I have begun to publicly criticize the gov-

erning party, which embodies the worst bureaucratic features of the Soviet Communist Party and has turned into a mechanism for maintaining its own monopoly of power, a machine that mindlessly endorses whatever decisions and orders come down to it from on high?

Dear Valeriy Dmitrievich, Your Honour! Do believe me when I say that I have written everything above solely in the interests of truth and justice. It is nothing personal. I do not indulge in anger or hold grudges. I wish you good health and hope you have a wonderful New Year and Christmas.

The need for dialogue between the government and society

What is likely to be the result of the current course of the state authorities if the president does not adjust it? I have no doubt that maintaining the status quo is to Russia's detriment. I spoke on this subject in a public lecture for young people that I gave in March 2013 at the Novosti news agency. It is a day I remember well. My talk and the question and answer session after it lasted almost two hours.

Here are the main points I made to the young people who filled the hall:

Politics is increasingly becoming a simulation of democracy. All the power is concentrated in the hands of the executive branch, the president. Parliament merely rubber-stamps his decisions.

We lack an autonomous judiciary.

The economy has been monopolized and is like a junky addicted to oil and gas exports. The initiative of entrepreneurs is fettered, and small and medium-sized businesses face enormous hurdles.

There is an unacceptably large gap between the incomes and living standards of the most well-off stratum of the population and everybody else. Corruption has reached extraordinary levels.

Such areas as education, health and science give grounds for very great concern.

Since 2004–5, I have been speaking constantly about these

problems. They are issues that have been raised very audibly by others besides myself, but the government has not responded meaningfully to the signals coming from society. Ultimately, that behaviour has caused society to react.

Society woke up. It claimed its rights. People again demanded change, but instead of initiating a dialogue, the government resorted to subterfuge with the sole aim of keeping itself in power at all costs. It has succeeded for a time in resisting the tide of protest, but Russia's problems have not gone away, and if nothing changes, they can only get worse.

That means that Russia is again facing the historic task of breaking through to genuine democracy.

People can influence the course of history only by participating in politics. The reality is that they have almost no opportunity to influence decision-making through genuinely effective party and social organizations that represent their interests. They are obliged to look for other ways, through the Internet, through spontaneous or organized protest demonstrations, or angry calls to radio programmes.

What is needed, however, is authentic political participation. That, however, is funnelled off, as if into a sinkhole, by United Russia and other official or quasi-official organizations.

If anybody falls out of the officially approved establishment, he is subjected to a rapid process of marginalization and banned from the political stage. ...

Aping the Communist Party, United Russia has become the 'leading and directing force' in Russian politics, but the actual problems facing people are not dealt with and break through to the surface, requiring intervention 'at the highest level'. Before our startled gaze, micromanagement of politics from the top degenerates to the level of directing the traffic and compiling railway timetables.

All this is explained away on the grounds of the need to maintain stability. Yes, of course we need stability, but the stability of democracy, which is achieved through dialogue, through the contending of responsible political forces, by making provision for the formulation and advocacy of competing programmes.

That is something we do not have, although we came part of the way in that direction, halfway, perhaps. Maybe less. If we do not go further, we may slide back and be forced to rediscover the road some time in the future. ...

We cannot afford to lag behind. Without political modernization, we will be mired in the past and will drift downwards in the international league table. I believe that both the present government and society face a historic choice. It is vital that both should understand that Russia's complex problems can be resolved only by means of democratic cooperation. The rift between government and people can no longer be tolerated. ...

I am sure that if the government chooses the path of dialogue with the active, concerned part of society, it will meet a positive response. From young people too.

The young have taken an active part in the rise of the civil protest movement. I was heartened by their energy and how they behaved at meetings. The whole experience of my life in politics warns, though, that it will be difficult: major change is not easily gained. Energy and enthusiasm need to be backed by persistence, the ability to organize yourselves, to think clearly, to listen to and take account of the opinions of others. In short, the need is to learn to fight for democracy while practising democracy.

One very important point I want specifically to mention and emphasize: avoid rifts. There should be no gap between the generations or between different trends within the forces of democracy.

You will need to show maturity and true patriotism, that is, to remember your responsibilities to the country, to society, and to the future of Russia. If you can do that, you will have shown that people can change history, and that Russia's citizens are well able to take the country's future into their own hands and build it on the path of democracy.

The truth of the matter is that that is our only viable option.

III TODAY'S UNEASY WORLD

The Relevance of New Thinking

The years since I left the Kremlin have been a time of enormous changes. I could not stand aside from what was happening; I reacted constantly to events and tried, within my abilities and opportunities, to influence them. I initiated and supported international projects, which continued, in the new circumstances, what had been begun in the years of Perestroika.

I wondered what would be the best way to talk about the dozens, indeed hundreds, of meetings, trips, conferences, speeches and articles I devoted to world events. How could I avoid losing sight of the wood for the trees?

So I asked myself what had been the main thing, the thread running through my international activities over the years. The answer came to me instantly: I had been standing up for, trying to develop and apply to the conditions of a rapidly changing world the New Thinking of the Perestroika era, the ideas and principles that I and my colleagues had offered the world in the latter half of the 1980s. I would like to reiterate them here, because I am certain that it was New Thinking that made possible putting an end to the Cold War. I believe the world still very much needs it today.

The New Thinking of the Perestroika period is not a set of dogmas or a code of practice. It developed and was supplemented by new ideas that reflected the course of world events. However, its basis remained unchanged: recognition of the interconnection and interdependence of the world, of the indivisibility of global security, of the importance of universal human values and interests. In February 1986, I declared it from the rostrum of the Twenty-Seventh Congress of the Communist Party of the Soviet Union. It became the outlook of the Party, and had momentous significance.

New Thinking was not a sudden revelation that arose out of nothing. It had a pre-history, precedents. On not a few occasions when I have been giving lectures or talks in the United States, I have quoted a speech given by President John F. Kennedy at the American University, Washington, DC in June 1963. He called then for us 'not to see conflict as inevitable, accommodation as impossible, and communication as nothing more than an exchange of threats'.[1] At the height of the Cold War, he managed to break free from the vicious circle of demonizing 'the enemy' and striving for world hegemony. The future world, he said, will not be 'a Pax Americana enforced on the world by American weapons of war'. Either there would be peace for all, or there would be no peace at all. When we criticize the communists, he was saying, we must not demonize Soviet people: they are the same as us.

Other precursors of New Thinking were such outstanding thinkers and politicians as the social democrats Olof Palme and Willy Brandt. Before others did, they were able to perceive and understand the challenges of modern times. Hence the innovative concept of 'common security' in the nuclear age that was propounded and advocated by Palme, and the ideal of overcoming the confrontation between East and West, of pan-European cooperation, of a Greater Europe, which was elaborated by Brandt, François Mitterrand and Helmut Schmidt.

New Thinking also incorporated important principles of international cooperation, which, even during the Cold War, were developed at the United Nations. Its humanist approach was in harmony with the appeals and demands of anti-war movements and the leaders of world religions.

A synthesis, New Thinking is modern humanism, its purpose to move us towards a more stable, safer, more just and humane society. Acknowledging the interconnection and interdependence

[1] John F. Kennedy, Presidential library and museum, Commencement Address at the American University, 10 June 1963 (transcript); http://www.jfklibrary.org/Asset-Viewer/BWC7I4C9QUmLG9J6I8oy8w.aspx. Accessed 16 July 2015.

of the world and the primacy of universal values and interests by no means implied a lack of respect for the sovereignty of states and national interests. Nobody was disputing their importance, any more than the importance of class, corporate and other interests. Now, however, they had to take account of new circumstances, when the interests common to all mankind needed to be given priority. The imperative needs were to prevent nuclear war, and to save mankind from ecological disaster.

We believed this could be achieved only through the joint efforts of all countries and peoples, and from this specific aims and features of the foreign policy of Perestroika followed:

- rejection of ideological confrontation of the West;
- rejection of a militarized approach to foreign relations;
- a policy of halting the arms race, eliminating weapons of mass destruction, reducing armed forces and embarking on disarmament to a level of 'reasonable sufficiency';
- a desire to integrate our economy into the world economy and include Russia in civilization in general;
- recognizing freedom of choice for all, including choice of social system;
- abstaining from the use of force in international relations to impose one's power on others;
- non-interference in the internal affairs of sovereign states;
- promoting preventive diplomacy and establishing trust as a crucial factor in global politics;
- showing a willingness to cooperate with all comers to take joint action on problems not previously included on the international agenda, like human rights, ecology and humanitarian matters.

This was new for us, and presupposed change both in foreign and domestic policy. At the same time, I quite deliberately emphasized to our partners in negotiations and to the leaders of Western states that modern global interdependence left nobody any option but to change. Subsequent events were to show not all our partners invariably observing the principles of New Thinking, and sooner or later the world and they themselves had to pay for that.

After resigning the presidency at the end of 1991, I naturally found myself in a very different situation, but considered I had a duty to try to ensure that New Thinking became firmly established in the world, despite the change in the global balance of power caused by the disappearance off the map of the Soviet Union. The situation was not straightforward. The Cold War had ended even before the dissolution of the USSR, as our Western partners acknowledged. Russia and the countries of the West no longer viewed each other as enemies, and there were opportunities for cooperation, both bilateral and in addressing global challenges.

One of my first guests at the Foundation, Henry Kissinger, began our conversation by saying that the new Russia now making its debut on the world stage had no enemies. She could be confident that her security was assured for the foreseeable future. 'And that', he added, 'is largely due to your efforts.' I agreed with him, but with the important caveat that security, good relations and cooperation with other countries do not arrive once and for all. For them to be permanent, there need to be policies based firmly on the foundation of what has been achieved and which adequately reflect those changes.

Challenges of globalization

Meanwhile, the world was changing rapidly. Processes begun earlier gained momentum from the ending of the Cold War. Global confrontation, if unable to halt them, had certainly inhibited them. Now they accelerated and spread virtually across the planet. Academics and politicians called them globalization, and it became the dominant trend of world development.

From the outset, I and my colleagues at the Gorbachev Foundation made this phenomenon a top priority in our researches. I believed that globalization offered an opportunity for transition to a securer, more stable world order and, ultimately, to a new civilization synthesizing the main ideals and values of different cultures and ideologies. We chose as the Foundation's motto, 'Towards a New Civilization!'. Even so, I was far from idealizing the way globalization was proceeding, and presented my thoughts on this at a conference we held in summer 1992.

> The objectively conditioned movement of the human community to interaction and interdependence is occurring so rapidly that it is forcibly uprooting the familiar way of life of hundreds of millions of people, forcing them to break with longstanding behavioural stereotypes and ways of thinking. The instinctive reaction of an ordinary person who feels helpless as he is buffeted by the winds of change is to retreat into his own little world, traditionalist, religious or national. This is the explanation of the swell of fundamentalism, religious fanaticism and crude nationalism flooding many regions of the world.
>
> Our world is in a major transition to a new symbiosis of peoples. This gives rise to pressing problems in need of careful analysis and coordinated solutions. One of these, perhaps the most perplexing, is how to correlate available resources with the desire of a multi-billion and rapidly increasing world population to live a decent, dignified life. ...
>
> After the collapse of the bipolar world, a multipolar, pluralistic world is just beginning to emerge, in which an increasing role will be played by a united Western Europe, China, Japan and a number of other countries. ... Despite all the obstacles and opposition, a system for international regulation of important social issues is emerging and will continue to do so. This process, for all its ambivalence, will take place, I believe and hope, through voluntary delegation by individual states of powers essential for resolving problems that can only be addressed at an international level. It is to be expected that the range of these powers will increase, which will surely be possible only on a voluntary basis. ... Mutual trust will be essential if international institutions are to be effective. In turn, trust will be generated if those involved in the process formulate their policies on the basis of transparent, democratic procedures.

I feel I managed in that speech to outline both the promise of the process of globalization and the knotty problems arising as it proceeded. Initially, it was presented as an unambiguously positive process opening up limitless possibilities for all. To some extent, that was an honest mistake, but in part it was promoted in order to exploit the new situation and establish a monopoly of leadership by the West, and primarily the United States.

Globalization became the object of one of the Gorbachev Foundation's main research projects. We were among the first to draw attention to negative aspects that became increasingly prominent as globalization accelerated, and to point out the considerable risks. Polarization of global wealth and poverty increased at a dangerous rate.

The problems of globalization and its consequences came to be an invariable item on the agenda at international forums, including those at the highest level. In September 2000 they were discussed at the Millennium Summit, held in New York at the headquarters of the United Nations and attended by 160 heads of state and governments. They were mentioned in the Millennium Declaration adopted there and approved by the UN General Assembly.

In parallel, also in New York that September, the State of the World Forum 2000 was held with participation of prominent members of the world's political elite. I was one of its initiators, chaired it and gave the opening speech, in which I urged that there was a need to find some way of regulating the blind, uncontrolled process of globalization.

The outcome of our project was a collective work, *Facets of Globalization: Difficult Issues of Contemporary Development*.[2] That volume tries not only to analyse the phenomenon of globalization, its complexities, pluses and minuses, but to outline the concept of 'globalization with a human face', socially and environmentally responsible globalization. This first attempt to suggest an alternative could not hope to provide answers to all the issues and problems, but was responding to a real public demand: the movement for an alternative globalization was gaining momentum and identifying serious problems. It increased in strength after the global economic crisis of 2008 exposed

[2] M. S. Gorbachev, ed., *Grani globalizatsii. Trudnye voprosy sovremennogo razvitiia*, M.: Al'pina Publishers, 2003.

the inadequacies of assumptions currently underlying world development.

One of the most important political conclusions, staring us in the face as we examined what was happening in the world, was that no country, or even group of countries, would be able to cope with the major challenges of the new millennium on its own. These were the challenges of security, poverty, economic backwardness and the environmental crisis. They are interconnected and ultimately require an integrated response. Their sheer scale and the risks they are fraught with are, in my belief, unprecedented. I have discussed them on numerous occasions with politicians, scientists and social activists, have taken part in dozens of conferences and forums, given interviews, published articles, and had my conviction confirmed again and again that, without New Thinking, the world will fail to respond adequately to them.

The challenge of security

Challenges to security come in various guises, of which the most dangerous are weapons of mass destruction and terrorism. The worry is compounded by the possibility that ultimately the most terrible weapons may fall into the hands of extremists.

For me, the issue of nuclear disarmament runs through all the years and decades of my career. One of the great achievements of New Thinking was ending the nuclear arms race. After decades of relentless build-up, stockpiles began to be reduced. The turning point came at the 1986 Reykjavik Summit. Although it proved impossible to finalize agreement there because of Ronald Reagan's desire to get us to agree to continued testing and deployment of anti-ballistic missile systems, not only on earth but even in space, it was at Reykjavik that the scope of a 50 per cent reduction of strategic offensive weapons and the elimination of intermediate range missiles were agreed. These were subsequently formalized in the Intermediate-Range Nuclear Forces Treaties of 1987 and the 1991 Strategic Arms Reduction Treaty (START). In autumn 1991, President George Bush and I exchanged letters of intent to eliminate the greater proportion of tactical nuclear weapons. All these agreements were subsequently implemented. It was an unparalleled reduction of such deadly weapons in such a short time frame.

It seemed at first that ridding the world of weapons of mass destruction would continue along the lines we had managed to establish. In 1992, Presidents Yeltsin and Bush signed the START-2 Treaty, and the Chemical Weapons Convention was drafted. Shortly afterwards, however, the process began slowing down before stalling completely. The START-2 Treaty languished in the US Congress and the Russian Duma for several years, and was not ratified by Russia. The delay was particularly due to the protracted economic crisis in Russia. Neither was a Comprehensive Nuclear Test Ban Treaty agreed. Negotiations on monitoring compliance with the Biological Weapons Convention also got nowhere, blocked by the United States.

The reduction and elimination of weapons of mass destruction became a hostage to the general state of international relations, and in the 1990s, instead of gradual improvement and the growth of trust, the direction of travel was reversed. I have no doubt that the main reason for that was a misreading by the West, and particularly the United States, of the circumstances of the collapse of the Soviet Union and the ending of the Cold War.

The West claimed a victory, as if the Cold War had ended not as the result of joint efforts, not through negotiation, but thanks to power politics. This led them to conclude that they should further increase their strength and military superiority. They abandoned the joint commitment, documented in a statement in Geneva by the leaders of the USSR and the United States, that our countries would not seek military superiority over each other. This affirmation was, however, no less important than another historic provision of that joint declaration, acknowledging that nuclear war must never be allowed, and that in such a war there could be no winner.

The world witnessed the capital of trust accumulated in the second half of the 1980s being frittered away, as the prospect of a new, more secure world order was replaced by the spectre of chaos and a world in which might was right. The use of force against Yugoslavia, the expansion of NATO and missile strikes against Iraq during the second half of the 1990s demonstrated how the United States intended to handle security issues. The voices of Russia, China and even of some US allies were ignored. The policy of unilateralism formulated, incidentally, before George W. Bush arrived in the White House, became an ongoing negative factor in world politics. Might was right: other countries duly took note.

In the late 1990s, India and Pakistan tested nuclear weapons and North Korea followed suit. There were questions about Iran's nuclear programme and whether it really was intended, as claimed by the Iranian leaders, solely for peaceful purposes. There are dozens of potential threshold nuclear countries in the world that could, if they so chose, create nuclear weapons. The example of South Africa which, after the abolition of apartheid, renounced nuclear weapons and destroyed them, has had no successors. The threat of nuclear proliferation and a new arms race became a reality.

In international politics the goal of eliminating nuclear weapons has, in effect, been abandoned. Instead, in the military doctrine of the nuclear powers it is again regarded as an acceptable means of waging war, for a first or even a 'preventive' strike. This change first occurred in US military doctrine, before its example was followed by others.

We have to face the fact that the opportunities that arose with the ending of the Cold War have not been pursued. Indeed, frankly, they have been squandered.

Ban the bomb!

I believed, and still do, that the only way to save the world from the danger posed by nuclear weapons is to get rid of them completely. In the final analysis, that is the only way, and in early 2007 something happened that indicated this was understood in elite political and intellectual circles of the United States, the country that had in the past made the greatest 'contribution' to the nuclear arms race.

On 4 January 2007, the *Wall Street Journal* published 'A World Free of Nuclear Weapons', signed by such well-known US politicians from both major political parties as George Shultz, Henry Kissinger, William Perry and Sam Nunn. The fact that these 'four wise men', political heavyweights not given to utopian projects and who have unique experience of forming the policies of previous administrations, decided to go public on such an important issue as the need to repudiate nuclear weapons, testified to an important change of attitude among the American establishment. This was momentous.

I responded with an article, also published in the *Wall Street Journal*, on 31 January. I reminded its readers that, at their forum in Rome in November 2006, Nobel Peace Prize winners had issued a special appeal in respect of the nuclear threat. I reminded them too of the campaign, in which I participated, initiated by the world renowned physicist and Nobel Peace Prize winner Sir Joseph Rotblat (who died in 2005), to inform the public about the nuclear threat. I reminded them of the great work undertaken by Ted Turner's Nuclear Threat Initiative. We shared a common understanding that the Non-Proliferation Treaty could not be allowed to gather dust and that the main onus for ensuring that did not happen was on the members of the 'nuclear club'. I wrote:

> We must put the goal of eliminating nuclear weapons back on the agenda, not in some distant future but as soon as possible. It links the moral imperative – the rejection of such weapons from an ethical standpoint – with the imperative of assuring security. It is becoming clearer that nuclear weapons are no longer a means of achieving security; in fact, with every passing year they are making our security more precarious.

Again, as in the mid-1980s, there is an issue of political will, of the responsibility of leaders of major states to overcome the gulf between talking about peace and security and the very real threats hanging over the world.

I called for a dialogue to be launched 'within the framework of the Nuclear Non-Proliferation Treaty, involving both nuclear weapon states and non-nuclear weapon states, to cover the full range of issues related to the elimination of those weapons'. The goal would be to develop a common concept for moving towards a world free of nuclear weapons, and the key to success would be 'reciprocity of obligations and actions':

> The members of the nuclear club should formally reiterate their commitment to reducing and ultimately eliminating nuclear weapons. As a token of their serious intent, they should without delay take two crucial steps: ratify the Comprehensive Test Ban Treaty and make changes in their military doctrines, removing nuclear weapons from the Cold War-era high alert status. At the same time, the states that have nuclear-power programmes would pledge to terminate all elements of those programmes that could have military use.

Banning nuclear weapons is not just a slogan but a specific, practical task. How is it to be accomplished, what is obstructing movement in that direction? These issues were the focus of intense, persistent discussion in the World Political Forum that I and a group of friends and allies established. The idea of setting up the forum found political support in many countries, and the inaugural conference took place in Turin on 18 May 2003. In my opening speech I said:

> The main objective of our Forum is to help to re-start dialogue as the only means of addressing the problems accumulating in the world; to develop new rules of conduct for states in order to present them to governments, political forces and the public at large, in the hope that they will find new approaches to solving crises on an international level, generating the political will to reform international institutions, and create a new, just and secure world order.

To put it in a nutshell, we wanted to help politics to keep up with the pace of global change.

One of the Forum's most important initiatives was a conference on 'Overcoming Nuclear Dangers', held in Rome on 16–17 April 2009. We organized it in collaboration with the Nuclear Threat Initiative and the Italian Ministry of Foreign Affairs. Participants included George Shultz, William Perry, Sam Nunn, Hans-Dietrich Genscher, Ruud Lubbers, Alexander Bessmertnykh; such members of the US and Russian legislatures as Dianne Feinstein, Mikhail Margelov and Konstantin Kosachev; and leading scholars and experts. The conference gained momentum after the 5 April statement in Prague by Barack Obama, newly elected president of the United States, in which he called for a world without nuclear weapons. This aim was confirmed at a meeting of the presidents of the United States and Russia in London. These events made it all the more important to discuss practical ways of achieving this.

In my declaration at the opening of the conference, I said: 'Nuclear weapons are an extreme manifestation of the militarization of international relations and political thinking. We have not successfully dealt with this burdensome legacy from the twentieth century.' Decisive action was needed. The co-chairman, George Shultz, was in full agreement, declaring that eliminating nuclear weapons was an idea whose time had finally come, but that time was also against us. Prudent action was needed immediately.

This was true, but could it be considered realistic if, after ridding the world of weapons of mass destruction, one country would still be in possession of more conventional weapons than the combined arsenals of almost all the other countries in the world put together? If it were to have absolute global military superiority? In my speech, I warned that the answer could only be negative. I reminded the conference that when, in years gone by, we had proposed moving forward to a non-nuclear world, our Western partners had raised the issue of the Soviet Union's superiority in conventional weapons. We had not tried to evade it and had entered negotiations that led to a mutual reduction of conventional arms in Europe. Today we needed the West to adopt a similar approach.

I returned regularly to the topic of nuclear disarmament, in October 2009 setting out my position in detail at the UN Office in Geneva. In the presence of representatives of dozens of countries and the UN secretary-general, Ban Ki-moon, I said it was essential that this global organization should play its part fully:

> The UN is the framework within which we can and must address such questions as, for example, involving second-tier nuclear powers in the process of nuclear disarmament. After Russia and

the United States conclude a treaty on a new, legally binding and verifiable major reduction of their nuclear arsenals and the United States ratifies the Comprehensive Nuclear Test Ban Treaty, this question will become particularly pressing.

I believe, I said, that after that, the other nuclear powers, both official members of the nuclear club and others, should at the very least declare a freeze on their nuclear arsenals and express their readiness to enter into negotiations to limit and reduce them.

I also proposed discussing within the UN framework the military concepts and doctrines inherited from the Cold War era. I suggested the topic might be raised at the Security Council's Military Staff Committee, which, as long ago as 1988, I had proposed in a speech to the UN General Assembly should be brought out of mothballs.

In April 2010, the presidents of Russia and the United States signed a new Strategic Arms Reduction Treaty to replace START-1. Almost immediately the agreement came under attack and was criticized from both right and left. Some claimed the proposed reductions were dangerous, others that they did not go far enough and boiled down to no more than creative accountancy. In an article published in both the *New York Times* (22 April 2010) and *Rossiyskaya Gazeta*, I stoutly defended the treaty. I wrote that, although the reductions proposed really were modest compared with what had been achieved in the agreement, which President George Bush and I signed in 1991, it nevertheless represented a major breakthrough.

First, it resumes the process initiated in the second half of the 1980s, which made it possible to rid the world of thousands of nuclear warheads and hundreds of launchers.

Second, the strategic arsenals of the United States and Russia have once again been placed under a regime of mutual verification and inspections.

Third, the United States and Russia have demonstrated that they can solve the most complex problems of mutual security, which offers hope that they will work together more successfully to address global and regional issues.

Finally, and perhaps most importantly, with the New Strategic Arms Reduction Treaty, the two biggest nuclear powers say to the world that they are serious about their Nuclear Non-Proliferation Treaty obligation to move toward eliminating nuclear weapons.

In connection with the signing of the treaty, the Obama administration proposed to Russia and China to initiate a dialogue on the issue of strategic stability. I commented that this should not be limited to strategic arms issues. 'More general problems must also be addressed if we are to build a relationship of partnership and trust. Foremost is the problem of military superiority.'

I pointed out that the US National Security Strategy adopted in 2002 explicitly proclaimed the principle that the United States should enjoy global military superiority: 'This principle has in effect become an integral part of America's creed. It finds specific expression in the vast arsenals of conventional weapons, the colossal defense budget and the plans for weaponizing outer space. The proposed strategic dialogue must include all these issues.'

Consequences of NATO expansion

The correlation between reduction and elimination of weapons of mass destruction and the general state of international relations and security is something any sober-minded politician should be keeping in mind. The generation of politicians that replaced ours failed signally to improve security in Europe and the rest of the world. The worst blunder was the decision to expand NATO and turn it into a 'guarantor' of security not only in Europe but beyond its borders.

Speaking in October 2009 at the Council of Europe, I gave that organization its due in building a Greater Europe, but added: 'Europe still has not resolved its major issue of providing a solid basis for peace, of creating a new security architecture.' I recalled the Charter of Paris for a New Europe, signed in 1990, which was to lay the foundation for that architecture. Immediately after the end of the Cold War, we discussed how to create new security procedures for our continent. There was talk of a European

Security Council, a kind of directorate with sweeping powers. The idea had the support of such major politicians as Hans-Dietrich Genscher, Brent Scowcroft and Roland Dumas, but events took a different course.

The leaders of NATO, with the United States taking the leading role, decided to expand the bloc to include the countries of Central and Eastern Europe, citing security considerations to justify the decision. Security, however, is needed only if there is a threat, so who was threatening whom? Who was threatening Poland, Hungary or the Czech Republic, countries that rushed to be first in the queue to join NATO? If there was such a threat, why did they not sound the alarm, convene emergency meetings of the institutions of the then Conference on Security and Co-operation in Europe, the Council of Europe or, come to that, the UN Security Council?

What was going on? Assuredly, many countries of Eastern and Central Europe applied for membership of NATO, and perhaps, knowing their history, it was difficult to expect that they would have a balanced and rational approach to the question after lacking independence for decades. That does not, however, mean that the overarching requirements of equilibrium and security should have been subordinated to their emotions. Alongside these there were entirely pragmatic vested interests involved that had little to do with security issues.

Russia, after initially failing to take a stand (on a visit to Poland in August 1993, Yeltsin even signed a declaration to the effect that if Poland preferred to join NATO, that would not be contrary to Russian interests), subsequently came to her senses and announced her opposition to the policy of expanding the North Atlantic alliance. Her views were effectively ignored. It was said that Russia had no right to veto decisions involving other states. This assertion, at first sight unchallengeable, implied that Russia was somehow not a party to general security matters.

The most the Americans would agree to was to sweeten the pill, but that made no real difference: Russia's relations with the West were irreparably damaged. Did those who so advocated NATO expansion give any thought to the configuration of political forces in Russia at that time? Was the West really blind to the kind of sentiments NATO expansion aroused among influential circles in Russia?

It has to be said that attitudes in the West to NATO's plans were far from uniformly supportive. I can instance my conversations with such prominent politicians as the former Italian prime minister, Giulio Andreotti; the former British prime minister, Edward Heath; the former US ambassador to the USSR, Jack Matlock; the doyen of American diplomats, George Kennan; and leading politicians of Spain, Portugal and France.

By then I had many times visited the United States, had discussions with numerous leading politicians of both parties, with businessmen, intellectuals and ordinary Americans. I found few people in favour of NATO expansion to the East. There were, of course, those who, without any particular enthusiasm, were prepared to go along with it, but most Americans clearly had doubts about its wisdom, and many were passionately opposed. They were ignored.

In Russia, NATO's expansion plans became an acute domestic problem. They were immediately seized on by those in favour of confrontation with the West, and by those who were intent on using the 'external threat' to their own advantage. There was much agitation among enthusiasts of blaming everything on Gorbachev, and people who simply did not know their facts and claimed I had failed to take measures that could have prevented the expansion of NATO. In the course of reunifying Germany I should have haggled harder and ruled out the possibility of any expansion of NATO in the future.

These charges were completely absurd. German reunification was completed at a time when the Warsaw Pact was still in existence, and to demand that its members should not join NATO would have been laughable. No organization can give a legally binding undertaking not to expand in the future. That was a purely political question, and all that could be done politically in the conditions of the time, was done. The agreement on the final settlement with Germany stated that no additional NATO troops would be deployed on the territory of the former GDR, and neither would weapons of mass destruction. That meant that NATO's military infrastructure would not move eastwards.

The decision to expand NATO, taken after the break-up of the Soviet Union, was contrary to the spirit of those undertakings, as I have repeatedly pointed out when parrying baseless accusations. The main problem was that the policy of the leaders of NATO harboured a real threat, and not only to Russia. There was a danger that, half a century after the start of the Cold War, the world could again be plunged into something analogous.

The expansion of NATO fundamentally undermined the European modus vivendi established by the Helsinki Final Act of the Conference on Security and Co-operation in Europe in 1975. It was a complete reversal of the strategy, jointly developed by all the states of Europe, to move beyond the Cold War. It shook the foundations of the Treaty on Conventional Armed Forces in Europe, as a new line dividing Europe was drawn. NATO started behaving like a policeman charged with maintaining order in Europe and even the world. That began as early as the first half of the 1990s, with intervention in the conflict as Yugoslavia disintegrated.

Most acute and bloody was the conflict in Bosnia-Herzegovina, where the Western countries, instead of doing their utmost to support the efforts of the mediators, Cyrus Vance, former US Secretary of State, and Lord Owen [a former leader of the British Social Democratic Party], only made the situation worse. For the first time in its history, the North Atlantic Treaty Organization began direct military intervention, and, moreover, with a clear bias against the Bosnian Serbs. In 1995, Serbia was forced to accept NATO's terms and the American-imposed Dayton Agreement.

NATO's new strategy, adopted on the alliance's 50th anniversary at a session of the North Atlantic Council in Washington in spring 1999, provided for the possible stationing, deployment and use of NATO forces beyond the borders of the territories for which the bloc was directly responsible, anywhere in the entire European and Atlantic area. This new strategy was promptly applied in Kosovo, where Albanian separatists were fighting to detach the province from Yugoslavia.

In the end, after NATO's intervention and the bombing of Belgrade, Yugoslavia was forced to concede and Kosovo was declared independent. The Serb minority there was reduced to the status of hostages and a dangerous precedent was created of military action undertaken against a sovereign country without authorization by the UN Security Council, in violation of the UN Charter and international law.

The world after 9/11

Despite this, the international community had an opportunity to return to the path of joint maintenance of security. It arose in the aftermath of the tragic events of 11 September 2001.

I well remember how I heard about the terrorist attack on the World Trade Center in New York. I was working in my office at the Gorbachev Foundation when my assistant came in. 'Mikhail Sergeyevich, something incredible is happening. A plane has crashed into a skyscraper in New York. Let's turn on the television.' And indeed, I could not believe what I was seeing on the screen. When I was in New York to address the United Nations in 1988, I had visited the World Trade Center and met businessmen there. Now those towers were on fire and belching smoke, the kind of spectacle you would have imagined possible only in a horror movie. That same day I sent a telegram of condolence to President Bush via the US Embassy in Moscow:

> I am shocked by this unprecedented crime against the United States and all mankind. I offer you and all Americans my profound condolences, and I know that today all people of goodwill are united in solidarity with the citizens of America. Humanity is facing an unheard-of challenge. Only through joint efforts will we be able to stop this insanity.

I expressed my sympathy and solidarity with the American people also in a letter published in the *New York Times*. It evoked many responses from citizens across the United States.

The fact that seemingly impregnable America had been struck right in its heart demonstrated clearly that nobody in the world is now invulnerable; anyone can become the victim of terror. The sense of sympathy and solidarity felt by most people around the globe was entirely natural. It was natural too that America's call for an international anti-terrorist coalition was positively received. The world witnessed something quite unprecedented: a common agreement between America, Russia, Europe, India, China, Cuba, the greater part of the Islamic world, and other regions and countries. This happened despite all the serious differences dividing them. Unique in modern history, it resembled the coalition against Hitler during the Second World War.

The first foreign leader to phone George W. Bush to express support and solidarity with stricken America was Russia's president, Vladimir Putin. Announcing that he was joining the anti-terrorist coalition, President Putin began cooperating in the fight against terrorism. I fully supported him, believing that at this moment we needed to put aside the irritants that had been bedevilling Russian–American relations recently. In an article published in dozens of newspapers in different countries, I developed the idea of a coalition for a new world order.

If the fight against terrorism comes down only to the exercise of violence, the world will lose out. If it is part of our joint efforts to build a just world order, everyone will be the winner.

Russia has joined the anti-terror coalition not just in words but in deeds: she extended real help to America from the outset of the UN-sanctioned military action in Afghanistan against the Taliban regime, sharing intelligence, coordinating her stance with that of the West and her neighbours, affording the right to overfly Russian territory, providing humanitarian assistance to the Afghan population and arms to the Northern Alliance. Following up on this, the Russian president took such unilateral steps to accommodate the US as closing down the electronic surveillance centre in Cuba and our naval base in Vietnam.

Not everybody in the Russian elite and the country was happy with this policy. Some were still stuck in the categories of the old thinking, others sincerely questioned whether it was right for the most powerful country in the world to be bombing impoverished Afghanistan. Others again muttered that here we were supporting America in its hour of need, but would it reciprocate on issues of importance to us?

In my article, I urged that these questions should not simply be dismissed.

> Russia, I have no doubt, will be a major partner in the fight against international terrorism, but no less important is that her views should be taken into account in the building of a new world order. Such irritants in Russo–American relations as the expansion of NATO and the anti-missile defence issue, and many other problems not only between Russia and America, will be more easily resolved if there is a shared overall strategy of moving towards a new global community.

As time passed, however, I and those hoping for a far-reaching change of direction in world politics began to have doubts. Would the coalition survive? Would those who were partners in it stick to the principle of collective action in the fight against the global threats facing mankind?

These doubts grew as the military action against Afghanistan became increasingly protracted, making it clear that the hope of rapid success was fading. Increasingly, the talk was of extending the military action in time and space. The longer the war, the more difficult it would become to maintain the unity of the grand coalition, I warned in an article in November 2001. It might come to grief because of political and geopolitical policies designed to satisfy the ambitions of regional leaders, or because of other interests. Or, indeed, because of an attempt, under the guise of combating terrorism, to gain greater control over other states and expand spheres of influence. It seemed to me important to analyse the underlying causes and consequences of the September 11 disaster. In the same article I wrote:

> September 11 marked the end of the ideology of a unipolar world, a turning point that also marked the end of 'unilateral globalization'. I think it is a tragic date, burying a philosophy born after the ending of the Cold War and the disintegration of the Soviet Union.

32 *Mikhail Gorbachev, Founding President of Green Cross International, 1993.*

33 Mikhail Gorbachev and Yasuhiro Nakasone, former prime minister of Japan, Tokyo, 11 April 1992.

34 Meeting with Kiichi Miyazawa, prime minister of Japan, Tokyo, 13 April 1992.

35 *Fulton, Missouri, USA, May 1992.*

36 *Meeting with Ronald Reagan during the 1992 visit to the USA.*

37 *Speech at the 250th Anniversary of the Birth of Thomas Jefferson, Virginia, USA, April 1993.*

38 Henry Kissinger, Mikhail Gorbachev and Hans-Dietrich Genscher, Germany, May 1993. Photo U. Jacobshagen.

39 Mikhail Gorbachev with Nobel Peace Prize winners Shimon Peres and Yasser Arafat, Israel, 11 January 1999.

40 *Nobel Peace Prize Laureates Betty Williams, Shimon Peres, Rigoberta Menchú, Mikhail Gorbachev, David Trimble, F.W. de Klerk and Joseph Rotblat, Rome, 22 April 1999.*

41 *With Helmut Kohl and George Bush Senior at the presentation of the Point Alpha Prize, Germany, 16 June 2005.*

42 World Summit of Nobel Peace Laureates. Betty Williams, the Dalai Lama, Mikhail Gorbachev, Muhammad Yunus and Mairead Maguire, 15 December 2007.

43 After the launch of Call Me Ted, *by CNN founder Ted Turner, Gorbachev Foundation, 4 November 2009. Photo: Dmitry Belanovsky.*

44 *Meeting at the White House with US President Barack Obama, with Joe Biden and Michael MacFaul, Washington, D.C., 20 March 2009.*

45 *Mikhail Gorbachev and Angela Merkel at celebrations of the twentieth anniversary of the fall of the Berlin Wall, Berlin, 9 November 2009.*

46 *Tenth World Summit of Nobel Peace Laureates, with F.W. de Klerk and Lech Wałęsa, Berlin, 11 November 2009.*

47 *Book launch of* Alone With Myself, *Moscow, 13 November 2011.*
Photo: Dmitry Belanovsky.

48 *Public lecture at Novosti News Agency, Moscow, 30 March 2013.*
Photo: Dmitry Belanovsky.

A whole decade had been lost.

> The celebrations over the death of communism went on rather
> too long and caused people to lose sight of the complexity of the
> world with all its problems and contradictions. People forgot
> about poverty and underdevelopment. They forgot about the need
> to construct a new world order, fairer than the one we had left
> behind.

Again and again, I urged that the fight against terrorism should
not be reduced to a purely military response, and in particular
that it should not be used as cover for promoting purely selfish
interests. Gradually, however, my worst fears proved only too
well founded.

After some initial success in Afghanistan, which proved ephem-
eral, US leaders again became persuaded that the United States
could cope with any situation by relying on its own military
might. They increasingly resorted to unilateral decisions and
actions, and they announced that the United States was unilaterally withdrawing from the Anti-Ballistic Missile Treaty, which
ceased to be operative in June 2002. They refused to implement
the Comprehensive Nuclear Test Ban Treaty, withdrew from the
United Nations' Kyoto Protocol on climate change (George W.
Bush revoking his predecessor's signature), and refused to recognize the jurisdiction of the United Nations' International Criminal
Court.

The world began to be drawn into a new round of militarization, growth of military budgets, development and production of
ever more sophisticated 'smart' weapons. Preparations began for
a military operation against Saddam Hussein's regime in Iraq.

The invasion of Iraq was the culmination of the US policy of
unilateral action. I heard about it at Tokyo railway station, when
I received a mobile phone call from the correspondent of Interfax.
I immediately described it as a mistake that would have immense
negative consequences for the United States and the rest of the
world. These are making themselves felt to this day.

Poverty is a political problem

In the first decade of the twenty-first century, then, it became clear that the world's politicians were failing to cope with the challenges of security, nuclear weapons or terrorism. Matters were no better in respect of two other crucial global problems: the challenge of poverty and underdevelopment, and the global environmental crisis.

In October 2004, we devoted the Assembly of the World Political Forum to the problem of poverty. Interest in the topic and the level of participation were wholly exceptional. Among the speakers at plenary meetings were the deputy UN secretary-general, Anwarul Chowdhury; the former prime minister of Malaysia, Mahathir Mohamad; former prime minister of Pakistan, Benazir Bhutto; the former German foreign minister, Hans-Dietrich Genscher; former UN secretary-general, Boutros Boutros-Ghali; vice-president of South Africa, Jacob Zuma; former Japanese prime minister, Toshiki Kaifu; former prime minister of India, Inder Kumar Gujral; former prime ministers of France, Lionel Jospin and Michel Rocard; former director-general of the World Trade Organization, Mike Moore; assistant UN secretary-general, Jeffrey Sachs; former Polish president, Wojciech Jaruzelski; former president of Portugal, Mário Soares; the personal representatives of the presidents of Nigeria and Kyrgyzstan; and other politicians, as well as representatives of social, governmental and religious organizations and the media.

Poverty is a political issue, I said in my speech at the opening of the assembly, and that became the leitmotif of the assembly. I believe the main thrust of my speech remains important today:

> In the 1990s, the hope was prevalent that this problem would solve itself as the economies of all countries developed on the 'only true basis' of the Washington Consensus. We remember how enthusiastically this view was supported by business, especially the transnational corporations. That kind of one-sided approach, however, always produces dismal results.
>
> Those who suffered most from this abstract theory were the developing countries, but the damage was not restricted to them.

To a large extent it was responsible for missing the opportunities that arose from the ending of the Cold War. Today it is clear new approaches are needed.

At the Millennium Summit at the United Nations in 2000, the heads of the world's states and governments took an important step forward by proclaiming their political will to solve the problem of world poverty and took on specific, quantified commitments to fight this evil. Now, only a few years after that event, for hundreds of millions of people in the third world, especially in Africa, those targets remain mere good intentions. Promises to develop fair trade conditions for developing countries, to give them access to markets, and for debt relief are not being kept.

Now, when the world has sufficient resources and there are specific ways to overcome poverty whose efficacy has been proven, the failure to resolve this problem relates primarily to a lack of political will. ...

Poverty is also a political issue because, if it is not resolved, the result will inevitably be a new division of the world, with consequences even more fraught than those of the division we overcame through our joint efforts to end the confrontation between East and West. The division of the world into islands of prosperity and zones of poverty and despair is more dangerous than the Cold War, because it is impossible to separate them from each other. Desperation provides conditions for extremism and terrorism to flourish, to say nothing of the floods of migration, the epidemics, and the emergence of new centres of instability.

Finally, poverty is a political issue because it is inseparable from the issues of democracy, human rights and fundamental freedoms. Democracy and development are in no way contradictory, but where the issue of poverty is not tackled for decades, people are prepared to sacrifice democracy and put their trust in politicians with authoritarian tendencies. The retreat of the wave of democracy that transformed the world at the end of the 1980s and early 1990s is largely due to this.

I am certain that democracy cannot be imposed by tanks and preventive strikes. It must grow as each country and its people develop, but we can create more favourable conditions for it to grow, and chief of these is overcoming poverty.

What I sensed in the speeches of the politicians and experts attending the forum was great concern at the critical situation of poverty in the world. Analysing the experience of different countries in the fight against poverty, they made their different suggestions for ways to resolve the problem, but what they were all agreed on was that poverty underlies virtually all the problems confronting humanity at the present stage of its development: the degradation of the environment, the lack of security and stable economic growth, terrorism, social marginalization and many other negative aspects of globalization.

I stressed that we must listen to the signals being sent by the anti-globalization movement. Although among the protesters calling for 'alternative globalization' there certainly were hoodlums, aggressive troublemakers and outright rabble-rousers, the vast majority of the hundreds of thousands of people taking to the streets were honest, concerned people putting forward an entirely reasonable demand: that globalization should not be a one-way process making the rich even richer and neglecting the poor. Here is the real situation:

- nearly a billion people in the world are starving, while one person in four in the United States suffers from obesity;
- of 34 million people with AIDS, 23 million live in Africa;
- Tokyo alone has as many telephone lines as the whole of Africa;
- 57 million children are deprived of the opportunity to attend school;
- in Botswana, average life expectancy is 41 years.

Eradication of poverty and hunger was the top Millennium Development Goal among those approved by world leaders at the Millennium Summit in 2000. Among the most immediate tasks were a plan by 2015 to reduce by half (compared with 1990), the proportion of people living in poverty, and to reduce by half the proportion of people suffering from hunger. What were the results? According to a 2013 UN report, the first task has been achieved: the proportion of people living on US$1.25 a day (the threshold of extreme poverty) fell from 47 per cent in 1990 to 22 per cent in 2010.

As we see, we are nevertheless still very far away from eradicating poverty. We are also far from eliminating hunger. Against the notable progress in China, India and a number of other countries, the situation in most African countries is all the more depressing. Aid from rich to poor countries, instead of increasing, has declined.

The global gap between the extremes of wealth and poverty continues to grow. According to *Forbes Magazine*, during 2013 the number of billionaires on the planet rose to 1,426, a more than threefold increase over the number at the end of the twentieth century. Their total capital amounted to $5.4 trillion, an increase on the previous year of $800 billion! The wealth of the billionaires is more than three times that of the poorer half of the global population.

This unheard-of concentration of wealth in the hands of a few undermines democracy, threatens the fabric of societies, and rules out equal opportunities for all. Mass poverty, meanwhile, is a drag on economic development, leads to instability, and facilitates the spread of crime and terrorism. Allowing mass poverty to continue while this accumulation of personal wealth at the other end of the spectrum proceeds unchecked is a serious challenge to the global community, a threat to peace and the security of the world.

There is, however, another issue that cannot be ignored in any honest discussion of the state of the world. I remember a conversation I had in 1992 with former US Secretary of State George Shultz. I pointed out to him: 'You Americans want to export your way of life to the rest of your world, but you consume 44 per cent of the world's electricity. If other countries were to live by your standards, the planet's resources would be totally exhausted within a few years.' I had in mind that for the world to continue in accordance with the old model would not only result in depletion of natural resources, but would also lead to environmental catastrophe. In all the years that followed, we have been witnessing a growing rift between man and nature. Some have looked on impassively, with indifference, while others have tried to halt this dangerous process. I have sided firmly with those who are disturbed by the environmental crisis and are trying to do something about it.

Responding to the Environmental Challenge

In 1992, a Conference on Environment and Development, the first 'Earth Summit' of heads of state and government, was convened by the United Nations in Rio de Janeiro. In parallel, a forum was held of representatives of public organizations, cultural figures and parliamentary and religious leaders from some dozens of countries. They discussed the role that should be played by civil society in the struggle against environmental threats. The participants of this forum sent me a letter, reminding me of an initiative I had suggested in 1990 at a forum of the Foundation for the Survival and Development of Humanity: to create a global environmental organization, like the International Red Cross in the humanitarian field, that would become a centre for efforts to save the planet from environmental disaster. They asked me to head efforts to create an International Green Cross. The wording of the letter was so genuine and insistent that I could not refuse.

Since childhood I have been very close to nature. I knew from my own experience how dependent human beings are on its condition and the changes taking place in it. I remembered only too well the dust storms in my native Stavropol, but it was only in Moscow, when I had access to the documents, that I learned of the environmental impact of the hydroelectric power stations on the Volga, and the slow destruction of the Aral Sea as a result of water being taken from the Syr Darya and Amu Darya rivers for irrigation. When we proclaimed the policy of Glasnost, among the first to make use of the opportunity to express their opinion were citizens protesting about pollution of the air and of freshwater reservoirs, the wasteful exploitation of forests and other damage inflicted on the environment. The situation had become so serious that, at the insistence of local people, dozens of polluting industrial enterprises were shut down. Mulling over whether to assume the duties of head of a global organization for the protection of nature, I was well aware that I would not get away with being a mere figurehead. This was going to be hard work. I could see that the environmental challenge might well prove the most demanding of all the tasks mankind would face in the twenty-first century. In an interview for the Japanese newspaper, *Asahi Shimbun* [*Morning Sun*], I said the environment was now my day job.

The date Green Cross International was founded is considered to be 18 April 1993, when the organization held its first general assembly in the Japanese city of Kyoto. This event was preceded by heated discussion about what kind of organization it should be. Some argued that it should be a kind of emergency response corps, sending 'green helmets' into environmental disaster areas. Others suggested we should follow the model of Greenpeace, mobilizing people for ambitious protest operations. I did not feel either option was very promising and found support from people with great experience and a profound understanding of the issues. The outstanding Norwegian scientist and explorer, Thor Heyerdahl, said at the organizational meeting before the first assembly: 'If we are going for "green helmets" I will not be in there with you. The need is for something different, an organization whose purpose is to change the way people think, to effect a transition to environmental awareness. The need is for specific projects leading to that goal.' As the discussion proceeded, with the lively participation of representatives from the United States, Russia, Japan, the Netherlands and Switzerland (and these countries were subsequently to provide the organizational muscle of the Green Cross), our view found favour.

We set forth the organization's philosophy in the Green Cross International Charter:

Life is precious. All forms of life have their own intrinsic value and share our planetary home in an interdependent community in which all parts are essential to the functioning of the whole. We have a moral and ethical obligation to preserve life in its integrity and maintain our planet healthy and secure for present and future generations.

The process began of forming national branches of the organization, in the course of which I visited many countries and took part in their founding conferences. Green Cross International sees its mission as being to respond to the combined challenges of security, poverty and environmental degradation. To achieve this, we:

- promote legal, ethical and behavioural norms that ensure basic changes in the values, actions and attitudes of government, the private sector and civil society, necessary to develop a sustainable global community;
- contribute to the prevention and resolution of conflicts arising from environmental degradation and shortages of natural resources;
- provide assistance to people affected by the environmental consequences of wars, conflicts and man made calamities.[1]

For many years, I served as president of Green Cross International and chairman of its board of directors. In 2008, we reorganized the management: I retained the honorary position of founding president and remained a member of the Board of Directors; Alexander Likhotal (Russia) was elected president and Jan Kulczyk (Poland) was elected chairman of the board. I am grateful to them and to dozens of other people who have supported me in this major project and who today continue it with energy and enthusiasm.

During its existence, Green Cross International has initiated a series of programmes for 'environmental healing' of the Earth. One of the most important has been the Legacy Programme, which had the aim of dealing with the environmental legacy of the Cold War and the arms race (eliminating stockpiles of chemical weapons, toxic contamination, etc.). In 2000, I undertook a major initiative to overcome the inertia building up in the process

---

[1] Charter of Green Cross International, Geneva, 16 January 2010, p. 1; http://www.gcint.org/wp-content/uploads/2015/06/GCI_Charter_2010.pdf. Accessed 21 August 2015.

of eliminating chemical weapons, of which the United States and Russia had together accumulated more than 65,000 tonnes. Destruction of Russia's stockpiles of chemical weapons had been halted due to lack of funds, and also as the result of demands and questions raised by other parties to the UN Convention on the Elimination of Chemical Weapons, which had not been addressed for several years.

I sent letters to the leaders of Russia, the United States, the United Kingdom, Switzerland and other countries appealing to them to give firm financial commitments in relation to the destruction of chemical weapons. In response, the Russian government substantially increased funding for its programme. Important steps were also undertaken by the US government.

Another important Green Cross International project was the Earth Dialogues, a series of public forums devoted to the ethical aspects of sustainable development. The first dialogue was held in Lyon in 2002, with the French prime minister and several other ministers participating. Lyon was followed by Barcelona, New York and Lahore, and similar events were held in Russia and Italy. In 2006, I participated in an Earth Dialogue in Brisbane.

My work in the international environmental movement led to involvement in the Earth Charter project, whose aim was to draft a kind of environmental code of best practice for the planet, a declaration of basic principles and values to enable the creation of a just, sustainable and peaceful global community in the twenty-first century.

The idea of an Earth Charter was first put forward in 1987 by the World Commission on Environment and Development (the Brundtland Commission). It was supported in 1992 by the then secretary-general of the UN, Boutros Boutros-Ghali, at the Earth Summit in Rio de Janeiro, but it was only in 1994 that Maurice Strong, secretary-general of the Earth Summit, and I, through organizations each of us had founded (the Earth Council and Green Cross International), breathed life into the project as a civil society initiative. The government of the Netherlands offered to provide financial support.

The final version of the Earth Charter was officially presented to the international community on 29 June 2000 at a launch ceremony in the Peace Palace in The Hague in the presence of Queen Beatrix of the Netherlands. The General Conference of UNESCO subsequently approved a resolution supporting it.

The efforts of ecologists and the environmentally aware section of the world community to get the idea of environmentally sustainable development put into practice ran into major obstacles. Although the United Nations fleshed it out into a specific action programme, a single-minded determination to promote the free play of market forces sent global development in the wrong direction, towards reduced sustainability.

This seriously alarmed many people, including me. When it came to the 'Rio + 10' conference in Johannesburg in 2002, I prepared the notes for a speech, but to my great regret was not able to attend.

We at Green Cross International were very concerned that the forum might not succeed. I sent more than 100 letters to heads of state and governments outlining the standpoint of our organization and received replies from the presidents of Russia, France and Poland, from the prime minister of Great Britain and many others. They all recognized the need to put environmental issues at the heart of politics and the social agenda.

More than 100 heads of state and governments went to Johannesburg, but many who were expected refused to attend. This was a bad sign, and indeed, hopes that the Johannesburg summit would be a turning point failed to materialize. Disagreements and vested interests again prevailed. The documents adopted were largely declarative, lacking specifics or binding provisions, and were really just one more disappointment.

The water crisis

Given the situation, action on specific environmental problems took on particular importance. One of those I had to deal with was the issue of the growing global shortage of fresh water. In July 2002, I took part in an international conference on Water for the World, organized through Green Cross International. The following year I took part in the World Water Forum. These began to be held regularly and attracted authoritative experts and politicians able to propose practical solutions.

In February 2009, in Brussels, an international conference on Peace with Water was held at the European Parliament, on the initiative of the World Political Forum. Its purpose was to develop proposals on conservation of water resources for consideration by those taking part in negotiations on a new international climate agreement. The water crisis, I said at the conference, is a combination of environmental, social, economic and political factors. According to UN estimates, nearly 900 million people do not have access to clean water and 2.6 billion live in insanitary conditions. Demand for water is constantly rising. Of the water in developing countries, 80 per cent is used for agricultural irrigation. The problem is being aggravated by global climate change. Access to water is beginning to cause international conflicts. Politics is being slow to respond to what is truly an emergency situation, despite numerous studies and reports from experts and environmental organizations. As founding president of Green Cross International, I coauthored such a report, together with three former political leaders of Sweden, Botswana and the Philippines, back in 2000. It was well received, but its recommendations have not been implemented.

The central principle we need to get acknowledged, we said, is that water, as a supremely important resource for all mankind, is common property and access to it must be declared a basic human right. This view was widely endorsed and the governments of many countries, as well as a number of business leaders, spoke out in support of it.

Green Cross International launched a Water for Life initiative that proposed developing an international convention on the right to water. It took many years to accomplish this but, finally, in 2010, the United Nations did adopt a resolution to include the right to water and sanitation as a fundamental human right. The international community found it difficult to agree on this important step, but eventually took it.

Practical implementation of the principle is even more difficult. Yet even quite simple solutions that do not require huge investment can save many human lives. As the result of just one Green

Cross International pilot programme in Ghana, 40,000 people living in the Volta River Basin have gained access to clean drinking water and sanitation. Another important area for our efforts is preventing conflicts over access to water resources, and exploitation of them as a means to exert political pressure or enforce ultimatums.

The threat of climate change

Another critical issue is global climate change. Every year brings further evidence that global warming, in which, in the view of most scientists, the main role is played by human activities, is causing anomalous weather patterns, leading to loss of life and bringing with it severe economic and social consequences. The 2010 Northern Hemisphere summer heat waves have by no means been the only disaster. Mudslides in China, unprecedented drought in Australia and India, floods in Pakistan and Central Europe – the list could easily be continued.

Meanwhile, the development of alternative and renewable sources of energy is sluggish. Progress in individual countries has little impact on the global situation. After all that has happened to the global economy in recent years, few people are likely to credit claims that the free market can solve all the problems.

The answer is for states to show collective political leadership and responsibility. They must take on a political commitment commensurate with the seriousness of the threat. We have to resolve the problem of 'climate injustice', where climate change has the most serious consequences for developing countries that do not have the resources necessary to counter them. The leaders of Western countries need honestly to admit the scale of the challenge and the need for systemic rather than cosmetic measures. A new global agreement must be based on scientific data, not on a compromise between group interests.

The major developing countries, by now comparable in terms of emissions with the industrialized countries, need also to take on serious commitments. The growth of the economic power of countries like China, India and Brazil must be matched by growth in their sense of ecological responsibility. Joining the fight against climate change is in their own interests. It is, nevertheless, for the rich countries to act first. Their inaction over the past 20 years gives them no right to lecture others on the subject.

In the final analysis, everybody will have to make sacrifices and learn to reach compromise solutions that take account of the interests of the major players in the world economy. Not that these always coincide perfectly.

We need a new model of development

The financial crisis that started in 2008, and which, in my opinion, is not yet over, demonstrated how closely intertwined are the three major challenges of the modern globalized world. Undeniably, militarism, expensive military interventions and the growth of military spending all played a crucial role in the explosive growth of budget deficits, most notably in the United States, that triggered the crisis. Another reason was the economic model itself, premised on overconsumption and excessive profits. It is this same model that condemns us to the continuing degradation of the environment. It is all one big tangle.

The crisis took world leaders completely by surprise. At the G8 summit in Japan just a couple of months before it started, they seemed to have no awareness of tell-tale signs of what was to come. Their reaction to the crisis when it came was little more impressive.

From the outset, I said that we could not restrict ourselves only to firefighting, and I had some questions I wanted to put to the 'Group of Twenty' leading economic powers in response to the crisis. The mere fact that the leaders of the G8 had now to be joined on an equal footing by the leaders of China, India, Brazil and nine other countries was very telling. That is simply how it now has to be, reflecting a shift in the global economic and political balance.

In early 2009, New York Times Syndicate published my article, listing questions I had for the G20, in newspapers around the world. The first of these was 'whether the decisions adopted in London can resolve the global financial and economic crisis, setting the world economy on track to sustainable growth'. My own opinion was that the decisions taken at the first summits of the G20 could only be a first step. 'Crisis prevention should not be the G20's main task. What's needed is a transition to a new model, integrating social, environmental and economic factors.'

Another question concerned the place of the G20 within the system of global institutions. 'What is this group?' I asked. 'A "global politburo", a "club of the powerful", a prototype for a world government? How will it interact with the United Nations?' I wrote:

> No group of countries, even if they account for 90 per cent of the world economy, can supersede or replace the United Nations. But clearly, the G20 could claim collective leadership in world affairs if it acts with due respect for the opinions of non-members. ... To avoid mistakes the G20 must be transparent and work closely with the UN. At least once a year, its summit meetings should be held at UN headquarters. It should submit a report for substantive discussion to the General Assembly.

I thought that the G20 could not ignore political problems closely linked with the fate of the world economy.

> One of the problems ripe for debate is the militarization of world politics and economics. Militarization deflects resources from the real economy, stimulates conflicts and creates an illusion that military rather than political solutions are viable. By initiating a serious discussion within the G20, world leaders can build momentum for the work of those UN organizations that are responsible for progress in this area.[2]

Within the framework of the World Political Forum and the World Summit of Nobel Peace Laureates, we carefully studied the course of the crisis and social processes accompanying it. During a trip to the United States in 2011, I saw protest demonstrations of the Occupy Wall Street movement that had sprung up and

[2] Mikhail Gorbachev, 'What Role for the G-20?', *New York Times*, 27 April 2009.

spread to many other countries. Millions of people were asking why it should be primarily ordinary people who were having to tighten their belts when they had not been responsible for the crisis. Extremists and irresponsible elements tried to hijack the protests, and that could, of course, only be condemned, but there were those who tried to use that as a pretext to write off the protest movement in its entirety.

I believed, and still do, that people have a legitimate democratic right to protest about extreme inequality and injustice in the distribution of wealth in society. In November 2011, I said at a conference of the Forum in Montpellier that the people who came out on to the streets and were 'occupying Wall Street' quite rightly blame the crisis on the mammoth corporations that push tax loopholes favourable to themselves through parliaments.

Politics, I pointed out, is confined in an iron cage by the demands and dogmas of neo-liberal economics, but every day it becomes increasingly obvious that these dogmas do not stimulate, but stifle, economic development.

The development model based on giving priority exclusively to the economic factors of profit and consumption, shovelling around huge amounts of money while ignoring social and economic responsibilities, has manifestly failed. It is fraught with catastrophic consequences. Transition to a different model, in stages but fairly urgent, struck me as inescapable. That, as I wrote in an article published in the *International Herald Tribune* and *Rossiyskaya Gazeta* in late 2009, will require a change in our system of values, a search for new drivers and incentives for economic development:

> The global economy must be reoriented toward the public good. It must emphasize issues like a sustainable environment, healthcare, education, culture, equal opportunities and social cohesion – including reducing the glaring gaps between wealth and poverty.
>
> Society needs this, and not just as a moral imperative. The economic efficiency of emphasizing the public good is enormous, even though economists have not yet learned how to measure it.

We need an intellectual breakthrough if we are to build a new economic model.[3]

Another issue needing to be rethought in the light of the crisis was the role of the state. 'Return of the State' was the title of an article I wrote at the very beginning of the crisis. More than 30 years ago, I said, 'an attack was launched on the role of the state. Economists, businessmen and politicians declared it to be the source of nearly all the economy's woes.' In those years, the electorate was choosing to vote for politicians who promised to cut back state bureaucracy and give greater freedom to entrepreneurs. This was exploited by people who, under the slogan 'a rising tide lifts all boats', wanted to give maximum freedom of action to large corporations, to exempt them from important obligations to society, and to dismantle structures safeguarding the welfare of workers.

Next, as the wave of globalization swept over the world, monetarist principles and a weakening of the role of government started to be introduced on an international scale. The Washington Consensus, I wrote, was an expression of these principles, imposed on many countries. What was the result?

Squeezing the state out of various areas of business and finance led to many organizations functioning entirely without regulation. Bubbles followed one after another: the dotcom bubble, the stock market, mortgage lending and financial bubbles. Although sooner or later all these bubbles burst, in the process a small group of individuals succeeded in accumulating fabulous wealth while the living standards of the majority, at best, stagnated. The obligation to assist poorer countries was simply ignored.

Weakening of the role of the state has fostered rampant financial fraud and corruption and facilitated the invasion by organized crime of the economies of many countries, as well as disproportionate growth in the role of corporate lobbies. Lobbyists are in reality a gigantic bureaucracy outside the state with huge resources at their disposal and levers for influencing

[3] Mikhail Gorbachev, New York Times, 9 December 2009.

politics. This distorts the democratic process and has serious consequences for society.

The crisis brought a period of sobering up. It was states and their leaders who were obliged to take over responsibility for rescuing the economy from the most dangerous deadlock in decades. Unfortunately, world leaders have not so far gone beyond fire-fighting measures, but sooner or later they will have little option but to return to doing their duty by society and the environment.

Only the state can lay down the ground rules in such matters, aggravated by the crisis, as equitable sharing out of the tax burden, stimulating economic growth, and ensuring the necessary level of social welfare safeguards. Only the state can deliver access for everyone to education and healthcare, and the development of fundamental science. Only the state can mobilize the resources and tools to promote and implement innovative technologies. Only the state is capable of establishing the robust standards and regulations without which there is no hope of effectively combating the ecological disaster threatening the world.

And, of course, only through the efforts of states, constantly driven on by the active involvement and unrelenting pressure of global civil society, will we find our way to a new political framework for international security and world governance. This must be based on repudiation of confrontational thinking, of the urge to dominate international affairs, on respect for freedom of choice and a plurality of cultures and models of development, a willingness to engage in dialogue and extensive cooperation. Which again brings us back to the ideals and principles of New Thinking.

Over the years, I have pondered how relations between states will evolve in the foreseeable future, and what role in building a new global architecture will be played by the countries that bear the greatest responsibility for good order in the world. Let me say at once that all nations, large, medium and small, can and must contribute to the process. The principle of sovereign equality of states, set down in the UN Charter, remains as valid today as ever it was. There is, however, also no doubt that the world's major powers, and Russia among them, must play the leading and most demanding role. It is they who have most to answer for to history.

The unipolar world, with one country invariably having the last word, did not come to pass. In the last two decades we have witnessed a gradual shift in the global balance of power. The 'collective West', the United States and the European Union, have increasingly to consider the opinions of other players on the stage of world politics. Primarily, that means Brazil, Russia, India, China and South Africa, all of whom are seeking to coordinate their policies within the new and, in my opinion, promising association of BRICS. At the same time, the centre of gravity of the global economy is increasingly shifting towards the Asia-Pacific region, where Japan remains prominent, but where other powerful countries are appearing: not only China, but also the countries of the Association of Southeast Asian Nations and, on the other side of the ocean, the countries of Latin America. All this is, of course, certain to have political repercussions.

In the past decades I have visited almost all the countries mentioned, met their leaders, representatives of civil society, scientists, artists and young people. I feel very fortunate to have had that opportunity. Nothing can replace seeing the world for yourself, sensing through personal contact what people are feeling, and entering into dialogue with them.

Meetings in America

George Shultz and Ronald Reagan

Remembering my first trips after relinquishing the presidency, rereading my speeches, press reports and interview, I can see that much of what was said is still relevant today. I hope that my reflections on the part played by the principal actors on the stage of world politics in the movement towards a new, more secure and just world order will be of value to those who take the responsibility for peace on our planet upon themselves.

In all the changes in the world, the United States remains the most important player, in politics, the world economy, science and technological innovation. To attempt to deny that would simply be unrealistic. Much depends on how the United States uses its potential, whether constructively through cooperation and dialogue, or by imposing its will on others. I took that as my starting point in preparing for my first 'post-presidential' visit to America.

I had no shortage of invitations, and was able to accept about a dozen of them. Then there was the question of when to go. I even had a visit from the US ambassador to Moscow, Bob Strauss. He conveyed President Bush's request that my trip should not take place until after an official visit by Yeltsin. The ambassador made it clear that this was being done at the insistence of the Russian side. I found such touchiness rather surprising, but Yeltsin and his entourage were already trying to isolate me and went to great lengths to avoid all contact. In practical terms there was no problem, because Yeltsin was going to the United States in February 1992 and my visit was scheduled for the first half of May.

It has to be said that later, during my trip, there were occasional, well, hiccups, caused by the eagerness of the Russian authorities of the time to cut Gorbachev down to size. The Russian ambassador to the United States, Vladimir Lukin, was instructed not to take part in any activities related to my visit. He was absent from the dinner to which President George Bush invited me at the White House, but then asked for a meeting at the hotel where I was staying in Washington, DC. Frankly, I found this silliness distasteful, and it did nothing to enhance the reputation of the Russian state authorities.

For me, the main thing was for the visit to be conducted in a way that would maximize its benefits for Russia and relations between our two countries. An extensive programme of meetings and speeches was arranged, and in two weeks we travelled 14,000 kilometres. I and my companions visited 11 of the greatest US cities: Los Angeles, San Francisco, Chicago, Atlanta, New York, Boston, and others. There were many speeches and meetings, including a speech to leaders of the US Congress. Former Secretary of State George Shultz, who headed the committee preparing my visit, did a great deal to achieve this result.

I would like to single George out. I remember our first meeting in 1985 very well. It occurred during his visit to Moscow to attend the funeral of General Secretary Konstantin Chernenko. Of course, we already knew that he belonged to the realists in Ronald Reagan's administration and advocated looking for a way out of the current deadlock in Soviet–US relations. From that first acquaintance it was difficult to tell how well we might be able to cooperate.

At the time, there were not a few among the leaders and our experts who believed we would get nowhere with Reagan and would just have to wait for a different, less conservative, less anti-communist president. I disagreed. I felt strongly there was no time to lose. I said that to George Shultz when we met, and it seemed to me I had found someone interested in continuing that conversation.

Preparations began for the first Soviet–American summit in six years. Shultz came to Moscow and Shevardnadze went to Washington, DC. It was heavy going. We had a sense that the idea of a substantive meeting, not just a first acquaintance but a serious discussion leading to meaningful results, was coming up against major obstacles in Reagan's administration. The Americans had a particularly sour reaction to our proposal that the summit should conclude with a joint statement announcing a programme to break the deadlock in negotiations on disarmament and restoring normal relations between our countries. Who needs rhetoric? What the Americans needed was action. By action, they meant unilateral concessions by the Soviet Union, while their own position remained unchanged.

In the end, however, common sense prevailed. Literally at the last moment, Shultz told us that the Americans were prepared to work on the joint statement. We discovered that Secretary of Defence Caspar Weinberger and other 'hawks' in the administration were furious that Shultz had managed to persuade President Reagan to take this step.

When we began work on the text, we found Shultz to be a constructive partner. We were able to document the vitally important principles that nuclear war was totally unacceptable and that the two sides would not strive to gain military superiority over each other. We recalled that work many times in our conversations in later years, and I am glad to say that Shultz never departed from those principles.

We agreed that the negotiations would be conducted through official channels, that our chief negotiators would be the USSR Minister of Foreign Affairs and the US Secretary of State, and also our countries' ambassadors in Moscow and Washington. Shultz was against secret diplomacy, 'back channels' and similar methods. I was all in favour of his approach. Negotiations should be conducted honestly and, as far as possible, openly, without offstage plots and surprises.

In the course of my numerous meetings with George Shultz, I gradually built up an understanding of his negotiating style and approach to the big issues of world politics. He showed himself to be a true diplomat, able to defend his negotiating stance, while at the same time looking out for points of contact with the position of the other party. It was crucial that at moments of heightened tension, which most often resulted from attempts by opponents of improved Soviet–American relations to put a spanner in the works, George showed restraint and tolerance and tried to keep the temperature down. This was much in evidence, for example, during the 'spy ring scandal' in autumn 1986, which almost torpedoed the Reykjavik summit.

Before Eduard Shevardnadze left for the UN General Assembly session in New York in September 1986, I instructed him to convey to Shultz the question, partly rhetorical but important, of who needed to provoke a bout of spy mania on the eve of a meeting on which the fate of negotiations on nuclear disarmament depended. I was not, of course, expecting a direct answer to the question, but to give Secretary of State Shultz his due, he participated personally in negotiations which succeeded in untying the knot. It was a real diplomatic marathon, and reports of the conversations were forwarded urgently to Moscow. Ultimately, a solution was devised that enabled both sides to save face.

In the spring of 1987, when George Shultz arrived in Moscow to discuss preparations for my first visit to the United States, literally on the eve of his arrival, a new 'sex for secrets' spy scandal broke. Opponents of better Soviet–American relations behaved like personal enemies of Shultz. The Secretary of State found himself in a difficult position and obliged to read out in Moscow a text with accusations against the Soviet Union. We could see he was doing so without the least enthusiasm. Most of our time was spent on specific issues relating to the negotiations on nuclear weapons. We were able to make progress not only on the issue of medium-range missiles, but also on a number of problems concerning strategic weapons.

Many years later, George and I met in Moscow and were reminiscing about the dramatic months before the signing in Washington of the first agreement on real nuclear disarmament, the Treaty on the Elimination of Intermediate- and Shorter-Range Missiles. George told me:

> The amazing thing is that when everyone realized we were on the verge of signing the treaty, it became apparent that many people in the United States and many Western leaders were opposed to the 'zero option' of withdrawing all Soviet and American inter-

mediate nuclear missiles from Europe. Yet at one time that had been proposed by President Reagan himself. It seemed to me a matter of honour to complete the job, but by no means everybody agreed. We had opponents in our administration as well as outside it. Kissinger was against; Scowcroft was against; Mitterrand and Thatcher were against it too. It took a whole lot of effort and political will to get that treaty finally signed.

In early 1988, it became clear that Shultz wanted Ronald Reagan's presidency to end with the signing of the strategic arms reduction treaty. It seemed that was also what the president wanted, but it was Shultz who shouldered the main burden. He came to Moscow several times, accompanied by large groups of experts, and the negotiating was very intense.

Meeting Shultz during those months I could see that the burden was taking a toll on him physically. He often looked fatigued. In his memoirs, he later wrote candidly about how bitterly opponents of the treaty had resisted it in Washington, and this at a time when 98 per cent of the provisions of the treaty had already been agreed. This time, alas, the Washington 'hawks' defeated the Secretary of State. He told me later that it had been his greatest disappointment in all his years in Reagan's administration.

My visit to the United States in May 1992 began with a meeting with Ronald Reagan, which was to prove our last. Ronald and Nancy invited us to the Reagan Presidential Library in Simi Valley, California. I have been in several American presidential centres, and each in its way reflects not only the career but also the personality of the president. Nancy showed us the place next to the Reagan Library where, as she put it, 'we shall some day be laid to rest'. 'But', she added, 'we are in no hurry.'

We also visited the Reagan ranch near Los Angeles. Over the years of our joint efforts we had come to understand each other better. It was not easy for a right-wing American conservative and a person whose career had developed inside the Soviet Communist Party to achieve mutual understanding and trust, but we were conscious of our responsibilities towards our countries and the world, and that made the difference.

I remember a few years ago asking George Shultz: 'What if the president had been someone other than Reagan, do you think we would have been able to make progress on nuclear disarmament and get that first treaty signed?' After a moment's reflection, he replied:

> I guess not. Reagan was the most conservative US president for many years. No one on the right could accuse him of being too soft or failing to stand up sufficiently for US interests. If instead there had been a Democrat in his place, those same right-wing politicians, and many other Republicans, would have pounced on him and made it impossible to get the treaty ratified.

The Reagan Presidential Library awarded me a Freedom medal. I wanted to make my speech on receiving the award more personal than the usual diplomatic courtesies. I reminded my audience that by no means everywhere in the world had the four freedoms triumphed that Franklin D. Roosevelt had proclaimed in 1941: freedom of speech, freedom of worship, freedom from want, and freedom from fear. All these freedoms, I said, are constituents of the concept of freedom of choice. Our generation had not found it easy to turn the course of global events in a direction that would make it possible to implement those principles.

We grew up in a climate of confrontation that distorted our thinking and our political vision. I will say frankly, none of us politicians here were entirely free of the taint of confrontational stereotypes but, at first barely noticeably, but then with growing awareness, we began to recognize it was essential to break out of that vicious circle.

I believe that came about because we listened to ordinary people.

> It was the popular consciousness that rejected and overcame the stereotypes of the Cold War, the image of an enemy, the reflex hostility towards the other side. In even the darkest years, many Americans and Russians were drawn to each other in friendship and refused to view each other through the perspective of preparation for war.

The Cold War and how it had been overcome was the main topic of my speech in Fulton, where we went from California. Westminster College in this small town in Missouri is where, 46 years before me, Winston Churchill gave his famous speech about the descending of an 'iron curtain' in Europe. On the slope of a gentle hillside were long rows of benches for an audience of some 15,000 people, many of whom had come from other cities.

At the back of the platform from which I was speaking rose a massive concrete wall with gaping openings in the shape of human figures. The artist's imagination had found a succinct way of expressing the drama of the Cold War, the irrepressible desire of human beings to break through the wall of alienation and confrontation. It was symbolic that the designer of this monument was a granddaughter of Winston Churchill. She was present in the audience and, of course, there was good reason for her sculpture to have been erected in Fulton.

In his speech, Churchill had called for the world to be saved from the communist threat. The decisive role, he believed, would be played by power, and primarily by armed force. Indeed, he titled his speech 'The Sinews of Peace'. Reminding my audience of this, I told them of my own view of the situation at that time. 'The world community had a unique opportunity to steer the world in a different direction and radically alter the role of force and war. That, of course, ultimately depended on the Soviet Union and the United States.' That opportunity had not been taken. Stalin's government saw the victory over fascism as tantamount to a victory for socialism and embarked on a course of spreading its own kind of 'socialism' to the rest of the world. The West too, however, and first and foremost the United States, also blundered. 'The conclusion that military aggression by the USSR was likely to follow, was fallacious and dangerous. That was out of the question.'

The outcome of mutual distrust and misinterpretation of events was the Cold War. 'Under the guise of protestations of peace-loving intentions and the need to protect the interests of the world's peoples, both sides took decisions that split the world. Their antagonism was misrepresented by both sides as a necessary confrontation between good and evil.'

I urged my listeners to acknowledge an important reality: it was not possible in this day and age for 'particular states or groups of states to reign supreme on the international stage'. My speech in Fulton was less a polemic against Churchill than against those hatching plans for global domination.

This speech was followed by meetings at two major American universities, Stanford in California and Emory in Atlanta, Georgia. University and student audiences are always wonderfully attentive and lively. Such wise and experienced politicians as Jimmy Carter and George Shultz as well as university professors and government representatives were there, and actively joined in the debate.

One of the main points I wanted to make in my speeches was that we cannot afford to adopt a fatalistic attitude towards the future. Those who believe it is unpredictable and that human beings are powerless to alter the inexorable course of events are plain wrong. It is no good trying to support this view by referring back to history. History was not fated. We had succeeded in overcoming the 'logic of fatalism' and put an end to the Cold War, but now, I warned, events were developing ever more rapidly, and we must change in order not to allow the intellectual and moral development of mankind to lag behind changing existential conditions. Mankind has no right to refuse to rationally regulate impersonal processes. That would be a fatal mistake.

I spoke to the students about the state under the rule of law (a topic suggested by George Shultz) and about democracy. 'There is nothing automatically safeguarding democracy from defeat. It will always find itself being tested. It has no shortage of open or covert opponents and false friends. Democracy does not just arrive by itself. It needs constantly to be cultivated and nurtured.'

The twin American capitals of New York and Washington, DC were, of course, the most critical stops of the trip. They are where the American elites are concentrated, with their enormous potential, but also certain quirks and delusions. Would I succeed in conveying my thoughts and conclusions to these influential people?

Speaking at the Council on Foreign Relations in New York, I focused mainly on the relationship between the United States and Russia. As far as I can tell, I said, two basic approaches have evolved to relations between our countries: 'The first aims to profit from the current state of the Russian Federation by preventing her from enjoying to the full the status of a great power. The second is based on the premise that a strong, rejuvenated, democratic Russia is in the national interests of the United States.' I urged my audience of experts in international relations and military politics to make a firm decision. The top priority should be

> to focus on the need for a radical change of attitude in strategic military thinking. I have to say that, with some exceptions, it remains – at least in military circles – determined by regarding each other as potential adversaries. The challenge is to formulate jointly a doctrine to ensure mutual security, encompassing military affairs and intelligence gathering. Science may also have a contribution to make.

Reading that speech today, I can only regret that those suggestions were not acted on at the time, and today it seems completely utopian to many. I believe that now, when the situation is largely changed, this is a task that will have to be returned to, if only to avoid making new mistakes.

The discussion at the Economic Club of New York was meaningful and at times heated. It was taking place at a complicated and bewildering moment. Economic reforms had begun in Russia and I was in favour of their overall direction, but critical of the 'shock therapy' approach. I was equally critical of the hopes placed on the magic wand of recommendations from American advisers and donor aid. I told the assembled businessmen and economists:

> No donor is going to be able to cure an ailing body if it does not itself fight disease and mobilize its own organic defences. Not even the wealthiest donor has the power and resources to restore such a vast territory as Russia and the Commonwealth of Independent States to health. The most promising approach is stable, mutually beneficial cooperation. 'Not donations, but trade and investment' is how I would summarize my view.

Unfortunately, American business was clearly in no hurry to enter Russia. I pointed out that there was almost no American capital invested. Such diffidence on the part of American entrepreneurs might lead to imbalances that would benefit neither them nor Russia. I urged them to act. 'Today a campaign in the East is a bold venture, but not a gamble. There is risk, but it is entirely quantifiable. Anyone who comes into the Russian market and, despite all the difficulties, stays, will soon be in a position to implement large-scale projects.'

Regrettably, not many American corporations went down that road, but for those that did, it paid off, as I was told by the chief executive of Boeing Commercial Airplanes, Alan Mulally, when we met some years later. He spoke admiringly of Russian engineers and said many components of the latest Boeing aircraft were being manufactured in Russia. This, of course, raises the question of why Russia's leaders missed the opportunity to develop our own aircraft industry. I believe our dealings with the world's giants could have been handled much more to Russia's benefit.

In Washington I had a meeting with President George Bush, visiting the White House, which I had previously visited during my two official visits, in a private capacity, without any claim to an official role. It was nevertheless no mere diplomatic courtesy visit. I spent more than two hours in the residence of the president of the United States, and our conversation was serious and meaningful.

First there was lunch in one of the rooms, attended by Barbara Bush, James Baker, Brent Scowcroft, an adviser and close friend of the president, the president's brother, Preston, and son George W. Bush, at that time still only preparing to run for governor of Texas. George W. Bush behaved modestly and gave the impression of being very polite.

We talked about the prospects for relations with Russia, Scowcroft particularly asking questions. He wanted to know how robust the Commonwealth of Independent States was organizationally, and asked whether it was necessary to build a relationship with it. That was a difficult question to answer. Of course, I could see even then that the CIS was something of a formality. I advised that, after the collapse of the Soviet Union it was now necessary to have relations with the individual states, but primarily, of course, with Russia. It would be there that the main events that would decide the fate of democracy in the vast post-Soviet space would be played out. It would be with Russia too that the major issues of military politics would have to be agreed, and in cooperation with Russia that regional problems would have to be addressed. At the same time, I said I was sure that the states that had emerged after the dissolution of the USSR would eventually have to find some form of integration, and America should not interfere with that.

Then there were just the three of us, Bush, Baker and myself, and we recalled what we had managed to do together. This was not mere reminiscence, however. We talked about my impressions on this trip and exchanged views on international issues. James Baker expressed astonishment that the question of who owned and controlled the nuclear weapons in the CIS inherited from the Soviet Union seemed not to have been cleared up. Leonid Kravchuk and other Ukrainian figures appeared to be envisaging almost joint control: 'three fingers on the button'. Clearly, the only sensible solution was to concentrate all nuclear weapons in Russia. I was shocked that 'the heirs of the Soviet Union' proved incapable of reaching agreement by themselves and needed Baker's mediation.

I talked to Bush and Baker frankly about my concern over events in Yugoslavia. So far, in Russia we had got by without a lot of bloodshed, I said, but in Yugoslavia everything was building up towards a major disaster. Bush replied that he was concerned about this himself and the US did not want to force the pace. I told him about my talks in the Kremlin in November 1991 with the leaders of Serbia and Croatia, Slobodan Milošević and Franjo Tuđman. It seemed to me then, and later, that the international community was not doing enough to move developments in Yugoslavia in the direction of negotiations.

Partners should be equal

I was to speak in the US Congress, and prepared meticulously. I was given a warm and dignified reception at the highest level. Members of the House of Representatives and the Senate assembled in the historic setting of the Statuary Hall and I was welcomed by the leaders of the majority and minority parties. I knew many of those present from meetings and negotiations in Moscow and Washington. I recognized that this was not so much personal to me as to the change for the better in the relationship between our countries.

Tom Foley, the speaker of the House of Representatives, referred to that in his welcoming speech:

> Many Americans first began to hope for true world peace, for an end to the Cold War against all previous experience, despite years of frustration and superpower stand-off, when they understood that Mikhail Gorbachev genuinely saw disarmament and the end of US–Soviet tensions as the only solution to his country's economic and social problems and those of the rest of the international community.

Foley's speech showed a much deeper understanding of what happened in 1991 than many of our so-called analysts:

> It was with great apprehension for President Gorbachev's safety and the safety of his family that many Americans watched and waited during those anxious hours of the August 1991 attempted coup. The swift flow of events that followed brought an end to the Soviet Union, a dissolution that President Gorbachev had not wanted to see. Yet it was his commitment to the welfare of the peoples of the Soviet Union that ensured a peaceful and orderly transition to the 12 new independent states of the Commonwealth of Independent States. The peoples of those new nations owe Mikhail Gorbachev thanks for the peaceful relations that have ensued with the United States and its allies. So too does the entire international community, so too does the United States of America.[1]

---

[1] Mikhail Gorbachev, 'Address to Both Houses of Congress', 14 May 1992; http://www.c-span.org/video/?26080-1/address-houses-congress. Accessed 26 July 2015.

Politicians, I said in my speech, have a responsibility to ensure that their nation has a correct understanding of its own vital interests. 'It is dangerous to pretend these coincide with the opportunistic, selfish needs of particular influential groups or sections of society.' The Russian Federation, looking to establish itself as a new state with its own national interests, is seeking a partnership of equals with the United States. This is also in the interests of America, not least, I said, because 'Russia will undoubtedly be a large, prosperous state whose weight in the world will be in accordance with its immense potential.' I expressed that view in the United States on many occasions, both during my first trip and later. It is a conviction I still hold.

Returning to the main theme of my speech, the issue of an equal and mutually beneficial partnership between our countries, I said:

I am, of course, aware that there are people in the United States who believe the interests of your country would be better served by a weak, fragmented Russia relegated to a secondary role in world affairs. I will not argue with them, but just ask two questions that I think are important.

The first. Is it really wise to base a policy on an impossibility? It will be impossible to keep Russia out of global politics. In the longer term that is a fruitless endeavour whose only result will be to damage the prospects of democracy in Russia.

The second question is, does the United States not actually need a good, rather influential partner in order to conduct a rational foreign policy? There is no reason why Russia should not be such a partner. She is not opposed to the United States, has no wish to compete with America and, in any case, the era of superpowers looks increasingly like becoming a thing of the past.

Reading these words, spoken more than 20 years ago, some will doubtless wish to accuse me of naivety in the light of much that has happened in the world and been done in US foreign policy in the meantime. I do not take them back. The United States chose to go in the opposite direction, behaved like a 'hyperpower', and got its fingers badly burned in the process. The world will, in the end, be obliged to return to the principles of international law, equal partnerships and shared security. Today, many in America have come to recognize this. It would, of course, have been much better if it could have been recognized sooner and by all of them.

My trip was coming to an end. The last venue was Boston, for a dialogue with the students and professors of Harvard University and a visit to the John F. Kennedy Presidential Library. For many of my generation, Kennedy was special. I still remember the impression his death made on us and cannot believe, as I have said openly, that his assassination was the deed of a loner. Some years ago, I visited the Sixth Floor Museum at the School Book Depository building in Dallas, now a memorial to Kennedy, and looked down at the street from the window from which Oswald shot. A chill ran down my spine. I wrote in the visitors' book, 'He looked far ahead and wanted to change a great deal. Perhaps that is the key to the mystery of the death of President John F. Kennedy.'[2] Later, when I met Oliver Stone, who directed a film about Kennedy, I told him what I had written. Stone agreed.

The hours spent at the Kennedy Library were amazingly warm and sociable. Our trip had ended, I said, among friends. We were welcomed by the president's widow, Jackie Kennedy, a woman of great charm, his brother Senator Ted Kennedy, whom I already knew well and appreciated, and other members of the extensive Kennedy family which has suffered so many tribulations. Raisa and I made no attempt to conceal our respect for them.

I felt it was important to talk of the continuing relevance of the heritage of John F. Kennedy. I recalled his words two years into the presidency that the problems had been more difficult than he anticipated, and that the resources of the United States for solving them were not limitless. I said these words encourage us to reflect seriously. 'Already in those days the world badly needed states to cooperate in combating the challenges it faced. The world needed thinking that looked beyond pretensions to dominate and solve all problems single-handed.'

[2] Gorbachev on JFK; http://jfkfacts.org/tag/mikhail-gorbachev. Accessed 26 July 2015.

I recalled, as I was often to do subsequently to American audiences, the president's advice, referred to above, at the American University in Washington, DC on 10 June 1963, 'not to see conflict as inevitable, accommodation as impossible, and communication as nothing more than an exchange of threats'.

That is precisely what we were guided by when we embarked on the huge challenge of changing the international climate together with Presidents Reagan and Bush. Even more relevant is that President Kennedy's appeal was backed by an audacious specific proposal to conclude a nuclear test ban treaty and the US decision to conduct no more such tests in the atmosphere.

In the light of how swiftly negotiations proceeded to conclusion of the Limited Nuclear Test Ban Treaty, banning nuclear tests in the atmosphere, underwater or in space, it is particularly noticeable how many opportunities were missed during the decades that followed, I said.

The politicians of that later period proved capable only of keeping the world away from a global nuclear disaster: they were unable to halt the build-up through inertia of nuclear stockpiles and the growing threat of catastrophe. What was it they lacked? I believe they lacked the ability to look beyond immediate problems, to make a moral choice and act accordingly.

On this last day of my major visit to America, I attempted a summary. I shared my impressions with the guests at this concluding lunch:

I have had revealed to me a huge, multifaceted land. The greatest impression is from conversations with ordinary Americans, people I met in the streets of the cities we visited. I saw not an arrogant America, looking out with smug self-satisfaction on the rest of the world, but a reflective, thoughtful America. The United States is pondering its problems and questions of justice. It is turning its attention to those who, to date, have been bypassed by the American dream, and while this society retains its dissatisfaction and capacity for critical self-evaluation, we can be confident that America will overcome its problems and cope with its difficulties.

Many Americans I spoke to told me that the ending of the Cold War had changed their lives. The explanation was simply that for decades people had been living under the constant shadow of the nuclear threat. In the United States, just as in the Soviet Union, people were instructed on how to behave in the event of a nuclear attack, what supplies they would need to stock up on, how to shield themselves from deadly radiation (assuming they were not killed instantly). The end of the Cold War freed them from a nagging fear which, over time, they might get used to or forget but which was always subconsciously there.

The role of the United States in the world

Since then, I have been back to the United States many times, visiting dozens of towns and states, giving lectures to students, business associations, Russia analysts and international relations researchers, and social activists. Americans are good listeners: you can always tell from the reaction of the audience how they are responding to what has been said. After the talk there is always time to answer questions, most of which show a genuine desire to make sense of what is happening in the world and to understand the speaker's standpoint.

American newspapers, as a rule, report the talks objectively and in detail, and after these sessions I am curious to know what people are saying about them. I remember the comment of one American who had come from another city to hear me in Denver, Colorado. He said, 'When Gorbachev is visiting, I always try to get to his talks even if I have to travel miles. I don't always agree with what he says, but always find it interesting. I respect his opinion because I can see he is stating it honestly and directly. Including when he is criticizing America.'

I have, of course, often criticized US policy. When you meet Americans you notice that literally all of them, ordinary people and politicians alike, believe that America is a special country, exceptional, as Barack Obama once said, and that it has a right to lead the world. That can sometimes grate, but what is more important, I think, is not which words are used but what kind of world leader America wants to be: an exclusive, monopolistic leader or a leading partner cooperating with other countries and taking account of their opinions. After the Soviet Union disappeared off the political map, that question became supremely important.

My spring 1992 visit to the United States coincided with the presidential election campaign which, this time, in addition to the two main party candidates, President and Republican George Bush and Democrat Bill Clinton, included a third candidate, multimillionaire Ross Perot. One journalist even asked me, no doubt in jest, whether I might stand as vice-president on Perot's ticket. I told him I had higher ambitions than that, having already been a president.

More seriously, the first election campaign in the new circumstances showed that Americans expected their politicians to focus mainly on domestic social and economic issues rather than foreign policy. I was often asked, though, for my thoughts on Russia's role in the world now that the Cold War had ended. My answer was that America should not try to play the role of global policeman. I detected that, in any case, American people were disinclined to support any such behaviour.

The opinion polls were suggesting George Bush was lagging behind Bill Clinton. That may be why, in the final stages of the campaign, he rather went over the top and, in a bid for votes, started talking about how the United States had won the Cold War. It did not help him to win the election.

I expressed my view on this subject unambiguously: the ending of the Cold War had not been a victory for one side or the other. It had been our shared victory, a victory for common sense. If one side was going to declare itself the winner, if the opinion took root that America was always right, that her democracy was the most democratic and her ideals the most ideal, and if she decided to promote her ideals through the use of force as the most effective argument in international affairs, disaster would be sure to follow. The only proper way, I stressed again and again, was cooperation and partnership based on the principles of international law.

Bill Clinton won the 1992 election. He had no international experience and at first focused, with considerable success, on America's domestic problems. Economic growth resumed, education, science and new technology were given significant support, and that served to ensure that four years later he was re-elected with a substantial majority. As far as his foreign policy was concerned, as I told him bluntly when I got to know him better after his presidency, there was much I disagreed with strongly.

The US political elite, having claimed victory in the Cold War, drew the 'appropriate conclusions' from this delusion. Overconfident about its power, it embarked not only on military intervention in the Yugoslav conflict, but launched missile strikes against Iraq. Its 'victory complex' did nothing for relations with Russia.

On the surface, everything seemed to be going on satisfactorily. A regular exchange of visits took place, like a well-rehearsed stage production, with hugs and mutual praises, but this became an irritant. There was no sense of genuine equality, no real sense of partnership, and when, in the second half of the 1990s, the US Ambassador in Moscow asked me what advice I would give President Clinton, who was about to visit Russia, I said it would be best not to pat Russia on the back. Compliments on the policy of shock therapy, I told him, which had weakened Russia and plunged huge numbers of our citizens into poverty, would only annoy people who were beginning to wonder if a weak, half-strangled Russia was what America wanted.

Behind the facade of amity, American policy took no notice of Russia's interests. This was apparent not only in the decision to press ahead with expanding NATO. An attempt to isolate Russia from the new states of the former Soviet Union was increasingly obvious. Anti-Russian sentiment and behaviour were encouraged in Ukraine; there was an anti-Russian tinge to the US flirtation with the president of Uzbekistan; negotiations over oil in the Caspian Sea region excluded Russia completely. Russia's weakness was exploited in order to exclude her from influence in global politics. In the late 1990s, a respected Russia analyst delivered a paper with the title, 'World Without Russia?'.[3] Politicians, he claimed, might have to get used to the idea that the world's major issues would have to be resolved with little or no Russian involvement.

I spoke against this possibility. In my speeches while travelling around the United States, in articles and interviews, I argued that Russia would revive. In her history there had been times of troubles and severe ordeal, but she had always emerged from them to became a strong, influential power, a nation without which no world order was imaginable.

'America needs its own Perestroika'

In the final stages of his presidency, Bill Clinton seemed to have understood that a foreign policy of unilateral interventions was, in the long run, unsustainable. At the 1999 Istanbul summit of the Organization for Security and Co-operation in Europe, he recalled the Charter of Paris for a New Europe and spoke of the need for mutual consideration of the interests of all countries. The baton was, however, already passing to a new president, George Bush Junior.

What course of global action would the new president choose? What kind of relations would he develop with Russia? It was impossible to know the answer in advance. On the one hand, he was saying US foreign policy should be more humble and modest. As secretary of state he appointed Colin Powell, whom I knew well as a politician whose thinking was realistic and balanced. One could hope that George W. Bush had inherited the gene for moderation from his father. On the other hand, it was known that he was susceptible to the influence of neo-conservatives, supporters of an aggressive foreign policy, of whom there were many in his entourage. Chief among them was the vice-president, Dick Cheney, whom I well remembered from his role in the

[3] Thomas Graham, Jr, 'World without Russia', Jamestown Foundation Conference, Washington, DC, 9 June 1999; http://carnegieendowment. org/1999/06/09/world-without-russia. Accessed 26 July 2015.

administration of George Bush Senior as someone who thought in Cold War categories.

In April 2001, I was on one of my trips to the United States, crossing the country from north to south and east to west. I was told that the State Department and the White House were interested in talking to me. Needless to say, I did not decline the invitations, the more so because this was before the first meeting between George W. Bush and Vladimir Putin.

My talk with Colin Powell was thorough and detailed, and certainly not limited to reminiscing about our joint efforts to end the Cold War and nuclear arms race. In respect of relations with Russia, Powell seemed to me to be thinking constructively, emphasizing opportunities for working together to resolve regional problems, particularly in the Middle East. The secretary of state very much wanted his term in office to culminate in a settlement of the Israel–Palestine conflict, but subsequently he found himself drawn into quite other matters.

My visit to the White House, which I had not entered since 1992, began with a conversation with Condoleezza Rice, who had been appointed national security adviser to the president. She had begun her career in national politics in the administration of George Bush Senior, taking part in the negotiations on disarmament. Bush and his adviser on national security matters, Brent Scowcroft, had a high opinion of her. The newspapers wrote that she had claims to great influence on the president.

Some time after the beginning of our conversation, President Bush, Vice-President Cheney and White House Chief of Staff Andrew Card came in. Such an august delegation was a signal in itself, and our meaningful conversation was no mere diplomatic nicety. Bush said he understood the importance of Russia and her role in the world and was minded to cooperate with her. There needed to be a meeting with President Putin as soon as possible, he said, and hoped there would shortly be an announcement about it.

What he then went on to say was obviously intended to be conveyed to the Russian president: 'I am a direct man. Putin is also a direct man. I think we will manage to cooperate.' That was, of course, an important signal and I communicated it to the addressee. On 7 May, when I returned to Russia, I had a meeting with Vladimir Putin during which I passed on to him my impressions from the trip and, in detail, my conversations in the State Department and the White House.

I am absolutely certain there were opportunities at that time for a move to all-round, serious interaction between Russia and the United States and, more broadly, with the West. These increased after the events of 11 September 2001 and Vladimir Putin's subsequent overtures towards the United States. They came to nothing. Despite all efforts, with many summit meetings, no real collaboration came about and there was no improvement in relations. Why? I think because, despite the assurances of a willingness for cooperation and partnership, US realpolitik was directed towards creating a unipolar world.

In February 2007, President Putin raised this in a speech at the Munich Conference on Security Policy. He spoke about the unilateral, non-legitimate use of military force in international affairs, about ignoring principles of international law, about the fact that the dominance afforded to military power was fuelling the urge in a number of countries to acquire weapons of mass destruction. He spoke of efforts to turn the Organization for Security and Co-operation in Europe into a tool for securing the interests of one country or a group of countries. He expressed Russia's objection to the continuing enlargement of NATO and the US withdrawal from the Anti-Ballistic Missile Treaty.

In response, Putin was practically accused of restarting the Cold War. I did not agree with those accusations. 'The president of Russia', I said in an interview for *Argumenty i Fakty*, 'was talking in Munich about something quite different: how to prevent the appearance in the world of new lines of division and a resumption of confrontation. The danger of that is real enough.' I pointed to the fact that surveys in several countries had shown that people there shared our president's concern about the situation in the world. In Germany more than 60 per cent of respondents agreed with his point of view.

There were some fairly blunt phrases in Putin's Munich speech, but that was entirely understandable: in spite of all his overtures to the United States during the presidency of George W. Bush, the US administration has not compromised with Russia on a single one of the issues important for our country's security. On the most important, the issues of enlargement of NATO and anti-ballistic missile defence, we have simply come up against a brick wall. I think this was just one manifestation of triumphalism after a supposed 'winning' of the Cold War and 'superpower illusions' (using the succinct wording of former Ambassador Jack Matlock), which reached their apogee during the Bush administration.

It was during this period that we began to hear talk to the effect that the United States was no longer just 'the only remaining superpower', but a 'hyperpower' capable of building a new kind of empire. Global politics very quickly supplied proof that this was not the case. In an article published in 2008 in the world's leading media, I wrote:

> [America] will have to decide whether she wants to be an empire or a democracy, whether she wants world domination or international cooperation. That is precisely how the issue stands: either – or, because the one cannot be combined with the other any more than you can combine oil with water.

The aspiration to dominate the world proved an unsustainable burden even for the United States with all its huge potential. The result, as Putin said in Munich (and I mentioned this in literally every speech I gave in the United States), was that the world has not become safer. On the contrary, the consequences of the policy have been disastrous for America itself. There has been an increase in anti-American sentiments in every region of the world, and acute financial and economic problems associated with astronomical spending on arms and military campaigns thousands of miles away from the American continent. Many social problems remain unresolved in the richest country in the world. Most importantly, as I wrote in an article published in the *International Herald Tribune*, 'the rest of the world did not agree to play the role of "extras" in a film script written by Washington'.

Speaking in the United States, I never tired of reminding Americans of John F. Kennedy's words in his 1963 speech in Washington to the American University:

What kind of peace do I mean? What kind of peace do we seek? Not a Pax Americana enforced on the world by American weapons of war. Not the peace of the grave or the security of the slave. I am talking about genuine peace, the kind of peace that makes life on earth worth living, the kind that enables men and nations to grow and to hope and to build a better life for their children – not merely peace for Americans but peace for all men and women.[4]

In other words, there will either be peace for all, or peace for none.

I would ask my audience a question, 'Do you want an America that acts as a global policeman, imposing democracy on other peoples with tanks and missiles?' Never once did I find anyone wanting to answer that question affirmatively. Probably some agreed with me and others, at least, thought it over. The unwisdom of the pursuit of 'a monopoly of leadership' and its dire consequences were becoming increasingly obvious to many Americans, both members of the political elite and, particularly, ordinary citizens. People were aware of the need for change.

Before the beginning of the 2008 presidential campaign, two young people in the audience asked me after a speech in St. Louis: 'What advice would you give America today, when we all feel that something is not right in our country?' I tried to dodge the question by saying this was something new – usually it was America that gave advice to other countries – but my questioners persisted. So I said: 'I am not going to try to tell you what you should do or offer you a blueprint, but one thing I am sure about is that America needs its own, American, Perestroika.' People rose from their seats and gave those words a standing ovation.

The election of Obama

It was no surprise that, during their campaigning, both presidential candidates, Barack Obama and John McCain, spoke of the

---

[4] John F. Kennedy Presidential Library and Museum, Commencement Address at the American University, 10 June 1963 (transcript); http://www.jfklibrary.org/Asset-Viewer/BWC7I4C9QUmLG9J6I8oy8w.aspx. Accessed 16 July 2015.

332 Today's Uneasy World

need for change. Even the Republican McCain felt obliged to distance himself from his predecessor.

Obama's victory in the 2008 presidential election was an important milestone. I remember a conversation I had with an old friend, an American who always voted Democrat. During the primaries he supported Hillary Clinton. 'Obama appeals to me', he said, 'but I just do not believe a black candidate with a name like Barack Obama could be elected president in our country.' And yet, a few months later, that is exactly what happened.

Obama's election generated great expectations around the world. Awarding him the Nobel Peace Prize was a kind of advance payment, an expression of hope and support for someone who was promising to end wars and focus on 'nation-building', that is, finding solutions to urgent problems not on faraway continents but at home.

I paid attention to the advice some veteran US policymakers were giving Obama during the first days of his presidency. Zbigniew Brzezinski, for example, advised him to pay particular attention to relations with China. A speech by Brzezinski in Beijing could be seen as a call for the creation of a kind of 'G2' consisting of America and China. Reacting to that proposal, I wrote: 'Of course, China's global economic and political importance will keep growing, but I think those who would like to start a new geopolitical game will be in for a disappointment. China is unlikely to accept; more generally, such games belong to the past.'

Henry Kissinger's proposals too were effectively assuming a new geopolitical division of the world which was unlikely to bring us to anywhere we would want to be. What we need, I wrote, is new, modern approaches. I pinned great hopes on Obama, and was not alone in that.

I have had two meetings with President Obama. The first was in spring 2009 during a trip to the United States. I first talked in detail to Vice-President Joe Biden, and we covered a whole raft of problems, after which I had a brief conversation with the president. Taken together these conversations merited a telegram, which I duly sent the following day from our embassy to President Medvedev. What seemed particularly important to me was that Obama understood the need to break the stalemate in reducing nuclear stockpiles. For that, I said in our talk, the United States needed to take some constructive steps on anti-missile defence. I had the impression that the president and vice-president were both listening.

My second conversation with the president came during his visit to Moscow in summer 2009, and confirmed my impression that he was a serious person with a modern outlook, open to dialogue and capable of taking far-reaching decisions.

Obama was an hour late arriving at the old Gostiny Dvor commercial centre, where he addressed students and where we met. The delay was caused by a long conversation with Prime Minister Putin. I told the president I fully understood the importance of this conversation for both of them. He replied: 'I was more inclined to listen, because it seemed to me it was very important to Putin to have an opportunity to get many things off his chest. We had a frank and friendly discussion and I was pleased with it.'

The president added that he had a lot of concerns and complicated matters to deal with back home, but thought it very important to come to Russia and not put off making a start on improving relations after eight years during which the previous administration had let them drift. I supported the president and said that, of course, there are always many problems and, as we had discussed in our first meeting at the White House, approval ratings may fall but action has to be taken here and now, without any pauses for reflection such as had been favoured by the administration of President Bush Senior. I told Obama he would see in his meetings with representatives of Russian society that people here wanted good relations with the United States, but on an equal footing, with Russia being listened to.

In our short conversation I managed to raise several important issues: nuclear disarmament and its link with anti-missile defence and the problem of conventional weapons; the triangular relationship of Russia, the United States and China; and President Dmitry Medvedev's initiative for a new pan-European treaty. I said it was important for dialogue between the United States and Russia not to be restricted to acute immediate problems like the nuclear programmes of North Korea and Iran, and for both sides to feel they were achieving real benefit from it.

Obama said he would pay constant personal attention to relations with Russia, and I think that, subsequently, this was clearly evident.

I believe Barack Obama succeeded in doing a lot during his first presidential term, despite extreme opposition from conservatives and the far right. That was true of both his domestic and foreign policy agendas. At home he introduced and pushed through important social reforms, particularly in respect of healthcare. His political stance was that the market system should be subject to rational regulation, whereas Mitt Romney, his opponent in the second election campaign, advocated giving priority to market forces which would supposedly sort everything out for the best if they were just left alone.

Obama has had his successes in foreign policy too. He honoured his promise to withdraw from the conflicts in Iraq and Afghanistan. He openly supported the idea of a world without nuclear weapons, spoke out in favour of ratifying the Comprehensive Nuclear Test Ban Treaty, and decided against deploying anti-ballistic missile systems in Poland and the Czech Republic. It is too soon to judge whether Russia and the United States will find a mutually acceptable solution to the ABM problem. Other systems are being deployed in Europe that may yet affect the overall strategic balance. Nonetheless, Obama's decision was an important step in the right direction and paved the way for signing of the New Strategic Arms Reduction Treaty in Prague in 2010.

When Obama was victorious in the November 2012 election I sent him a message in which I expressed confidence that 'the prerequisites are there for our countries to cooperate, both bilaterally and on the international stage', and that, cooperating on a basis of mutual respect and trust, they 'can do much to advance their own interests and those of the whole world'.

In late summer 2013, Obama found himself in an awkward situation in connection with the Syrian crisis. Responding to reports that Syria had used chemical weapons, he rushed, without waiting for the conclusions of UN experts, to lay responsibility on the Syrian government and declare he was prepared to authorize a missile strike even without the authorization of the UN Security

Council. When I was asked to comment on this, I called on the president to tread warily and make sure he fully understood the situation. At the time, most commentators were saying a military strike on Syria was unavoidable, but I was hoping for a different response. I suggested the opportunity should be taken at the imminent G8 summit in St Petersburg for the presidents of the United States and Russia to meet.

This happened, and it would seem that it started the search for a solution to the problem. Before that, Obama had proposed to Congress, including his opponents from the Republican Party, that they should take a vote and arrogate responsibility to themselves. Instead, he gained a tactical advantage, a temporary pause which, especially thanks to Russia's initiative in joining the search for a solution to the conflict, allowed the problem to be dealt with through political and diplomatic channels.

The Future of Europe

All these years, Europe has been a major focus of my reflections, speeches and contacts. What will happen to the pan-European project? Will the move towards a Greater Europe continue? These questions have occupied me, not least because I was directly involved in the initiatives that gave impetus to what happened and is happening in Europe.

Speaking in December 1984 in the United Kingdom Parliament, I uttered a phrase that attracted a lot of attention: 'Europe is our common home.' That went on to become an important plank of Soviet foreign policy and integral to our new diplomacy.

The 1975 Helsinki Final Act of the Conference on Security and Co-operation in Europe, and then the Charter of Paris for a New Europe, adopted at an OSCE summit in November 1990, opened up the possibility of overcoming the artificial alienation of Russia from Europe caused by ideological confrontation and the preceding decades of the Cold War. After the collapse of the Soviet Union, however, the Helsinki process stalled and people stopped mentioning the Charter for a New Europe. European integration came to centre exclusively on the European Union and a policy of drawing the countries of Eastern Europe and the former Soviet republics into it. Europe increasingly came to mean Western Europe, in effect denying Russia the status of a European nation. New barriers replaced the old: less obvious, perhaps, but entirely real.

We continued, of course, to hear talk of willingness to develop relations with Russia and the importance of cooperation, but it seemed little more than a nod in the direction of political correctness. I saw this as a worrying development, and tried to draw our Western partners' attention to possible undesirable consequences, to coax them back to a pan-European perspective, and make them see how essential and potentially rewarding increased cooperation with Russia might prove.

In summer 1993, the Stockholm International Peace Research Institute invited me to give a lecture on the topic of 'European Security' in their series dedicated to the memory of the assassinated Swedish prime minister, Olof Palme. I wanted to convey my anxiety to the audience, and expressed a firm belief that developing pan-European integration would be essential if we were to successfully tackle the new challenges in different parts of Europe, not least the issue of relations with Russia. I felt those were shortsighted who wondered whether supporting the revival of Russia was wise, and whether it might not be better to keep her as a weak neighbour and source of raw materials for Western Europe.

We were approaching or had reached a threshold for deciding the future of Europe for years to come, I warned at a conference in Barcelona in April 1994. I repeated that message in Frankfurt in September 1996, speaking at a forum I had helped to establish there two years before. This time the topic was, 'A United Europe: Reality or Utopia?' The question had been raised of whether there was such a thing as Greater Europe. Those trying to draw Europeans into discussing this topic were implying, of course, that Europe ended at the Russian border.

My old acquaintances, Henry Kissinger and Zbigniew Brzezinski, spoke along those lines. If General de Gaulle had had a vision of a 'Europe from the Atlantic to the Urals', then my opponents were more in favour of a 'Europe from Brest to Brest'. Others spoke as if there were already three or four Europes, but in all the arguments there was a sense that Russia was being fended off as something dangerous.

I have never doubted that Greater Europe already exists, its shared civilization a fact of history. Its foundation is its Christian roots and European cultural heritage, which means that Europe's future must be built not only from the West eastwards but also from the East westwards.

I said I saw European union not as just parallel development of separate nations on the territory of our continent, but as movement towards a qualitatively new history. It is obvious, I said at that forum in Frankfurt, that the path to a united Europe is going to be long and arduous. We should have no illusions on that score, but to reject the goal is dangerous and, at the very least, unproductive.

My thinking was shared by another of the forum's participants, Hans-Dietrich Genscher, whom I had first met in 1986, and already then found we had much in common. He was a man chastened by experience and politics, a man of profound intelligence, capable of seeing far into the future.

Most national politicians in Western Europe favoured a different logic. After the Maastricht Treaty, which came into force in 1993, the European Economic Community became the European Union, which implied more fundamental integration. It continued to expand and, after the number of West European member states reached 15, the process spread to countries of Eastern Europe. In 2004, the EU admitted ten new states, including Hungary, Poland, the Czech Republic and Slovakia, and the three former Soviet republics of Latvia, Lithuania and Estonia. In 2007, they were joined by Bulgaria and Romania.

At the same time, the degree of integration increased to affect all the main aspects of national life, economic, political, legal and social. The European Union became a major economic power and an independent and substantial player in global politics. This was a new situation that had to be given due weight. In 1997, three years after it had been concluded, the Agreement on Partnership and Cooperation between the European Union and the Russian Federation came into force. The Cooperation Council held its first meeting the following year.

The policy of rapidly expanding the European Union was not without problems. It became clear that the pace and scale of the process had not been carefully thought through. Without doubting its positive aspects, I had to point out that, although the first decade of the twenty-first century had seen the European Union advance triumphantly, problems had been accumulating which eventually broke through to the surface. Economic growth began to slow. EU countries became less competitive relative to other rapidly developing economies.

Speaking in 2009 at a public meeting in Strasbourg, I said:

Every process, every association has limits to its speed and scope. The ability to absorb change is not limitless, and expectations that all the continent's problems can be solved by integrating Europe only from the West have proved overoptimistic.

A more moderate pace of integration would allow more time to develop a model for relations with Russia and other countries which will not in the foreseeable future be joining the European Union.

It is obvious that the approach of swallowing most other European countries into the EU as rapidly as possible, while leaving relations with Russia unstable and uncertain, has run its course.

People appeared on both sides who questioned the need for close cooperation between Russia and the EU. In a 2005 article in *Rossiyskaya Gazeta*, I noted that among Russian politicians and analysts the view was gaining ground that we should probably take a break in developing our relations with the EU, be in no hurry to integrate further, and turn our attention in other, more promising directions. Some European politicians were beginning to express doubts about whether closer relations between the EU and Russia were even possible.

Criticism of Russia, sometimes justified but more often over-hasty, was accompanied by lofty generalizations. Russia was deemed incapable of mastering democratic principles and institutions, establishing civil society, abandoning imperial ambitions, and accordingly had little to offer Europe. I asked what could be behind these recriminations and the policies to which they gave rise. My answer was, 'I believe there is a desire to keep Russia half-strangled for as long as possible.' Not a pleasant conclusion, but one for which there was then, and still is, good reason.

The next question I posed was whether it was wise to alienate a partner like Russia, 'a partner that, on most international issues, takes a stance close to, and often complementary to, the policy of the European Union, and accordingly affords opportunities for both sides to promote their policies more effectively'.

I remember participating in 2002 in a forum in Passau in southeast Germany on 'The Individual in a United Europe'. Helmut Kohl and I were asked point blank what forms convergence and partnership between Russia and the EU could take. I always enjoy taking part in discussions with Kohl. His remarks reflect his great experience of affairs of state, but he also has a dazzling personality, instant reactions, and is never at a loss for words. Kohl said new, effective relations with Russia were essential and I agreed with him. At that, a young man said: 'Well, if you both think Russia and the EU have a lot in common and should come closer, why not admit Russia to the EU?' You should have seen Kohl's reaction! Despite his enormous bulk, he almost jumped out of his seat and blurted something like: 'That is not going happen: it could never possibly come about.' I was stunned, but that was his completely honest reaction.

Unfortunately, in the years since then, relations between Russia and the EU have become no more straightforward. In fact, they have become more convoluted. New questions are asked and doubts expressed about how European Russia is interested in being. Some observers found grounds for such doubts in Vladimir Putin's speech to the members of the Valdai Club in October 2013. There, he criticized Europe not only in political and economic terms, but also on ideological and philosophical grounds. Some are concluding that Russia is 'withdrawing from Europe' and looking elsewhere.

I think it is important for that not to happen. More precisely, I believe we should prevent it from happening. Both sides need to think this through carefully, and vigorously renew efforts to find ways to be partners. In the longer term, Greater Europe and the countries of the North American continent need to aim to establish a transcontinental community, a partnership extending over a huge geographical area.

At one of the assemblies of the World Political Forum, I recalled the goal of creating a belt of security and cooperation from Vancouver to Vladivostok. A difficult but feasible task in which I hope new generations will be successful.

Germany

Speaking of Europe, I need to give a special mention to Germany, with which Russia has a very particular kind of relationship.

It was Germany I visited in May 1992 on my first trip abroad after resigning the presidency. I was flying on a standard, scheduled flight. In the past, as general secretary and later as president, my status had entitled me to a personal aircraft. Raisa and I were not too bothered by this, never having been particularly attached to privileges of that kind. The only snag was that, after take-off, we found a whole bevy of Russian and German journalists had booked seats on the same flight. They had been detailed by their editors to 'accompany' the Gorbachevs, and now, at 35,000 feet, they came in relays to say hello to me or Raisa, to chat and, if possible, fit in a flying interview.

Before we arrived, the German press had been cautious in its comments. Germans still had, of course, reason to be grateful to Gorbachev for his contribution to German reunification, but now he was out of office and his visit was purely symbolic. The newspapers implied that no great public interest should be expected, and that its political significance would probably be negligible. Moreover, as we discovered, ambassadors of the Russian Federation had been given strict instructions to offer no assistance to Gorbachev if he were to visit the country in which they were posted.

The helicopter taking us from Frankfurt to Bonn landed directly in front of our hilltop hotel. We already knew the Hotel Petersberg, the official residence for guests of the federal government. We had stayed here during an official visit in autumn 1990 and this was where the grand treaty on Soviet–German relations was signed. This time too we were accommodated in the presidential apartments.

I had a long, frank discussion with Helmut Kohl. He is rightly ranked among the major figures of world politics of the second half of the twentieth century. On visits to Moscow, Helmut invariably looked me up at the Gorbachev Foundation. In 2002, in our small dining room there, we arranged an intimate supper with just him, his assistant, myself, my daughter Irina, and a member of the Foundation staff. He cheerfully drank two or three glasses of vodka, followed by beer. Kohl was very proud of his role in the creation of the Euro, and signed a 20-Euro banknote, added the date, 1 January 2002, and gave me it as a souvenir.

Another episode I remember had taken place a few years earlier, in 1998. That summer, Cologne was celebrating the 750th anniversary of the foundation of its renowned cathedral and Raisa and I were invited. We arrived in good time and were sitting in pews at the front, next to our good friends the German social democrats. These included Johannes Rau, the minister-president of North Rhine-Westphalia. The cathedral gradually filled up and behind we heard what sounded like the clatter of hooves as a large group moved towards the front rows. Federal Chancellor Kohl and his retinue had arrived. When he saw me, he stopped in theatrical amazement. Our invitation on this occasion had come from Germany's social democrats and Kohl had not been advised personally of my arrival, although he might have read about it in the newspapers.

If he did already know, he gave no sign of it, registered astonishment, and gave me a mock rebuke for all to hear: 'Mikhail, next time you come to Germany, do warn me in advance so that we can arrange a meeting.' He was evidently displeased to have found me consorting with his political rivals. Elections to the Bundestag were just a couple of months away, and the main contenders, the CDU-CSU and SPD, were in the middle of a battle to decide the outcome. It was unclear who would win, but, after 15 years as Chancellor, Kohl evidently considered himself invincible. Nodding just a little dismissively to Johannes Rau and his comrades, he addressed me again, and again for all to hear: 'Tell your neighbours there in the pew to forget it: the outcome of the elections is a foregone conclusion!' He swept off.

Helmut Kohl was chancellor of Germany for 16 years, an unsurpassed record for West Germany, but lost the elections by a landslide. The social democrat, Gerhard Schröder, became chancellor. A year later, Johannes Rau was elected federal president.

In March 1992, two-thirds of my conversation with Helmut Kohl concerned the progress of reforms in the Commonwealth of Independent States. My account of the consequences of the Soviet Union's collapse made quite an impression on him. For example, the fact that someone living in Moscow could not transfer money to his own mother in Ukraine. The Germans did not need to have it spelled out to them what it means when a country is torn apart: they had only very recently got rid of the Berlin Wall.

After a private talk at the Schaumburg Palace, the official residence of the German chancellor, the Kohls invited us back to their home for dinner. Our relationship with Helmut and Hannelore Kohl meant this was entirely natural. Kohl had visited my native Stavropol region, and Raisa Maximovna and I had been to the home of Kohl's mother in Deidesheim during our official visit in autumn 1990.

Late that evening we got back to Hotel Petersberg to find a dozen and a half Russian and foreign journalists waiting for us in the lobby. Back to business. Most of the labour was mine, but the questions were of all kinds and Raisa had to step in too.

'Mikhail Sergeyevich', one of the journalists said, 'quite apart from political issues, your friends in Germany want to know how you are both personally feeling after leaving the political stage?' I turned to my wife. 'I would like Raisa Maximovna to answer that.' 'Incidentally', the journalist added, 'how is your health, Raisa Maximovna?' She was often asked that. People knew that after the August 1991 coup, when there was a real threat to the life of our whole family, she had had serious health problems, been in hospital several times and received treatment at home. By this time the worst was behind us, so she did not dwell on it:

How are we feeling? We have very mixed feelings. As far as my health is concerned, after what happened in Crimea during the coup everything is pretty much back to normal. If you want to know how we are feeling more generally, things are of course very difficult, even depressing. I don't mean in our personal life so much. Not everyone may agree, but I will say it anyway: after all that Mikhail Sergeyevich started in 1985, many things have changed, and now we are very disturbed about what is going on in Russia. Because today almost no one in our country is living well, so how could we be feeling happy?

In the Petersberg lobby, journalists came to sit close to us one after the other. The clock struck midnight, 2:00 am in Moscow ...

The second day of our visit was taken up with talking to the leaders of West Germany's main political parties. It was not only presently active politicians who wanted to meet us. We had a conversation with Chancellor Helmut Schmidt. He was a social democrat, but, after resigning in 1982, seemed more or less to have retired from politics. He published and contributed to *Die Zeit*, a weekly newspaper much respected in Germany, particularly in elite intellectual circles. Even after becoming an 'ordinary citizen', Schmidt remained a highly respected authority.

Each of the 16 West German *Länder*, or provinces, had an office in Bonn, and the minister-president of the Saarland, Oskar Lafontaine, gave a lunch in our honour at their legation with the leaders of the Social Democratic Party. The most striking figure at the table was Willy Brandt, honorary chairman of the party and someone who has his place in the history of Germany and Europe. It was he who, with like-minded colleagues, succeeded in ending the seemingly unchallengeable 20-year dominance of the Christian Democrats to become the first Social Democratic chancellor of the Federal Republic of Germany.

It was Brandt too who, during an official visit to Poland, as a sign of penitence, demonstratively knelt down at the monument to the victims of the Warsaw ghetto, although he personally would seem to have had nothing to repent. At a young age, the left-wing socialist Herbert Frahm (Brandt's real name) fled from the Nazis to Norway, then Sweden, and became a political refugee.

Brandt was the first major West German politician to visit the German Democratic Republic. It was he who gave the impetus to West Germany's 'New Eastern Policy', when, despite the atmosphere of the Cold War, he began building good relations with the Soviet Union and the other East European countries.

Willy Brandt and I had long had an affection for each other. I knew he was seriously ill, but at the dinner he and all the others seemed to have forgotten about that. There were jokes and jibes and tall stories and a wonderfully easy atmosphere. Brandt drank a couple of glasses of wine and laughed happily and infectiously. On this occasion there was hardly any mention of politics. Only when the dinner was almost over did Brandt extend to me an invitation to come to Berlin in the autumn to the next congress

of the Socialist International to give a major speech. I promised I
would, and kept my promise. Alas, Brandt was unable to attend
that congress, his illness having entered its final phase.

We bade each other a warm farewell in Bonn, neither of us
aware that we would never meet again.

That evening, the official programme specified there was to be
'a dinner hosted by Minister of Foreign Affairs Genscher and Mrs
Genscher for M. S. Gorbachev and R. M. Gorbacheva at the home
of the Minister of Foreign Affairs'. Among all our warm German
acquaintances, Barbara and Hans-Dietrich Genscher are linked
to us, I am not embarrassed to say, by a bond of true friendship.
Of course, it helped that I saw Genscher as someone who had a
profound understanding of our policy of New Thinking. That
did not mean our relations were always blissfully idyllic: I had
the interests of my country to defend and Genscher those of his.
Sometimes these did not coincide. At times, Genscher was defending the position of Chancellor Kohl in dialogue with me when
it was not difficult to imagine that his own views differed from
those of his chief. Genscher gave no hint of that, however, and
conducted himself with meticulous political propriety.

Early the next day, we visited Villa Hammerschmidt, the
presidential palace. Richard von Weizsäcker, the president of
West Germany and, after 1990, the first president of reunified
Germany, and his wife invited me and Raisa to breakfast.

In 1941, at the age of 20, Weizsäcker was an officer in Hitler's
Wehrmacht on the Eastern Front, in Russia. He was no admirer
of Hitler, but neither was he a member of the Resistance,
although some of his friends were involved in plans to assassi-
nate the Nazi dictator. Weizsäcker learned from his experiences,
proof of which was evident after he became president of the
Federal Republic of Germany. It was he who formulated a
different understanding of the significance of 8 May 1945 for
the present generation of Germans: 'As time has passed, it has
become increasingly plain that we all need to declare today, 8
May, the day of our Liberation, the day we were all of us liberated from the inhuman system of national socialism's violent
domination.' Anyone familiar with the post-war development
of West Germany will confirm that, even in a country that had

advanced along the road to democracy, for a politician of such a rank this was a bold political act.

From Bonn we travelled to Munich. At the airport, in spite of the rain, hundreds of people were waiting just to say a kind word, shake our hands, or give us some small souvenir. Throughout our three days in Bavaria, we felt we were at the epicentre of some great earthquake, not frightening, not terrible, but engulfing us in paroxysms of friendliness. On Max-Joseph-Platz we had a ceremonial meeting with the townspeople. Thousands had gathered. Every window of the adjacent houses was thronged with people who wanted to watch the proceedings. Great bunches of people festooned every conceivable eminence, kerbs, concrete flower containers and balconies. The people of Munich greeted their guests from windows and roofs, waving flags, scarves and even bedsheets.

On 6 March, the minister-president of Bavaria invited us to a lunch at the Antiquarium, a huge vaulted hall built in the sixteenth century as a museum for antique sculptures, but soon converted into a banqueting hall. Destroyed during the war, it was restored and is now used for the minister-president's receptions.

After lunch, we were to visit the town hall on Marienplatz. We went out on to the balcony under the famous chimes of the Town Hall. I was asked to say a few words to the city's residents gathered in the square and waiting for me to appear. I said the first words in German: 'Liebe Münchner!' 'Dear people of Munich!' This gained me an ovation. My speech could hardly have been more brief. I said only: 'I am extremely moved by your wonderful reception. This expression of your warm feelings for me and my wife gives us great joy.' The burgomeister welcomed us in the great hall, where prominent citizens had assembled:

> You see the reception you have received. The impulse you gave to democratic changes in Eastern Europe, the taking down of the Iron Curtain, the bringing together of East and West was and is something we in Munich will never forget. Most memorable of all has been the courage with which you supported the longing of us Germans to be reunited, and for that we are especially grateful to you.

On Saturday, we were offered an entirely tourist programme: Neuschwanstein Castle, located in the pre-Alpine region, then the Wieskirche which, we were told, is the most beautiful rococo church in Bavaria, and in the evening a visit to the theatre. We were relieved to be having a day off after all the excitement of the previous day's receptions in Munich. We thought this would be a respite, but it was not to be.

The helicopter bringing us to the foot of the 'Cliff of the Swan', 100 kilometres south of Munich, landed in what appeared to be deserted mountainous terrain, but within a couple of minutes there appeared out of nowhere dozens, then hundreds, of people who surrounded it and began chanting the, from yesterday already familiar, 'Gorby! Gorby!'

Soon the helicopter took us on to another niche at the foot of the Wieskirche church. We were now no longer taken aback when we saw how many people were waiting, but the surprises were not over yet: a whole class of children from a nearby school welcomed us with a huge banner that read, in Russian, 'Welcome, Gorby and Raisa!'. The burgomeister of Wildsteig, Josef Taffertshofer, greeted us in Russian.

Accompanied by the priest, we went into the church as the organ began to play. Many people were intrigued to see how the former general secretary of the CPSU would behave in a church. The following day the newspapers reported, 'In the recently restored church, Gorbachev, whose outlook is atheist, joined in reciting the prayer of the United Nations.' Father Georg Kirchmeier had learned the prayer in Russian and recited it together with us, although we had to read it from a leaflet. It is only a few lines, and I will quote them here in full:

Lord! Our Earth is only a little star
Twinkling in the universe.
Yet we can make of this if we care to a planet
Undisturbed by war
Unperturbed by want or fear
Whose creation will not suffer because of wars,
Will not go hungry and fearful,
Not be separated by meaningless division

Today's Uneasy World

By race, colour, or worldview.
Give us the courage and insight,
So that we who are already embarked on this case,
So that our children and our children's children
Are proud to bear the name – a man.[1]

The following morning we left hospitable Bavaria. Our route was northwards, to North Rhine-Westphalia. The *Land*'s capital is the fine city of Düsseldorf, but our destination was the less well-known city of Gütersloh in eastern Westphalia, home to the publishing concern of Bertelsmann, whose board of directors had a programme for our visit scheduled, as in Bavaria, down to the last minute.

In Gütersloh, we found a real sense of solidarity with Russia. We met Peter Dangman of the Humanitas association, who sent 22 aircraft laden with charitable aid to Russia. Another civic group, Help Without Frontiers, in two years sent 140 tons of food and medicines to St Petersburg. Mr and Mrs Higson and the British-German Society sent 7.5 tons of relief supplies to Ukraine. It is impossible to list all the acts of kindness. On this, our first unofficial visit, we found immense willingness on the part of the Germans to come to the aid of our compatriots, and they were keen to show us that. Our next, and final, destination was Hamburg. Knowledgeable people warned us that Hamburg was not Bavaria: it was 'the North', where people were reticent about showing their feelings. In fact, however, Hamburg defied all the predictions and met us with what I can only describe as Italianesque *brio*.

Hamburg made a great impression on both of us. I had never realized the city was so beautiful. I had imagined its mighty industry would have left its stamp on everything, but found instead that its natural surroundings had been preserved with extraordinary success, and that its architecture was not in conflict, but very much in harmony with them.

In the evening, tired by our official meetings, we decided just to go for a stroll round the city. This was easier said than done.

[1] The words appear to be taken from a speech by Franklin D. Roosevelt at the signing of the UN Charter in 1945 [translator's note].

An unplanned walkabout caused some perplexity among the German security officers charged with protecting these guests, and it was decided we should at first only go for a drive. We went round the Inner Alster lake, past a monument to Bismarck, and suddenly came out onto a broad, brightly lit street with all the colours of the rainbow, where crowds were taking the air at this hour of the evening. We agreed not to get out of the car and drove on to St Michaelis Church, a baroque church and one of the city's symbols. From there we did get out for a stroll. The weather was drizzly, which it often is in Hamburg. We spotted welcoming light shining from the windows of a pub. 'Let's go in', Raisa suggested.

Everyone agreed, although our German detectives 'strolling' behind wondered whether to call for backup, just in case. It was warm and cosy in the pub, but not busy, with only two of the tables occupied. The owner recognized us and was at first taken aback, perhaps surprised that a visit of this kind could just happen, but pulled himself together and served us with professional amiability and without fuss (although he did absent himself for a moment to fetch his camera).

The next day I took part in a discussion at the Institute for Peace Research and Security Policy, which at the time was headed by Egon Bahr, a well-known social democratic politician who made a great contribution in the early 1970s to developing the New Eastern Policy of Willy Brandt's government.

That morning we also visited the Ohlsdorf cemetery on the outskirts of Hamburg, where 384 Soviet soldiers who died in German captivity during the Second World War are buried. We laid a wreath at the monument, inscribed to 'Soviet soldiers, victims of fascism'. The Germans tend their graves carefully, seeing it both as a human duty and a gesture of reconciliation.

Our programme included a trip on the yacht of Hamburg's governing Senate but, just as we were due to go on board, there was a great flurry of large wet snowflakes. This was promising to be some lake trip! Raisa made what might have seemed a rather sensible suggestion: 'Perhaps we should cancel it?' 'Absolutely impossible,' she was told. At every pier on the lake and the adjoining canal we were to sail past, already, in defiance of the weather, many people had gathered to greet us. It really was out of the question to let them down.

Among the events, there was a grand reception in Grüner and Jahr's huge House of the Press, built in exuberant accordance with the norms of modernist architecture. At the end, there was a short concert, the highlight of which was a performance by Wolf Biermann and Nina Hagen. Nina Hagen was a young actress and singer, the daughter of Eva-Maria Hagen, a famous actress in the days of the German Democratic Republic. Wolf Biermann was a man with a guitar, what in Russia we call a bard, and he too had lived almost his entire life in the GDR. He sang barbed protest songs, for which he had constantly been subjected to such restrictions as house arrest.

He and Nina Hagen surprised us by performing in German and Russian something I had never heard before: 'A Song about Gorbachev'. We were given a Russian translation of the text, and Wolf gave us a note of how it had come to be written. It read:

Dear Raisa and Mikhail Gorbachev,

Four years ago, Mirra Slawutzkaja, a German Jew who had worked in the Comintern for Dimitrov and Togliatti, and then from 1936 to 1956 continued her education for 20 years in the Far East Academy of Social Sciences [by which I took Wolf to be referring to the Gulag. – MG], brought with her from Poland a cheery song about Gorbachev. Nina Hagen asked me to translate it, but to be honest, I thought the words were rather silly, so I wrote completely new German words and new music, which you can hear on a record called *Gut Kirschenessen* (*Good to Know*).

We have performed the song at hundreds of concerts to thousands of people in Germany, including the former GDR. Most of them liked it. They like the fact that, when singing of the world today, we do not only complain and whinge, but say there is a man we praise who did a little to save it. Whether it was enough, whether it was done in time or too late, time will tell, but that is up to us.

In May, I shall be singing in Moscow for the first time. If you can find the time and have the inclination, you will be able to

hear a few of my other songs and compare them with those of
Okudzhava and Vysotsky.

With my kindest regards,
Wolf Biermann

The song is quite long, so I will not quote it in full. Like much else,
it is symptomatic of the times. From Biermann's letter it would
seem to have been written in 1989 or thereabouts and reflects the
euphoria, the doubts and anxieties of that time:

Mikhail Gorbachev,
Are you fish or are you flesh?
Look out that no one sits on you
And do not sit on us.
Mikhail Gorbachev,
Stay smart, stay sly,
Be a child and be a man,
Be brave as woman.
Oh, oh, Gorby,
All our hopes are now
That Mother Russia
is on the move.
Oh, oh, guys,
Fan the fire!
That little spark of *Ogonyok*,
Warms my heart and gives me hope.

Mikhail Gorbachev,
Everywhere in East and West
You have friends, but enemies too,
Who call a plague down on your head.
Mikhail Gorbachev,
I, though, wish you luck,
May you carry on along your path
And not get a bullet in your head.

Gorby, do not falter.
If you need support,
My poor strength is yours.

On a solid foundation

'Europe, Germany and Russia between the Past and the Future.' This was the title I gave to my speech in Frankfurt-on-Main at the celebrations of the 20th anniversary of German reunification. The first thing I said, after congratulating the Germans on this occasion, was: 'You have done yourselves proud. The commitments that you, the German nation, undertook you have successfully fulfilled. You are an example to all countries following the path of democracy or seeking it.'

For all that to come about, much had had to change in the world, with huge changes in Soviet society and among the peoples of the Soviet Union. At the same time there had had to be changes in international relations, the end of the Cold War, and changes in the two German states. For us, the leaders of that generation – George Bush, Margaret Thatcher, François Mitterrand, Helmut Kohl – Germany presented a major challenge. For many years it had been an acute European and global problem, a bare nerve in international politics, I said.

I recalled the milestones along the way that led to the historic threshold crossed when Konrad Adenauer visited Moscow in the mid-1950s and the establishment of diplomatic relations between the USSR and West Germany, the Eastern Policy of Willy Brandt and Leonid Brezhnev's meetings with Helmut Schmidt. I spoke of the role of the German Democratic Republic in overcoming the hatred of Germany left by the war in the hearts of many Soviet people, especially those who had fought in the war. As late as June 1989, Helmut Kohl and I were agreeing that reunification of Germany would be a matter for the twenty-first century.

But within a few months, in November, the Berlin Wall came down. It is not that we were mediocre prophets. No, the people expressed their will loudly and clearly. The citizens of the GDR took to the streets to demand reunification without delay. They had the support of the entire population of West Germany: 'We are one people!' was the slogan of the hour.

This was particularly evident during a torchlight procession on the occasion of the German Democratic Republic's 40th anniversary. Representatives of all the regions of the GDR came together in Berlin. Together with the country's leaders and other guests, I was standing on the podium. I saw the faces of thousands of young people and sensed their mood. One of the slogans they were shouting was: 'Gorbachev, stay here another month!' People were openly chanting in support of reunification. I was standing next to Wojciech Jaruzelski and the Polish prime minister Mieczysław Rakowski. Mieczysław turned to me and said, 'You do know this is the end?' I replied: 'Yes, I understand what is happening.'

No one can ignore such determination on the part of the people, and we recognized it. If we had embarked on democratic change to give people freedom in our own country, we could not refuse it to citizens of the other countries of Central and Eastern Europe, and could not deny the German people the right to reunification. In my Frankfurt speech, I repeated words I had said many times before:

> When people ask me who was the main protagonist of reunification, I say, the people. Two peoples. The Germans who resolutely and peacefully expressed their will to reunite, and the Russians, who showed understanding of their aspirations and believed that today's Germany is radically different from the Germany of the past, and supported the will of the German people. Without that, the Soviet government could never have acted as it did.

Nowadays, when you read some of the commentaries or memoirs of those days, you might imagine the process of German reunification was plain sailing, that it dropped like manna from heaven, that it was all just the result of a lucky coincidence or even of the naivety of some of those involved. Not so. I said:

> It was far from easy and was fraught with major risks for many European leaders and their countries.
> In every country that had endured aggression there remained an almost genetic fear of strengthening Germany, which would be

an inevitable consequence of reunification of the GDR and West Germany.

We may smile today at French President François Mitterrand's joke that he loved Germany so much he would prefer there to be two of them. We might wonder at Margaret Thatcher's edginess, if we overlook the fact that she, like millions of Britons, lived through the cruel bombing of the British Isles by German aircraft. To say nothing of Russia, which suffered the heaviest losses, casualties and destruction in the Second World War.

It must surely be clear that the negotiations were far from easy. There were heated arguments, clashes of opinion, and at times it seemed everything would collapse in misunderstanding and failure. And yet, finally, there was success. In the years immediately after reunification, Germany faced serious ills but overcame all the fundamental problems. I recalled that Raisa and I were in Bonn in the early 1990s and were told by Helmut Kohl: 'You know, Mikhail, we expected to face difficulties in the economy because huge expenditure was needed. We had to accept that, and the whole country shouldered the burden. What I found extraordinary, though,' he continued, 'was that East and West Germans met like different peoples. Only 40 years had passed, yet we are still only finding our feet. We see many things quite differently.'

How easy it is to cleave something with a single blow, and how difficult afterwards to put it back together! I was conscious that this was only part of the problem. Later, in 1997, I was in Leipzig, also on 3 October, the anniversary of reunification. In my speech, I recalled what Kohl had said, and after the talk my audience asked questions and made comments.

I listened and sensed that they were dissatisfied and upset. I said, 'Just tell me if you are against reunification. I don't suppose it is too late for us to split Germany in two again.' 'No, no, of course not. But still, there is not enough employment for everyone and the attitude towards us East Germans is not very fair. We have a lot of problems.'

'You know,' I admonished them, 'I can only say that all these are at least your own problems. If you like, I will make you an

offer. We can have this all looked at in Russia and get a decision on whether to swap your problems for ours.' That got a
laugh, and we parted with a better understanding of each other's
situation.

In my speech, I talked about Russo-German relations and noted
they had been developing successfully all these years. In that connection I mentioned my involvement in the Petersburg Dialogue
forum established by Germany's ex-Chancellor Gerhard Schröder
and Russian President Vladimir Putin. At Putin's request, I was
the Russian co-chairman of the forum for eight years, while my
health allowed.

Year by year it was attended by an increasing number of
highly authoritative representatives of civil society on both sides,
including scientists, businessmen and leaders of nongovernmental
organizations, members of the youth Workshop of the Future,
cultural figures, and representatives of the media, education
and healthcare. In 2006, we were able to claim: 'The Petersburg
Dialogue has been a great success. It is appreciated by society in
both our countries and has every prospect of continuing to work
fruitfully for the benefit of the citizens of Russia and Germany.'

The work of the Petersburg Dialogue has received public
recognition. The European Cultural Foundation gave it a pres-
tigious award in a ceremony held in the Church of Our Lady in
Dresden. This is one of Dresden's finest architectural treasures. It
was destroyed during the Second World War and rebuilding had
been completed shortly before, coinciding with the 800th anniversary of the founding of Dresden. Besides being an architectural
masterpiece, it was a masterpiece of restoration. As co-chair-
men of the Petersburg Dialogue, I and Lothar de Maizière,
former prime minister of the GDR, accepted the award from
German ex-President Richard von Weizsäcker on behalf of the
forum.

Chancellor Angela Merkel plays an important role in the
development of Russo-German relations. We have met on many
occasions and discussed meaningfully and frankly the ties between
our countries and civil society in Russia and Germany. Angela has
told me about her life, growing up and developing as a person
and future politician in East Germany. Today she is a strong,

visionary politician, not only in Germany but also in Europe, and seems to me an ideal example of the role of the human factor in politics.

I believe we can expect major joint initiatives from Russia and Germany in the building of Greater Europe, a Europe without lines of division, where the legacy of the Cold War will finally be overcome. If two such countries work jointly towards that objective, there will be a great chance of success.

Major figures in European politics

In Greater Europe, as I envisage it, the role of sovereign states must be retained. Pan-European organizations and integrated associations cannot replace them or squeeze them off the international stage. Countries like Britain, France and Poland, because of their great traditions and extensive contacts, have every right to play an important part in the development of Europe, and Russia should pay particular attention to relations with them.

I have strong, longstanding relations with these countries and their leaders. I have been a regular visitor to them also since leaving the Kremlin. Much links me with the United Kingdom and London, which is where I first encountered Margaret Thatcher, a unique and outstanding politician. I have been to London many times, and enjoyed memorable visits to Edinburgh, Glasgow and Aberdeen. I have warm memories of charity evenings to raise money for the Raisa Gorbachev Children's Institute of Transplantology and Haematology, which were attended by the elite of British society: prominent politicians, cultural figures, businessmen and writers.

Almost every time I was in London, I met Margaret Thatcher. In the United Kingdom, her legacy as prime minister is controversial and our contacts were by no means all sweetness and light. I have not forgotten how, during my first visit in 1984, at an official dinner at Chequers, we quarrelled so violently that we turned our backs on each other. Raisa, sitting on the other side of the table talking to Denis Thatcher, told me afterwards she had noticed and feared it might torpedo the visit. There were other fraught moments in our relations, but there was no denying that

Margaret Thatcher was an outstanding political leader with a clear outlook, strong will and determination to achieve her goals.

She never wavered in her support for Perestroika, never questioned our sincerity, accepted that the Soviet leadership was firmly committed to reform, that success in that area was a possibility and that it would benefit everyone, including the West. Moreover, she never tried to offer glib advice about how we should act.

I remember shortly before my resignation she said at a pan-European meeting in Paris: 'I understand that things are not easy for you at present, but what you are doing is laying foundations for many decades into the future. I am sure everything will work out.'

She was far from approving uncritically of all the ways Western leaders behaved towards us after she was forced to resign as prime minister. Shortly before I was due to leave after the London G7 summit in July 1991, she asked to meet me at the Soviet Embassy and, without warning, started laying into other Western leaders for failing to genuinely support Perestroika. 'Look what they have done!' the already former prime minister, Baroness Thatcher, exclaimed. 'Now, just when things are most difficult for you, they have confined themselves to rhetorical support. As politicians they are not worth tuppence! They are incompetent. They have let you down!'

Of course, like any other leader, she did not always get things right. Suffice it to recall her reaction to the Reykjavik summit: 'One more Reykjavik and we will be finished!' I told her more than once that she seemed to enjoy sitting on a nuclear powder keg. Her neo-liberal approach to the economy, although it played a role in correcting the British system as she found it, has not on the whole stood the test of time and exacerbated many social problems.

We remained friends for many years. In October 2005, I stopped in London on my way to the United States to give Margaret my best wishes on her 80th birthday. My daughter Irina was with me and we pondered long and hard over what to give her, before settling on a beautiful vase of fine porcelain. Of course, our conversation was not confined to birthday pleasantries and we discussed current political events, issues and leaders. Margaret

358   Today's Uneasy World

was very definite and critical and suddenly said, 'Mikhail, do you really not wish you could be at the helm again?' I was surprised. To be honest, Margaret did not look all that well and her memory sometimes let her down. In any case, I felt we had to give a new generation of leaders their chance, and said as much. 'Well I do!' Thatcher replied emphatically.

I have often met Margaret Thatcher's successors and visited No. 10 Downing Street. All of them have tried to do their best for their country, but in terms of force of personality and leadership qualities, Thatcher remains unchallengeable.

A leader of similar historical significance was François Mitterrand in France. In our conversations there was always time to discuss big ideas and concepts. He reflected profoundly on the future of Europe and the world and formulated far-reaching ideas. One of the most central was his idea for a European confederation, which was close to my own proposals to build a common European homeland. It is a pity Mitterrand's successors were unable to develop and place it firmly on the European agenda, but I believe the time for such visionary thinking will yet come.

Mitterrand wanted France's voice to have a special tonality on the world stage, for his country to raise major issues affecting the interests and future of all mankind. In our conversations, global problems always featured prominently: the need to overcome poverty, and threats to the environment. He remained true to the ideal of social justice. At the London G7 meeting, which I joined, he was one of those who spoke in favour of substantial measures to support the reforming Soviet economy.

Mitterrand was seriously ill for the greater part of his second term as president, and that was noticeable during our meetings. The last was in 1995 in Colorado Springs. We had been invited there by George Bush Senior, along with Margaret Thatcher and Brian Mulroney, the ex-prime minister of Canada, to record the memories of world leaders for a television programme. Before the recording, Baroness Thatcher was very anxious, but Mitterrand was outwardly calm. Raisa was talking to him when she suddenly sensed he was unwell. She asked him what was wrong. 'It is old age, Madame Gorbacheva', he replied and then, summoning up his willpower, accompanied us through to the television studio.

For over an hour, under the powerful, even dazzling, lights he joined in the discussion, answering the presenter's questions. A few months later he was gone.

Another major figure among my European partners was Wojciech Jaruzelski. My contacts with Poland were primarily through him. I met him as the head of the Polish state during the mid-1980s, which were fateful years for Europe. It was an uneasy period, and at such times trust between leaders of states is particularly important. It was established between me and General Jaruzelski almost immediately. This was a time when the relationship between our country and Poland was freed from the shadow cast by the so-called [Brezhnev] Doctrine of Limited Sovereignty. Relations between our countries have an onerous historical legacy, darkened by major tribulations and tragedies. We must never forget these, but they must not be allowed to permanently poison relations between our peoples. The first, indispensable step was truthfulness. Jaruzelski and I agreed to establish a joint commission of historians and, when documentary evidence was found in our archives testifying that the Stalin regime had been guilty of the Katyn massacre of the Polish elite, I passed it on to the president of Poland. In my eyes, Jaruzelski was a staunch Polish patriot, a major politician who understood the importance of good neighbourly relations with Russia in his country's national interests and for peace and cooperation in Europe. That is why I could not help but express astonishment at the campaign launched against him later, which turned into something little short of inquisitorial persecution.

In April 2007, I sent a letter to the Marshal of the Sejm of the Republic of Poland and the deputies of the Sejm. I wrote:

> Today, more than a quarter of a century after the 1981 events in Poland, to seek to interpret the role of Wojciech Jaruzelski in the events of that very difficult period in an extremely biased manner, even alleging criminal behaviour, is, in my opinion nothing better than an unseemly attempt to settle political scores.

I drew the deputies' attention to the role General, later President, Jaruzelski had played in the movement towards political reconciliation and national harmony in Poland, facilitating the first bloodless transition to democracy in Eastern Europe and the attainment of national independence and sovereignty.

I remain convinced that a continuing urgent task for relations between our peoples is to strengthen understanding, good-neighbourliness and mutually beneficial cooperation. 'Nobody else is going to do this for us citizens of Russia and Poland', I wrote in my letter to the Polish parliament. My experience and deep conviction is that this is, without exaggeration, the historic duty of true patriots of Russia and Poland and our duty to future generations of Russians, Poles and, to a large extent, the whole of Europe.

Looking East

China

Since resigning the presidency, I have had no occasion to visit the People's Republic of China. My unforgettable visit in May 1989 was the only one, but in the course of it, after meetings and negotiations with Deng Xiaoping and other Chinese leaders, relations between our countries were restored and set on a friendly footing after 30 years of estrangement.

People often ask me why I did not conduct our reforms in the same way as Deng Xiaoping conducted his in China, and my reply is that it would only have been possible if the people living in Russia were Chinese. Different countries, different cultures, different initial circumstances: it would take a long time to list them, and, on top of all that, before the reforms began in China there was a 'cultural revolution' that shook to the foundations the entire political elite, the party bureaucracy and all the institutions of government and society. I too was sometimes urged to 'open fire on enemy headquarters'. We chose not to.

Needless to say, the reforms there are an immense achievement, a huge step forward. What has occurred in China and India is the world's most spectacular achievement in the fight against poverty and backwardness. Literally hundreds of millions of people have been lifted out of poverty. China has become the workshop of the world, creating modern infrastructure and with cities sprouting outwards and upwards.

China's leaders have not forgotten what was done in the years of Perestroika to normalize relations between China and the USSR. Here is a quote from a book written by Qian Qichen, the Chinese Minister of Foreign Affairs in 1988–98:

It is, of course, for our descendants to assess Gorbachev's strengths and weaknesses as a historical and political figure. Nevertheless, the historic mission he took upon himself on this trip to Beijing deserves to be inscribed in heavy black ink in the annals of the history of Sino-Soviet relations.

Later in the book, he says: 'In this way, normal interstate relations of friendship and good neighbourliness developed.' The Chinese minister makes one further very important comment:

> The framework established then for normalizing Sino-Soviet relations provided a basis for rapid development of Sino-Russian relations, all the way to establishment of a relationship of strategic cooperation and partnership founded on equality and mutual trust. If we had missed the favourable opportunity offered at that time, bilateral relations between the two countries might have developed in an entirely different direction.

Qian Qichen quotes what I said at the press conference in Beijing 'Normalization of Sino-Soviet relations is not directed against the interests of any third countries, is not prejudicial to the interests of any third countries, and is an organic development of trends in the modern world.' I repeated this to President George Bush Senior, and have no doubt that is the way the relationship should be developed in the future.

I am glad that the impulse given by my visit to China and the talks I had with Deng Xiaoping has survived, and that relations between Russia and the People's Republic of China are now developing on a basis of strategic partnership.

In the 1990s my books were not published in China, but in 2002 Xinhua News Agency published *Reflections on the Past and Future*, a book very important to me. It contains my thoughts about history and revolution, and how the modern world is developing. After that, my other books were translated into Chinese and published there. Chinese journalists and diplomats began to ask my opinion and there was meaningful communication with Chinese scholars and politicians at the World Political Forum.

In connection with the centenary of the birth of Deng Xiaoping

Xinhua News Agency asked me to share my reminiscences of the meeting with him, my opinion of the reforms he initiated and the state of Russo-Chinese relations. I think it is worth quoting the gist of my response, which dates from 19 August 2004.

Fifteen years ago, at the invitation of China's leaders, I undertook an official state visit to the People's Republic of China. This came after nearly 30 years of confrontation between our countries.

For the visit to take place successfully, a lot of preliminary work had to be done by both sides. Through joint efforts, the necessary conditions were in place by May 1989. We arrived in China at a sensitive time of unrest, particularly among students, but not confined only to them. Nevertheless, we and China's leaders, especially Deng Xiaoping, believed the visit should go ahead. ...

I consider the results of our negotiations in Beijing to have been a major success. We achieved one of the greatest changes for the better not only in our relations but in global politics generally. We sketched out and subsequently implemented plans, meticulously scrutinized by experts, to demilitarize the huge Soviet–Chinese border and resolve a number of contentious border issues. Our attention was also, of course, focused on the challenges of economic cooperation and development of scientific and cultural ties.

All China's leaders were involved in the negotiations but, of course, Deng Xiaoping was playing first violin. In his words, we 'brought closure to the past and opened up the future.' We cast aside mutual suspicion, old scores and grudges.

At that time, Deng Xiaoping was almost 85 years old, but he radiated immense energy. I was struck by his frankness and the pragmatism of his judgements. Assuredly, both China and the Soviet Union had had to come a long way before a meeting at this level and with this kind of climate could be held.

Deng Xiaoping's reforms and his openness to the rest of the world had a huge impact not only on the situation in China, but also in world affairs. I think a really important part of the philosophy he professed was his deep understanding of the need for China to keep the peace, and its responsibility for bringing about positive change in the world as a great power and permanent member of the United Nations Security Council.

Under Deng Xiaoping, China consistently opposed domineering and hegemonism in international relations, while at the same time setting an example with a constructive approach to building a new world order founded on equal, mutually beneficial cooperation and respect for the diverse cultural history of the world. As I listen today to the declaration by Chinese leaders of their commitment to a multipolar world and strengthening the authority of international law and the United Nations, I recognize this as his very constructive legacy.

Deng Xiaoping will go down in the history of world politics primarily as a great reformer of China and architect of its modernization and openness. I have followed the reforms in China very closely, and been impressed by their pragmatism and effectiveness. I also share Deng Xiaoping's conviction that it is futile to copy foreign models and examples uncritically, without due respect for national individuality.

The great merit of Deng Xiaoping, his political colleagues and successors, the present leaders who seem to me to have a new outlook, is that in the world's most populous country they have managed to maintain a balance between political and social stability, thereby ensuring high rates of economic growth and participation of China in the global economy.

I welcome the energy that has characterized Russo-Chinese relations in recent years. I welcome the committed, business-like approach on both sides, with frank dialogue to clarify difficult issues. This is how it should be between partners and friends. This was published in the Chinese press.

I cannot fail to mention here my liking for another great Chinese politician, Zhao Ziyang, the former general secretary of the Communist Party of China's Central Committee, who died in 2005. At the request of Interfax, I recalled our meetings in 1989 and spoke of the positive impression left by our conversation. 'Our meetings', I reminisced, 'were taking place against the background of demonstrations many thousands strong in Tiananmen Square, and Zhao Ziyang was following them closely and anxiously. I believe that, of all the Chinese leaders, he was closest to those protesters and was emotionally inclined to democracy.' At the same time, at every press conference Zhao Ziyang stressed that he stood alongside Deng Xiaoping. It seemed to me he found that situation very painful.

China will face enormous, extraordinarily complex issues some time in the future. No nation's history develops in a continuous straight line: it comes to forks in the road, when difficult decisions have to be taken. Sooner or later China will have to decide the country's future political arrangements: not to put too fine a point on it, whether or not to become a democracy. We should recognize that we all have an interest in the stable development of this great land. The question of political reform, of how and when to embark on such a fraught move, is something only the Chinese can decide for themselves.

In China's current political model, based on a one-party system, there are some important aspects that have already served the country well as it modernizes. I am thinking of the regular turnover, every ten years, of the upper echelons of the Party and state leadership. The retirement of Deng Xiaoping, then Jiang Zemin, then Hu Jintao demonstrated that generational change, turnover of the top team, does not undermine stability but, on the contrary, maintains it and avoids stagnation. The new leaders are free to take new decisions and the old leaders are accorded respect and dignity. This and other features of the Chinese political model show an ability to learn from mistakes, not least the mistakes of Russia. It seems to me that, when the time comes, the Chinese will show themselves able to respond flexibly to the requirements of a new stage in the country's development.

I believe China will play an increasingly important role in global politics and in dealing with global environmental issues. In my interviews I have often said that we cannot make the same environmental demands of countries like China and India that we do of the industrialized countries that are most to blame for global warming, but the Chinese understand that, as their economic might increases, so they must take increasing responsibility for the environment. They will be further prompted to do so by the dire environmental pollution in many Chinese cities.

I note that the world's great powers are minded to cooperate with China. It is vital that in the process they do not start playing geopolitical games and trying to gain advantage for themselves by setting up various axes and triangles. On this, I find myself in complete agreement with George Bush Senior. I have talked to Barack Obama about this and found he too agreed.

In March 1994, the main Taiwanese newspapers invited me to visit Taipei. The highlight of the visit was perhaps a speech I gave in the memorial hall dedicated to the first president of the Republic of China, Dr Sun Yat-sen. The vast hall was full, and representatives of all the Taiwanese media were in attendance. My topic was 'The Prospects for a World Community'. I said there was every prospect of a global community now the Cold War was over, with the world no longer divided into blocs and groups bent on intimidating, suppressing and annihilating each other. A profound change of direction had come about in how the world was developing, whether some people liked it or not, under the impact of Perestroika in the USSR.

After the speech, I was asked a lot of questions. One was: 'How do you picture China after Deng Xiaoping?' In reply, I wished Deng Xiaoping the best of health and, no less importantly, all success with the great and far-reaching reforms begun under his leadership. The whole audience gave these remarks a standing ovation.

I had an interesting meeting with General Jiang Weiguo, the Director of the Institute of Strategic Studies, who was the son of Chiang Kai-shek. The general, who had visited Moscow, was responsible for the defence of Taiwan and so had an informed view on the dangers of nuclear confrontation. 'Few people can imagine what it might develop into,' he said. He believed even a local nuclear conflict would be likely to develop into a global nuclear catastrophe. He spoke nostalgically about how much the communists in Russia and the revolutionary Kuomintang had had in common at one time, and was in favour of strengthening and developing relations between Russia and China. In the course of our meeting, he uttered never a word of criticism of Beijing.

I vividly remember the people I met in Taipei, most of whom considered Taiwan to be part of China. Sometimes their warmth reminded me of the people I had met in Beijing and Shanghai in 1989.

There are many sides to Asia, which is increasingly becoming the centre of world politics. I have always been fascinated by it and in the years after I left office I have stayed in touch with such politicians in India as Sonia Gandhi, Charan Singh and I. K. Gujral; and with political leaders in Japan and other Asian countries. I have tried to keep up with what is happening in these countries, but what I am mainly interested in, of course, is how they are getting along with Russia. I have no doubt our relations with India will develop steadily. They are already very good, and new opportunities for us to cooperate are now arising there.

Russia and Japan

The situation is more difficult with Japan. There is great potential for our relationship, but major obstacles in the way of developing it. The main one is well known: the 'territorial problem'. When I went to Japan in 1992, I still had fresh in my memory the many hours of discussion of the issue with Prime Minister Toshiki Kaifu during my visit in April 1991.

The Japanese side raised the question of the 'Northern Territories' very stridently, demanding that we should confirm a Soviet–Japanese Declaration of 1956 which foresaw the possibility that the islands of Habomai and Shikotan might be transferred to Japan. My position was unequivocal: the Joint Declaration of 1956 had become null and void as a result of changed circumstances since that time. 'Let us', I urged the Japanese prime minister, 'develop relations between our countries, reach a new level of trust and mutual cooperation, and perhaps when our cooperation covers the Far East, Siberia and the European regions of Russia, this dispute may no longer be so bitter and we will be able to find a solution satisfactory to both Russia and Japan.'

Now, just one year later, I was back in Japan. A public committee under former Prime Minister Yasuhiro Nakasone had been established to prepare for and coordinate my visit. Nakasone was a high-profile and greatly respected politician. In conversations with him and many other Japanese politicians I noticed two points of interest.

The first was that the changes that had occurred during the years of Perestroika had created an opening for putting Russo-Japanese relations on a new footing. I detected a change of tone on the most sensitive issue, those four islands in the Kuril chain. As I said at a press conference on my return to Moscow, I had the impression that instead of the previous rigidity, a more flexible policy might be considered that did not exclude compromises and transitional arrangements. Accordingly, our work in April 1991 during my many hours of talks with Prime Minister Kaifu showed some initial results. But second, I added: 'We have to be realistic and not fall prey to wishful thinking. The politicians on the other side are very rigid, very specific, very rigorous and they will demand equal rigour from our side. So perhaps all we can say for now is that this is in the early stages.'

The trip took place in a good atmosphere, with a lot of interest from the Japanese public. We personally received a lot of sincere sympathy and kind feelings from thousands of people. For me, this was all rather unexpected. The only person to show no interest whatsoever in my visit was the ambassador in Japan of the Russian Federation.

Since then, I have visited Japan often. I have many friends there, and the Gorbachev Foundation maintains relations with Japanese universities and research institutes. Together with Daisaku Ikeda, the leader of one of Japan's major religious political movements Soka Gakkai, I coauthored a book of dialogues titled *Moral Lessons of the Twentieth Century*, in which I gave a detailed exposition of one of my most important tenets: the need to bring politics closer to morality.[1]

During my visits to Japan, I spoke to hundreds of Japanese people, and I can testify that most of them respect my position on the issue of the islands, which I first stated in 1991. I see a continuity with the principles laid down back then in the current position of the Russian government.

Russia and Japan to this day do not really enjoy good-

[1] Mikhail Gorbachev and Daisaku Ikeda, *Moral Lessons of the Twentieth Century: Gorbachev and Ikeda on Buddhism and Communism*, London: I.B. Tauris, 2005.

neighbourly relations, but good-neighbourliness and cooperation are in the interests of both our countries. A rapprochement
between Russia and Japan is indispensable also to maintain equilibrium in the region.

Simmering Regions

Egypt and Syria

Looking back today, I cannot help wondering whether global politics will continue to be dominated by force, primarily military. Is it really not yet abundantly clear that it does not solve, but instead aggravates problems and conflicts, and is completely inapplicable to the new, primarily environmental, problems and challenges we face? Must we really depart again and again from the principles of New Thinking, dialogue and multilateral cooperation, in order to be persuaded again and again that they are imperative? Year after year, and indeed decade after decade, that is what is repeated in the Middle East.

From my contacts with the leaders of countries in the region – and I have met on several occasions the late King Hussein of Jordan, his successor Abdullah II, the Israeli president, Shimon Peres, and the Palestinian leaders – I have come firmly to the conclusion that peace in the region is possible. At the Madrid Conference of 1991, co-sponsored by the USSR and the United States, the outlines for future peaceful negotiation were agreed, but then the United States again decided to go it alone and impose peace and order in the Middle East unilaterally. I could not help recalling what the then secretary of state, George Shultz, had told me in Moscow in 1988: 'We tried to resolve the Middle East problem on our own. We wanted to squeeze the Soviet Union out of the region. I myself flew between the capitals of the Middle East and devoted dozens of hours to shuttle diplomacy. In the end we concluded we should not attempt to squeeze you out. Let's work together on this.'

Alas, the temptation to act unilaterally proved too great. The United States decided to 'democratize' the region with missile strikes, followed by military intervention in Iraq with results that are well known. This brings me to the whole question of the future of democracy, and ways of achieving democracy, in this endlessly simmering region and in the world at large. It is a question we discuss continuously at the World Political Forum, and one of the central issues of the present century.

Democracy, I said at one of the Forum's conferences, has certain basic principles and values, but there is nothing uniform about it: 'It has to reflect the cultural characteristics, the traditions and mentality of peoples. Only then will it succeed, only then will it avoid the slippery slope to authoritarianism. That is particularly the case for countries in transition.' I offered another no less important proposition:

> As committed supporters of democracy, we have to recognize that people's attitude towards it also depends on how successfully matters of vital importance to them are managed. Accordingly, we can see that democracy is currently on trial both at the national level and internationally. If democracy fails to address the problem of poverty, people start looking to authoritarian politicians for answers. That is why we are currently seeing a slowing of the move towards democratization, and in some cases a receding of the democratic tide.

The Arab Spring, whose events we all watched closely, confirmed the truth of these conclusions.

Early in 2011, I responded to the popular protests in Egypt with an article published in the *International Herald Tribune* and other newspapers around the world. 'A lot of anxiety has surfaced', I wrote, 'in comments by politicians and the media. Many voice the fear that the popular movement could lead to chaos and then to fundamentalist reaction and confrontation between the Islamic world and the international community.' It has to be admitted, there were solid grounds for such fears.

> First in Tunisia and now in Egypt, the people have spoken and made clear that they do not want to live under authoritarian rule and are fed up with regimes that hold power for decades.

In the end, the voice of the people will be decisive.

For too long, conventional political thinking about the Arab world was based on a false dichotomy: authoritarian regimes or fundamentalism, extremism, terrorism. The people who filled Tahrir Square in Cairo and the streets of other Egyptian cities wanted to end this charade.

I wrote in that article :

> [T]he equation to be solved in Egypt and other countries of the Arab East has many unknowns. The most unpredictable is the Islamic factor. What is its place in the people's movement? What kind of Islam will emerge?
>
> The history of Islamic culture includes periods when it was a leader in the development of world civilization. Its contributions to science, education and literature cannot be disputed. Islamic doctrines strongly advocate social justice and peace. An Islam that emphasizes those values can have great potential.
>
> Already, democratic processes and genuine socio-economic achievements in countries like Turkey, Indonesia and Malaysia offer optimism.

In Egypt, subsequent events confirmed the apprehensions of those who suspected that change would be difficult and painful, and beset by failures and setbacks. One of the reasons the wind of change did not sweep the Arab world and soon weakened, apart from the fact that not all countries are equally ripe for change that in the longer term is inevitable, was probably the intervention of external forces that only hampered and distorted the process. This was particularly glaring in Syria.

On the one hand, Syria is one of those countries where the ruling regime has held on to power for decades, where the leaders come to identify themselves with the nation and fail to respond adequately to accumulating social and economic problems. Sooner or later, social unrest is inevitable. On the other hand, external interference in the affairs of such countries has practically never ended well. It is unacceptable not only because it is against international law, but also because its instigators have no understanding of the complexities of the situation, the intertwined and entangled relationships, interests, historical grievances, religious and cultural tensions. In this respect, Syria is a prime example. But as soon as the unrest began in Syria, outside forces started competing with one another to aggravate it, their priority being to ensure they had a strong position in 'Syria after Assad'. This approach is one of the main problems in the Middle East, and indeed elsewhere.

The UN Security Council paid lip service to the idea of convening a conference on the future of Syria, bringing together all the interested parties, but it was not realized. Former UN Secretary-General Kofi Annan was appointed joint special envoy of the UN and Arab League to Syria to bring about a settlement of the conflict, but he had to abandon his mission. While in Moscow recently, he told me with dismay that he had no sense of genuine support from the leading powers in his efforts to initiate dialogue.

Matters reached a dangerous level, beyond which there was a likelihood of missile strikes, loss of life and a widening of the conflict. Ongoing military action, hundreds of thousands of refugees, the unwillingness of the greater part of the Syrian opposition to come to the negotiating table in Geneva: all together add up to a situation that may at any moment deteriorate into a regional catastrophe.

In Egypt, the reasons for the breakdown of the democratic process are mainly domestic. People are not always ready to avail themselves skilfully and responsibly of the opportunities that their freedom offers them. Leaders are not always forthcoming who are capable of leading them through the vicissitudes of the process of transition. In my 2011 article I wrote: 'Just as everywhere else, the only way forward in the Arab world, with its tortuous history, unique culture and numerous risks and dangers, is towards democracy, with the understanding that the path is difficult and that democracy is not a magic wand.'

During the first phase of the events, the main forces of Egyptian society were united, but already when it was time to draft a new constitution, and subsequently, before and after the presidential election, differences began to surface. Protests began, clashes between the representatives of different groups and faiths, and people were killed. The Coptic Christians were in a particularly bad situation. Most seriously, people had no sense that the transition to democracy was delivering, if not an improvement in their lives, then at least the prospect of improvement. The president, although democratically elected, failed to behave like a genuinely democratic leader. The urban middle class and the military joined forces against him and, when he was overthrown, there was almost no one willing to give him support.

It is very difficult to say now how events will develop. The rolling back of a wave of democracy is not uncommon, but this does not mean the leaders of authoritarian regimes can look forward to an easy life. All these regimes have one shared weakness: the gap separating those in power from society at large, a breakdown of feedback of popular opinion, which, sooner or later, causes the government to get out of control.

Of course, the leaders can continue to tell themselves things are not that bad and that they 'have the situation under control'. But they cannot but wonder just how stable that control is. I have little doubt that, deep down, they know it will not last forever, that it is increasingly an illusion. So then the question is, what to do next? Continue by inertia, further strengthening the structures and machinery of authoritarianism? Or look for ways to make the transition to democracy?

The second way is far from easy, and even agonizing. It implies that, sooner or later, power will pass to the opposition. Misconduct will be exposed; the chains of corruption leading to the top will be broken; someone will have to answer for everything. That is not an attractive prospect for an authoritarian regime.

Nevertheless, you need to have the courage to go for real change, because ruling without accountability for the rest of time is, in any case, not an option.

Russia and Ukraine

I have to admit that I did not anticipate the events that are severely testing not only the relationship between Russia and Ukraine, but also the prospects for global politics in general, and which could bring the world to the brink of a major disaster.

Everything I see happening causes me immense pain. The stakes are too high, the risks and dangers too great. I feel an obligation to explain how I see the situation, and my ideas on how to find a way out of it. For every Russian, Ukraine and our relationship with it is very special. Historical, cultural and family ties between our countries, which for so long existed within the framework of a single state, are so longstanding and close that we empathize very directly with what is happening on our neighbour's territory.

The crisis was precipitated by Ukraine's signing an association agreement with the European Union. I was disturbed from the outset that this matter was not considered in the context of the other, no less important, issue of how that would affect Ukraine's relations with Russia. A framework for negotiation and coordination was needed that created a triangle of Russia, Ukraine and the European Union and paid due attention to the interests of each of the parties.

That, unfortunately, was not done. The European Union rejected the very idea of cooperating with Russia and involving her in negotiations. President Yanukovych of Ukraine intrigued, put his own political interests first and finally decided against signing an agreement with the EU. Many people in Ukraine disagreed with that decision and found it inexplicable. Demonstrations and protests were peaceful at first, but later the initiative passed to radicals, extremists and provocateurs. The situation became increasingly tense, but I hoped, nevertheless, that Ukraine's politicians would themselves find an honourable way out of the situation. It was soon apparent that they were not up to the job.

The course of events was becoming increasingly threatening and, on 23 January 2014, I sent an open letter to Presidents Vladimir Putin of Russia and Barack Obama of the United States, urging them to take the lead in negotiations, put an immediate end to the violence and prevent bloodshed on a massive scale. The letter read:

It is within your power to achieve this aim. The parties to the conflict should sit down at the negotiating table. The main thing is to prevent a dangerous escalation.

It is impossible not to see that the course of events in Kiev is a threat not only to Ukraine and its neighbours, but also to Europe and the rest of the world.

People are understandably distressed. Russia and Ukraine have been very close for centuries and it is not just a matter of historical links. People are bound by close family ties.

I do not have to look far for examples. In my own family, my mother was Ukrainian, my father Russian. My late wife was Ukrainian. There are thousands of such examples. There are literally blood ties between our people and our peoples. It is unforgivable for Ukrainians to be fighting other Ukrainians, but as the situation has developed it seems that, without help, without the assistance of authoritative representatives of our two countries, a disaster could develop. Vladimir Vladimirovich, Mr Obama, I appeal to you to find a way to take decisive action to help Ukraine back to the path of peaceful development.

I pin great hopes on you.

My letter was truly a *cri de coeur*, but it fell on deaf ears. Events continued to develop as if under their own momentum, as out of control as an avalanche. The unforgivable thing I warned the two presidents about became a reality. While the foreign ministers of three EC countries, Germany, France and Poland, conducted talks in Kiev, the chaotic situation in Ukraine worsened. The agreements they reached proved ineffective, Yanukovych fled the country, and the parliament, pressured by radicals, started rubber-stamping resolutions that infringed the rights of many citizens and jeopardized the status of the Russian language.

Even in these circumstances, I remained hopeful that the crisis could be halted and things begin to return to normal. In an interview for Associated Press news agency on 23 February 2014, I again called for outside mediation. I insisted that everything possible must be done 'to ensure that the crisis in Ukraine does not lead to a tragic division. People must be given an opportunity to reach agreement.' I have no doubt that if this principle had been taken as a basis from the outset, many bad things could have been avoided, but with every day that passed the situation deteriorated. Events developed close to a worst-case scenario.

Why?

In the West, by which I mean the ruling elites of the United States and the countries of NATO, everything was blamed on Russia. Everywhere they saw the 'long arm of Moscow', but this conflict was not of Russia's making. It has its roots within Ukraine itself.

I see the main, deep cause of the Ukrainian events in the disruption of Perestroika and the mindless, reckless 'disbanding' of the USSR. The primary responsibility for that lies with Russia's then leadership, which exacerbated centrifugal processes in the Union. At the same time, I remind my readers that the Ukrainian leaders sabotaged transformation of the Union, both before the August 1991 coup and after it, in spite of the fact that the text of a Union Treaty had been agreed with a majority of the republics. I fought to preserve the Union state with all the political, and I stress, *political*, means at my disposal. I proposed negotiations with Ukraine on an economic union, a common defence and foreign policy. In the course of such negotiations we could have resolved all the thorny questions, like the status of Sevastopol and Crimea, and the Black Sea Fleet.

My suggestions and warnings at that time went unheeded. Forgetting that in relations between peoples you need to apply the utmost circumspection, to evaluate the consequences of every move, the Supreme Soviet of the Russian Federation rose to its feet to applaud its approval of the destruction of the Union. Some may say that this is all in the past now. Actually, no, the past has many threads tying it to the present; it gives us cause again and again to recall old mistakes politicians made.

How is the conflict in Ukraine to be resolved and the international consequences overcome of the crisis those events have caused? There is only one way: dialogue, a search for consensus.

What is essential is a coherent, constructive dialogue both at the international level and between the political forces in Ukraine. The foreign 'players' have much to answer for over their behaviour at every stage of the Ukrainian crisis. The country has been tested to destruction and now it is time for some constructive help. Next, we need the broadest possible dialogue between all responsibly minded forces in Ukraine on how to rescue the country and rebuild a national consensus. After all that has happened, the mutual recrimination, the hostility, the bloodshed, that is going to be extremely difficult. We should have no illusions, but at the same time, there is no alternative. We have to get on with it.

In May 2014 Ukraine elected a president who found himself saddled with huge responsibilities. Much will depend on how responsibly and equitably the newly elected parliament behaves. It is vital to get a genuinely representative forum functioning as soon as possible.

I well remember in 1988 discussing the idea of such a forum with the Polish president, Wojciech Jaruzelski. I told the general he could count on total support and understanding on our part. At that time, a great deal of mistrust, even hostility, had built up in Poland between the government and the opposition, but both managed to put the national interest first.

Above all else, Ukraine needs nationwide agreement on its constitutional arrangements and the basic direction of its domestic and foreign policy. The Ukrainians themselves are the only people who can reach such a consensus, but an absolute prerequisite is that the interests of all nationalities, sections of the population and regions must be taken into account. As far as the foreign policy of the Ukrainian state is concerned, one of its first priorities should be getting its relations with Russia right. I have no doubt the majority of Ukrainians not only know that, but desire it. That is something the West too needs to understand: it is time its leaders stopped trying to draw Ukraine into NATO.

I would very much like to believe that Ukraine will get over its feverishness, that the Minsk Protocol of 5 and 19 September 2014 will prove the first step on the road to reconciliation and a better life for all the country's citizens, and that relations between Ukraine and Russia will again be those of two truly fraternal peoples.

The Ukrainian crisis has provoked a serious and dangerous deterioration of relations between Russia and the West. US President Obama has declared that Russia must be isolated; he and other Western leaders have refused to negotiate with the Russian president in the G8 group of nations. Economic sanctions against Russia have been introduced, cooperation in many areas greatly restricted, and decisions are being taken to strengthen the military presence of NATO in countries adjacent to Russia. All this is very reminiscent of the Cold War era.

What can and must be done to stop a dangerous slide, to avoid a new division of Europe and the world? I note that both Russia and the countries of the West have stated that they do not want a new Cold War. All is not yet lost: a certain level of communication persists.

There have been signs of attempts to break the vicious circle bedevilling relations between Russia and her Western partners. Escalation of mutual sanctions has been halted, thanks to restraint on the part of Russia. Brussels has expressed willingness to negotiate a free trade zone between the European Union and the Customs Union of Russia, Belarus and Kazakhstan. Cooperation is improving, albeit with difficulty, within the framework of the Organization for Security and Co-operation in Europe to consolidate the ceasefire in Ukraine.

We must, however, face up to the truth and acknowledge that it has not so far proved possible to pull relations back out of their nosedive. That is damaging both for Russia and her Western partners, and for Europe as a whole. Instead of leading change in a globalized world, Europe has become an arena of political upheavals, rivalry for spheres of influence and, finally, military conflict. The inevitable consequence is a weakening of Europe in the face of a rapid rise of other centres of power and influence. Europe is losing its distinctive voice in world affairs.

Today, it is tremendously important to look at things in a sober and balanced way. We need to remember that there are global challenges and interests common to all mankind, problems that it will be impossible to solve if the leading powers in the world fail to cooperate. In other words, it is time to turn again to the basic postulates of the New Thinking we proposed to the world when tensions between East and West were at their height.

At that time the main danger was of global nuclear conflict. We succeeded in reducing that threat, but the problem of nuclear weapons and the threat of a new arms race have not gone away. At the same time, other threats have become more acute: most glaringly, global climate change. The predictions of scientists become increasingly alarming with every year that passes. A report of the United Nations Environment Programme predicts an increase in the average global temperature of 5° Celsius by 2050 and the melting of all the ice in the Arctic Ocean. Mankind has never faced these conditions before.

To this we must add other global problems: the increasing shortage of fresh water and food resources, the problems of international terrorism, cybersecurity and the prevention of pandemics. Are we really going to allow cooperation in all these areas to fall victim to the present crisis in relations between the great powers?

People say the current deterioration results largely from the fact that Presidents Putin and Obama 'don't get on' on a personal level, so until there is a change of leaders no worthwhile improvement can be expected. I think this approach is profoundly erroneous. We do not choose our international partners, and if that relationship does not gel, it is the duty of the leaders to their citizens and to the world to get over their private feelings and behave like statesmen.

I am certain there must eventually be a return to the principles of New Thinking in international affairs. It is indispensable if we do not want to destroy the world we all live in. I urge everyone to waste no more time. Today that is the top priority.

History is not fated

Almost every year I meet my friends, fellow Nobel Peace Prize laureates. These summits have been attended by such figures as Jimmy Carter, Shimon Peres and Yasser Arafat, and representatives of Nobel Prize-winning organizations like Médecins Sans Frontières and the Association of Doctors for the Prevention of Nuclear War.

Every time I meet and talk with them, I come away with new ideas and renewed faith that, in the difficult and not always predictable circumstances of the modern world, we must not give way to disillusionment and panic. History is not fated. There is always a place for initiative, creativity and action. All the Nobel Prize winners I meet want, each in their own way, to continue to be part of the process of human history and, to the best of their ability, exert influence on the course of events. This is a manifestation of active, global civil society, which knows it cannot just delegate responsibility for the world to the professional politicians of today.

There is no question but that the politicians have a difficult job to do, and quite often think that we, with our declarations and initiatives, merely get under their feet. But is it not a fact that politicians, by ignoring the demands and warnings of civil society, have made numerous mistakes, for which most often it is not they who pay, but ordinary citizens, sometimes in their hundreds of thousands, in their millions? That is why we do not keep quiet.

We conclude our meetings by adopting papers, declarations and statements on issues that are causing us concern. Sometimes they relate to issues current at that moment, violent conflicts. Not infrequently, we speak out about fundamental issues of principle and critically important aspects of the contemporary world. Working on our statements is always a creative process of the colliding and reconciling of the views of people not content to stand on the sidelines. The statements I especially remember are those where the Nobel laureates have pronounced on issues I have been reflecting on for decades, namely, how morality relates to politics and the problem of keeping things manageable in a globalized world.

In 2003, the Nobel Prize winners stated:

> Our generation bears an ethical responsibility towards future generations to ensure that we are not passing on a future of wars and ecological catastrophe. For policies to be in the interests of humanity, they must be based on ethical values.
>
> We express our profound anxiety that current policies are not creating a sufficiently secure and stable world for all. For this reason, we need to reset our course based on strong ethical foundations.
>
> Compassion and conscience are essential to our humanity and compel us to care for one another. Cooperation amongst nations, multilateralism, is the logical outgrowth of this principle. A more

equitable international order based on the rule of law is its needed expression.

We stressed that recent events 'confirm that problems with deep economic, social, cultural or religious roots cannot be resolved unilaterally or by armed force'. We called for rejection of 'doctrines that lower the threshold of use and promote the creation of new nuclear weapons. This is particularly dangerous when coupled with the doctrine of pre-emption.' We concluded that it was essential to undertake a decisive renewal of global politics. We stated: 'Humanity has developed sophisticated technologies for destruction. Appropriate social and human technologies based on cooperation are needed for survival.'

For too long, politicians and a significant section of society have believed that politics and morality are incompatible. I have never been able to agree with that. The golden rule of morality is: 'Do unto others as you would have them do unto you.' Another formulation is: 'Do not do to others what you would not want done to yourself.' We stated: 'Ethics in the relations between nations and in government policies is of paramount importance. Nations must treat other nations as they wish to be treated. The most powerful nations must remember that, as they do, so shall others do.'

Another important point in the declaration states that we believe that both the exploitation of new, unprecedentedly increased opportunities for humanity and the countering of dangers that threaten us all demand an end to laissez-faire, and the responsible management of global processes. For globalization to contribute fully to sustainable development, the international community 'needs to establish more democratic, transparent, and accountable forms of governance'.[1] Exactly what I understood by this, I made clear in my speech: 'Responsible management does

---

[1] '4th World Summit of Nobel Peace Laureates: Final Statement – Ethics and Policy, 30 November 2003', Rome, in *International Peace Bureau Contributions to Nobel Peace Laureates Summits 2002–2006*; http://gs institute.s3.amazonaws.com/assets/docs/IPB_NobelSummitReports.pdf (p. 28). Accessed 7 August 2015.

not mean a world government. We are talking about something different: the preservation and improvement, renewal and adaptation of every level of the complex machinery that currently ensures a degree of orderliness in global processes.' If instead we saw only a continuation of efforts to give absolute priority to the national interests of a single country or group of countries, that would lead to unmanageable chaos. That, I said, is the choice facing mankind today. The right of might, leading to destructive chaos, or an orderly transition to a new model of global development: a new model of international relations based on the principles of international law and cooperation between states, unshakable, but at the same time constantly adapted and adapting itself to new problems and new challenges. This model would have to be created through the joint efforts not only of states, but also of the institutions of civil society and mass public movements.

I drew attention to the fact that this was beginning to be acknowledged by representatives of the world's business and political elites. The 2010 World Economic Forum in Davos was held under the motto, 'Improve the State of the World: Rethink, Redesign, Rebuild', which was effectively the programme of Perestroika. Immediately before the forum, its founder, Klaus Schwab, called on its participants to find new models for a collective approach to global challenges and a new model of leadership that would be effective in the world today. I have no doubt that the new model called for will incorporate the basic postulates of New Thinking, the experience of the years when we were successful in changing the direction of mankind and ending the Cold War.

In conclusion, I want to ask whether there is any sign in the thinking of politicians and the actions of world leaders of a move away from militaristic approaches premised on the use of armed force, any sign of the world changing course in the way international affairs are conducted.

Right now, I am not ready to give an answer to that question because positive steps are so far too timid and inconsistent. Too often, attempts to reach agreement or find compromise solutions are still terminated or gutter out almost before they are begun. Too massive are the interests vested in the arms race, the arms trade, polluting industries, religious strife and unequal relationships. And yet, there are grounds for cautious optimism.

Chief among these is the fact that today we simply cannot afford to be pessimistic or defeatist or to panic. That, luckily, is not the only reason. It is simply not true that we never learn from history. The second half of the twentieth century, although it was spent under the shadow of the Cold War and the threat of nuclear conflict, was at least not a repetition of the first half of a century scarred by the catastrophe of two world wars. By our joint efforts we kept the world away from the brink and did ultimately bring the Cold War and the nuclear arms race to an end. Although we failed to take full advantage of that great achievement, I believe that all is not yet lost. The possibility of moving forward to a rational and equitable world order is still there.

I am convinced that history is not fated. No doubt it has its own logic, its laws. There is what is called the 'irony of history', its caprices, but, more importantly, in the way historical processes develop there is always room for alternatives. The same outcome in history can be achieved at a very different price, depending on the methods used. A great deal depends on the actions of particular individuals, particular leaders, on the choices a society makes (which we can influence), on our own sense of responsibility, wisdom, goodwill and determination.

An optimist, in my understanding, is not someone like Voltaire's Candide, who at first views the world through rose-tinted spectacles and parrots the mantra that 'all is for the best in this best of all possible worlds' when beset by one misfortune after another. An optimist is someone dissatisfied with the existing state of affairs who is not resigned to it and consciously looks, to the best of his or her ability, for opportunities to make the world a better place, who helps to find practical solutions to the problems facing people here and now.

In that sense, I declare myself an optimist.

Conclusion

I began contemplating the need for reforms in the USSR during the years of stagnation and, of course, I was not alone in that. Proposals for modernizing social and economic relations and institutions were being worked on by top-class experts, and there were attempts to introduce novel initiatives in a number of regions. These were viewed with displeasure by the country's leaders, who, especially after the unrest in 1968, mostly inclined to conservatism. Their approach is conventionally associated with the name of Leonid Brezhnev.

I remember Brezhnev at different periods of his life, when he was open to innovation and later, when he had closed his mind to it and was effectively a hostage of those around him, who took advantage of his debility and later illness to further their own interests. A state of stagnation suited them very well, enabling them to further their careers and promote their interests and pet projects, including some that were dangerous and harmful for Russia. It is enough to recall the mass production and deployment in the European part of the country of SS-20 missiles, souring our relations with Western Europe and leading to deployment of US ballistic missiles with a five-minute flight time to Moscow. Then there was Afghanistan, the mere mention of which is, I think, enough.

When Yury Andropov came to power, he set about sorting out the problematical legacy of Brezhnev, particularly in terms of personnel. He understood, though, that it was not just a matter of individuals. It is worth remembering the excitement in the thinking part of Russian society when he commented in one of his articles that we did not really know the society in which we were living. That was seen as recognition at last of the urgency of the problems facing Russia and the inevitability of change.

Over a period of several years I was in contact with Andropov and met him informally. I know he cultivated scholars, writers and people in the arts. He felt a need for that kind of interaction, evidently finding the rituals of Party officialdom burdensome. During the last years of Andropov's life, I was constantly in touch with him. Nowadays, we often hear people wondering what would have happened if history had allowed him more time. Could he have gone for major changes in the development of Russia? I reached my own conclusions about that and will repeat them here.

In terms of personality and intellect, Yury Vladimirovich stood out head and shoulders above the rest. Nevertheless, he was a leader fixed in his time. His intention was to introduce change using the old methods, administrative leverage, slogans about improving discipline and 'restoring basic order'. He believed that was what Russian people were used to and ready for, and that was what he hoped to achieve. I do not believe he would have gone further.

Andropov's views and ideas had been moulded by his long service as director of the KGB, and before that, as Soviet ambassador to Hungary during the 1956 events. The fight against dissent; rigorous measures, even including confining people in psychiatric hospitals, against the dissident movement, whose size in Russia was actually quite modest; passing laws and taking administrative measures to regulate intellectual and cultural life: all this was done on the initiative of the KGB he directed. Andropov was one of those who prepared and oversaw the Soviet invasion of Afghanistan in 1979. I do not believe he would have been able to leave all that behind.

As regards Konstantin Chernenko, he found himself promoted to the highest post in the USSR when he was already seriously ill. It is clear enough that he was in no state to attempt to change the situation. It was impossible then even to raise the question of root-and-branch economic and political reform.

In the literature of political history, the beginning of Perestroika is dated from my election as general secretary of the CPSU Central Committee. That is true to the extent that my election indicated the Party's leaders had come to recognize that renewal was essential. As regards me personally, I inclined to democracy from an early age. I was a student at Moscow University where, even during the Stalin period, an intellectual climate of enquiry survived in Moscow. For me, this was a new, expansive world of information and culture, an opportunity to rub shoulders with a wide range of people. It shaped my personality as someone prepared to think for themselves. After graduating, I returned to Stavropol and began working in the Komsomol and later in Party institutions, which at that time really were 'answerable for everything'. That gave me experience of working in the real world and being responsible for other people.

My years working in the region, and then, within a few years, in the highest echelons of power, led me to an acute, alarmed awareness of the problems that had built up in the USSR, and of the urgent need to finally tackle them. It would be an exaggeration, though, to say that at the time I was elected general secretary I had already formed a specific plan or the concept of Perestroika.

Ahead of me, in spring 1986, was the CPSU Congress at which the word 'Perestroika', restructuring, was pronounced, at first applicable only to the activities of the Communist Party. On 8 April 1986, however, speaking in the city of Togliatti, I was already talking of Perestroika in the broader sense in which the term has gone down in history. By this time, there was a group of people among the leaders of the Party and the country who understood that change was inevitable, and that reflected a general mood in society. People rejected unfreedom, the rigid framework constraining their initiative and opportunities. They demanded change. There was a very widespread feeling that 'This is no way to live!'

The system created in the USSR under the banner of socialism, at a very high price of extraordinary efforts, sacrifices and casualties, made it possible to lay the foundations of the country's industrial might. In emergency situations it worked, but under more normal conditions it held the country back.

The question is often asked of whether we realized the extent of the upheaval on which we were embarking. Yes, we did, but initially only in general terms. I can testify that the leadership of the time recognized that the reform must be profound and

far-reaching, and that we must not stop, not limit ourselves to
half-measures as had been the fate of previous attempts to transform the Soviet system.

It was clear enough what we needed to reject and abandon:
a rigid ideological, political and economic system; head-on confrontation on the international stage; and the arms race. There
was public support for this from a society ready for a renewal of
life, and for a time it was favoured with tacit neutrality, and even
condoned, by people who subsequently proved still to be hardline
Stalinists.

It was much less straightforward to find an answer to the other
question of where we should be going and what we should be
aspiring to. We came a long way in a short time, starting with
the intention only of accelerating socio-economic development
by introducing new systems in mechanical engineering, machine
tool manufacturing and other vitally important industries. We set
about replacing personnel. We supposed that this would create
the prerequisites for moving forward to new ways of organizing
production and applying them to every sector of the economy.
However, we ran into obstruction from the current administrative-command system of managing the economy and every aspect
of society, which rejected or inhibited all innovation. Having
started with the intention of overhauling the existing system, we
came to see that it needed to be replaced. It needed new 'load-
bearing structures', new pillars. What did not change was the
humane character of Perestroika, with its corollary that change,
even the most radical, must be evolutionary in order not to break
the country's back, to avoid destructive upheavals, major disruption and, of course, bloodshed.

We pictured and began Perestroika as a process of renewing
socialism. That was the only viable option. For me, the idea of
cleansing socialism of the totalitarian legacy of the Stalin era was
something personal, arrived at through all I had experienced in
the course of my life. Those who see Gorbachev as a radical liberal who has repudiated socialist ideals are simply wrong, but also
mistaken are those who consider him an unregenerate communist
who has learned nothing during the years of Perestroika.

I am not someone who readily sloughs his skin, changing his

beliefs as he might a pair of gloves. My transition from the boy who wrote essays at school on the topic 'Stalin Is Our Military Glory, Stalin Is the Soaring of Our Youth' to rejecting Stalinism and waging war on the totalitarian system was hard and far from painless. A major part in it was played by my turning to the last works of Lenin, his admission that 'we made a mistake in deciding to move directly to communist production and distribution'. There is no denying that the Bolsheviks made a complete hash of things with War Communism.

I think Lenin was appalled by the results: the collapse of the economy, famine in the cities, the Kronstadt mutiny, peasant uprisings; and he concluded: 'You cannot jump ahead of the people.' Lenin's comments on the need for 'a fundamental change of our entire point of view about socialism', as well as his words about a transition from the earlier, revolutionary approach to 'a completely different, reformist way forward' had a profound impact on me.

No small part in my understanding and rethinking of socialism in the modern world was played by the Prague Spring of 1968. Its motto was 'Socialism with a human face'. Later, people in many countries, including Russia and especially among the intelligentsia, rejected that ideal. That was very unwise. They turned their backs on socialism with a human face, and instead got capitalism with an inhuman face.

Implementing reformist ideas at that time proved impossible: the process of change was halted by the sending in of Soviet troops to Czechoslovakia. To this day, I remember the workers at the Zbrojovka Brno arms and vehicle factory turning their backs on us when we tried to start a conversation with them during a Soviet Communist Party visit to Czechoslovakia in 1969. I have no reason to think they were enemies of socialism: they just wanted to decide the future of their country themselves. Our leaders at the time failed to understand the democratic changes begun in Czechoslovakia, and saw them only as underhand scheming by the 'enemies of socialism'.

The motto of our Perestroika, 'For a humane, democratic socialism', was consonant with the ideas of the Prague Spring, the thinking of our intelligentsia in the 1960s and of the

Eurocommunists in the West. It was no mere slogan, but an aspiration at the heart of what we were seeking, a concept rejecting a rigid dichotomy between socialism and capitalism.

We set ourselves the task of democratizing every aspect of society, overcoming the alienation of people from politics and the state in order to give them the opportunity of exerting real influence on decision-making and awaken their initiative. We saw the main engines of change as Glasnost, transparency; in genuine dialogue between state authorities and society; open discussion of all problems; repudiation of censorship and pressure from the Party and government on the media (which, incidentally, remains relevant today, when the opportunities for such dialogue are being constricted and forced into official frameworks); in recognizing the rights to free assembly, movement and religion, and setting up public associations and allowing them to function without interference.

Of fundamental concern to the proponents of Perestroika was the question of the pace of change. It remained controversial throughout the Perestroika period, and is no less contentious today. Opinions vary widely. In hindsight, it seems to me that we forced the pace, and perhaps too ambitiously for a society in which radicalism existed side-by-side with traditions of conservative thinking and communal culture, of pinning hopes on a 'good tsar', and limited ability to organize things independently.

That certainly caused problems for Perestroika, particularly in its second phase when turbulent political developments exposed many painful problems, which had surreptitiously accumulated in the course of years past. For all the differences in the two phases of Perestroika, however, what they had in common was the direction of greater humanity in which the process of change was heading, the evolutionary approach, the faith in the Russian people and their ability to determine their own history, trust in their choices.

Gradually, but by historical standards very quickly, it became clear to the instigators of Perestroika that there needed to be a change in the role of the Soviet Communist Party. The Party needed to be freed of its functions as a supreme arbiter standing above all other state and public institutions. It needed to be replaced by a state governed under the rule of law. At the June 1988 Party conference we succeeded in gaining approval of that course, and from then onwards the momentum towards democracy and freedom gradually became irreversible.

I am often asked why we did not implement reform of the economic system in parallel and in association with the political transformation. Was the fact that it was archaic and not fit for purpose not obvious to everyone? We need to remember that the initial decisions to embark on transition to a market economy were agreed in 1987 at the April Plenum of the Party's Central Committee, but proved impossible to implement: resistance by conservative forces in the government and economic bureaucracy was too great, and they were too firmly entrenched in power. To our misfortune, at just this moment there was a sharp fall in the price of oil and other fuels and of commodities on global markets, which forced us to reduce imports. Disruption of the consumer market, money supply and industrial production was aggravated by increasingly active forces of separatism and the breakdown of economic ties between the republics, territories and regions.

Perestroika could not but affect interethnic problems, involving the most complex and delicate area of relations within our society. Our policy here was unambiguous: we favoured decentralization, and empowerment of such national institutions as the Union republics, territories and regions, while preserving and strengthening the Union. In this area, we underestimated many problems and overestimated the strength of the 'friendship of the peoples', but I firmly believe that the overall direction of our policy was right.

Perestroika had a profound impact on our foreign policy and the role of our country in the system of international relations. In this field we backed our words with action. On 15 January 1986, I called for a radical reduction of nuclear weapons, leading to their eventual total abolition. This was followed by far-reaching agreements with the United States. We abandoned the 'Brezhnev doctrine' in relations with the socialist countries, normalized relations with China, and took a constructive position on the issue of German reunification.

A simple listing of the main policies and actions of Perestroika makes clear that it was in tune with the real and urgent needs of our society. So why was it interrupted? To this question I give the straightforward answer that Perestroika was halted by people who disagreed with its policies and by political forces that opposed it.

Opposition to Perestroika was manifest virtually from its inception from the 'right', that is, the conservative wing within the Party and state bureaucracy, including the Party's Central Committee, some members of the Politburo, the government, the Supreme Soviet, and from leading Party and government officials both in Moscow and the regions. The renewal and replacement of those in positions of leadership encountered stiff opposition and suffered from misjudgements. Many of those promoted during Perestroika (Lukianov, Yanaev, Pavlov, Kryuchkov and others) subsequently proved to be inimical to it. As members of the leadership team, they held Perestroika back, and when it became plain that the country was about to move decisively towards democracy and new social relations, the opponents of Perestroika went on the attack.

I have regularly pointed out, and do so again, that they were scared of open political battles, and every time they tried to fight me openly at plenums of the Central Committee, at congresses of People's Deputies or in the Supreme Soviet, they lost. The majority always supported me. So they recklessly attempted a coup d'état and made complete fools of themselves in the process.

Perestroika had other opponents too. Increasingly, it came under fire from the opposite direction, the radically inclined liberals. The worsening economic climate meant that radicalism rapidly gained public support. Its proponents advocated total destruction, 'down to the foundations', of the Soviet system, and high-speed imposition from above of capitalism, of which most of them had only the most primitive notion. As subsequently became only too clear, they also had not the foggiest notion of what the period of 'transition' to a market economy would involve.

The radicals found their leader in the person of Boris Yeltsin, who cultivated the image of a 'disgraced leader'. That is how the former hardline communist boss of Sverdlovsk and Moscow, a man with a glaringly authoritarian way of thinking and acting, was adopted as the battering ram of an ostensibly democratic opposition.

No one can deny Yeltsin his role in thwarting the August 1991 coup. That averted the threat of a reimposition of the pre-Perestroika way of doing things. Subsequent events showed, however, that there was too high a price to pay for Yeltsin's intervention: that price was the dissolution of the Soviet Union and the 'shock therapy' reforms of the 1990s.

Today, it is impossible to deny that the destruction of the Union had disastrous consequences both for the economy (leading to failure of the reforms as inter-republican economic links were ruptured), and for the move towards democracy, establishment of the rule of law and promotion of human rights in the new independent states. In most of these, unbudgeable regimes appeared that were far from democratic and inhibited development of civil society.

Perestroika was thus interrupted by blows from both conservative and ultra-'liberal' forces. To undo what had been done during the years of Perestroika has, however, proved impossible. The achievements of Perestroika, and above all citizens' newfound freedom, have become deeply rooted in society. The results of Perestroika on the international stage are equally enduring. These are advances that nobody can write out of history.

There is no Great Wall of China, no impermeable firewall between the Perestroika period and the last 20 years or so. It would be wrong to write off everything that has been done in the post-Perestroika period as pernicious, but it would also be a mistake to overlook the differences between the two eras. The policies during Perestroika and those 'post-Perestroika' pursued different goals and employed different methods. Assuredly, in the course of the 1990s reforms, property relations and political institutions changed, but these were not truly democratic changes. That had an impact both on how the reforms turned out and the price paid for them.

We in the Perestroika years put our faith in gradual, evolutionary change and tried to avoid breaking the country's back in the process: those who succeeded us chose instead the approach of first smashing everything to pieces. We considered it essential during the transition to a market economy to retain the regulatory role of the state: the reformers of the 1990s believed in the magical powers of the 'free market'. We wanted to retain all that was good in relations between the republics of the Union and in our relations with neighbouring countries: the leaders of the Russian Federation opted for disintegration.

Many of Yeltsin's actions were prompted purely by a desire to appear stronger and more radical than Gorbachev, and the democratic nature of the reform process fell victim to his approach. It is the undemocratic nature of his actions that is responsible for failures and problems that persist to this day, and that will be felt far into the future. These are:

- social polarization, the huge gap between rich and poor;
- corruption;
- the dominance of the bureaucracy; and
- deindustrialization of many regions of Russia.

The problems are not solely socio-economic. Even more damaging are the deformation of the political process, falsification of election results, armed conflicts and the growth of criminality.

In the light of the situation today, I consider one of the main lessons of Perestroika and the period that followed to be that evolutionary change is preferable to the radical, revolutionary approach. Those initiating change may set themselves what are essentially revolutionary tasks, but should remember that the best way of achieving them is through evolutionary reform. That is the only way of obtaining genuinely sustainable results.

Change is rarely painless. It affects people's lives and interests, and that is why we need to do everything possible to mitigate painful consequences. There should be no attempt to go for a 'big bang' at the outset.

I remember a few years ago at Harvard University, where I had given a lecture, I was approached at a reception arranged by the university's president by Richard Pipes, a well-known historian and author of many works on the history of Russia and the 1917 revolution. During Ronald Reagan's presidency, he was a presidential adviser and considered a hardliner. He said:

> Mr President, I have to apologize to you. When you were on a visit to Washington in 1987, we were talking at a White House reception and you asked if I had read your book *Perestroika: New Thinking for Our Country and the World*.[1] I said I had and you asked what I thought of it. I said frankly that I had not been particularly impressed. The truth was that the thoughts there seemed to me insufficiently bold and radical. Recently, however, I was reading the correspondence between Catherine the Great and Diderot and I was struck by what she wrote: 'You, M. Diderot, propose sweeping changes, but you write on paper, which is very durable, whereas I must write on human skin, and that is very sensitive.' I understand you much better now.

Truly, reform in any country cannot be carried out using a stereotype, in accordance with the Washington Consensus or the recipes of the International Monetary Fund. That is only too reminiscent of our own attempts to graft the Soviet model onto other countries. Foreign advisers rarely have an understanding of the obstacles from history and the particularities of the culture and mentality of the nation where the reforms are being conducted. It has to be admitted that we, the reformers in the second half of the 1980s, did not take full account of them either. That was even more true of the radicals who came to power after us.

The changes that will come in Russia and that she so desperately needs cannot and should not be a repeat of Perestroika. There is no question, however, but that changes will come, and the longer they are delayed, the more painful they will be.

Just like Perestroika, these changes will come about not in a vacuum, but in the context of all the other processes taking place in the world. These are primarily the ongoing process of globalization and the accelerating pace of changes that the world's politicians are struggling to keep up with. They are the search to

---

[1] Mikhail Gorbachev, *Perestroika: New Thinking for Our Country and the World*, NY: HarperCollins, 1987.

find responses to the global challenges of security, poverty and the environment.

These are not processes that began yesterday: they were having a major impact on the world and on our country in the years of Perestroika. Since the end of the Cold War, they have only speeded up. There is, however, one feature that makes their current phase different, and that is that today the model guiding the development of civilization, elaborated during the twentieth century and entrenched in its last decades, is showing ever more alarming signs of dysfunctionality.

The economic crisis that began in 2008 is the crisis of a civilization. Although it may seem to be over the worst, politicians should not allow themselves to be fooled. There is an urgent need to devise a new model for global development. If we stay with the present model, the world will be doomed to further worsening and aggravation of global threats and challenges. The economy and politics are now linked even more closely. If globalization leads us further towards a world economy of super-profits and hyperconsumption, and world politics fails to find a path towards a more just and secure world order, mankind will face a period of global chaos and social upheaval. These cautions are not alarmist, not panic-mongering, but the apprehensions of someone who has seen and experienced much in the course of his life.

I do not have a recipe for the new development model. It can be arrived at only through concerted effort, through demanding intellectual and political searching. A general consensus needs to be arrived at on what kind of world people want to live in. In my view, that world cannot be based solely on personal, selfish interests, on constant growth of material needs and their satisfaction through endless industrial expansion. Is it not already clear where that leads? The world is being turned into a gigantic machine grinding up mineral resources and leaving behind mountains of waste, which are disposed of by being buried and which pollute the earth, the air and water resources. All the while, in the rapidly developing countries and regions, people cannot breathe the air. Of course, the challenge can partly be met with the aid of new technologies, tax incentives and the like, but almost certainly that will be insufficient. Ultimately, what is needed is a reorientation of the world economy, moving the focus of attention away from excessive individual consumption to such public goods as environmental security, human health, the quality of people's lives and development of the human personality.

I may be accused of utopianism, even of a return to communist illusions or, at best, of underestimating self-interest as a driver of economic development. We all know, it may be said, where that leads, and did lead in Russia. It will be argued that hundreds of millions of people do not yet have even their most basic needs satisfied. These are cogent arguments. In seeking to devise the new model for civilization, we certainly need to take account of the mistakes of the past even while addressing the tasks of the present. That is precisely why the model should be a synthesis of different values: social democratic, traditionalist conservative, liberal, environmental and national. The advocates of all ideologies need to be aware that right now modern civilization has no answers to many questions, and to find them, a synthesis of approaches is needed. Ideologies must evolve.

The search for a new development model for civilization is no easy task and many believe it to be beyond our power. But let us think back to the late 1970s and early 1980s when the world faced a threat to the very existence of mankind. Mountainous stockpiles of deadly weapons had been built up and the arms race was accelerating. Tension was growing, hundreds of nuclear missiles were in a state of readiness to be launched instantly. It seemed impossible to get out of that situation and that the world was moving steadily towards catastrophe, but together we managed to pull back from the abyss, to halt the Cold War and initiate a process that culminated in a vast reduction of nuclear stockpiles.

No more today can we afford to panic, to drift downriver with the current. Drawing on the experience of those years, we need to seize the new opportunities that appeared with the end of the Cold War and take decisive action.

Russia, with her as yet far from realized potential, will be able to participate in the search for answers to these universal challenges, but to do so she needs to become strong and must modernize. I believe Russia can and will achieve that, but I see her being successful only if she follows the path of democracy.

Of late, the word 'democracy' has figured rarely in the speeches of Russian politicians. Disillusionment with democracy is also rife among the citizens of Russia, and not only of Russia. A rolling back of the wave of democracy after its tumultuous inroads in the late 1980s and early 1990s has been a global phenomenon. There are serious reasons for that, of which the most important has been that the democratic leaders were not always competent to deal with the situation and often fell short of expectations. I am convinced, however, that there is no alternative to democracy.

Different countries come to democracy by different routes and practise its principles in different ways. In historical terms, many countries that today boast a stable, successful democracy only recently passed through difficult and even horrifying times. This is true both of Germany and Chile, of Argentina and Japan. A little over a century ago, the Scandinavian countries were experiencing famine. Nowadays democracy is practised in all these countries in the forms best suited to their national circumstances. Russia too will have to build a democracy that takes account of and builds on its cultural characteristics, traditions, mentality and national character.

There are, however, certain features without which a system cannot be democratic. Some of these are of particular importance for Russia because we cannot yet claim they are found in our present way of life. These are: regular, honest elections ensuring a periodical turnover of those in power; stable constitutional order and a balance of powers between the three branches of government; competition between political parties; respect for the basic human rights and freedoms; a just and impartial legal system and a developed civil society. Russia needs to build the institutions of a democratic society.

What is behind the success of countries where democracy is not only stable but most effective, where it provides its citizens with a decent standard of living and stable economic growth? I have in mind the Scandinavian countries, for example, or Finland, the Netherlands and Germany.

These countries have their own characteristics. They do not necessarily have closely similar economic and taxation policies or models of society, but we find in all of them a strong, vibrant civil society and a strong state. Something else they have in common is that, for many decades, they have not borne the burden of militarism and excessive military spending.

We in Russia have not yet found the 'algorithm' for stable democracy, but that is not some sort of fate hanging over the country. Even less is it the result of 'historical inability' or unreadiness of our people for democracy. 'Democracy is not for Russians.' Whether that claim comes from the right or the left, it is still balderdash.

In the course of their long history, the Russian people have incorporated and defended vast territories, given the world outstanding politicians, thinkers, writers, composers and artists. We are a talented people, capable of great feats of endurance and dogged, routine hard work. Russians, both at home and abroad, achieve enormous success when they are able to work in normal conditions. What is needed to bring out the talent and abilities of our people to the full? It seems to me the answer is obvious: we need to improve relationships within society, and we need to improve the political system.

We need strong presidential authority. In Russia, it is crucial that people should trust the president and be able to believe him. Yes, Russia needs a strong leader, but not a Führer, not a Stalin. Calls to 'Bring back Stalin' are a dangerous folly and manifest a lack of common sense.

Throughout almost the whole of Russian history, the identity of the man who came to power has been of immense importance. Character, preferences and psychological peculiarities of the tsar, the leader, the general secretary or the president left their mark on literally everything happening in the country, on the lives of millions of people. I have no doubt that in the twenty-first century Russia must overcome excessive dependence on this subjective factor.

Of course, given Russia's traditions, the mentality of the people, the vastness of the land, and the role and responsibilities of the Russian state in the world, the president cannot be a purely symbolic figure as in most European countries. At the time of Perestroika we were slow in coming to see the need for strong presidential power. We were not given enough time to deal with that problem. Russia does need a strong president, but we cannot have all the levers of political power in the hands of one person. Even the president only has two hands and one head: God makes no exceptions. Of course, there may be certain circumstances in which manual control and emergency measures are called for, but those circumstances should be clearly defined by law.

Russia needs a strong, independent parliament. Today, Russia's parliament is almost constantly criticized, severely, and in my opinion most often justly. On one occasion, a speaker of the State Duma said: 'Parliament is no place for discussion.' It was probably a slip of the tongue but, no less probably, a Freudian slip. The Russian parliament, as presently composed, has passed without debate laws that divide society and compromise the state authorities in the eyes of the thinking public. At some point, these errors will have to be corrected.

For the Federal Assembly to became a genuine institution of government, it is essential for the attitude to parliament of the executive branch, of the president, to be changed. Is it really in the president's interests for parliament to be rubber-stamping decisions as it does at present? Parliament should have a strong and intelligently thought-through mechanism for parliamentary investigations, hearings on the most important issues facing the country.

Today, both chambers of the Federal Assembly in reality consist of appointees. The political parties do not play the role in the life of the country and in parliament that they should in a democratic country. Creating genuine, strong, responsible political parties with their own ideology is one of the most important challenges facing our society and our 'political class' in the coming years.

What will be the basis on which political parties are formed? I imagine they will be based, first, on genuine interest groups within society where interests are varied and may well not coincide. Second, on the basis of political sympathies: social democratic, conservative, liberal and others. The outcome should be the appearance of several strong parties that can credibly aspire to gain a majority in parliament.

I have often pondered Lenin's words (I return to him again and again, as a politician and thinker deserving of his place in history) to the effect that socialism is the living creativity of the masses. I see that, as proof, that he saw socialism as a system for people, hence democratic. The most important word in that maxim is 'creativity'.

We cannot, of course, just ignore the problem of governability, which is particularly important in the case of Russia. It is a problem because of the sheer size of the country and because of its multi-ethnic character, and it can only be resolved on a basis of federalism. To complicate matters, the kind of federalism that works, for example, in the United States or Germany is not sufficient for us, because Russia includes nation-states. Any talk of abolishing them is dangerous and pernicious. The focus should rather be on ensuring that they are as autonomous as possible, while remaining an integral part of Russia.

The problem of governability is closely tied up with another thorny issue: the fight against corruption. After all, if the state cannot deal with this problem in years, indeed, decades, it forfeits the trust of the people.

That is why you cannot just put up with it, as some suggest, asserting that it will never be eradicated in Russia. It must be combated, but police measures, prohibitions and prison sentences will not solve the problem. The main weapon against corruption is efficient democratic institutions and a healthy economy that gives people the means to show initiative, to establish their own business, and that curbs the appetites of greedy officials.

I have no doubt that we in Russia will eventually find an optimal combination of economic freedom and state regulation. I remember how dramatically everything changed after the Central Committee plenum on agriculture in 1953, six months after Stalin's death. Country people, who until then had been little better than slaves, had their hands untied and were allowed to work properly. Everything changed, everything that had been forgotten reappeared!

Or take the Shchekino Method in the 1970s, which produced much higher productivity for the same outlay, and using the same resources and machinery, by giving workers the incentive to reorganize the way they worked. Creative approaches soon appeared. That was a first experiment of giving people economic freedom in industry. Even in the Soviet period it was possible to pass the initiative to individuals. That is even more the case now.

Why is it not happening? I have no doubt that here too everything depends on the politics. The current stagnation of the Russian economy results from the fact that for many years there has been no fundamental change in ideas of how it should develop. Also, the 'economic team', the main theoreticians and those who implement their ideas, is largely unchanged. Monetarist thinking dominates. There is a stubborn reluctance to regulate the economy, whether by stimulating demand, effective use of accumulated reserves or infrastructure projects. The economy remains straitjacketed by hardline monetarism.

Recently, appeals have more frequently been addressed to the head of state to change macroeconomic policy, but I believe that genuine competition in economic thinking will only be possible within a different political framework. We need political parties capable of putting forward alternative economic programmes, and a periodical handover of political power to make possible necessary changes of policy. In the absence of those changes, appeals to 'the man at the top' will do little good.

A crucial role in building a strong modern state in Russia can only be played by the judiciary. Without impartial courts, without justice, the rule of law is impossible. This goal, first called for in the years of Perestroika, is very far from having been achieved. Worse, in recent years there has been serious maladministration in this area. Respect for the legal system has been undermined and it will be no easy matter to restore it.

For Russia, with its vast territory and unique position in the world, the issue of security, its own and that of the world, is always a concern. It is an issue that, in the twenty-first century, can only be addressed through joint political efforts. The last few decades have confirmed how right were Olof Palme, John F. Kennedy and other leaders who were ahead of their time. 'International security must rest on a commitment to joint survival rather than a threat of mutual destruction,' Palme advised.[2] Kennedy called for 'not merely peace for Americans but peace for all men and women'.[3] 'Only together can we put an end to the era of wars. Our common goal must be cooperation, joint creativity, joint development', I said in my speech to the United Nations in 1988.

At the Twenty-Seventh Congress of the CPSU in 1986, we put forward the principle of restricting military capacity to a 'reasonable sufficiency' for defence on the grounds that 'the nature of modern armaments gives no scope for any state to hope to defend itself solely by means of military technology'. That remains true today. States should resolve defence issues primarily through political means, on the basis of the principle of sufficient defensive force and not inflating military budgets.

I am certain that Russia is capable of ensuring her security in this way. It is also incumbent upon her to make a significant contribution to establishing a secure world order. Today, Russia has a major, inalienable and constructive role to play in global politics. It is very important that the international community understands that she must be involved in resolving major global problems and that her contribution is properly recognized and appreciated.

Russia inherited from those who destroyed the Union a difficult set of problems in respect of relations with her immediate neighbours, who are bound to her by special historical ties. Some have joked that the motive behind establishing the Commonwealth of Independent States was primarily to spite Gorbachev. It is far from easy to build relationships on the imperative of unconditional recognition of the independence and sovereignty of the former Soviet states, while at the same time recognizing the need for close 'cooperation' (if some jibe at the word 'integration').

What matters is not the words, but the fact that a purely selfish

[2] Sadako Ogata, 'Assuring the Security of People: The Humanitarian Challenge of the 21st Century', UNHCR, 14 June 1995; http://www.unhcr.org/3ae68fa9c.html. Accessed 10 August 2015.
[3] John F. Kennedy Presidential Library and Museum, Commencement Address at the American University, 10 June 1963 (transcript); http://www.jfklibrary.org/Asset-Viewer/BWC7I4C9QUmLG9J6I8oy8w.aspx. Accessed 16 July 2015.

approach to relations between states that have for centuries been part of a united, if diverse, country, simply will not work. This history cannot simply be deleted, and that is why establishing close cooperation between Russia and her immediate neighbours is essential and inescapable. It must, however, proceed on the clear understanding that there will be no attempt at domination, and that in dealing with problems large and small mutual interests will be fully taken into account.

We live in a time of great change. The twenty-first century got off to a difficult start, full of surprises, and humanity finds itself facing urgent problems. On the eve of the new century, I said:

> The twenty-first century will either be a century of disastrous intensification of a deadly crisis, or the century in which mankind becomes morally more pure and spiritually healthier. I am convinced that we are all called upon to do our part to ensure the triumph of humanity and justice, to make the twenty-first century an age of renaissance, the century of mankind.

For our country, Russia, the twenty-first century may also be decisive. The present generation of Russian citizens, politicians and leaders may finally put our country on the road to stable democratic development. A renewed Russia may become a key participant in renewing the world. She has much to offer: natural and intellectual resources; the lessons from the past which we are, in spite of everything, learning; and an ardent desire to pave the way for a future of peace and justice for new generations.

Reflections of an Optimist

(As noted by Mikhail Kazinik and Dmitry Golubovsky)

As soon as people start asking you for wisdom, you think, 'Looks like I'm on my last legs.'

My very first memory is of famine. In 1933 I was just over two years old, and I remember my grandfather, Andrey, catching frogs in our small creek and boiling them in a pot. Their little white bellies turned upwards when they were being boiled, but I don't remember eating them. Much later, on a boat trip on the Seine and to the accompaniment of songs about Paris, Raisa and I did eat frogs' legs.

In 1935, I was seriously ill. It was just called 'being poorly'. I couldn't breathe. They put a candle by the cradle and cried but couldn't think what else to do. We lived in the countryside; it was 1935. You get the picture. Then a woman came in and said: 'You need to find some good honey and get him to drink a glass of that.' I remember it perfectly: the room there, the window here, and a little blue teapot they put on the window-sill, very, very dark blue, with the honey. I took it, drank it and the lid fell off. I can still hear the clatter it made, right now.

I get spasms in the night in August, ever since I worked on the combine harvester as a boy. If I close my eyes now, I can see the wheat in front of me, oceans of it. Especially in June when it grows, the ears form and seed and the quail get to work on them.

Both my grandad Andrey and my other grandad, Panteley, were poor peasants. Soviet power gave them land and ten years later they were classed as middle-income peasants. Grandad Panteley liked to say: 'Soviet power was the saving of us. It gave us land. The rest we did ourselves.'

I haven't been back to Privolnoye for five years now, and the other day decided I must go back again, in September or October. Those are the loveliest months: the harvest has been brought in and all you hear is the roar of tractors in the distance tilling the soil ready for winter, the birds are migrating, and that's how life goes on, one thing following the other.

A person with no sense of belonging somewhere will never amount to anything.

I don't like people who don't care how they relax or what company they keep. I am a different kind of person.

After the war, I worked for five years on the combine harvester with my dad. We became very close, talked a lot, and I asked him a lot of questions. We developed a man-to-man relationship. The most serious ticking-off I ever got from him was routed through my mother. I was 18 and he said: 'Tell Mikhail he is staying out too late. He should come back earlier.'

Life is passing and people are passing away.

In a television interview, Vladimir Pozner asked me: 'Supposing it was possible, and you were invited to phone someone no longer with us. Who would you like to talk to?' I answered: 'I think for Gorbachev everyone knows the answer – his wife.'

Raisa and I were together for 46 years, and for 40 of them we went for a walk every day, wherever we were. In all weathers: in blizzards, snow, rain, but Raisa especially loved blizzards. I would say: 'No, for heaven's sake, there's a blizzard outside!' She would just say, 'Come on, let's go!' and out we would go. I got used to walking in blizzards. When she died I stopped going for walks.

I used to wind Raisa up. One time I said: 'You don't want to make me angry.' I gave a menacing sigh and added: 'Because I just need to raise my fist, just bring it down once and that will be it. It won't take two blows.' She said: 'What, are you thinking of beating me. You've gone nuts!'

In old age it gets difficult to hold back tears.

I take better care of my health now. I want to keep a promise I made to my friends to invite them to my 90th birthday. It was a bit of a cheek, but I think that's the way to behave, setting goals that challenge you.

I slept well last night, but the night before was grim. I took a double dose of painkiller but couldn't come to an amicable arrangement with sleep. I dozed off towards morning and had the most amazing dream. The day before, I had watched a film about the Civil War. The commentary said 15 million people died in Russia in those years. Anyway, in my dream I was walking with someone and they showed me all the dead people. Countless numbers of them. At the end I came to a bright, open space and asked: 'What's over there?' My guide said: 'That's where the dead go.'

Often when I am asleep, I find the answer to questions that have been tormenting me while I was awake. Someone told me I should keep a pen and notebook by the bed to write it down. I tried that, but when I read what I'd written, I decided it hadn't been worth waking up for.

Morning is my favourite time. I wake at 6:00 or 6:30, throw off the blanket, smooth the bedclothes, lie down again and do exercises. Completely basic things, stretching, push-ups. I can't be sure whether the cat is imitating me when it stretches or I am imitating the cat.

I may be a hunter, but I'm not a destroyer.

A missile the Americans call the Satan and we call the R-36M has the power of 100 Chernobyls. In one missile! When you hear that while occupying the position I held, you feel a bit unhinged.

When I hear people talk about a 'Soviet stooge', I feel nothing. For a politician at my level the expression is meaningless.

In tenth grade I had to produce an essay for my school-leaving exams and chose to write on 'Stalin is our military glory, Stalin is the soaring of our youth'. It got a mark of 'Excellent'. Today I consider myself one of the staunchest opponents of the evils of Stalinism.

Russia's history is complicated. It is hard to say what was the golden age. Everything was always becoming, becoming, expanding, assimilating territory.

When people ask me what Russia will be like in 20 years' time, I can't bring myself to say things might be worse.

Russia's biggest problem is that the people are pushed out of politics.

There are similarities and dissimilarities between today's protests and those of the late 1980s and early 1990s, but what matters is something different: today's demonstrations are very earnest. It's not just a lot of yelling. This is thought-through protest giving voice to people's innermost feelings and wishes. That cannot just be ignored.

I sometimes hear it said that the slogan 'For Fair Elections!' is no longer topical. I don't agree. Under no circumstances should it be abandoned. It is the whole crux of the matter.

A proper leader wants a lively, fully functional, serious opposition. The weakness of Russia's current leaders is that they don't understand that. To put it mildly, they resent opposition.

I really wish the president would understand how important it is to step down at the right time, to put everything aside and make way for new faces. That takes courage, but it is the sort of decision that tells you a lot about a person and what they've got in them.

The best word for what is presently going on in our country is 'troubles'.

You need to walk the path of freedom.

The Americans made a big mistake. They shouted louder than anyone that we needed a new world order that would be more democratic and just, and then were the first to turn their backs on it.

It upsets me that Europe cannot put its house in order and finally become a global driver of change for the better.

My first trip to Canada was amazing. In 1983 I spent seven days there and an American radio station managed in that time to arrange my funeral. They reported I had drunk myself into a stupor at a party with the minister, had a heart attack and died. It's just what they do. They can't seem to grow out of it.

Pass the author his book! This is my first book of memoirs, published in 1995. I want to read you a passage from it about the land our hut stood on: 'There were apple and pear trees of different varieties. Which exactly was of no interest to me at the time. I remember only that they were delicious and, crucially, ripened at different times, so we had them all through the summer and autumn. Beyond the apples and pears were the plums, black and white. Beyond that the orchard gave way to an overgrowth of elm, a real jungle that took up almost a third of the land. I had my own hiding places there, and one time got my hands on a book called *The Headless Horseman*. I disappeared for nearly three days. My mother was going crazy, not knowing what to think, but until I had read that book from cover to cover I hid away.

Recently I have found myself going down from the first to the ground floor to do something, but by the time I get there I've forgotten what I went down for.

I am an optimist. I end many of my interviews by saying it, so let's finish on that.

Life teaches you more than any teacher.

(Published in the Russian edition of *Esquire*, September 2012.)

Index

Notes: MG and RG in various sub-entries and parentheses refer to Mikhail and Raisa Gorbachev(a) respectively. Chinese names are indexed as written, i.e. family name followed by given name – no comma separator. Japanese names are listed according to usual Western practice.

Vladimir (city) 87–8
Vladimirskaya, Yelena Borisovna 117
Vladivostok 11, 340
Vlasov, Yury 87
Vodolazov, Grigoriy 28
Volga region
  environmental impact of power
    stations 296
  not granting autonomous status to
    Germans 25
Volgodonsk 136
Volta River Basin 302
Voltaire 384
Voronezh Province 11
Voznesensky, Andrey 71
Vysotsky, Vladimir 351

Wadongo, Evans 238
wages 123, 181
  backlog of 105, 126
  living 164
  millions of people not paid for
    months 168
  minimum level of 24
  non-payment of 122
  not received for six months or more
    119
  overdue 122
  paid on time 161
  rising 168
Wałęsa, Lech 51, 237
Wall Street Journal 279–80
War Communism 389
Warsaw ghetto 344
Washington DC 123, 165, 310–11,
    313, 316, 318, 320, 395
  American University 272, 323,
    330–1, 403n
  Jamestown Foundation Conference
    (1999) 327n
  North Atlantic Council (1999) 287
  Treaty on the Elimination of
    Intermediate- and Shorter-Range
    Missiles 312
Washington Consensus 292, 306, 395
Washington Post 211
Water for the World conference
    (2002) 300–1
weapons of mass destruction 277, 286
  elimination of 273, 278, 284

  fuelling the urge to acquire 329
  reduction of 278, 284
  ridding the world of 278, 282
  see also chemical weapons
Weinberger, Caspar 311
Weizsäcker, Richard von 345,
    355
West Germany 342, 354
  diplomatic relations between USSR
    and 352
  post-war development of 345–6
  Willy Brandt's New Eastern Policy
    344, 349
  see also German reunification
White House (Moscow) 57
  assault on 64–5
  hundreds of people killed in 67
  mass beatings of citizens in
    approaches to 70
  sealed off by troops and armoured
    vehicles 66
  Yeltsin standing on tank outside
    112
Wildsteig 347
Wilmes, Maria 60
Workers' Russia 26
World Commission on Environment
    and Development (1987) *see*
    Brundtland Commission
World Economic Forum (Davos 2010)
    383
World Political Forum 292, 301, 304,
    340, 362, 371
  inaugural conference (Turin 2003)
    281
World Trade Organization 215
  see also Moore
World Water Forum 300–1

Xinhua News Agency 362–3

Yabloko Party 146, 173
Yakovlev, Alexander Nikolaevich 20,
    101, 152, 190
Yakovlev, Yegor Vladimirovich 34,
    140, 190
Yanaev, Gennadiy 392
Yanukovych, Viktor 375, 376
Yasin, Yevgeny 78, 79
Yavlinsky, Grigoriy 108, 115, 125